LEARN TO PROGRAM WITH SCRATCH

LEARN TO PROGRAM WITH SCRATCH

A Visual Introduction to Programming with Games, Art, Science, and Math

by Majed Marji

San Francisco

LONGWOOD PUBLIC LIBRARY

LEARN TO PROGRAM WITH SCRATCH. Copyright © 2014 by Majed Marji.

All rights reserved. No part of this work may be reproduced or transmitted in any form or by any means, electronic or mechanical, including photocopying, recording, or by any information storage or retrieval system, without the prior written permission of the copyright owner and the publisher.

Printed in USA
Third printing

18 17 16 15 14   3 4 5 6 7 8 9

ISBN-10: 1-59327-543-9
ISBN-13: 978-1-59327-543-3

SUSTAINABLE FORESTRY INITIATIVE Certified Sourcing www.sfiprogram.org SFI-00854

Text stock is SFI certified

Publisher: William Pollock
Production Editor: Alison Law
Cover Illustration: Tina Salameh
Developmental Editor: Jennifer Griffith-Delgado
Technical Reviewer: Tyler Watts
Copyeditor: Paula L. Fleming
Compositor: Lynn L'Heureux
Proofreader: Kate Blackham

For information on distribution, translations, or bulk sales, please contact No Starch Press, Inc. directly:

No Starch Press, Inc.
245 8th Street, San Francisco, CA 94103
phone: 415.863.9900; info@nostarch.com; www.nostarch.com

Library of Congress Cataloging-in-Publication Data

Marji, Majed, author.
  Learn to program with Scratch : a visual introduction to programming with games, art, science, and math / by Majed Marji.
    pages cm
  Audience: 11+
  ISBN-13: 978-1-59327-543-3 (paperback)
  ISBN-10: 1-59327-543-9 (paperback)
  1. Scratch (Computer program language) 2. Computer programming. 3. Computer games--Programming. I. Title.
  QA76.73.S345M38 2014
  794.8'1526--dc23

2013043492

No Starch Press and the No Starch Press logo are registered trademarks of No Starch Press, Inc. Other product and company names mentioned herein may be the trademarks of their respective owners. Rather than use a trademark symbol with every occurrence of a trademarked name, we are using the names only in an editorial fashion and to the benefit of the trademark owner, with no intention of infringement of the trademark.

The information in this book is distributed on an "As Is" basis, without warranty. While every precaution has been taken in the preparation of this work, neither the author nor No Starch Press, Inc. shall have any liability to any person or entity with respect to any loss or damage caused or alleged to be caused directly or indirectly by the information contained in it.

About the Author

Majed Marji holds a PhD in electrical engineering from Wayne State University and an MBA in strategic management from Davenport University. He has over 15 years of experience in the automotive industry, where he developed many software applications for real-time data acquisition, device control, test-cell management, engineering data analysis, embedded controllers, telematics, hybrid vehicles, and safety-critical powertrain systems. Dr. Marji is also an adjunct faculty member with the Electrical Engineering Department at Wayne State University. He has taught courses on communication engineering, machine vision, microprocessors, control systems, and algorithms and data structures, among other topics.

About the Technical Reviewer

Tyler Watts, EdS, is a creative-computing educator who teaches sixth through eighth graders in Kansas City (Kansas) Unified School District 500 and adult students at the University of Missouri–Kansas City. He has been using Scratch since 2009 as a tool to combat the digital divide and teach students how to think like computer scientists. Since Tyler's first year of teaching Scratch, he has learned the importance of weaning learners off of the "Scratch training wheels" and challenging them and molding them into digital creators. He feels that programming is a form of personal expression and teaches his students to approach it as they would any other art form and have fun.

BRIEF CONTENTS

CONTENTS IN DETAIL

2
MOTION AND DRAWING 25

3
LOOKS AND SOUND 47

6 MAKING DECISIONS 123

7 REPETITION: A DEEPER EXPLORATION OF LOOPS 155

9
LISTS 213

APPENDIX
SHARING AND COLLABORATION 243

INDEX 251

ACKNOWLEDGMENTS

Although the book's cover shows a single author, many people have had a hand in its creation. I would like to acknowledge the many professionals at No Starch Press who contributed to this work. Special thanks go to my editor, Jennifer Griffith-Delgado, and my production editor, Alison Law, for their significant contributions. Their helpful suggestions and expertise have led to a greatly improved book, and their commitment to excellence appears on every page. I would also like to thank Paula L. Fleming and Serena Yang for their work on the book.

I am truly grateful for the valuable feedback provided by the technical editor, Tyler Watts. His thoughtful suggestions have, in many instances, made their way into the book.

My final thanks go to my wife, Marina, and my two sons, Asad and Karam, who supported me throughout this long project. They've put up with so much to give me the time and space I needed. Maybe now I can catch up with the things I've missed!

INTRODUCTION

Scratch is a visual programming language that provides a rich learning environment for people of all ages. It allows you to create interactive, media-rich projects, including animated stories, book reports, science projects, games, and simulations. Scratch's visual programming environment enables you to explore areas of knowledge that would otherwise be inaccessible. It provides a full set of multimedia tools you can use to create wonderful applications, and you can do so more easily than with other programming languages.

In many ways, Scratch promotes problem-solving skills—important in all areas of life, not just programming. The environment provides immediate feedback, allowing you to check your logic quickly and easily. The visual structure makes it a simple matter to trace the flow of your programs and refine your way of thinking. In essence, Scratch makes the ideas of computer science accessible. It makes learning intrinsically motivating; fosters the pursuit of knowledge; and encourages hands-on, self-directed learning through exploration and discovery. The barriers to entry are very low, while the ceiling is limited only by your creativity and imagination.

A lot of books claim to teach you how to program using Scratch. Most target very young readers and present only a few simple applications that guide the reader through Scratch's user interface. These books are more about Scratch than programming. The goal of this book, by contrast, is to teach fundamental programming concepts using Scratch as a tool, as well as to unveil the capabilities of Scratch as a powerful vehicle for both teaching and learning.

Whom This Book Is For

This book is for anyone eager to explore computer science. It teaches the fundamentals of programming, and it can be used as a textbook for middle and high school students or as a self-study guide. The book can also be used at the college level to teach elementary programming concepts to students from different backgrounds or as a companion textbook that provides an introduction to such a course.

Teachers who want to use Scratch in the classroom can also benefit from the deeper understanding of programming to be found in this book. You'll develop the skills you need to engage students with Scratch in meaningful ways that are compatible with their needs.

The book assumes no prior programming experience and, for the most part, no mathematics beyond what is taught in high school. Some of the advanced simulations can be skipped without causing any learning gap.

A Note to the Reader

The beauty of being a programmer is that you can create. Think about it: You come up with an idea and use your keyboard for a couple of hours, and a new software project comes to life! Like any new skill, however, programming takes practice. Along the way, you'll most likely make mistakes—but don't give up. Take time to reflect on the concepts and experiment with different techniques until you master them. And then move on to learn something new.

Features

This book provides a hands-on, problem-solving approach to learning programming and related concepts in computer science. With this approach, I hope to cultivate readers' imaginations and make the computer-programming experience available to everyone.

With that in mind, the book is project oriented. I'll present concepts with detailed explanations, and then together, we'll develop a number of applications that illustrate those concepts. The emphasis is on problem solving rather than on Scratch's particular features.

The examples presented in these pages demonstrate the wide range of knowledge you can explore using Scratch. These examples were selected carefully to explain programming concepts and to show how you can use Scratch to increase your understanding of other topics.

The Try It Out exercises and the problems at the end of each chapter are designed to challenge your programming skills. They also suggest new ideas that incorporate the studied concepts into larger problems. I encourage you to attempt these exercises and to come up with your own programming problems. Solving problems of your own shows that you've developed a solid understanding of programming.

Organization of This Text

The first three chapters of this book introduce Scratch as a powerful tool for drawing geometric shapes and creating media-rich applications. They'll get you started quickly and easily, while the rest of the book focuses on the programming constructs supported in Scratch.

Chapter 1: Getting Started introduces Scratch's programming environment, the available command blocks, and the process of creating simple programs.

Chapter 2: Motion and Drawing reviews the motion commands and introduces Scratch's drawing capabilities.

Chapter 3: Looks and Sound discusses Scratch's sound and graphics commands.

Chapter 4: Procedures introduces procedures as a way to write structured, modular programs. We jump into procedures here to enforce good programming style from the beginning.

Chapter 5: Variables explores how you can use variables to keep track of information. This chapter also explains how to ask users questions and get answers, paving the way for building a wide range of interactive applications.

Chapter 6: Making Decisions outlines decision making and controlling the flow of programs.

Chapter 7: Repetition: A Deeper Exploration of Loops discusses in detail the repetition structures available in Scratch and explains how to use them through concrete examples.

Chapter 8: String Processing discusses the string data type and presents a collection of useful string-manipulation routines.

Chapter 9: Lists introduces lists as containers of items and demonstrates how you can use them to create powerful programs.

All chapters also include several complete projects that can be used as a guide for creating similar applications in many learning settings. By the time you finish this book, you should be able to tackle just about any programming project on your own!

Conventions Used

We use a few text styles to correspond with the text in the Scratch interface:

- Scratch block names are in this style: **when green flag clicked**.
- Sprite names and variables are in this style: Ball.

Filename.sb2

The file(s) that you need when reading a particular section are named in the margin (see the example on the left), and Try It Out exercises are shown like this:

TRY IT OUT

This is something for you to try.

Online Resources

Visit *http://nostarch.com/learnscratch/* to download the extra resources for this book. Once you've downloaded and unzipped the file, you'll see the following materials:

Bonus Applications This folder contains bonus Scratch applications that you can study on your own. The file *Bonus Applications.pdf* walks you through them with detailed explanations.

Chapter Scripts This folder contains all the scripts mentioned in the book.

Extra Resources This folder contains three PDF files that provide more in-depth information on special topics (the Paint Editor, mathematical functions, and drawing geometric shapes) that you may be interested in.

Solutions This folder contains the solutions to all problems and Try It Out exercises in the book.

Errata and Updates

We've done our best to make sure that the book contains accurate information. However, to err is human. Visit *http://nostarch.com/learnscratch/* for the latest updates.

1

GETTING STARTED

Have you ever wanted to create your own computer game, animated story, tutorial, or science simulation? *Scratch* is a graphical programming language that makes it easy to create those applications and more. In this introductory chapter, you will:

- Explore Scratch's programming environment
- Learn about different types of command blocks
- Create your first game in Scratch

When you make a Scratch application, you can save it on your computer or upload it to the Scratch website, where others can comment on it and remix it into new projects.

Excited? Then let's get started!

What Is Scratch?

A computer program is just a set of instructions that tell a computer what to do. You write these instructions using a *programming language*, and that's where Scratch comes in.

Most programming languages are *text based*, which means you have to give the computer commands in what looks like a cryptic form of English. For example, to display "Hello!" on the screen, you might write:

`print('Hello!')`	(in the Python language)
`std::cout << "Hello!" << std::endl;`	(in the C++ language)
`System.out.print("Hello!");`	(in the Java language)

Learning these languages and understanding their syntax rules can be challenging for beginners. Scratch, on the other hand, is a *visual* programming language. It was developed in the Massachusetts Institute of Technology (MIT) Media Lab to make programming easier and more fun to learn.

In Scratch, you won't type any complicated commands. Instead, you'll connect graphical blocks together to create programs. Confused? Look at the simple program in Figure 1-1, and I'll explain.

say Hello!
A Scratch program that contains a single block.
Hello!
The result of running the program.

Figure 1-1: When you run this Scratch block, the cat says "Hello!" in a speech bubble.

The cat that you see in Figure 1-1 is called a *sprite*. Sprites understand and obey sets of instructions that you give them. The purple block on the left tells the cat to display "Hello!" in a speech bubble. Many of the applications you'll create in this book will contain multiple sprites, and you'll use blocks to make sprites move, turn, say things, play music, do math, and so on.

You can program in Scratch by snapping those color-coded blocks together as you would puzzle pieces or LEGO bricks. The stacks of blocks that you create are called *scripts*. For example, Figure 1-2 shows a script that changes a sprite's color four times.

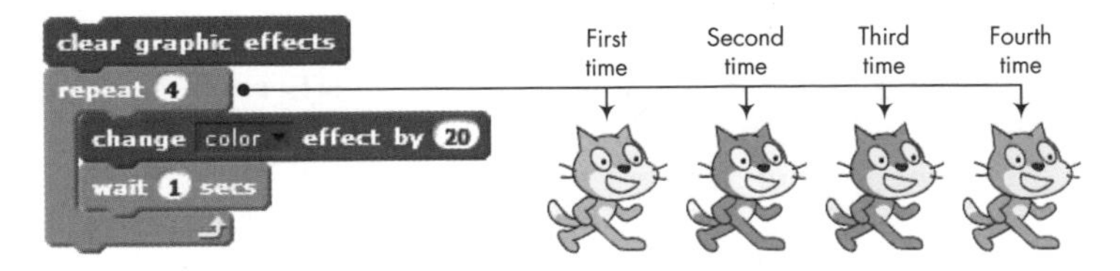

Figure 1-2: Using a script to change the Cat *sprite's color*

This script waits for one second between color changes, and the four cats you see here show the sprite's new color after each change.

TRY IT OUT 1-1

Though we haven't discussed the blocks in Figure 1-2 yet, read them, look at their shapes, and try to figure out the steps the script took to make the cat teal. (Hint: The first purple block returns the cat to its original color.) What do you think would happen if we removed the **wait** block from the script?

This book covers Scratch 2, which was released in May 2013. This version allows you to create projects directly in your web browser so you don't have to install any software on your computer, and we'll rely on Scratch's web interface for the material in this book.

Now, that you know a little about this language, it's time to kick off our programming journey and learn how to use it.

Scratch Programming Environment

To start Scratch, go to the Scratch website (*http://scratch.mit.edu/*) and click the *TRY IT OUT* link. This should take you to Scratch's project editor interface, shown in Figure 1-3.

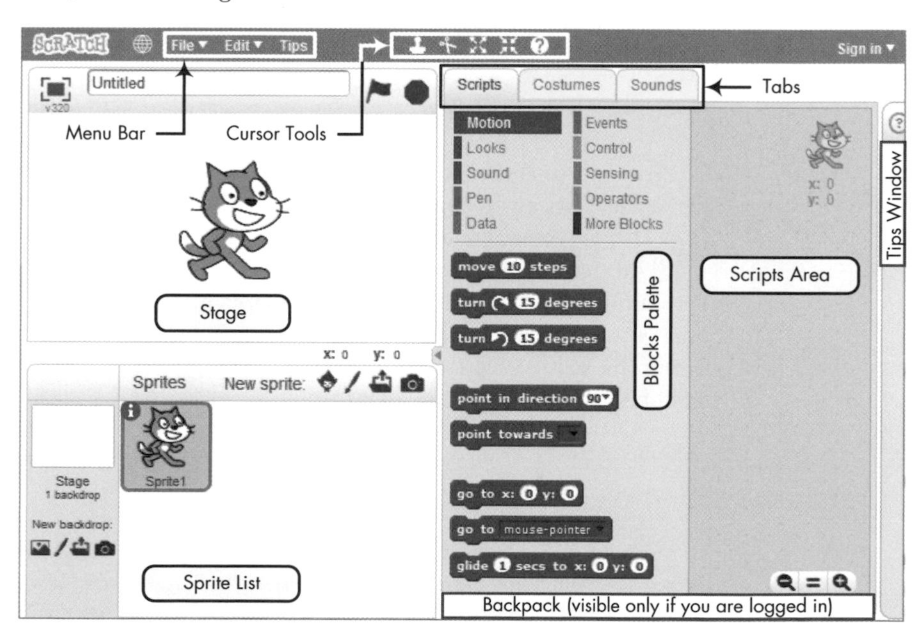

Figure 1-3: The Scratch user interface, where you'll build your programs

You should see a single window with at least the following three panes: the Stage (top left), the Sprite List (bottom left), and the Scripts tab (right), which contains the Blocks tab and the Scripts Area. The right pane also contains two additional tabs, Costumes and Sounds, which will be discussed later in this section. If you're logged into an account on the Scratch website, you should also see the Backpack (bottom right), which has buttons that let you share your project and use sprites and scripts from existing projects.

Let's take a quick look at the three main panes.

The Stage

The *Stage* is where your sprites move, draw, and interact. The Stage is 480 steps wide and 360 steps tall, as illustrated in Figure 1-4. The center of the Stage has an *x*-coordinate of 0 and a *y*-coordinate of 0.

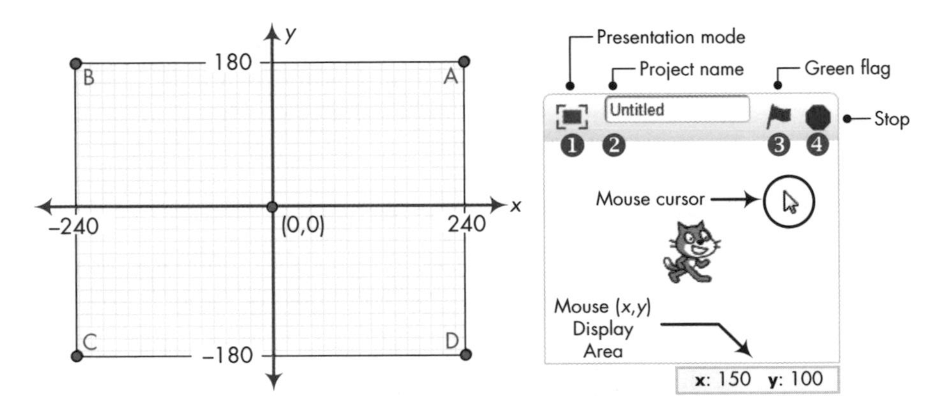

Figure 1-4: The Stage is like a coordinate plane with point (0,0) in the center.

You can find the (*x*,*y*) coordinates of any point on the Stage by moving the mouse cursor to that point and watching the numbers in the Mouse (*x*,*y*) Display Area, located directly below the Stage.

The small bar located above the Stage has several controls. The Presentation mode icon ❶ hides all scripts and programming tools and makes the Stage area take up almost your entire monitor. The edit box ❷ shows the name of the current project. The green flag ❸ and stop ❹ icons let you start and end your program.

> **TRY IT OUT 1-2**
>
> Move the mouse around the Stage and watch the Mouse Display Area. What happens when you move the mouse outside the Stage area? Now, switch to Presentation mode and watch how the screen changes. Click the icon in the top left of the screen or press ESC on your keyboard to exit Presentation mode.

Sprite List

The Sprite List displays names and thumbnails for all the sprites in your project. New projects begin with a white Stage and a single cat-costumed sprite, as illustrated in Figure 1-5.

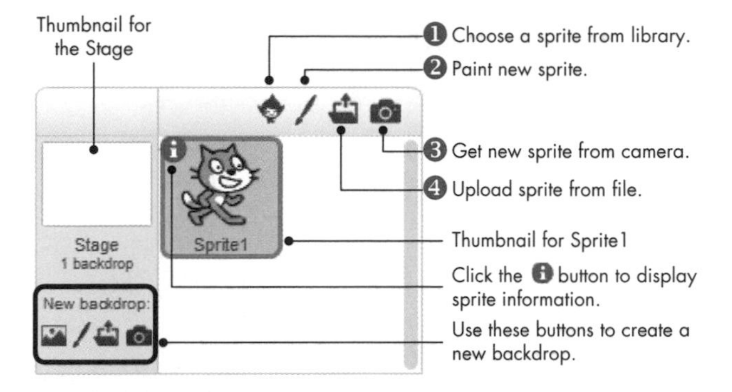

Figure 1-5: The Sprite List for a new project

The buttons above the Sprite List let you add new sprites to your project from one of four places: Scratch's sprite library ❶, the built-in Paint Editor ❷ (where you can draw your own costume), a camera connected to your computer ❸, or your computer ❹.

> **TRY IT OUT 1-3**
>
> Add new sprites to your project using some of the buttons located above the Sprite List. Rearrange the sprites in the Sprite List by dragging their corresponding thumbnails.

Each sprite in your project has its own scripts, costumes, and sounds. You can select any sprite to see its belongings. Either (1) click the sprite's thumbnail in the Sprite List or (2) double-click the sprite itself on the Stage. The currently selected sprite thumbnail is always highlighted and outlined with a blue border. When you select a sprite, you can access its scripts, costumes, and sounds by clicking one of the three tabs located above the Scripts Area. We'll look at the contents of these tabs later. For now, right-click (or CTRL-click if you're using a Mac) the Cat sprite's thumbnail to see the pop-up menu shown in Figure 1-6.

The duplicate option ❶ copies the sprite and gives the copy a different name. You can remove a sprite from your project with delete ❷, and you can export a sprite to a *.sprite2* file on your computer using the save to local file option ❸. (To import an exported sprite into another project, just click the Upload sprite from file button shown in Figure 1-5.) The hide/show option ❹ allows you to change whether a sprite on the Stage is visible or not.

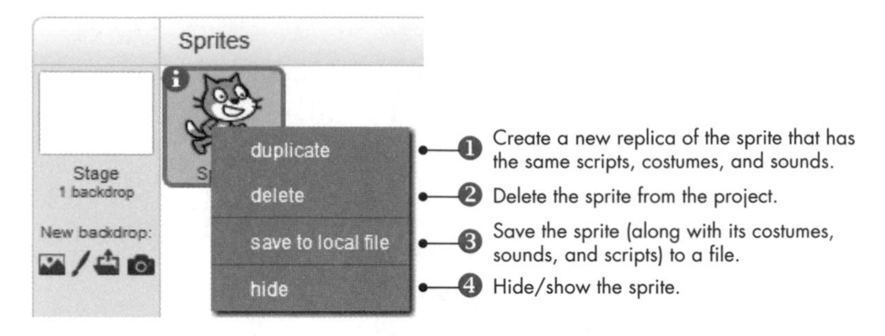

Figure 1-6: Right-clicking a sprite's thumbnail shows this handy menu.

Along with thumbnails for your sprites, the Sprite List also shows a thumbnail of the Stage to the left (see Figure 1-6). The Stage has its own set of scripts, images, and sounds. The background image you see on the Stage is called a *backdrop*. When you start a new project, the Stage defaults to a plain, white backdrop, but you can add new backdrop images with any of the four buttons below the Stage's thumbnail. Click on the Stage icon in the Sprite List to view and edit its associated scripts, backdrops, and sounds.

Blocks Tab

Blocks in Scratch are divided into 10 categories (palettes): *Motion, Looks, Sound, Pen, Data, Events, Control, Sensing, Operators,* and *More Blocks*. Blocks are color coded to help you find related blocks easily. Scratch 2 has more than 100 blocks, though some blocks only appear under certain conditions. For example, blocks in the *Data* palette (discussed in Chapters 5 and 9) appear only after a variable or a list is created. Let's look at the various components of the Blocks tab in Figure 1-7.

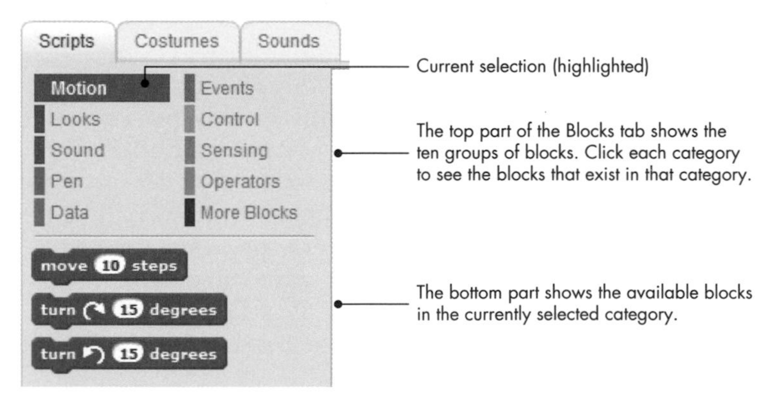

Figure 1-7: An enlarged view of the Blocks tab

Try clicking a block to see what it does. If you click **move 10 steps** on the *Motion* palette, for example, the sprite will move 10 steps on the Stage. Click it again, and the sprite moves another 10 steps. Click the **say Hello!**

for 2 secs block (in the *Looks* palette) to make the sprite display "Hello!" in a speech bubble for two seconds. You can also access the help screen of a block by selecting *Block help* (the question mark icon) from the toolbar and clicking the block you're confused about.

Some blocks require one or more inputs (also called *arguments*) that tell the block what to do. The number 10 in the **move 10 steps** block is an example of an argument. Look at Figure 1-8 to see the different ways blocks let you change their inputs.

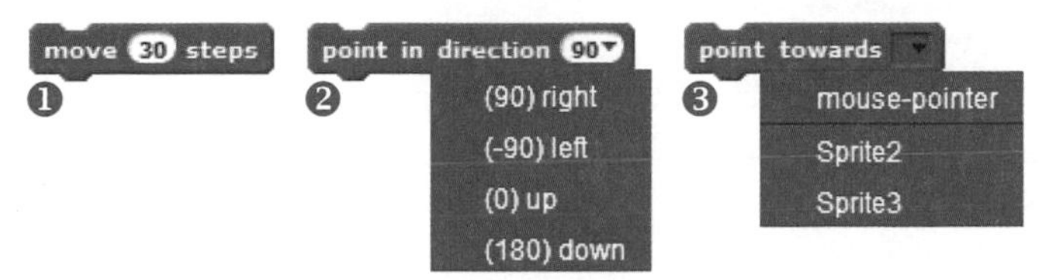

Figure 1-8: Changing the inputs of different types of blocks

You can change the number of steps in **move 10 steps** by clicking the white area where you see the 10 and entering a new number ❶, perhaps 30 as you see in Figure 1-8. Some blocks, like **point in direction 90**, also have pull-down menus for their inputs ❷. You can click the down arrow to see a list of available options and select one. This particular command has a white editable area, so you could also just type a value inside the white box. Other blocks, like **point towards** ❸, will force you to choose a value from the drop-down menu.

TRY IT OUT 1-4

Go to the *Looks* palette, change the values of block inputs, and click the blocks to see what they do. For example, experiment with the **set color effect to** block. Try numbers like 10, 20, 30, and so on until the cat returns to its original color. Try the options in the drop-down menu with different numbers. You can click the **clear graphic effects** block (also in the *Looks* palette) to remove your changes.

Scripts Area

To make a sprite do interesting things, you need to program it by dragging blocks from the Blocks tab to the Scripts Area and snapping them together. When you drag a block around the Scripts Area, a white highlight indicates where you can drop that block to form a valid connection with another block (Figure 1-9). Scratch blocks only snap together in certain ways, eliminating the typing errors that tend to occur when people use text-based programming languages.

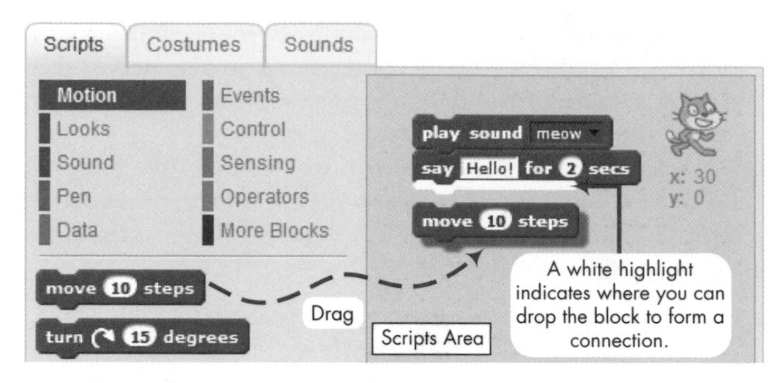

Figure 1-9: Drag blocks into the Scripts Area and snap them together to create scripts.

You don't need to complete scripts to run them, which means that you can test your script as you build it. Clicking anywhere on a script, complete or partial, runs the entire script, from top to bottom.

TRY IT OUT 1-5

Start a new Scratch project and create the script below for the Cat sprite. (The **forever** block is in the *Control* palette, and the other blocks are in the *Motion* palette.)

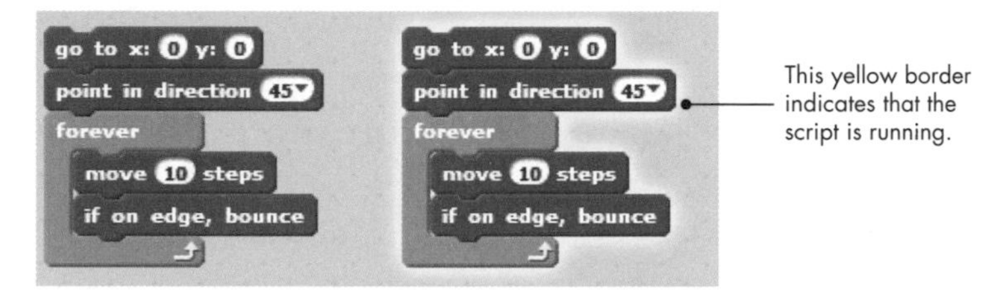

You'll learn about most of these blocks in Chapter 2. For now, click your new script to run it. (Scratch should highlight the running script with a glowing yellow border, as shown in the right side of the image.) You can even change a block's inputs and add new blocks to a script while it runs! For example, change the number in the **move** block and watch how the cat's motion changes. Click the script one more time to stop it.

You can also easily disassemble a stack of blocks and test each individually. This will be an invaluable strategy when you're trying to understand long scripts. To move an entire stack of blocks, grab the top block of the stack. To detach a block in the middle of a stack and all the blocks below it, grab it and drag it. Go ahead and try this out.

This feature also allows you to build your project one piece at a time. You can connect small chunks of blocks, test them to make sure they work as intended, and then combine them into larger scripts.

You can even copy a stack of blocks from one sprite to another. Just drag the stack from the Scripts Area of the source sprite to the thumbnail of the destination sprite in the Sprite List.

TRY IT OUT 1-6

Add another sprite to your project. Drag the script from the Cat sprite and drop it over the thumbnail of the new sprite. Your mouse arrow must be on top of the new sprite's thumbnail for the drop to succeed. Check the Scripts tab of the new sprite to make sure that it has an identical copy of the script.

Costumes Tab

You can change what a sprite looks like by changing its costume, which is just an image. The Costumes tab contains everything you need to organize your sprite's costumes; you could think of it like a clothes closet. The closet can have many costumes, but a sprite can wear only one at a time.

Let's try changing the Cat sprite's costume now. Click the thumbnail of the Cat sprite and select the Costumes tab. As illustrated in Figure 1-10, the Cat has two costumes: costume1 and costume2. The highlighted costume (costume1 in this case) represents the sprite's current costume.

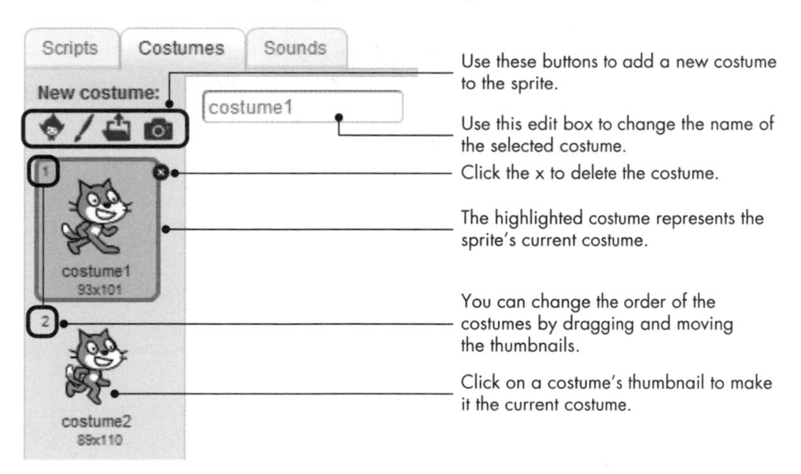

Figure 1-10: You can organize all the costumes for a sprite from the Costumes tab.

If you right-click on a costume's thumbnail, you'll see a pop-up menu with three options: (1) duplicate, (2) delete, and (3) save to local file. The first option adds a new costume with an image identical to that of the costume you duplicated. The delete option deletes the selected costume. The last option allows you to save the costume to a file. You can import that costume and use it in a different project using the Upload costume from file button (the third button in Figure 1-10). Go ahead and try these options out.

TRY IT OUT 1-7

Click the first button above the cat's image in Figure 1-10 to choose a new costume from Scratch's library. Then select any image you like from the window that appears. Apply some of the tips in Figure 1-10 to become more familiar with the costume options.

Sounds Tab

Sprites can also play sounds, which liven up your programs. You can, for example, give a sprite different sounds to use when it's happy or sad. If your game contains a sprite that looks like a missile, you could make the missile generate different sounds when it hits or misses a target.

The buttons in the Sounds tab will help you organize the different sounds your sprites can play. As shown in Figure 1-11, Scratch even provides a tool you can use to edit sound files. I won't discuss the details of this tool in this book, but I encourage you to experiment with it on your own.

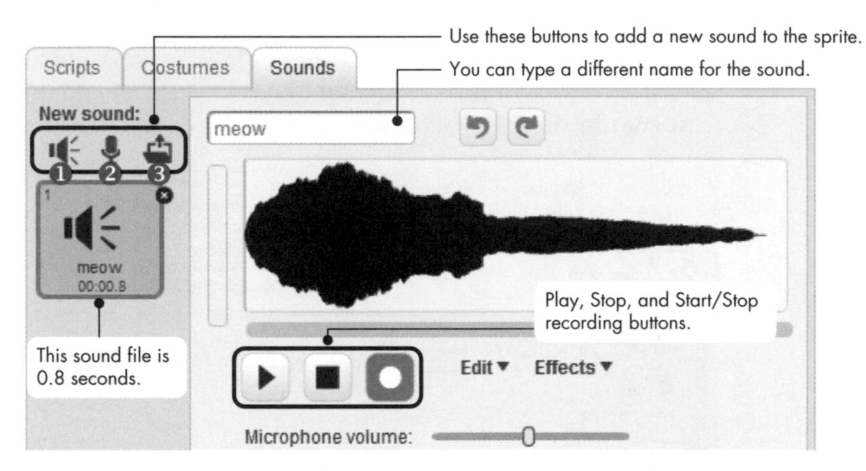

Figure 1-11: The Sounds tab allows you to organize the sounds of a sprite.

Most of the time, you'll need only the three buttons at the top of the Sounds tab. They allow you to choose a sound from Scratch's sound library ❶, record a new sound ❷ (if you have a microphone), or import an existing sound file from your computer ❸. Scratch can read only MP3 and WAV sound files.

TRY IT OUT 1-8

Select the Sounds tab and click the **Choose sound from library** button. Listen to the various sounds that are available in Scratch to get some ideas for your future projects.

Backdrops Tab

When you select the thumbnail of the Stage in the Sprite List, the name of the middle tab changes from *Costumes* to *Backdrops*. Use this tab to organize the Stage's background images, which you can change with your scripts. For example, if you're creating a game, you might show one backdrop with instructions to begin and then switch to another when the user starts the game. The Backdrops tab is identical to the Costumes tab.

TRY IT OUT 1-9

Click the **Choose backdrop from library** button below the thumbnail of the Stage in the Sprite List. Select the xy-grid backdrop from the window that appears and click OK. Scratch will add the xy-grid to your project and make it the default backdrop. (The xy-grid shows a 2-D Cartesian plane, which is useful when you're working with the Motion command blocks.) Repeat these steps and select any other backdrop that you like.

Sprite Info

You can view the sprite info area by clicking the small ❶ icon at the top-left edge of a sprite's thumbnail, as illustrated in Figure 1-12. This area shows the sprite's name, its current (*x*,*y*) position and direction, its rotation style and visibility state, and whether it can be dragged in Presentation mode. Let's briefly talk about each of these options.

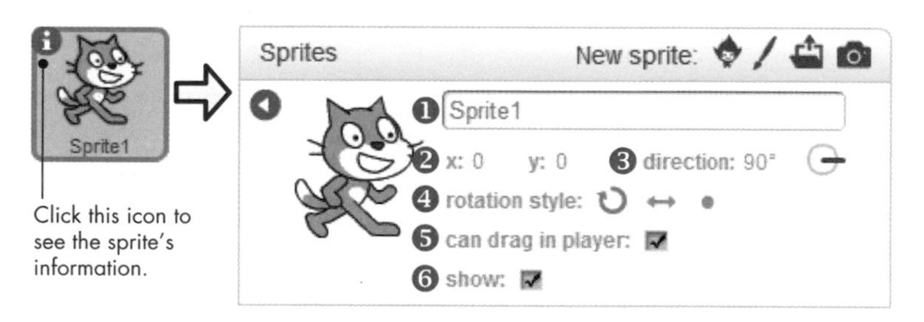

Figure 1-12: Sprite info area

The edit box ❶ at the top of this area allows you to change the sprite's name. You'll use this box many times in this book.

The *x* and *y* values ❷ show the sprite's current position on the Stage. Drag the sprite onto the Stage and watch what happens to these numbers.

The sprite's direction ❸ indicates which direction the sprite will move in response to a movement block. Drag the blue line emanating from the center of the circle icon to rotate the sprite.

The three rotation-style buttons ❹ (named Rotate, Left-right flip, and No rotate) control how the costume appears as the sprite changes its direction. To understand the effect of these buttons, create the script shown in Figure 1-13 and then click each of these buttons while the script is running. You can find the **wait** block in the *Control* palette.

The Can drag in player checkbox ❺ indicates whether or not the sprite can be dragged (using the mouse) in Presentation mode. Switch to Presentation mode with this box checked/unchecked and try to drag the sprite across the Stage to understand the effect of this checkbox.

The Show checkbox ❻ allows you to show/hide the sprite at program design time. Try it out and see what happens. You'll see several examples of hidden sprites that do useful work behind the scenes in many examples throughout this book.

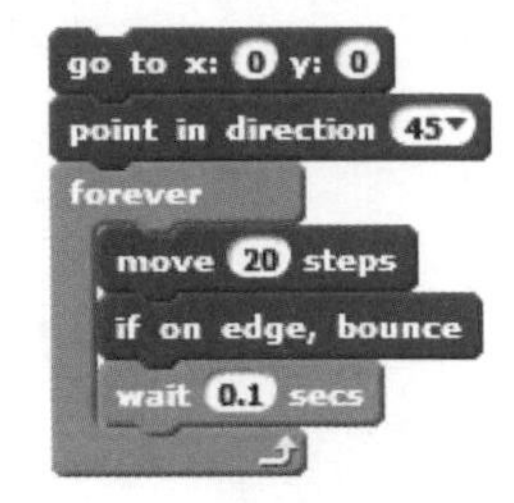

Figure 1-13: Script for demonstrating rotation styles

Toolbar

Let's take a quick look at Scratch's toolbar in Figure 1-14, starting with some of the buttons. (The toolbar will look slightly different if you are signed in, as covered in Appendix A.) Use the Duplicate and Delete buttons to copy and remove sprites, costumes, sounds, blocks, or scripts. The Grow button makes sprites bigger, while the Shrink button makes them smaller. Just click the button you want to use and then click on a sprite (or a script) to apply that action. To return to the arrow cursor, click on any blank area of the screen. You can use the Language menu to change the language of the user interface.

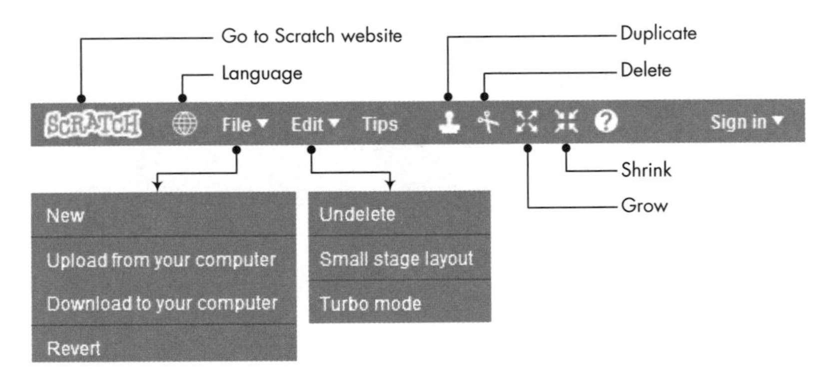

Figure 1-14: Scratch's toolbar

From the File menu, you can create new projects, upload (open) an existing project from your computer, download (save) the current project to your computer, or revert (undo) all your changes to the current project. Scratch 2 projects have an *.sb2* file extension to distinguish them from projects created in the previous version of Scratch (*.sb*).

In the Edit menu, Undelete will bring back the last block, script, sprite, costume, or sound you deleted. The Small stage layout option shrinks the Stage and gives the Scripts Area more room. Selecting Turbo mode increases the speed of some blocks. For example, executing a **move** block 1,000 times may take about 70 seconds in normal mode and about 0.2 seconds in Turbo mode.

Now that you've seen the essentials of the Scratch toolbar, we'll talk briefly about Scratch's built-in Paint Editor.

Paint Editor

You can use the Paint Editor (Figure 1-15) to create or edit costumes and backdrops. (Of course, you're free to use your favorite image-editing program, too.) If you want to learn more about Scratch's Paint Editor, check out *ScratchPaintEditor.pdf* (located in the online resources, which can be downloaded from *http://nostarch.com/learnscratch/*).

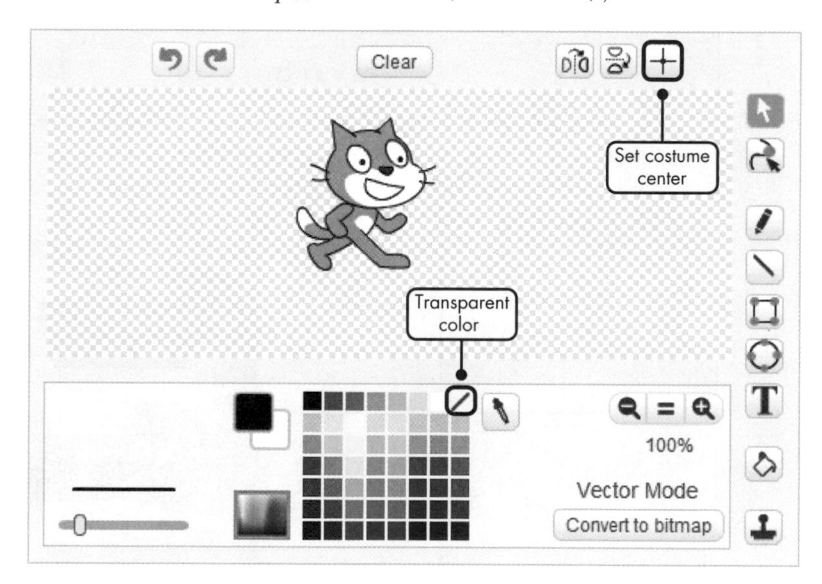

Figure 1-15: Scratch's Paint Editor

For now, there are two important features you'll need to know about: setting the center of an image and setting the transparent color. I'll explain these features in the following sections.

Setting the Center of an Image

When you command a sprite to turn (left or right), it will turn with respect to a reference point—the center of its costume. The Set costume center button (in the upper-right corner of the Paint Editor) allows you to choose that center. When you click this button, you'll see crosshairs on the drawing area, as shown in Figure 1-16. The center point is determined by the intersection of these two axes, so to shift a costume's center, just drag them to a new position. To hide the axes, click the same button again.

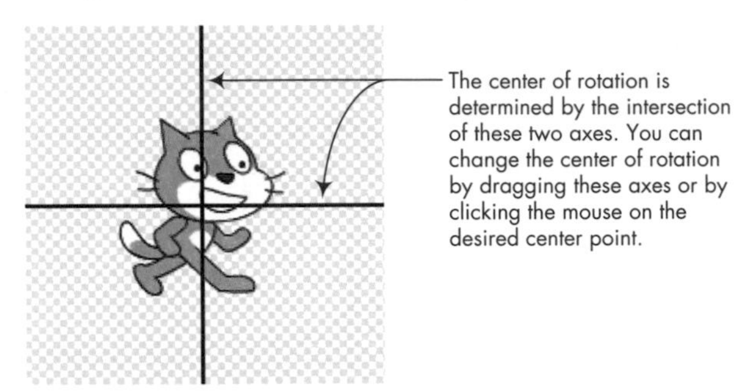

Figure 1-16: Changing a costume's center after clicking the Set costume center button

TRY IT OUT 1-10

RotationCenter.sb2

Open *RotationCenter.sb2* and run it. This application contains a single sprite with the costume and script shown below. The costume center is set in the middle of the square. Run the script and notice the pattern. Then edit the costume to set its center in the middle of the circle and run the script again to see how the picture changes.

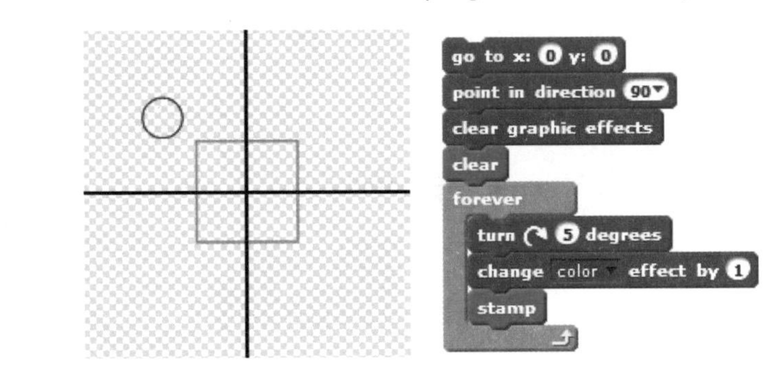

Setting Transparent Color

When two images overlap, the top image will cover some part of the bottom image. Similarly, sprites cover parts of the Stage. If you want to see what the Stage looks like behind an image, you need to use the Paint Editor to make at least part of that image *transparent*, as the penguin on the right is in Figure 1-17.

In the *Color* palette, just click the square with a diagonal red line and paint with that "transparent" color to make something invisible. You can think of this icon as a "No Color" sign, similar to a "No Smoking" sign with a red bar across a cigarette.

Figure 1-17: You can make any part of an image transparent by filling it with the "transparent" color.

Now that you know your way around the Scratch interface, we'll put that knowledge to good use and make something fun. Roll up your sleeves and get ready: We're making a game!

Your First Scratch Game

Pong.sb2
Pong_NoCode.sb2

In this section, you'll create a single-player game in which players will move a paddle to keep a bouncing tennis ball from hitting the floor, based on the classic arcade game Pong. The user interface for our game is illustrated in Figure 1-18.

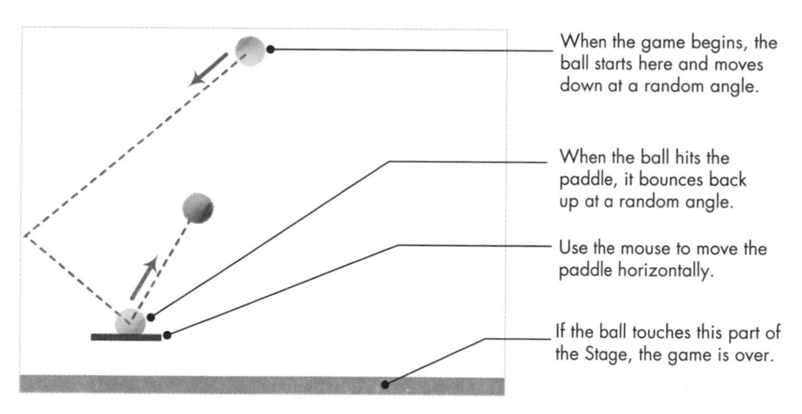

Figure 1-18: Our game screen

As shown in the figure, the ball starts at the top of the Stage and moves down at some random angle, bouncing off the edges of the Stage. The player moves the paddle horizontally (using the mouse) to send the ball back up. If the ball touches the bottom of the Stage, it's game over.

We'll build this game one step at a time, but first we need to open a fresh project. Select **File ▸ New** to start a new Scratch project. Then delete the Cat sprite by right-clicking it and selecting **delete** from the pop-up menu.

Step 1: Prepare the Backdrop

To detect when the ball misses the paddle, we'll mark the bottom of the Stage with a certain color and use the **touching color ?** block (from the *Sensing* palette) to tell us when the ball touches that color. Our current backdrop is white, so we can just draw a thin, colored rectangle at the bottom, as shown in Figure 1-19.

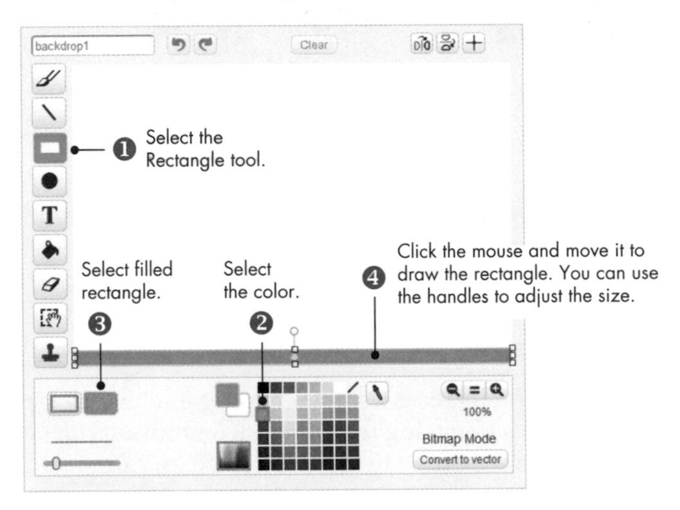

Figure 1-19: The steps for drawing a rectangle at the bottom of the backdrop image

Click the thumbnail of the Stage to select it and then go to the Backdrops tab. Follow the steps in Figure 1-19 to draw a thin rectangle at the bottom of the Stage's backdrop.

Step 2: Add the Paddle and Ball

Click the **Paint new sprite** button above the Sprite List to add the Paddle sprite to your project. Since the paddle is just a thin, short rectangle, repeat what you did in Step 1 to draw a paddle like the one in Figure 1-18. Color the paddle any way you want and set the center approximately in the middle of the rectangle.

Next, name the sprite something that explains what it is; I called it Paddle. Also, click the paddle image on the Stage and move it so that its *y*-coordinate is about –120.

Our game has a paddle now, but we still need a ball to bounce around, so click **Choose sprite from library** above the Sprite List to import one. In the dialog that appears, click the **Things** category and select the **Tennis Ball** image to add that sprite to your project. Rename the sprite as Ball.

Before you start working on scripts for the game, select **File ▸ Download to your computer** to save what you've done so far to your computer. In the dialog that appears, select the folder where you want to save your work, name the file *Pong.sb2*, and click **Save**. If you are currently signed in, you can also save your work on the *cloud* (that is, on a Scratch server). Whether you decide to save your files locally (on your computer) or on the cloud, make sure to save your work often.

With the Paddle and Ball sprites, the Stage should look similar to Figure 1-18. If you encounter any difficulties at this time, you can open the file *Pong_NoCode.sb2*, which contains everything we just created. You'll add the scripts to run the game next, but don't worry too much about the details of the blocks. We'll explore all of them later in the book, so for now, let's focus on learning to put a complete project together.

Step 3: Start the Game and Get Your Sprites Moving

As the designer for this game, you'll decide how players can start a new round. For example, the game could begin when you press a key, click a sprite on the Stage, or even clap or wave your hands (if you have a webcam). The green flag icon (located above the Stage) is another popular option, which we'll use here.

The idea is simple. Any scripts that start with the **when green flag clicked** trigger block start running when you press that button. The flag turns bright green and stays that way until the scripts finish. To see this in action, create the script shown in Figure 1-20 for the Paddle sprite.

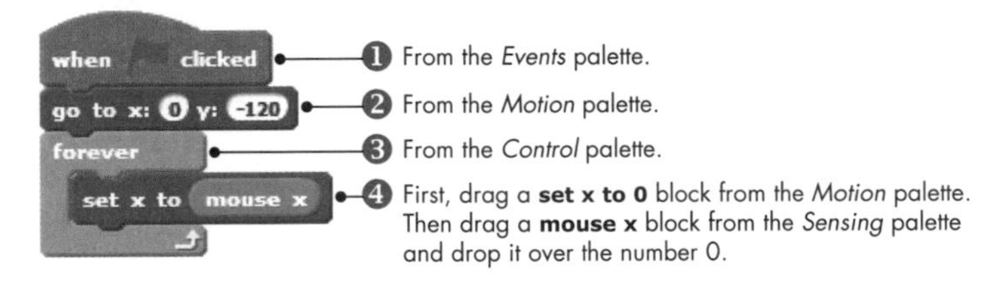
when clicked
go to x: 0 y: -120
forever
set x to mouse x
❶ From the *Events* palette.
❷ From the *Motion* palette.
❸ From the *Control* palette.
❹ First, drag a **set x to 0** block from the *Motion* palette. Then drag a **mouse x** block from the *Sensing* palette and drop it over the number 0.

Figure 1-20: The script for the Paddle sprite

When the green flag is clicked ❶, the **go to x: y:** block ❷ sets the paddle's vertical position to –120, just in case you previously moved it with the mouse. The paddle should hover just above the pink rectangle at the bottom of the Stage, so if your rectangle is thicker, change its position number to something that works for your design.

The script then uses a **forever** block ❸ to constantly check the mouse position. We'll move the paddle back and forth by matching the paddle's *x*-position to that of the mouse ❹. Run the script (by clicking the green flag icon) and try moving your mouse horizontally; the paddle should follow. Click the stop icon next to the green flag to stop the script.

The script for the Ball sprite is a little longer than the previous one, so I'll break it down into simple chunks. The ball should start moving when we click the green flag, so first, add the script in Figure 1-21 to the Ball sprite.

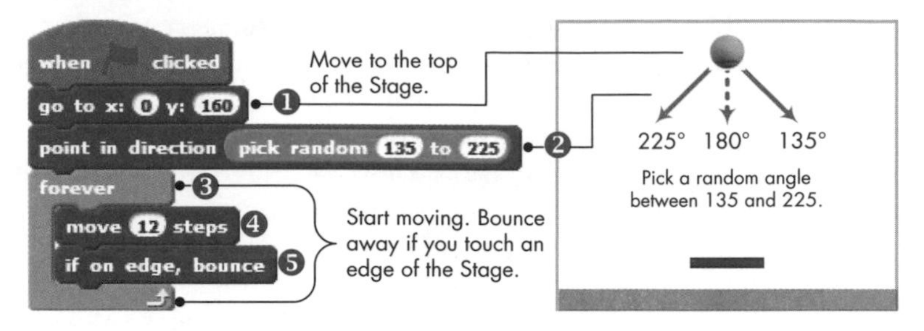

Figure 1-21: The first part of the Ball *sprite script*

First, we move the ball to the top of the stage ❶ and make it point down at a random angle using the **pick random** block ❷ (from the *Operators* palette). The script then uses a **forever** block ❸ to move the ball ❹ across the Stage and bounce ❺ off the edges. Click the green flag to test what you've written so far. The ball should move in a zigzag pattern, and the paddle should still follow your mouse.

> **TRY IT OUT 1-11**
>
> Replace the 12 inside the **move** block with different values, run the script, and watch what happens. This should give you an idea of how to make the game easier or harder to play. Click the stop icon when you're done.

Now, it's time to add the fun part—the blocks that make the ball bounce off the paddle. We can modify the **forever** block we just created so the ball travels upward when it hits the paddle, as shown in Figure 1-22.

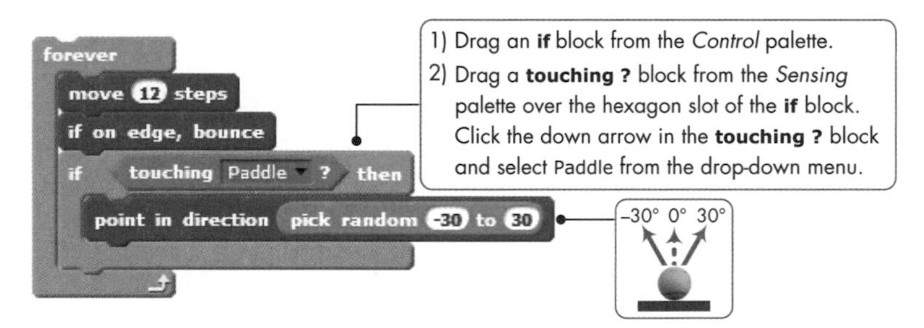

Figure 1-22: Adding code to kick the ball up

When the ball and paddle touch, we command the ball to point in a random direction between –30 and 30. When the **forever** block goes for the next round, it will execute the **move** block, which will now cause the ball to go up. Click the green flag again to test this part of the game. Click the stop icon when you are sure the ball is bouncing off of the paddle as it's supposed to.

The only piece we're missing now is some code to stop the game when the ball touches the bottom of the Stage. Add the script shown in Figure 1-23 to the Ball sprite, either right before or after the **if** block in Figure 1-22. You'll find the **touching color ?** block in the *Sensing* palette and the **stop** block in the *Control* palette.

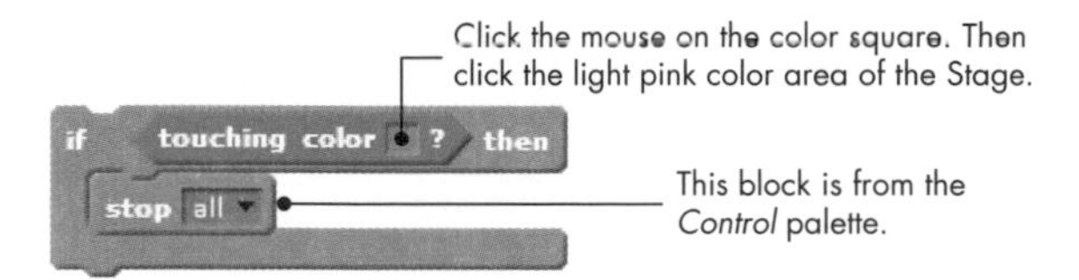

Figure 1-23: The blocks for ending the game

When you click the mouse over the colored square inside the **touching color ?** block, the cursor will change to a hand cursor. When you move that cursor and click over the light pink rectangle at the bottom of the Stage, the colored square inside the block should match the rectangle's color. The **stop all** block does exactly what its name says: It stops all running scripts in all sprites, and the Paddle and the Ball sprites are no exception.

This basic pong game is now fully functional. Click the green flag and play it a couple of times to test it out. After seeing that you can create a whole game with such a small amount of code, I hope you agree with me that Scratch is amazing!

Step 4: Spice It Up with Sound

Of course, games are more fun when they have sound, so let's add one final touch to play a noise every time we hit the ball.

Double-click the ball on the Stage to select it and then select the Sounds tab. Click the **Choose sound from library** button to add a sound to the Ball sprite. In the dialog that appears, select the **Effects** category, choose the **pop** sound, and click **OK** to add it to the Sounds tab. After that, go back to the Scripts tab and insert a **play sound** block (from the *Sound* palette), as shown in Figure 1-24.

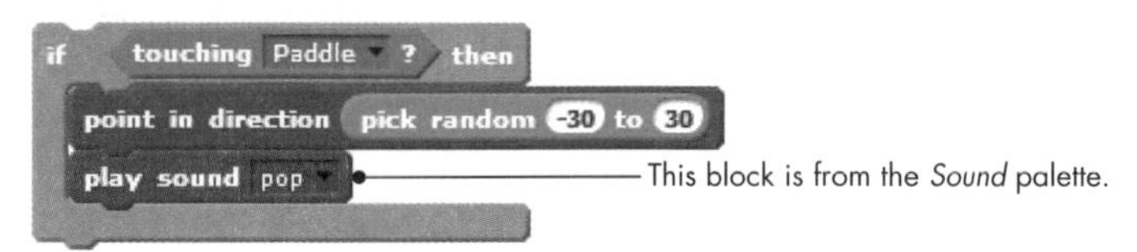

Figure 1-24: Playing a sound when the ball touches the paddle

Test the game once more, and this time, you should hear a short "pop" every time the ball touches the paddle.

Congratulations! Your game is now complete (unless, of course, you want to add more features to it), and you just wrote your first Scratch program. If you'd like to experiment some more, try duplicating the Ball sprite to have two (or more) balls in your game and see how that changes the way you play!

In the next section, I'll introduce the different types of blocks available in Scratch. As you continue through this book, you'll really dig into how those blocks work, but for now, we'll just go over them briefly.

Scratch Blocks: An Overview

In this section, you'll learn about the different blocks available in Scratch, their names, and their intended usage. The goal is to define some of the terms that you'll read in the next chapters. You can come back to this section as you progress if you need to refresh your memory.

As shown in Figure 1-25, Scratch has four kinds of blocks: command blocks, function blocks, trigger blocks, and control blocks. *Command blocks* and *control blocks* (also called *stack* blocks) have bumps on the bottom and/or notches on the top. You can snap these blocks together into stacks. *Trigger blocks*, also called *hats*, have rounded tops because they are placed at the top of a stack. Trigger blocks connect events to scripts. They wait for an event—such as a key press or mouse click—and run the blocks underneath them when that event happens. For example, all scripts that start with the **when green flag clicked** block will run when the user clicks the green flag icon.

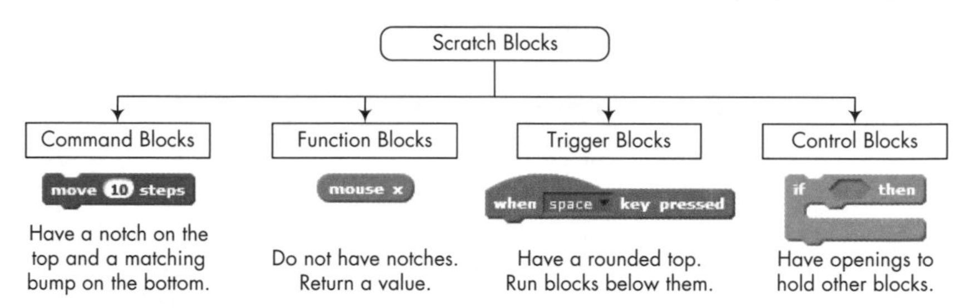

Figure 1-25: The four types of blocks available in Scratch

Function blocks (also called *reporters*) don't have notches or bumps. They can't form a layer of a script alone; instead, they're used as inputs to other blocks. The shapes of these blocks indicate the type of data they return. For example, blocks with rounded ends report numbers or strings, whereas blocks with pointed ends report whether something is true or false. This is illustrated in Figure 1-26.

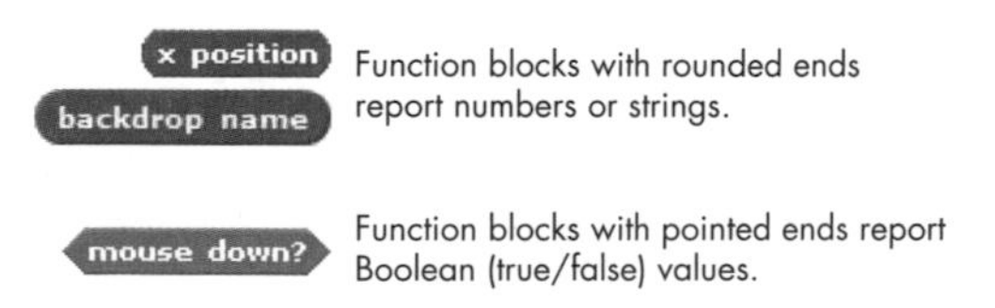

Figure 1-26: The shape of a function block indicates the type of data it returns.

Some function blocks have a checkbox next to them. If you check the box, a *monitor* appears on the Stage to display the current value of the reporter. Select a sprite and check the box on the **x position** block (in the *Motion* palette). Then drag the sprite around the Stage and watch that monitor. It should change as you move the sprite back and forth.

Arithmetic Operators and Functions

Now, let's take a quick look at the arithmetic operators and functions supported in Scratch. If you've lost your calculator, then your worries are over! You could make your own calculator in Scratch with the blocks from the *Operators* palette, which you'll explore in this section.

Arithmetic Operators

Scratch supports the four basic arithmetic operations of addition (**+**), subtraction (**-**), multiplication (*****), and division (**/**). The blocks used to perform these operations, called *operators*, are shown in Figure 1-27. Since these blocks produce a number, you can use them as inputs to any block that accepts numbers, as demonstrated in this figure.

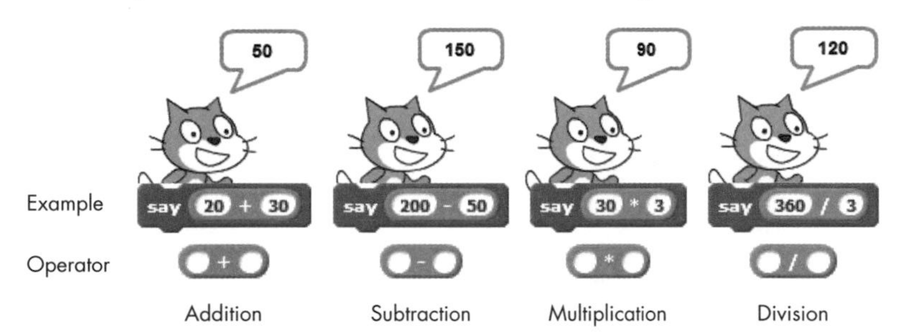

Figure 1-27: Arithmetic operators in Scratch

Scratch also supports the modulus (**mod**) operator, which returns the remainder of the division of two numbers. For example, **10 mod 3** returns 1 because the remainder of dividing 10 by 3 is 1. A common use of the modulus operator is to test the divisibility of one *integer* (whole number) by another (smaller) integer. A modulus of 0 indicates that the larger number is divisible by the smaller number. Does this give you an idea for checking whether a number is even or odd?

Another useful operator supported by Scratch is the **round** operator, which rounds decimal numbers to the nearest whole number. For example, **round(3.1)** = 3, **round(3.5)** = 4, and **round(3.6)** = 4.

Random Numbers

As you program more often, you'll probably need to generate random numbers at some point, especially if you create games and simulations. Scratch provides the **pick random** block specifically for this purpose.

This block outputs a random number each time you use it. Its two editable white boxes allow you to enter a range for that number, and Scratch will only choose values between the two limits (inclusive). Table 1-1 shows some examples of using this block.

Table 1-1: Examples of Using the Pick Random Block

Example	Possible Outcome
pick random 0 to 1	{0, 1}
pick random 0 to 10	{0, 1, 2, 3, ... , 10}
pick random -2 to 2	{–2, –1, 0, 1, 2}
10 * pick random 0 to 10	{0, 10, 20, 30, ... , 100}
pick random 0 to 1.0	{0, 0.1, 0.15, 0.267, 0.3894, ... , 1.0}
pick random 0 to 100 / 100	{0, 0.01, 0.12, 0.34, 0.58, ... , 1.0}

NOTE *The outputs of* **pick random 0 to 1** *and* **pick random 0 to 1.0** *are different. The first case will give you either a 1 or a 0, but the second gives a decimal value between 0 and 1. If any input to the* **pick random** *block contains a decimal point, the output will also be a decimal value.*

Mathematical Functions

Scratch also supports a large number of mathematical functions. The **sqrt of** block groups together 14 math functions that can be selected from the drop-down menu, including square root, trigonometric, logarithmic, and exponential functions. Refer to *MathematicalFunctions.pdf* for an extensive coverage of these functions.

Summary

This chapter provided a high-level overview of Scratch and its programming environment. You learned about the various elements of the user interface and even created a game! We also explored Scratch's mathematical operators and functions.

At this point, you've seen the most basic information you need to create some powerful scripts in Scratch, but that's only one step on the road to writing awesome programs. In the chapters that follow, you'll dig deeper into how you can use Scratch to develop your programming skills.

Problems

1. Write down the result of each block in the script below. Is there a pattern in these products?

```
say (1 * 1) for 2 secs
say (11 * 11) for 2 secs
say (111 * 111) for 2 secs
say (1111 * 1111) for 2 secs
say (11111 * 11111) for 2 secs
```

2. Is there a pattern in the products 9 × 9, 99 × 99, 999 × 999, ... , etc.? Use the **say** command to find the result of these products and check your answer.
3. Complete the following table by writing the value of each expression.

Expression	Value
3 + (2 × 5)	
(10 / 2) – 3	
7 + (8 × 2) – 4	
(2 + 3) × 4	
5 + (2 × (7 – 4))	
(11 – 5) × (2 + 1) / 2	
5 × (5 + 4) – 2 × (1 + 3)	
(6 + 12) mod 4	
3 × (13 mod 3)	
5 + (17 mod 5) – 3	

Now, use the **say** command and the appropriate operator blocks to check your answers.

4. Evaluate the following Scratch expressions using a pencil and paper. Let $x = 2$ and $y = 4$.

a) (6 * x)

b) ((2 * x) + (4 * y))

c) (x * x)

d) ((y + 4) / (x * x))

e) ((y * y) / ((2 * x) + 2))

5. Use the **say** command and the appropriate blocks from the *Operators* palette to calculate the following:
   a. The square root of 32
   b. The sine of 30°
   c. The cosine of 60°
   d. The result of rounding 99.459
6. Create a function block that calculates the average of the following three numbers: 90, 95, and 98. Display the result using the **say** block.
7. Create a function block that converts 60°F to Celsius. (Hint: $C = (5/9) \times (F - 32)$.)
8. Create a function block that calculates the area of a trapezoid with a height of 4/6 foot and bases of lengths 5/9 foot and 22/9 foot. (Hint: $A = 0.5 \times (b_1 + b_2) \times h$, where h is the height and b_1 and b_2 are the lengths of the two bases.)
9. Create a function block that calculates the force needed to accelerate a 2,000 kg car 3 m/s^2. (Hint: *Force* = *mass* × *acceleration*.)
10. The cost of electricity is $0.06 per kilowatt-hour. Create a function block that calculates the cost of using a 1,500-watt air conditioner for 2 hours. (Hint: *Energy* = *power* × *time*.)
11. With a simple mathematical trick, you can use the **round** operator to round a number to a specific decimal place. For example, you can round the number 5.3567 to the nearest tenth (that is, the first position to the right of the decimal point) using these three steps:
   a. 5.3567 × 10 = 53.567 (Multiply the number by 10.)
   b. round(53.567) = 54 (Round the answer from step a.)
   c. 54/10 = 5.4 (Divide the answer from step b by 10.)

   What changes would you need to make to the above steps to round to the nearest hundredth (i.e., the second position to the right of the decimal point)? Create a function block that rounds 5.3567 to the nearest tenth (or hundredth) and display its output using the **say** block.

2

MOTION AND DRAWING

Now that you know your way around the interface, you're ready to use more of Scratch's programming tools. In this chapter, you'll do the following:

- Explore Scratch's motion and pen commands
- Animate sprites and move them around the Stage
- Draw artistic, geometric patterns and create games
- Learn why sprite cloning is a valuable tool

It's time to put on your creative hat and jump into the world of computer graphics!

Using Motion Commands

If you want to make games or other animated programs, you'll need to use blocks from the *Motion* palette to move sprites around. Furthermore, you'll need to command sprites to move to a particular spot on the Stage or turn in a certain direction. You'll find out how in this section.

Absolute Motion

Remember, as you saw in Figure 1-4, the Stage is like a 480 × 360 rectangular grid whose center is point (0,0). Scratch has four *absolute motion* commands (**go to**, **glide to**, **set x to**, and **set y to**) that let you tell your sprite exactly where to go on that grid.

NOTE *If you want more details about these and other blocks, use the Scratch Tips window on the right side of the Scripts panel. If you don't see the Tips window, just click the question mark near the top-right corner of Scratch's Project Editor.*

To demonstrate these commands, let's say that you want to make the Rocket sprite in Figure 2-1 hit the star-shaped Target sprite at position (200,150). The most obvious way to do this is to use the **go to** block, as illustrated in the right side of the figure. The *x*-coordinate tells the sprite how far to move horizontally across the Stage, whereas the *y*-coordinate tells it how far to move vertically.

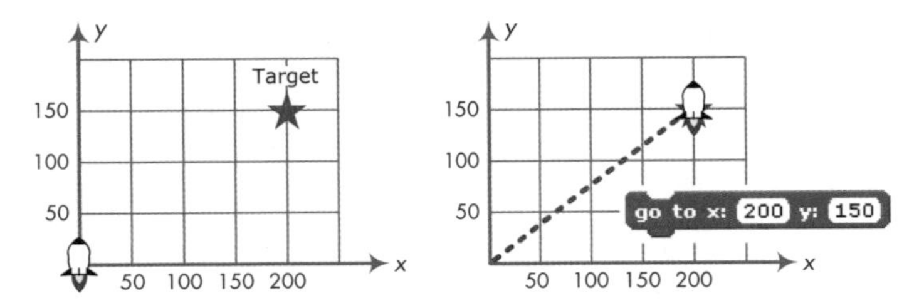

Figure 2-1: You can move a sprite to any point on the Stage using the **go to** *block.*

The Rocket won't turn to face the target, but it will move along an invisible line connecting its current position, point (0,0), to point (200,150). You can make the Rocket slow down by using the **glide to** command instead. It's nearly identical to the **go to** command, but it lets you set how long the Rocket will take to reach the target.

Another way to hit the target is to change the *x*- and *y*-positions of the Rocket sprite independently with the **set x to** and **set y to** blocks, as illustrated in Figure 2-2. Do you remember how you used the **set x to** block in the Pong game in Chapter 1? (See Figure 1-20 on page 17 for a review.)

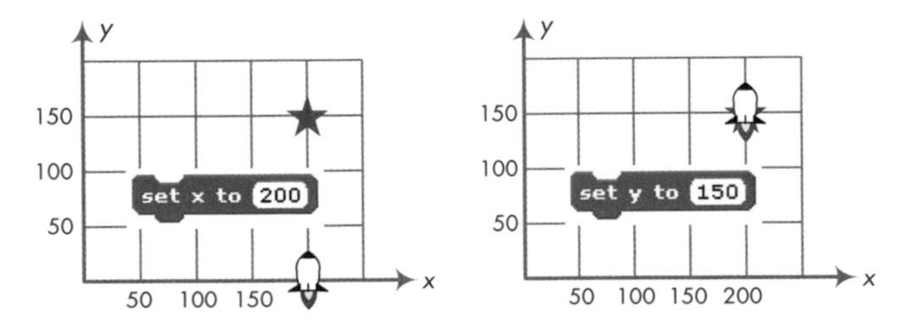

Figure 2-2: You can set the x- and y-coordinates of a sprite independently.

You can always see a sprite's current *x*- and *y*-position in the upper-right corner of the Scripts Area. If you want to display this information on the Stage, you can use the **x position** and **y position** reporter blocks. Click the checkboxes next to these blocks to see their values on the Stage.

NOTE *Motion commands work with reference to a sprite's center, which you can set in the Paint Editor. For example, sending a sprite to point (100,100) moves the sprite so that its center is at (100,100), as illustrated in Figure 2-3. Therefore, when you draw or import a costume for a sprite you plan to move around, pay special attention to its center!*

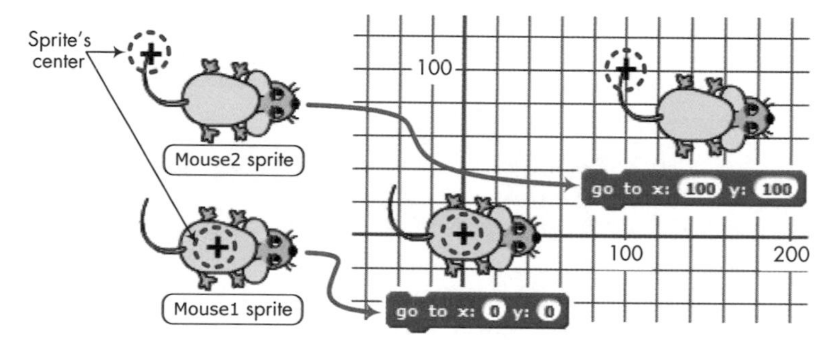

Figure 2-3: Motion commands reference a sprite's center.

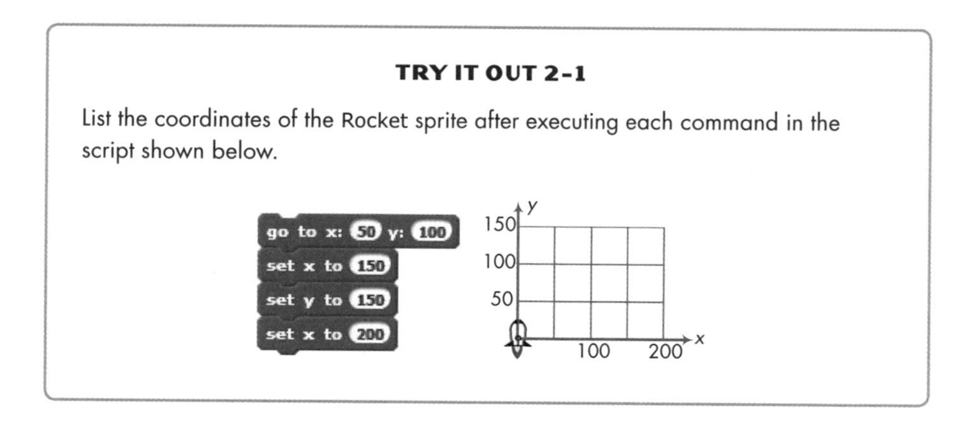

TRY IT OUT 2-1

List the coordinates of the Rocket sprite after executing each command in the script shown below.

Relative Motion

Now consider the grid depicted in Figure 2-4, which shows another Rocket sprite and target. You can't see the coordinates this time, so you don't know the sprites' exact position. If you had to tell the Rocket how to hit the target, you might say: "Move three steps, then turn right, then move two steps."

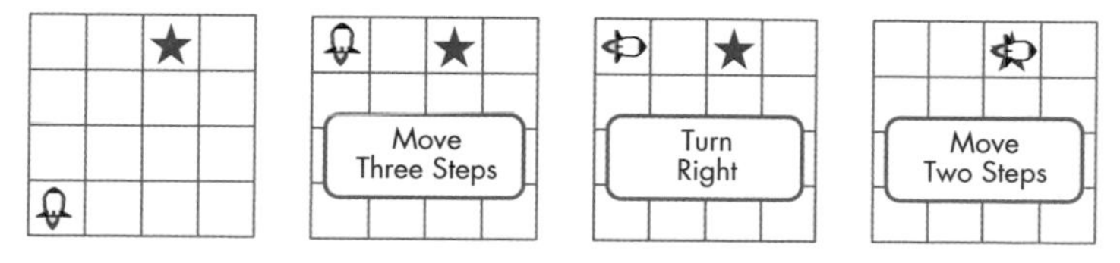

Figure 2-4: You can move a sprite on the Stage using relative motion commands.

Commands like **move** and **turn** are *relative motion* commands. The first "move" command above, for example, caused the Rocket to move up, while the second "move" command sent it right. The motion depends on (or is relative to) the sprite's current *direction*. The direction convention used in Scratch is illustrated in Figure 2-5.

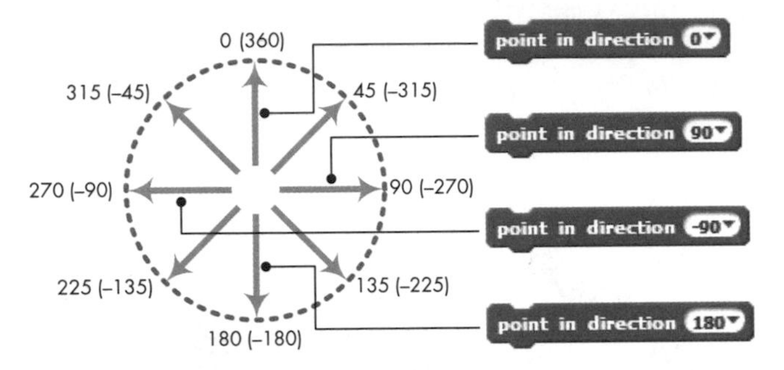

Figure 2-5: In Scratch, 0 is up, 90 is right, 180 is down, and –90 is left.

You can turn a sprite toward a particular direction (or *heading*) with the **point in direction** command. To choose up, right, down, or left, just click the down arrow and select one of these options from the drop-down menu. For other directions, type the value you want in the white edit box. You can even use negative values! (For example, typing 45 or –315 will both point the sprite northeast.)

NOTE *You'll find the sprite's current direction in the sprite info area. You can also click the checkbox next to the* **direction** *block (in the* Motion *palette) to see the direction on the Stage.*

Now that you know how directions work in Scratch, let's see how the relative motion commands (**move**, **change x by**, **change y by**, and **turn**) work. We'll start with the **move** and **turn** commands, which work with respect to the sprite's current direction, as shown in Figure 2-6.

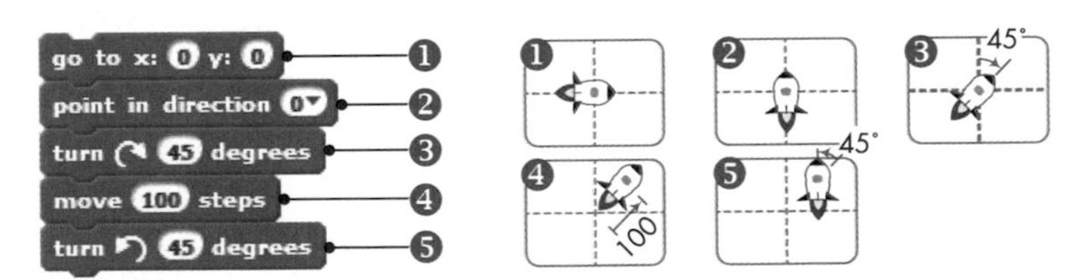

Figure 2-6: A simple script that illustrates using the **move** *and* **turn** *commands*

First, the **go to** block ❶ moves the Rocket so that its center is aligned with the center of the Stage. The second command block ❷ points the sprite up, and the third ❸ turns it 45° clockwise. Then, the sprite moves 100 steps ❹ in its current direction before turning 45° counterclockwise ❺ to stop in the up position.

DIRECTION AND COSTUMES

The **point in direction** command knows nothing about the sprite's costume. For example, consider the two sprites shown below.

Using the Paint Editor, we drew the bird's costume to face right and the insect's costume to face up. What do think will happen if you use the **point in direction 90** command (that is, point right) on each sprite?

You might guess that the insect will turn to face right, but actually, neither sprite will turn. Although 90° is labeled "right," that direction really refers to the costume's *original orientation* in the Paint Editor. So because the insect looks like it's facing up in the Paint Editor, it will still face up when you tell it to point to 90°. If you want your sprite to respond to the **point in direction** command as shown in Figure 2-5, you need to draw the sprite's costume so that it faces right in the Paint Editor (as the bird costume does in the above figure).

Sometimes you might only want to move your sprite horizontally or vertically from its current position, and that's where the **change x by** and **change y by** blocks come in. The script in Figure 2-7 illustrates the use of these blocks.

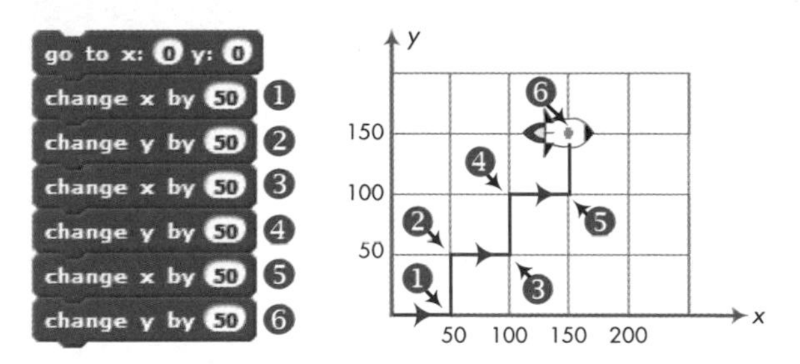

Figure 2-7: Navigate a winding path with **change x by** *and* **change y by**.

After the Rocket sprite moves to the center of the Stage, the first **change x by 50** command ❶ adds 50 to its *x*-coordinate to send it 50 steps to the right. The next command ❷, **change y by 50**, makes the *y*-coordinate 50, causing the sprite to move up 50 steps. The other commands work in a similar way. Try to trace the sprite's motion, illustrated in Figure 2-7, to find the sprite's final destination.

TRY IT OUT 2-2

Find the rocket's final (*x*,*y*) position when it executes each of the two scripts shown below. What mathematical theorem can you use to prove that the two scripts are equivalent?

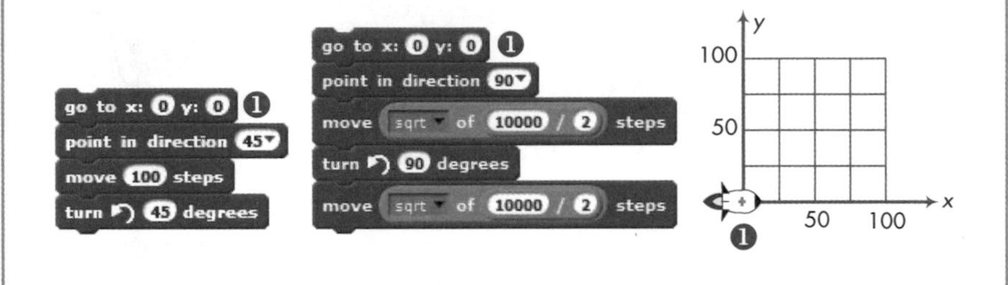

Other Motion Commands

TennisBallChaser.sb2

There are just four motion commands left to explore: **point towards**; a second type of **go to** block; **if on edge, bounce**; and **set rotation style**.

You've already learned about rotation styles, and you saw the **if on edge, bounce** command in action in Chapter 1 (see Figure 1-13 on page 12). To see the other two commands in action, let's create a simple application of a cat chasing a tennis ball, as illustrated in Figure 2-8.

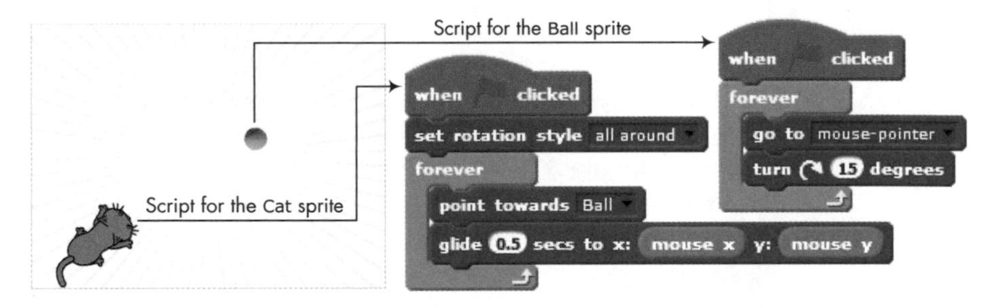

Figure 2-8: Programming a cat to run after a tennis ball

As shown, the application contains two sprites, named Cat and Ball, and two scripts. When you click the green flag icon, the Ball sprite follows the mouse pointer. The Cat sprite continuously points towards the Ball and moves toward it using the **glide** command. Go ahead and build this application to see how it works. You can find the **forever** block in the *Control* palette and the **mouse x** and **mouse y** blocks in the *Sensing* palette. You can find the complete application in the file *TennisBallChaser.sb2*.

In the next section, we'll look at the *Pen* palette and learn how to make a sprite leave a visual trace of its motion.

Pen Commands and Easy Draw

EasyDraw.sb2

The motion commands you used in the previous section allow you to move the sprite to any point on the Stage. Now wouldn't it be nice to see the actual path your sprite travels? Scratch's pen can help.

Each sprite has an invisible *pen,* which can be either up or down. If the pen is down, the sprite will draw as it moves. Otherwise, the sprite moves without leaving any trace. The commands in the *Pen* palette allow you to control the pen's size, color, and shade.

TRY IT OUT 2-3

Open the Tips window in Scratch, click the house icon, and click **Pen** for a brief description of each Pen command. The scripts below demonstrate most of those commands. Re-create these scripts, run them, and describe the output of each. Don't forget to set the sprite's pen down before running these scripts. (You can find the **repeat** block in the *Control* palette.)

```
go to x: 0 y: 0
clear
set pen color to [ ]
set pen size to 160
pen down
set pen color to [ ]
set pen size to 120
pen down
```

```
go to x: -200 y: 0
clear
set pen color to 0
set pen size to 20
repeat 200
    move 2 steps
    change pen color by 1
```

```
go to x: -200 y: 0
clear
set pen color to 70
set pen size to 20
set pen shade to 0
repeat 100
    move 4 steps
    change pen shade by 1
```

Let's explore some of the pen commands in detail and create a simple program to draw pictures by moving and turning a sprite on the Stage with the arrow keys. One press of the up arrow (↑) will move the sprite forward 10 steps. Pressing the down arrow (↓) will move the sprite backward 10 steps. Each press of the right arrow (→) will turn the sprite to the right 10°, and each press of the left arrow (←) will turn the sprite to the left 10°. So, for example, to make the sprite turn 90°, as shown in Figure 2-9, you would press the left or right arrow key nine times.

First, start a new Scratch project. Replace the Cat's costume with something that clearly shows if the sprite is pointing left, right, up, or down. The beetle or the cat2 costumes (from the Animals folder) are good choices, but feel free to pick any other costume you like. In the *Costumes* tab, click the **Choose costume from library** button and select an appropriate costume.

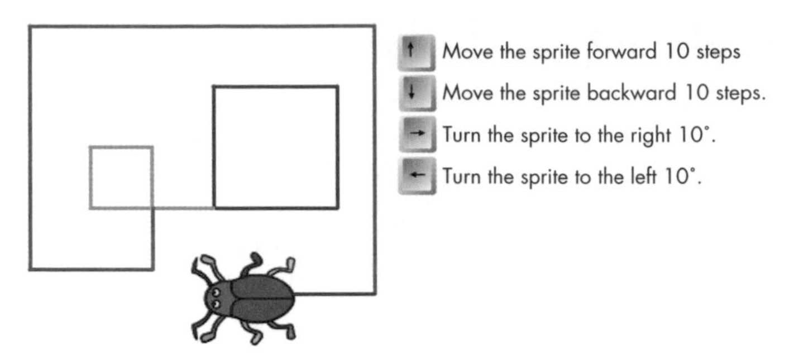

Figure 2-9: The Easy Draw application in action

Now, add the scripts shown in Figure 2-10 to your sprite. You can create the four **when key pressed** blocks from the **when space key pressed** block in the *Events* palette. Just click the down arrow and choose the arrow key you need.

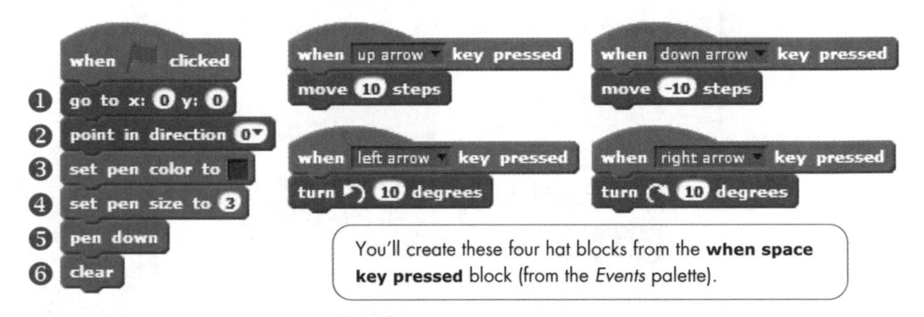

Figure 2-10: Scripts for the Easy Draw application

When you click the green flag, the sprite will move to the center of the Stage ❶ and point up ❷. Then the pen's color ❸ and size ❹ will be set, and the script puts the pen down ❺ to get ready for drawing. After that, the program clears any previous drawings from the Stage ❻.

All you have to do to clear the Stage and start a new drawing is click the green flag. Use the keyboard arrows to draw any shape you like. What shape do you think the sequence ↑→↑→ ↑→ … would create?

TRY IT OUT 2-4

Add an option to make the drawing pen wider when the letter *W* is pressed and narrower when the letter *N* is pressed. Think of other ways to enhance the application and try to implement them.

The Power of Repeat

Our programs have been relatively simple so far, but as you start writing longer scripts, you'll often need to replicate the same stack of blocks several times in a row. Duplicating scripts can make your program longer, harder to understand, and tougher to experiment with. If you need to change one number, for example, you'll have to make the same change in each copy of the block. The **repeat** command from the *Control* palette can help you avoid this problem.

DrawSquare.sb2

For example, let's say that you want to draw the square shown in Figure 2-11 (left). You could command the sprite to follow these repetitive instructions:

1. Move some distance and turn 90° counterclockwise.
2. Move the same distance and turn 90° counterclockwise.
3. Move the same distance and turn 90° counterclockwise.
4. Move the same distance and turn 90° counterclockwise.

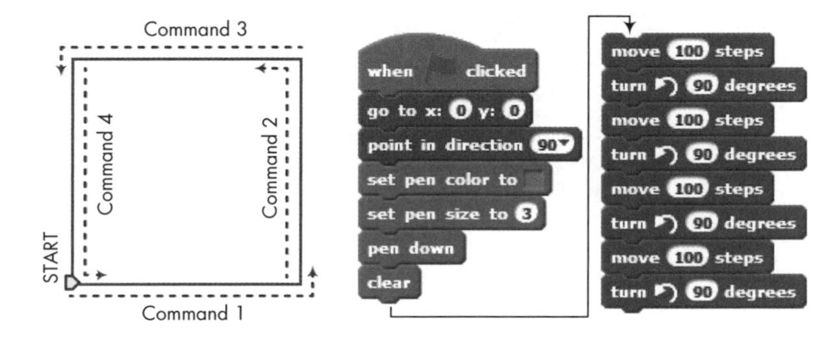

Figure 2-11: A square (left) and a script to draw it (right) using a sequence of **move** *and* **turn** *commands*

Figure 2-11 also shows a script that implements these instructions. Notice that it repeats the commands **move 100 steps** and **turn 90 degrees** four times. In contrast, we can avoid using the same two blocks over and over with the **repeat** block, which runs the commands inside it as many times as you tell it to, as shown in Figure 2-12. Using a **repeat** block can also make the instructions much easier to understand.

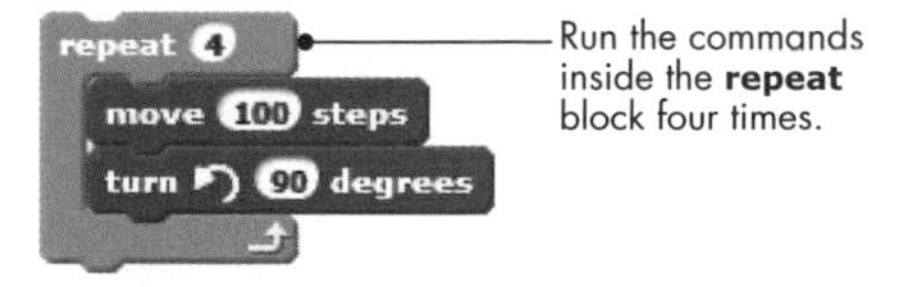

Figure 2-12: Using the **repeat** *block to draw a square*

The square you draw with the script in Figure 2-11 depends on the direction your sprite faces when you start. This concept is illustrated in Figure 2-13. Note that after drawing the square, the sprite will return to its starting point and face the same direction it did before it began to move.

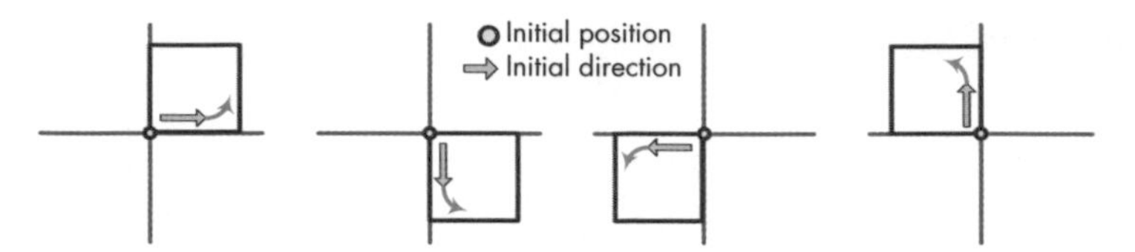

Figure 2-13: The sprite's initial direction changes the square's location.

Polygon.sb2

TRY IT OUT 2-5

You can easily modify the square-drawing script of Figure 2-12 to draw other regular polygons. The modified script has the form shown below. You can substitute any whole number for "number of sides" to specify the desired polygon and any value for "side length" to control the polygon's size. The figure also shows six polygons of the same side length that were drawn using this script. The sprite started at the position and heading indicated by the green arrow in the figure. Open the file *Polygon.sb2* and run it using different values for "number of sides." What happens when this number becomes large? This should give you an idea of how to draw circles.

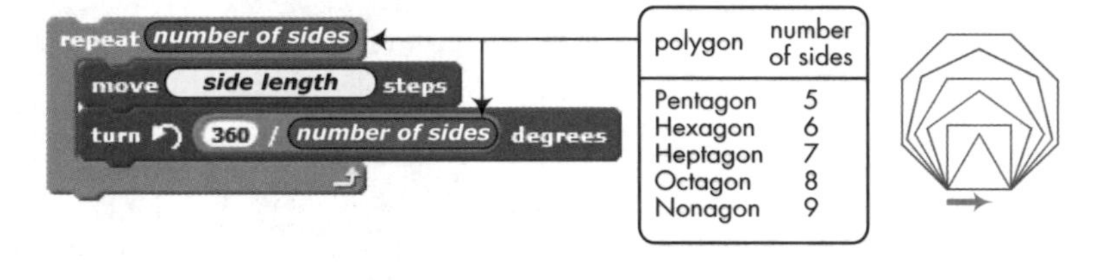

polygon	number of sides
Pentagon	5
Hexagon	6
Heptagon	7
Octagon	8
Nonagon	9

Rotated Squares

RotatedSquares .sb2

You can create amazing art by repeating a pattern in a certain sequence. For example, the script shown in Figure 2-14 creates an attractive pattern by rotating and drawing a square 12 times. (The blocks for initializing the pen and putting it down are not shown for the sake of brevity.)

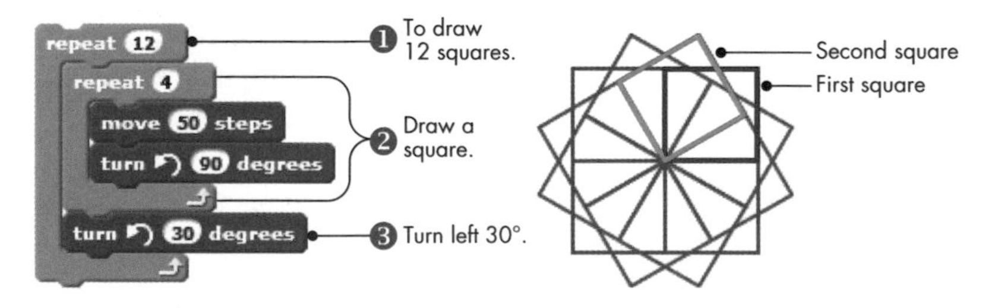

Figure 2-14: Drawing a rotated square

The outer **repeat** block ❶ executes 12 times. Each time inside the loop, it draws one square ❷ and then makes a 30° left turn ❸ to prepare to draw the next one.

TRY IT OUT 2-6

Notice that (12 repeats) × (30° for each repeat) = 360°. What do you think would happen if you changed the numbers in the program to 4 repeats and 90°? What about 5 and 72°? Experiment with different values for the **repeat** count and the **turn** angle to see what happens.

Exploring with Stamp

Windmill.sb2

In the previous section, you learned to use the **turn** and **repeat** blocks to transform simple shapes into complex patterns. But what if you want to rotate more challenging shapes? Instead of drawing the basic shape with **move** and **turn** commands, you can make a new costume in the Paint Editor and use the **stamp** block to draw multiple copies of it on the Stage. To illustrate this technique, let's write a program to draw the windmill shown in Figure 2-15.

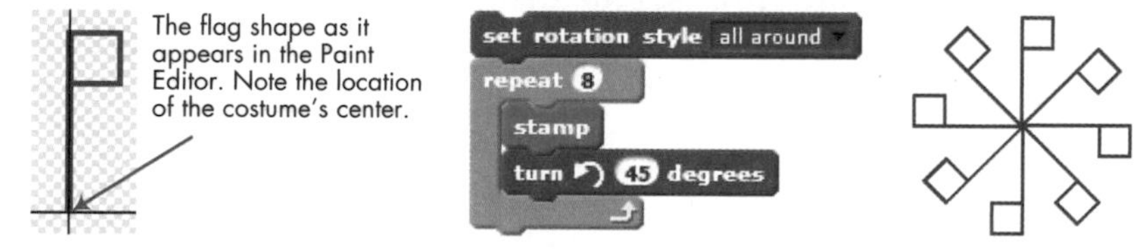
The flag shape as it appears in the Paint Editor. Note the location of the costume's center.
set rotation style all around
repeat 8
stamp
turn 45 degrees

Figure 2-15: The **stamp** *command allows you to create complex geometric patterns with ease.*

We drew the flag shape using the Paint Editor (see Figure 2-15, left) and used it as the costume of our sprite. We set the costume's center at the lower tip of the flag so we could rotate the flag around this point.

The script for drawing the windmill is shown in Figure 2-15 (middle). The **repeat** block executes eight times; each time, it stamps a copy of the costume on the Stage before rotating the sprite 45° to the left. Note that for this script to work, you must use the **set rotation style** block with the sprite's rotation style set to all around to allow the flag to flip as it rotates.

NOTE DrawingGeometricShapes.pdf *in the extra resources package (which you can download from* http://nostarch.com/learnscratch/) *provides comprehensive coverage of drawing geometric shapes such as rectangles, parallelograms, rhombuses, trapezoids, kites, and polygons, and teaches you how to create attractive polygon art.*

TRY IT OUT 2-7

The **change color effect by** block (from the *Looks* palette) allows you to apply graphic effects like color, whirl, and fisheye. Open the file *Windmill.sb2* and add this command inside the **repeat** block. Experiment with other graphic effects to make some more cool patterns. Note that for the **change color effect by** block to work, the flag's color in the Paint Editor can't be black.

Scratch Projects

In this section, we'll develop two short programs that should further your understanding of the **Motion** and **Pen** blocks you've learned so far. You can find the backdrops and sprites in the project files for this chapter, so we'll focus on writing the scripts we need to make these applications work. An explanation of an additional bonus game, called Survival Jump, is available in the extra resources. You'll find details in *BonusApplications.pdf* (*http://nostarch.com/learnscratch/*).

Some of these scripts will use command blocks that you haven't seen, but don't worry if you don't completely understand some things. You'll learn all about them in the coming chapters.

Get the Money

Money_NoCode.sb2

Our first application is a simple game in which the player needs to move the sprite by using the keyboard arrows to collect as many bags of gold as possible. As illustrated in Figure 2-16, the bag of gold appears at a random location on the grid. If the player doesn't grab the bag in three seconds, it moves somewhere else.

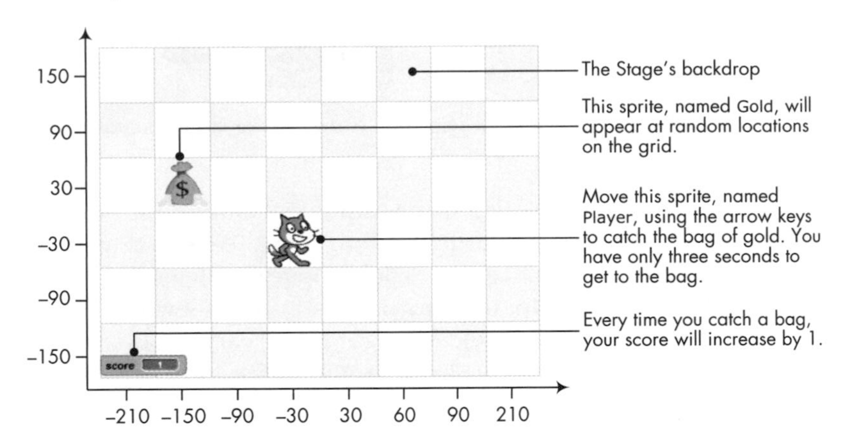

Figure 2-16: Help the cat grab as many bags of gold as possible!

Open the file *Money_NoCode.sb2*. The scripts are missing, but you'll create them now, and the file contains everything else you'll need.

NOTE *The coordinate axes shown in Figure 2-16 were added to help you understand the numbers used in these scripts. Come back to this figure as needed to refresh your mental picture of how the sprites are moving.*

Let's start by writing the scripts for the Player sprite, as shown in Figure 2-17.

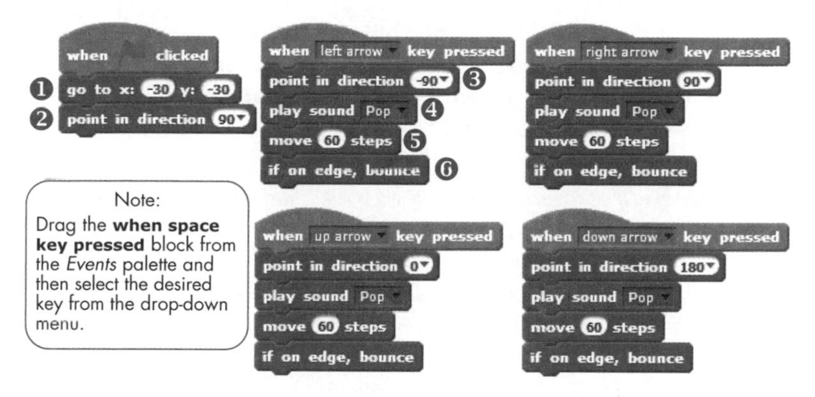

Figure 2-17: The scripts for the Player *sprite*

When the player clicks the green flag, this sprite moves to (–30,–30) ❶ and points to the right ❷. The other four scripts respond to the arrow keys. When an arrow key is pressed, the corresponding script changes the sprite's direction ❸, plays a short sound (using the **play sound** block ❹ from the *Sound* palette), and moves the sprite 60 steps ❺. The sprite bounces off the Stage's edge ❻ if needed. Because 60 steps correspond to 1 square on the grid of Figure 2-16, each time you press an arrow key, the Player sprite moves 1 square.

NOTE *Have you noticed that the four arrow-handling scripts in Figure 2-17 are almost identical? In Chapter 4, you'll learn how to avoid duplicating code this way.*

Go ahead and test this part of the game. You should be able to move the Player sprite around the Stage using the arrow keys on your keyboard. Once you have that working, we'll move on to the Gold sprite, whose script is shown in Figure 2-18.

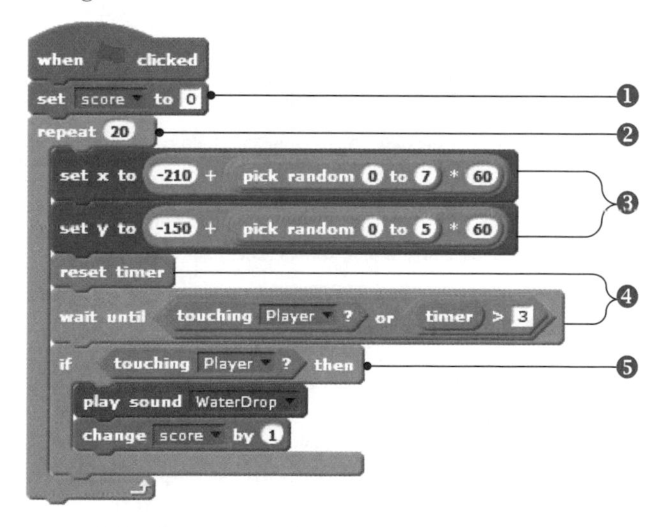

Figure 2-18: The script for the Gold *sprite*

Like the Player script, this script also starts when the green flag is clicked. It moves the bag of gold around. It also tracks how many bags have been collected with a variable named score, which I've created for you in the *Data* palette.

NOTE *Labels like* score *are called* variables. *They let us save information to use later in our programs. You'll learn everything about variables in Chapter 5.*

Since the game just started and we don't have any bags yet, we set score to 0 ❶. Next, we start a loop that will repeat 20 times ❷ to show a total of 20 bags to the player. (If you don't want 20 bags, feel free to use your favorite number instead.) Each time the loop runs, the bag of gold will appear at some random location ❸, give the player some time to grab it ❹, and increment score if the player is successful ❺.

We need the bag to appear randomly on one of the Stage's 48 squares. As you saw in Figure 2-16, the bag's *x*-position can be any of the following values: –210, –150, –90, ... , 210. These numbers are spaced 60 steps apart, so you can find each *x*-position starting with –210 by calculating

$$x = -210 + (0 \times 60)$$
$$x = -210 + (1 \times 60)$$
$$x = -210 + (2 \times 60)$$
$$x = -210 + (3 \times 60)$$

and so on. A similar expression applies to the *y*-position.

We can set the bag's *x*-position by generating a random number between 0 and 7, multiplying it by 60, and adding the result to –210. Figure 2-19 shows the detailed steps for creating the **set x to** block in our script; the **set y to** block is constructed in a similar manner.

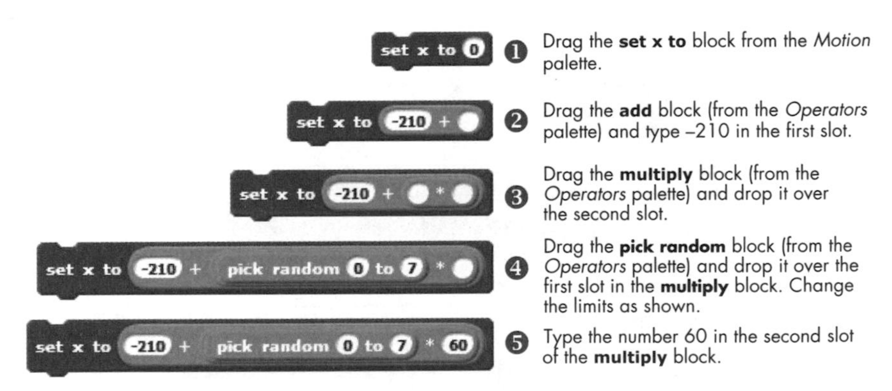

set x to 0
❶ Drag the **set x to** block from the *Motion* palette.
set x to -210 +
❷ Drag the **add** block (from the *Operators* palette) and type –210 in the first slot.
set x to -210 + *
❸ Drag the **multiply** block (from the *Operators* palette) and drop it over the second slot.
set x to -210 + pick random 0 to 7 *
❹ Drag the **pick random** block (from the *Operators* palette) and drop it over the first slot in the **multiply** block. Change the limits as shown.
set x to -210 + pick random 0 to 7 * 60
❺ Type the number 60 in the second slot of the **multiply** block.

Figure 2-19: Building the **set x to** *block from Figure 2-18*

After appearing at a random location, the bag of gold will give the player three seconds to grab it. (You can change this duration to make the game harder or easier to play.) To track the time, the script first resets Scratch's built-in timer to 0. It then waits until either the player grabs the bag by touching it or the timer exceeds three seconds. When either condition happens, the **wait until** block will let the script move on to execute the **if/then** block. The details for creating the **wait until** block are illustrated in Figure 2-20.

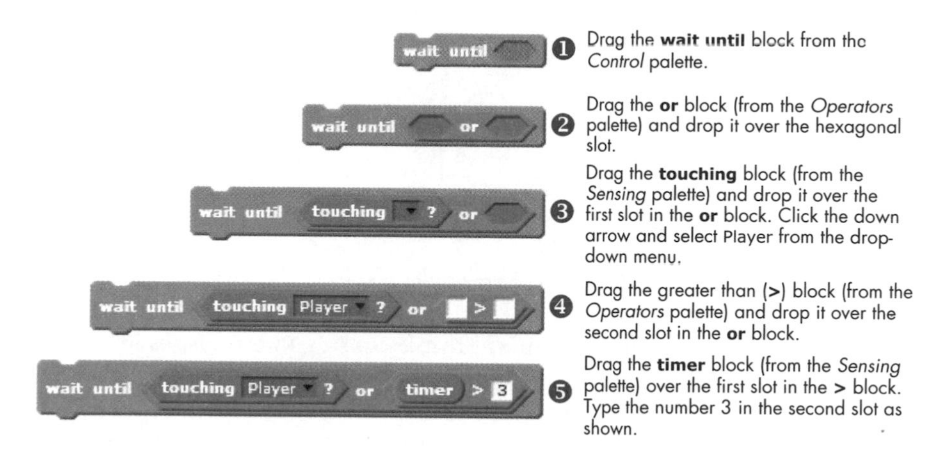

wait until
❶ Drag the **wait until** block from the *Control* palette.
wait until or
❷ Drag the **or** block (from the *Operators* palette) and drop it over the hexagonal slot.
wait until touching ? or
❸ Drag the **touching** block (from the *Sensing* palette) and drop it over the first slot in the **or** block. Click the down arrow and select Player from the drop-down menu.
wait until touching Player ? or >
❹ Drag the greater than (**>**) block (from the *Operators* palette) and drop it over the second slot in the **or** block.
wait until touching Player ? or timer > 3
❺ Drag the **timer** block (from the *Sensing* palette) over the first slot in the **>** block. Type the number 3 in the second slot as shown.

Figure 2-20: Building the **wait until** *block in the script of Figure 2-18*

NOTE *Blocks inside the* **if/then** *block will only run if the condition you specify in the header of the* **if/then** *block is true. Chapter 6 explains this block in detail, but for now, you know enough to use it to add your own touches to a program.*

If the player touches the bag, the commands inside the **if/then** block will run. In that case, the **play sound** block will make a WaterDrop noise, and the **change score by 1** block (in the *Data* palette) will add 1 to the score.

The game is now complete. Click the green flag to test your creation!

SCRATCH'S TIMER

Scratch maintains a timer that records how much time has passed since Scratch was started. When you start Scratch in a Web browser, the timer will be set to 0, and it will count up by tenths of a second as long as you keep Scratch open. The **timer** block (in the *Sensing* palette) holds the current value of the timer. The checkbox next to the block allows you to show/hide the block's monitor on the Stage. The **reset timer** block resets the timer to 0, and the time starts ticking up again immediately. The timer continues to run even when the project stops running.

Catching Apples

CatchApples_NoCode.sb2

Consider the Catching Apples game shown in Figure 2-21. In this game, apples appear at random horizontal positions at the top of the Stage at random times and fall to the ground. The player has to move the cart to catch the apples before they touch the ground, and each apple is worth 1 point.

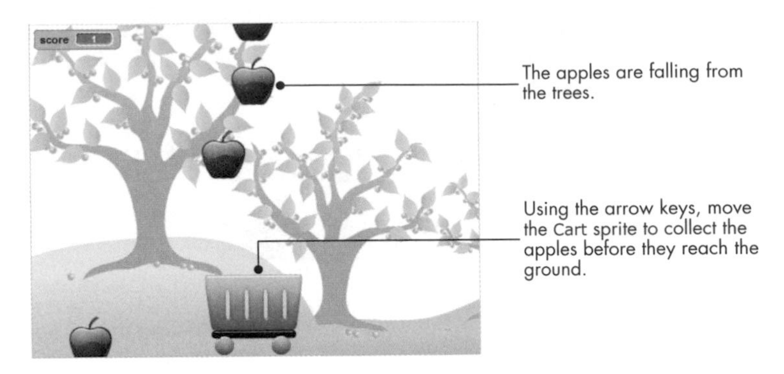

score 1
The apples are falling from the trees.
Using the arrow keys, move the Cart sprite to collect the apples before they reach the ground.

Figure 2-21: The Catching Apples game

At first, you might think such a game requires many sprites with nearly identical scripts. After all, there are a lot of apples. As of Scratch 2, however, that's not the case. With the *cloning* feature, you can easily create a bunch of copies of a sprite. In our Catching Apples game, we'll use a single apple sprite and create as many clones as we desire.

Open the file *CatchApples_NoCode.sb2*, which contains the setup for our game without scripts. To make things a little more exciting, the setup also includes a variable named score (created for you in the *Data* palette), which we'll use to keep track of the caught apples. First, however, you'll make the script for the Cart sprite as illustrated in Figure 2-22.

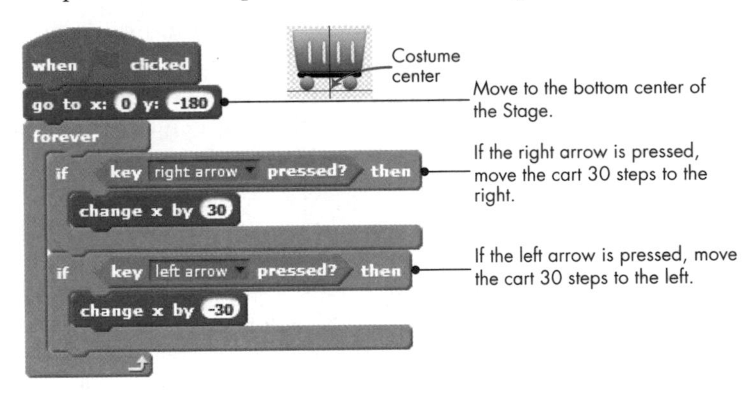

if key right arrow pressed? then

if key left arrow pressed? then

If the right arrow is pressed, move the cart 30 steps to the right.
If the left arrow is pressed, move the cart 30 steps to the left.

Figure 2-22: The script for the Cart *sprite*

When the green flag is clicked, we move the cart to the bottom center of the Stage. The script then continuously checks the state of the right and left arrows and moves the cart accordingly. I picked the number 30 based on trial and error, so feel free to change it based on your own experimentation.

Now comes the cloning business. Start by adding the script of Figure 2-23 to the Apple sprite. This script also starts running when the green flag is clicked.

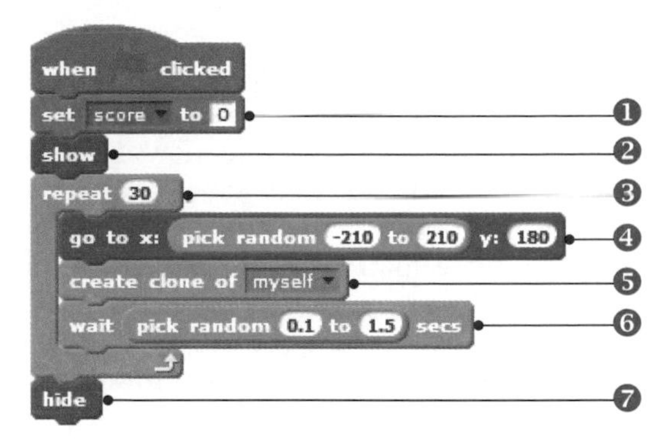

Figure 2-23: The first script of the Apple *sprite*

Since we haven't caught any apples yet, the script sets the score variable to 0 ❶. Next, it makes the sprite visible with the **show** block from the *Looks* palette ❷. It then starts a **repeat** block that will loop for 30 times ❸ to have 30 apples fall.

During each pass of the loop, the Apple sprite will move to a random horizontal position at the top part of the Stage ❹. It then calls the **create clone of** block (from the *Control* palette) to clone itself ❺, waits for a short random time ❻, and starts the next round of the **repeat** block. After completing the 30 rounds of the **repeat** block, the script hides the Apple sprite using the **hide** block ❼ from the *Looks* palette.

If you run the game now by clicking the green flag, 30 apples will pop up randomly at the top of the Stage and stay there—because we haven't told the cloned apples what to do. This is where the next script for the Apple sprite (Figure 2-24) comes in.

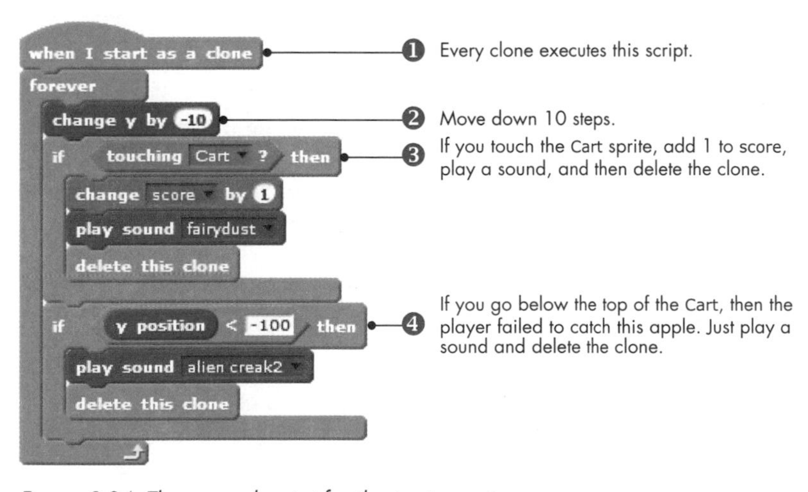

Figure 2-24: The second script for the Apple *sprite*

Thanks to the **when I start as a clone** block ❶ (from the *Control* palette), each clone will execute the script shown in this figure. Each Apple moves down 10 steps ❷ and checks whether it was caught or missed by the cart. If the clone detects that it is touching the cart ❸, that means it was caught. Therefore, it increases the score, plays a sound, and deletes itself (because it has no more work to do). If the clone falls below the cart ❹, then the player missed; in this case, the clone plays a different sound before deleting itself. If the clone is neither caught nor missed, then it's still falling, and the **forever** block goes around again.

Now that our apples know how to fall, the game is complete! Go ahead and test it out by clicking the green flag. If you want to experiment, try changing the wait time between cloning the different apples and the speed of moving the cart. Does that give you some ideas for changing the game's difficulty?

More on Cloned Sprites

Any sprite can copy itself or another sprite using the **create clone of** block. (The Stage can also clone sprites using the same block.) A cloned sprite inherits the original's *state* at the time it is cloned—that is, the original's current position and direction, costume, visibility status, pen color, pen size, graphic effects, and so on. This idea is illustrated in Figure 2-25.

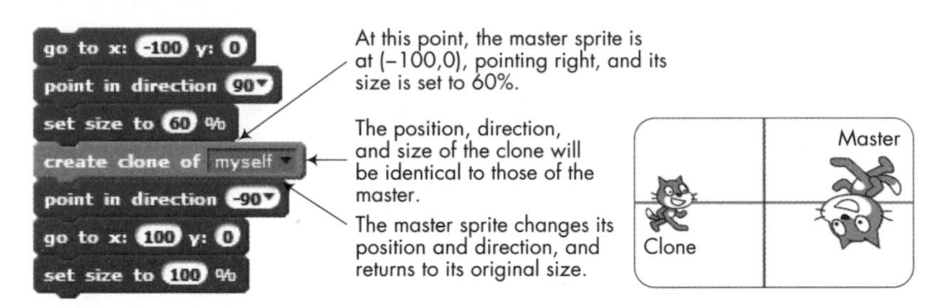

Figure 2-25: A clone inherits the attributes of its master.

Clones also inherit the scripts of the master sprite, as shown in Figure 2-26. Here, the master sprite creates two clones. When you press the spacebar, all three sprites (the master and the two clones) turn 15° to the right because they all execute the **when space key pressed** script.

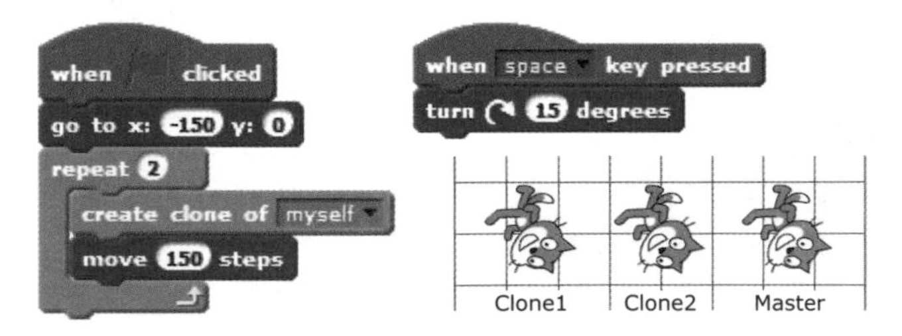

Figure 2-26: Clones inherit the scripts of their master.

Always pay special attention when using the **create clone of** block in a script that doesn't start with the green flag trigger, or you could end up with more sprites than you intended. Consider the program shown in Figure 2-27. The first time you press the spacebar, a clone will be created, and the application will have two sprites (the master and the clone).

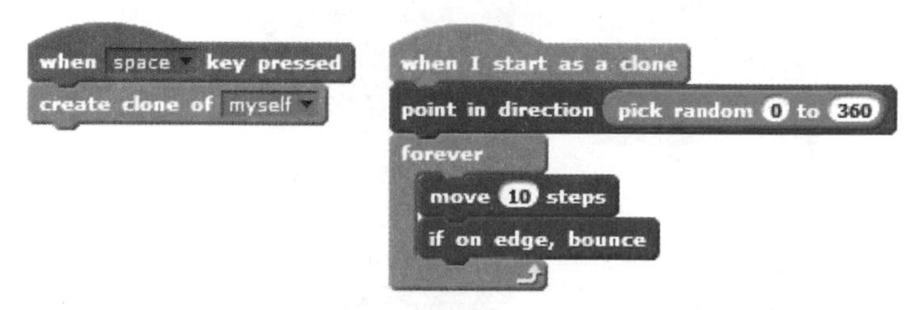

Figure 2-27: Cloning in response to a key press event

Now, if you press the spacebar a second time, you'll have four sprites in your application. Why? The master sprite will respond to the key press and create a clone, but the first clone will also respond and create another clone (that is, a clone of the clone). Press the spacebar a third time, and you'll have eight sprites in your application. The number of clones will grow exponentially!

You can solve this by only cloning sprites in scripts that start with the **when green flag clicked** block. These scripts are run only by the master sprite.

Summary

In this chapter, you learned how to move sprites to specific points on the Stage using absolute motion commands. You then used relative motion commands to move sprites with reference to their own position and direction. After that, you created some nifty drawings with the pen commands.

As you drew different shapes, you discovered the power of the **repeat** block, which allows you to create shorter and more efficient scripts. You also learned about the **stamp** command and used it with the **repeat** block to design complex patterns with ease.

At the end of the chapter, you created two games and learned about Scratch's clone feature. In the next chapter, you'll use the *Looks* and *Sound* palettes to create even more engaging programs.

Problems

1. Explain how the following script works. Write the (x,y) coordinates for all corners of the figure.

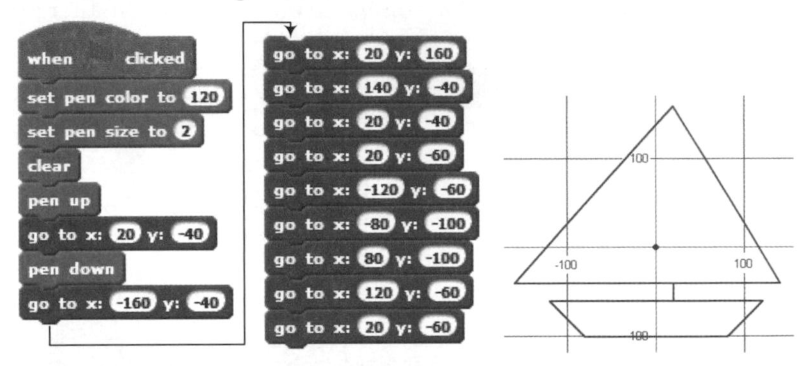

2. Write a script to connect each of the following sets of points in order and reveal the final shape:
   a. (30,20), (80,20), (80,30), (90,30), (90,80), (80,80), (80,90), (30,90), (30,80), (20,80), (20,30), (30,30), (30,20)
   b. (–10,10), (–30,10), (–30,70), (–70,70), (–70,30), (–60,30), (–60,60), (–40,60), (–40,10), (–90,10), (–90,90), (–10,90), (–10,10)

3. Write a script to draw each of the patterns shown below.

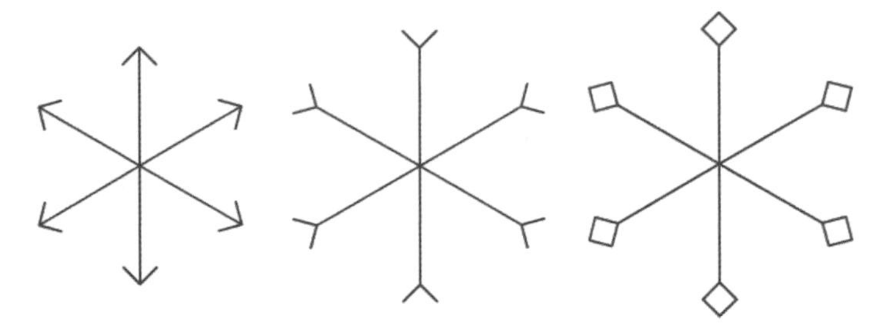

4. Consider the following script and its output. Re-create the script, add the necessary pen setup commands, run it, and explain how it works.

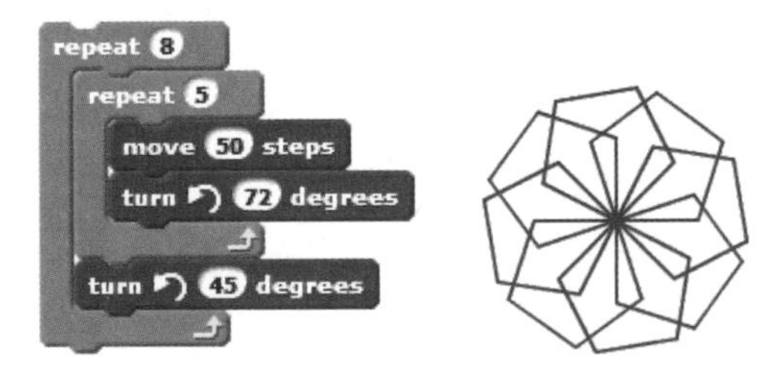

5. Consider the following script and its output. Re-create the script, add the necessary pen setup commands, run it, and explain how it works.

```
repeat 6
  move 80 steps
  repeat 60
    move 10 steps
    move -10 steps
    turn ↺ 6 degrees
  turn ↺ 60 degrees
```

6. Consider the following script and its output. Re-create the script, add the necessary pen commands, run it, and explain how it works.

```
repeat 8
  repeat 4
    move 10 steps
    turn ↺ 90 degrees
  move 60 steps
  turn ↺ 45 degrees
```

7. Create the script shown below, add the necessary pen commands, and run it. Explain how the script works.

repeat 12
move 100 steps
turn 150 degrees

8. Write a program that produces the output shown below.

BalloonBlast_NoCode.sb2

9. In this problem, you'll write the scripts needed to complete the Balloon Blast game shown below.

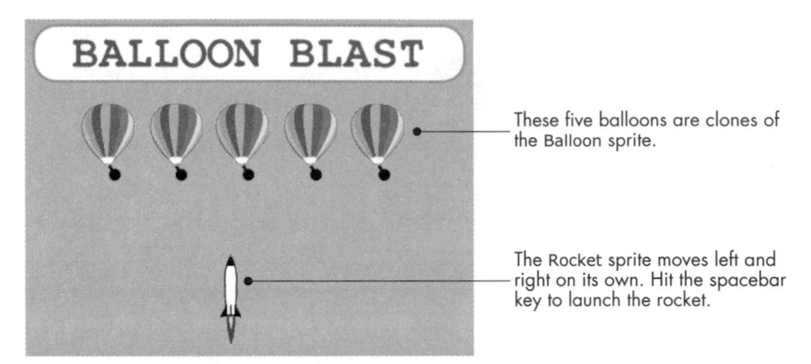

This game contains two sprites, named Balloon and Rocket. When you click the green flag, the Balloon sprite creates the five clones in the interface shown above. The Rocket sprite moves left and right on its own, bouncing off the edges of the Stage. You need to press the spacebar at the right moment to launch the rocket and pop the balloons.

Open the file *BalloonBlast_NoCode.sb2*. This file contains the code for creating the five clones when the game starts. Your task is to complete the game by adding the following two scripts.

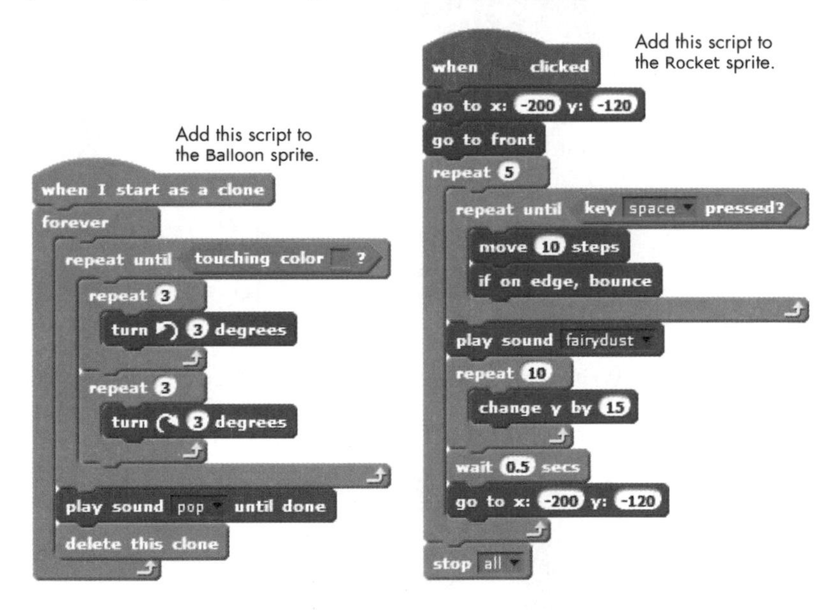

3

LOOKS AND SOUND

In the last chapter, you learned to move sprites on the Stage using the motion commands and how to use the pen to draw patterns. In this chapter, you'll learn about the various commands in the *Looks* and *Sounds* palettes. Along the way, you'll do the following:

- Create animations and image effects
- Learn how layers work in Scratch
- Play sound files and compose music
- Make complete animated scenes of your own

The commands in the *Looks* palette will let you create animations and apply graphic effects like whirl, fisheye, ghost, and so on to costumes and backgrounds. The commands in the *Sounds* palette are handy when you want to add sounds, voices, or music to your applications. Let's jump right in with some animation!

The Looks Palette

You can draw images directly on the Stage using the pen commands, but costumes provide another powerful, and sometimes much easier, way to add graphics to your programs. The commands in the *Looks* palette will let you manipulate costumes to create animations, add thought bubbles, apply graphic effects, and change a sprite's visibility. We'll explore those command blocks in this section.

Changing Costumes to Animate

Animation.sb2

You know how to send a sprite from one point to another on the Stage, but static sprites don't look very lifelike as they jump around. If you use different costumes and switch between them fast enough, you can make a sprite appear as if it were really moving! Open the file *Animation.sb2* to try out the animation in Figure 3-1.

Figure 3-1: You can create the illusion of animation by switching among different costumes.

This application contains one sprite with seven costumes along with one script. You can see the seven costumes in the *Costumes* tab and the script in the *Scripts* tab of the sprite. When you run the application by clicking the green flag, the stick figure will appear to walk on the Stage. The key to its motion is the **next costume** command, which tells the sprite to put on the next costume in its list. If the sprite is wearing the last costume in the list, it will roll over to its first costume.

When the green flag is clicked, the script starts a **forever** loop with a **wait** block at the end to create a delay of 0.1 seconds after each costume change. If you remove this delay from the script, the stick figure will appear to run instead of walk. Experiment with different values for the **move** and the **wait** blocks and see how they affect the animation.

Although you could draw this walking stick figure with the pen commands, you would need to write a long script. On the other hand, once you draw these costumes, programming the animation is a breeze. Remember that you can create images using your favorite paint program or with Scratch's Paint Editor.

ClickOnFace.sb2

If you want people to interact with a sprite, you could change its costume in response to a mouse click, as in the Click on Face application. This application contains a single sprite, named Face, which has the five costumes shown in Figure 3-2. It uses the **when this sprite clicked** block (from the *Events* palette) to tell the sprite when to switch costumes.

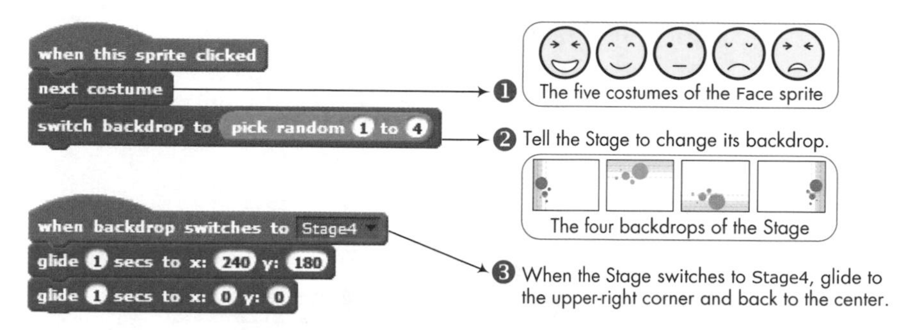

Figure 3-2: The smiley face and the backdrop change whenever the sprite is clicked.

When you run this application, every time you click the mouse on the face image, the image will change to the next one in the list. The script also uses the **switch backdrop to** block to command the Stage to switch randomly to one of its four backdrops. When the Stage switches to its Stage4 image, the Face sprite detects this event (using the **when backdrop switches to** trigger block from the *Events* palette). In this case, the face makes a trip to the upper-right corner of the Stage and then returns to the center.

TrafficLight.sb2

TRY IT OUT 3-1

The file *TrafficLight.sb2* contains one sprite that has three costumes (named red, orange, and green) and an incomplete script, as shown below. Complete the application by adding the necessary **wait** blocks to create a realistic traffic light animation.

```
when clicked
forever
    switch costume to red
    switch costume to orange
    switch costume to green
```

red orange green

NOTE *You can use the* **switch backdrop to** *command to change scenes in a story, switch levels in a game, and so on. Any sprite in your project can use the* **when backdrop switches to** *block to detect when the Stage has switched to a certain costume and act accordingly. See the Tips window in the Scratch interface for more details.*

Sprites That Speak and Think

You can use the **say** and **think** commands to make your sprite speak or think like a character in a comic strip, as illustrated in Figure 3-3 (left).

Figure 3-3: Use the **say** *or* **think** *commands to show a message in a speech or a thought bubble.*

Any phrase you type into these commands will appear above the sprite, and the message is displayed permanently. If you want to clear the message, use a **say** or **think** block with no text. You could also display a message for a fixed time instead with the **say for secs** (or the **think for secs**) command, as illustrated in Figure 3-3 (right).

Argue.sb2

TRY IT OUT 3-2

To see the **Say** and **Think** commands in action, open the file *Argue.sb2* and run it. This application simulates an endless argument between two characters, as illustrated below. Study the scripts to understand how they use accurate timing to synchronize the actions of the two characters.

Image Effects

GraphicEffects.sb2

The **set effect to** command allows you to apply different graphic effects to costumes and backdrops. Scratch gives these effects names like fisheye, whirl, mosaic, and so on. Figure 3-4 shows exactly what they do.

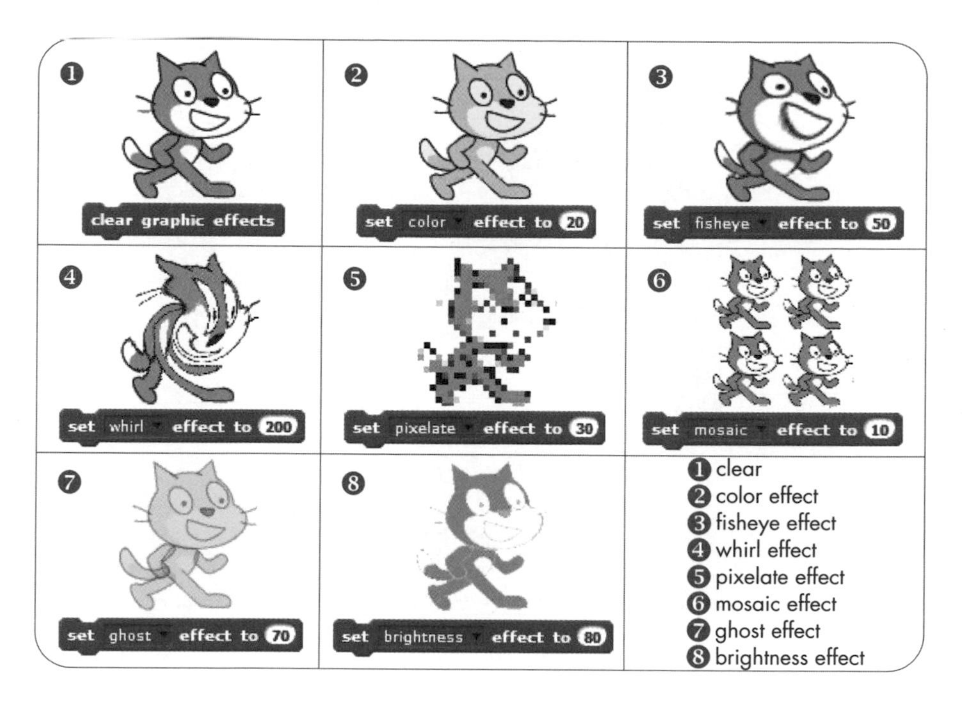

Figure 3-4: This figure shows what happens to the cat when you apply Scratch's graphic effects.

Click the down arrow in the **set effect to** block to choose the effect you want from the drop-down menu. You can also use the **change effect by** command to adjust an effect instead of setting it directly. For example, if the current ghost effect is set to 40, changing it by 60 would set the ghost effect to 100, causing the sprite to disappear (like a ghost). When you want to return an image to its original state, use the **clear graphic effects** block.

NOTE *You can apply multiple effects to a sprite at once by using several graphic effect commands in sequence.*

Size and Visibility

SneezingCat.sb2

Sometimes you may need to change the size of a sprite or control when it appears in your program. For example, you may want to have closer objects in a scene look larger, or you may want to show an "instructions" sprite only at the beginning of a game.

If you need to shrink or grow a sprite, the **set size to %** and **change size by** commands can help. The first sets a sprite's size to a percentage of its original size, and the second modifies a sprite's size by a specified amount relative to its current size. When you need to make a sprite appear or disappear, use the **show** block or the **hide** block, respectively.

To see these commands in action, open *SneezingCat.sb2*. In this application, we'll have the cat sneeze like a cartoon character by changing its size, as shown in Figure 3-5.

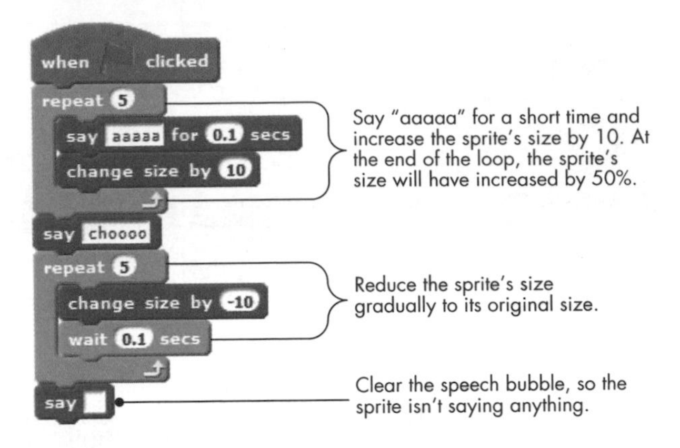
when clicked
repeat 5
say aaaaa for 0.1 secs
change size by 10
say choooo
repeat 5
change size by -10
wait 0.1 secs
say
Say "aaaaa" for a short time and increase the sprite's size by 10. At the end of the loop, the sprite's size will have increased by 50%.
Reduce the sprite's size gradually to its original size.
Clear the speech bubble, so the sprite isn't saying anything.

Figure 3-5: This script makes the Cat *sprite sneeze.*

The size of the sprite increases as it gets ready to sneeze, and after it sneezes, it returns slowly to its original size. Run the program and watch what happens to get a feel for these commands.

TRY IT OUT 3-3

Add a block to the end of the script in Figure 3-5 to have the Cat sprite finish its dramatic sneeze by vanishing afterward. Add another block to show the sprite at the beginning of the script.

Layers

The last two commands in the *Looks* palette affect the order in which sprites are drawn on the Stage. This order determines which sprites are visible when they overlap. For example, let's say that you want to create a scene of a girl standing behind a big rock. There are two layering possibilities, shown in Figure 3-6 (left).

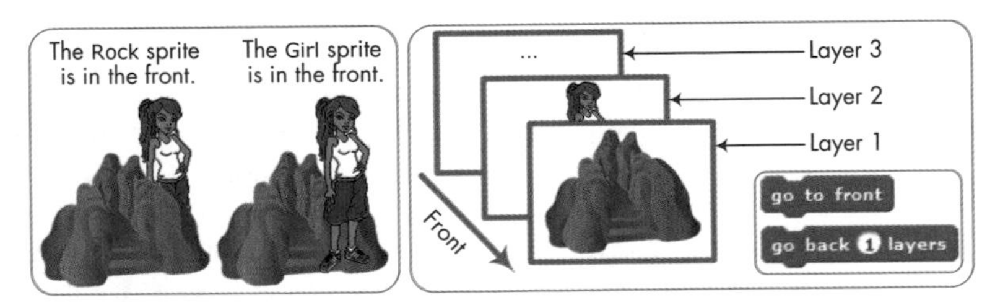
The Rock sprite is in the front.
The Girl sprite is in the front.
...
Layer 3
Layer 2
Layer 1
Front
go to front
go back 1 layers

Figure 3-6: The sprite in the front layer is completely visible and can cover parts of overlapping sprites.

If you want the girl to be behind the rock, you must bring the rock to the front drawing layer or send the girl to the back drawing layer. Scratch provides two commands that allow you to reorder the drawing layers, **go to front** and **go back layers** (also shown in the figure). The first tells Scratch to always draw a sprite on top, while the second sends a sprite back as many layers as you specify.

Layers.sb2

TRY IT OUT 3-4

The *Layers.sb2* application has four objects that move on the Stage. You can bring an object to the top by pressing the first letter of its color. Run the application to explore the effect of the **go to front** command.

We've covered animation with the *Looks* palette, but there's another thing that can liven up our applications. In the next section, we'll explore the *Sound* palette and its rich set of commands.

The Sound Palette

Games and other applications use sound effects and background music to add excitement. In this section, you'll learn to use Scratch's sound-related blocks, starting with how to incorporate audio files and control their playback. You'll then look at command blocks for playing drums and other musical instruments. After that, you'll find out how to control the volume and change the speed (or tempo) at which musical notes and drums are played.

Playing Audio Files

You can save audio files on your computer in many formats, but Scratch only recognizes two: WAV and MP3. There are three command blocks that allow you to use these sound files in your applications: **play sound**, **play sound until done**, and **stop all sounds**. Both of the first two blocks play a given sound. The **play sound** command lets the next command start before the sound finishes playing, while **play sound until done** won't move on to the next command until the end of the sound. The **stop all sounds** command immediately turns off any sound that is playing.

You can add background music to your application by playing an audio file repeatedly. The easiest way to do this is to use **play sound until done** to let the file to play completely, and then restart it, as shown in Figure 3-7 (left).

Figure 3-7: Two ways to create background music: Repeat the sound after it finishes (left) or start the sound over after playing it for a certain amount of time (right).

Depending on the audio file, this approach may produce a very short, but sometimes noticeable, pause between the consecutive restarts. You could also use the **play sound** command with a **wait** command to give yourself more control over the play duration, as shown in Figure 3-7 (right). By experimenting with the wait time, you may be able to shorten the pause to produce a smoother transition between the end of the current playback and the beginning of the next.

Playing Drums and Other Sounds

BeatsDemo.sb2

If you're developing games, you'll probably want to play a short sound effect when the player hits a target, finishes a level, and so on. It's easy to create these sounds with the **play drum for beats** command, which plays your choice of 18 drum sounds for a certain number of beats. You can also add pauses with the **rest for beats** command. The *BeatsDemo.sb2* application, shown in Figure 3-8, demonstrates the effect of the beats parameter.

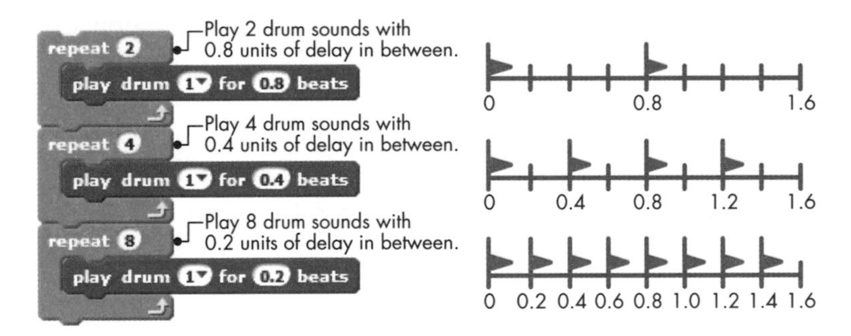

Figure 3-8: An illustration of beats in Scratch

The script contains three **repeat** blocks with repeat counts of two, four, and eight, respectively. Each **repeat** block plays the same drum sound using a different number of beats. If you think of the time axis as being divided into intervals of 0.2 units, the first loop will play two drum sounds that are 0.8 units of time apart. The second loop will play four drum sounds that are 0.4 units apart, and the third loop plays eight drum sounds that are 0.2 units apart. Each loop takes the same amount of time to complete; we're just hitting the drum a different number of times in the same time interval.

I said "units of time" instead of seconds because the actual time to finish each loop depends on the *tempo*, which you can set with the **set tempo to** command. Using the default tempo of 60 beats per minute (bpm), each loop in the above example will take 1.6 seconds to complete. If you set the tempo to 120 bpm, each loop will take 0.8 seconds to complete, while at 30 bpm, each takes 3.2 seconds, and so on.

Composing Music

FrereJacques.sb2

Scratch also contains two commands that allow you to play musical notes and compose your own music. The **play note for beats** command plays the note you choose, from 0 to 127, for a number of beats you specify. The **set instrument to** block tells Scratch which instrument the note should sound like. Let's use these commands to create a complete song. The script shown in Figure 3-9 plays the French children's song "Frère Jacques."

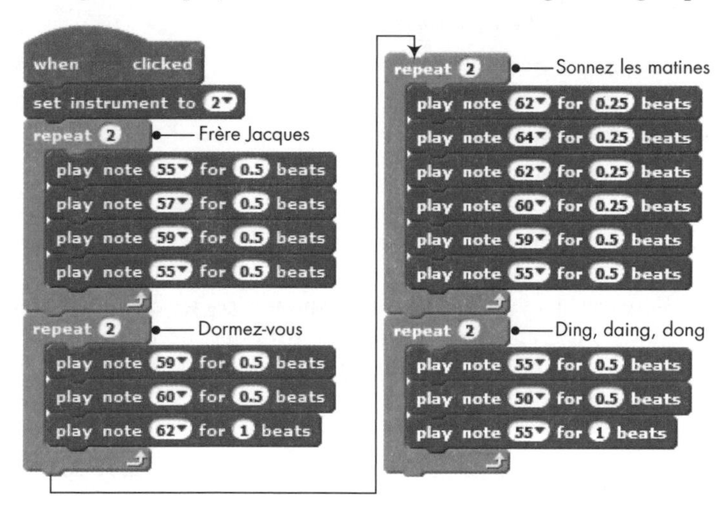

Figure 3-9: A script that plays "Frère Jacques"

Open this application, named *FrereJacques.sb2*, and experiment with different values for the **set instrument to** command to change the instrument that plays this song.

Controlling Sound Volume

Let's say that you want to make a sound fade in response to some event in your application. If you are launching a rocket into space, for example, you might want the rocket to sound loud when it takes off and become quieter as it moves farther away.

Scratch contains a set of commands to control the volume, or loudness, of audio files, drum sounds, and musical notes. The **set volume to %** command sets a sprite's loudness to a percentage of the speaker's volume. However, it affects only the sprite that uses it (or the Stage), so if you want sounds to play at the same time with different volumes, you'll have to use multiple sprites. The **change volume by** block reduces or increases the volume by the number you enter. Negative numbers make sounds softer, while positive numbers make them louder. You can even show a sprite's volume on the Stage by checking the box next to the **volume** block. These blocks are handy if you want to change the volume based on how close a sprite is to a target (as in a treasure-hunt game) or make parts of a song louder than others. You can also use these blocks to simulate an orchestra by playing different instruments (with different loudness levels) simultaneously.

VolumeDemo.sb2

TRY IT OUT 3-5

The file *VolumeDemo.sb2* simulates a cat walking into a forest. The application uses the **change volume by** command to make the cat's sound fade away as it goes deeper into the woods. Come up with some ideas to make this simulation more real and try to implement them.

Setting the Tempo

The last three blocks in the *Sound* palette are related to the tempo, or speed, at which drums and notes are played. Tempo is measured in beats per minute (bpm). The higher the tempo, the faster the notes and drums will play.

Scratch lets you choose a specific tempo with the **set tempo to bpm** command. You can also tell a sprite to speed up or slow down the tempo by a certain amount with the **change tempo by** command. If you want to see a sprite's tempo on the Stage, check the box next to the **tempo** block.

TempoDemo.sb2

TRY IT OUT 3-6

Open the file *TempoDemo.sb2* and run it to see the **set tempo to bpm** and **change tempo by** commands in action.

Scratch Projects

The commands in the *Looks* and *Sound* palettes will help you add lots of nifty effects to your applications. In this section, we'll put everything we've learned so far in this chapter together to create animated scenes of a person dancing and some fireworks. This should help you review some of the new command blocks and give you more practice with creating a complete Scratch project.

Dancing on Stage

DanceOnStage.sb2

In this section, you'll animate a Dancer sprite on the Stage. This application is illustrated in Figure 3-10, and the complete script is saved as *DanceOnStage.sb2*. We'll build the whole scene right here—follow along to see how it works!

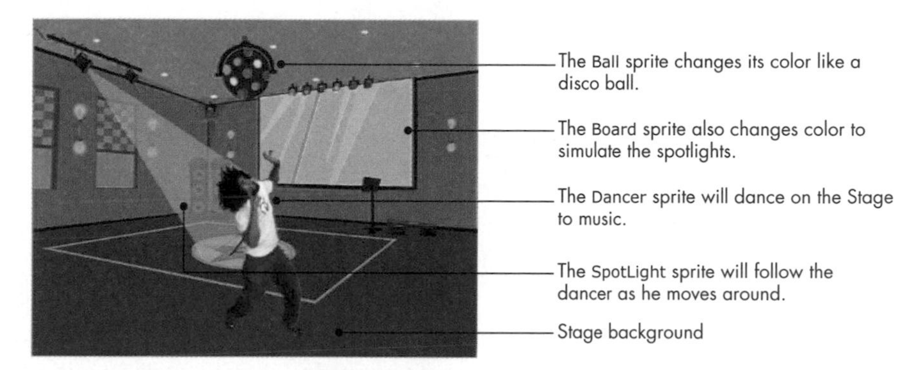

The Ball sprite changes its color like a disco ball.
The Board sprite also changes color to simulate the spotlights.
The Dancer sprite will dance on the Stage to music.
The SpotLight sprite will follow the dancer as he moves around.
Stage background

Figure 3-10: The Dance Party application in action.

First, start a new project. If Scratch is not already running, all you have to do is start it—this will automatically create a new project for you. Otherwise, select **New** from the **File** menu. In both cases, you'll have a new project that contains the default Cat sprite.

The backdrop that you'll use in this application is the party room from the *Indoors* category. Import this backdrop and delete the default white backdrop, which you won't need. The Stage should now look like Figure 3-11.

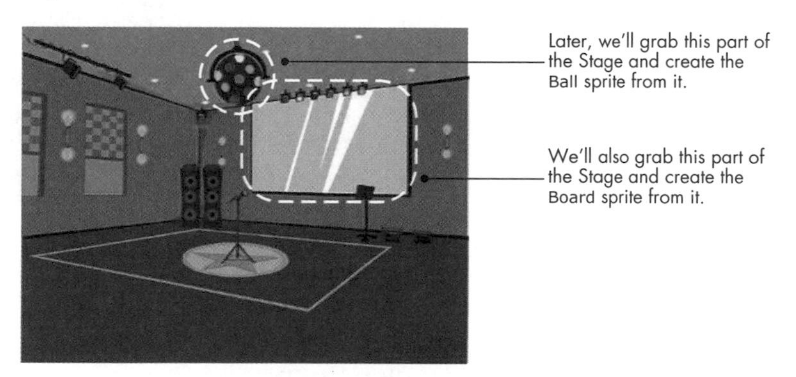

Later, we'll grab this part of the Stage and create the Ball sprite from it.
We'll also grab this part of the Stage and create the Board sprite from it.

Figure 3-11: We'll turn some sections of the party-room backdrop into sprites later.

Examine Figures 3-10 and 3-11 carefully and notice how the Ball and Board sprites look like parts of the backdrop. As you'll see in a moment, these two sprites were actually created from that image and placed on the Stage to cover the sections they came from. Creating the two sprites this way lets us change their color and make the Stage more realistic.

Now we need some background music. Let's use the *medieval1* file from the *Music Loops* category. Import this file to the Stage and then delete the default "pop" sound. Next, add the script in Figure 3-12 to the Stage. It uses the **play sound** command along with a wait time that lets the audio file restart smoothly. The wait time of 9.5 seconds was selected by experimentation.

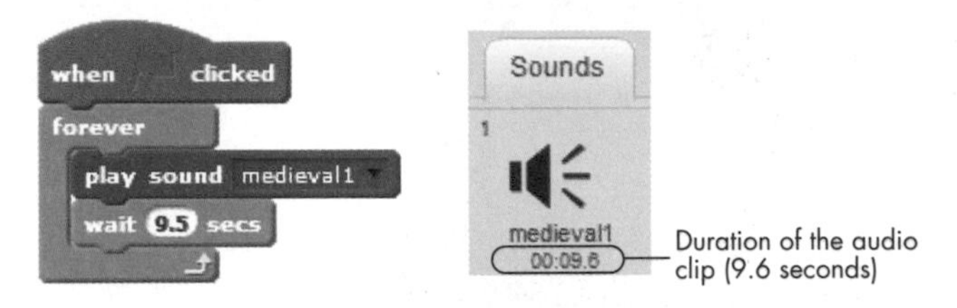

Figure 3-12: The Stage plays our background music.

Click the green flag to test what you've created so far. You should hear an audio clip repeating continuously. Stop the script when you're ready, and we'll add our dancer.

Replace the costumes of the Cat sprite with those of the Dancer. Import the dan-a and dan-b costumes from the *People* category, delete the two Cat costumes, and change the Cat sprite's name to Dancer. The script for the Dancer is shown in Figure 3-13.

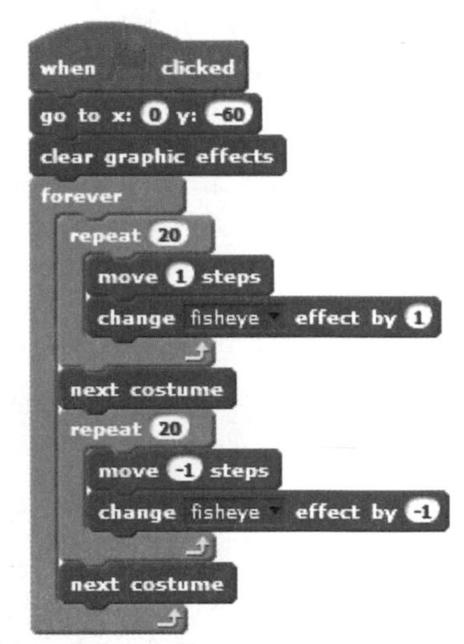

Figure 3-13: This script tells the Dancer *sprite how to boogie.*

The Dancer moves 20 steps to the right, changes its costume, moves 20 steps to the left, and changes its costume again. These steps are repeated forever to make him look like he's really dancing. The script also changes the fisheye effect slightly with every step for some variety. Click the green flag to test this new addition to the program. You should hear the background music and see the Dancer moving left and right on the Stage.

Now that you have a dancer for your party, let's add some colorful lights with the Ball, Board, and SpotLight sprites. To create the Ball sprite, click the thumbnail of the Stage to select it and then select the **Backdrops** tab. Right-click the thumbnail of the party room backdrop and select **save to local file** from the pop-up menu. This brings up a dialog that allows you to save the backdrop image locally. Remember where you saved this image because you'll import it back in a moment.

Click the **Upload sprite from file** button (above the Sprite List) and select the image you just saved. This creates a new sprite whose costume is the same as the backdrop image. Name this sprite Ball and edit its costume in the Paint Editor to remove everything but the colorful ball depicted in Figure 3-14 (left). Be sure to paint the space around the ball with transparent color. Next, place the Ball sprite on the Stage exactly over the spot in the backdrop where you took it from so that it looks like part of the image (see Figure 3-11).

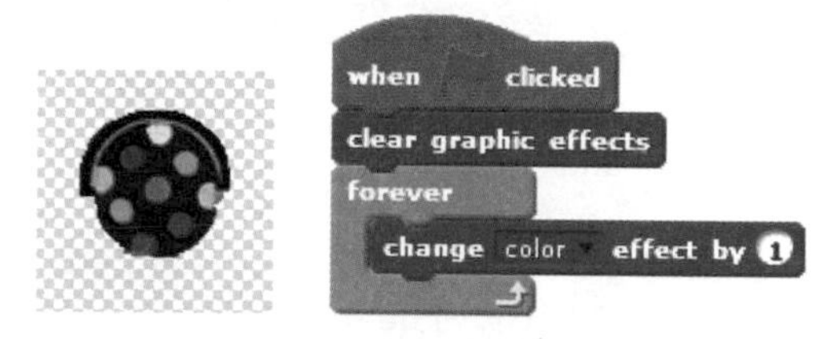

Figure 3-14: The costume for the Ball *sprite as it appears in the Paint Editor and its script*

Figure 3-14 also shows the script you should add to the Ball sprite. It changes the sprite's color effect continuously to give the illusion that the small circles are actually changing color.

Create the Board sprite the same way you created the Ball sprite. Figure 3-15 shows how this sprite should appear in the Paint Editor (left) and the script you'll need to animate it (right). I've added some colors to the costume (compare to Figure 3-11) to make the **change color effect** command effective.

Figure 3-15: The Board *sprite and its script*

Because the Board sprite overlaps with the Dancer, the script sends the Board two layers to the back so the Dancer will always be in the front. You can do the same thing by selecting the Dancer sprite and clicking the **go to front** block from the *Looks* palette.

The last sprite in this application is the SpotLight sprite. Figure 3-16 shows how this sprite appears in the Paint Editor, as well as the script you need to create. The center of the image is at the tip of the cone shape, which represents a light beam.

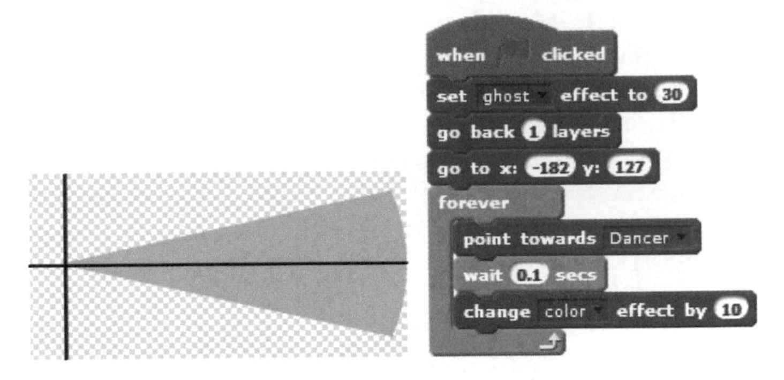

Figure 3-16: The SpotLight *sprite and its script*

The script first sets the sprite's ghost effect to 30 to make it transparent so that it won't obscure the backdrop. The script then sends this sprite one layer back, which places the light beam behind the dancer. The sprite is then positioned so that the light beam appears to be emanating from the spotlight (see Figure 3-10). You'll have to choose the *x*- and *y*-coordinates based on your drawing. After that, the script commands the light beam to follow the dancer (using the **point towards** command) and change its color forever.

Once you're done adding the spotlight, the application should be complete. Click the green flag to watch your dance party in action! In addition to the music and the dancing, you should also see the Ball, Board, and SpotLight sprites changing color as though real disco lights are in action.

In the next section, we'll look at a different application that highlights many of the graphic effects we studied in this chapter.

Fireworks

Fireworks_NoCode.sb2

Another application that lends itself naturally to the graphics blocks and other concepts discussed in this chapter is an animated fireworks scene. In this section, you'll make a simple firework animation that floods the sky with colorful sparks. The firework rockets will explode at random times, producing sparks that fall as though acted upon by gravity and fade slowly with time, as illustrated in Figure 3-17.

Clones of the Rocket sprite will explode and produce colorful sparks that fall to the ground.
The City sprite

Figure 3-17: The fireworks animation in action

Start by opening the file *Fireworks_NoCode.sb2*, which contains the initial setup of the application without any scripts. As shown in Figure 3-17, the application contains two sprites: the City sprite and the Rocket sprite. The City sprite shows an image of tall buildings that you can animate in any way you like. The Rocket sprite will continuously create clones that explode in the dark sky, producing the fireworks.

The Rocket sprite has the eight costumes shown in Figure 3-18. The first costume, C1, is just a small dot that we'll launch into the sky. When this dot reaches its destination, which is selected at random, it will switch to one of the other costumes (also at random) to simulate the initial explosion. We'll then use an appropriate graphic effect to make this explosion look more realistic.

Figure 3-18: The eight costumes of the Rocket *sprite.*

With this plan in mind, add the script shown in Figure 3-19 to the Rocket sprite. The script runs when the user clicks the green flag. After hiding the Rocket sprite, it starts a **forever** loop to create clones of itself at random times. Since the clones inherit the visibility state of the Rocket sprite, all created clones will be hidden at first.

```
when clicked
hide
forever
  create clone of myself
  wait pick random 0.2 to 2.5 secs
```

Figure 3-19: The first script of the Rocket *sprite*

We now need to tell the cloned rockets what to do. This script is shown in Figure 3-20.

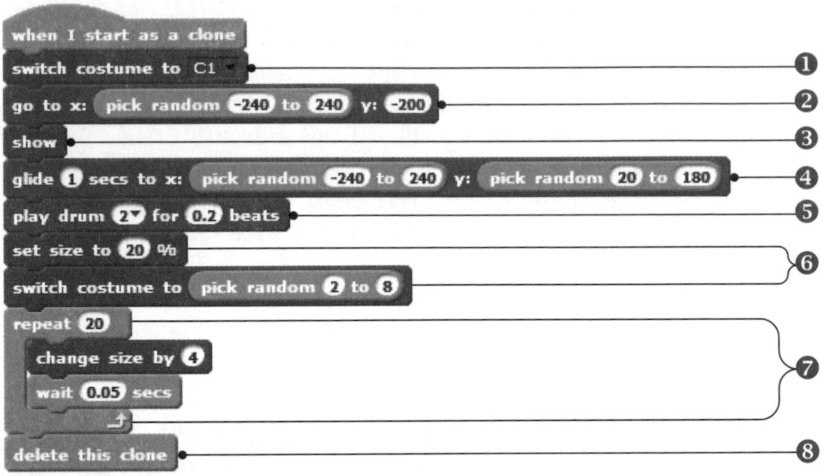

```
when I start as a clone
switch costume to C1                                        ❶
go to x: (pick random -240 to 240) y: -200                  ❷
show                                                        ❸
glide 1 secs to x: (pick random -240 to 240) y: (pick random 20 to 180)   ❹
play drum 2 for 0.2 beats                                   ❺
set size to 20 %                                            ❻
switch costume to (pick random 2 to 8)
repeat 20                                                   ❼
  change size by 4
  wait 0.05 secs
delete this clone                                           ❽
```

Figure 3-20: The start-up script of the cloned sprites

The cloned rocket starts by putting on its first costume ❶ (the small red dot). It then moves to a random horizontal position at the bottom of the Stage ❷, shows itself ❸, and glides to a random position ❹ in the upper part of the Stage (somewhere above the buildings). This part of the script simulates the launch of the rocket, and if you run it, you will see a red dot moving from the ground to the sky. When the dot reaches its final point in the sky, it explodes due to instructions in the second part of the script. First, the clone plays a short drum sound ❺ (to simulate the sound of an explosion). Fireworks explosions start small and expand, so the clone sets its initial size to 20%and picks one of its other costumes randomly ❻. It then starts a **repeat** loop ❼ to grow the firework. Every pass through the loop, the clone increases its size by 4. At the end of the loop, the clone deletes itself ❽.

That wraps up this fireworks festival! You should now be able to run the animation and show off the scene you created. With just a couple of scripts, we made a relatively complex animation.

Summary

In this chapter, we introduced many new programming blocks that can be used to add some pizzazz to our applications. With these blocks, we can add color, animation, graphic effects, music, and more.

We explained the blocks in the *Looks* palette and gave several examples of how to use them. You animated sprites by switching costumes, learned about drawing layers, and saw how layers affect the appearance of overlapping sprites.

We then covered the commands in the *Sound* palette and explained how to play audio files, drum sounds, and musical notes. You created a complete dance scene with commands from both the *Looks* and the *Sound* palettes, and you finished with a bang by making a fireworks animation application.

In the next chapter, you'll learn how to coordinate the work among different sprites using message broadcasting and receiving. You'll also learn how to break up a large program into smaller and more manageable pieces, called procedures. This concept is the key to writing more complex applications.

Problems

Zebra.sb2

1. Open the application *Zebra.sb2*, shown below. The application contains a single sprite (the Zebra), which has three costumes. Write a script that makes the Zebra move across the Stage and switch among its costumes to create the illusion of running.

Wolf.sb2

2. Open the application *Wolf.sb2*, shown below. When you click the green flag, the Wolf will play the WolfHowl sound, which takes about 4 seconds. Create a script that changes the Wolf's costumes in sync with the sound. (Hint: Insert a **wait** block with an appropriate time delay after each costume switch.)

ChangingHat.sb2

3. Open the application *ChangingHat.sb2*, shown below. The hat in this application is a sprite that has five costumes. Create a script to switch the Hat's costume when it is clicked. Then create a game in which the player dresses characters by clicking on different pieces of clothing.

Aquarium.sb2

4. Open *Aquarium.sb2*. The application contains six sprites, as illustrated below. Try out different graphic effects to animate the aquarium. Here are some suggestions:
   a. Use the whirl effect on the Stage. Start with a large number like 1,000 to give the figure a wavy appearance.
   b. Change the costumes for the Bubble1 and Bubble2 sprites at an appropriate rate.
   c. Move the Fish across the Stage while changing its costume.
   d. Apply the ghost effect to the Tree sprite.
   e. Use the color effect on the Coral and Bubble3 sprites.

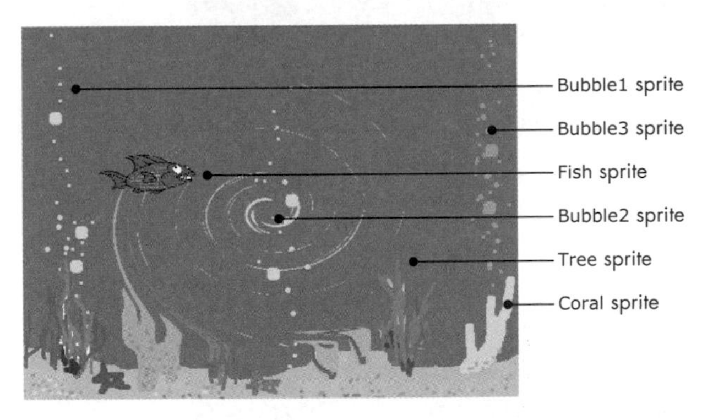

Words.sb2

5. Open the application *Words.sb2* (shown on the next page) and animate the words using size and rotation. Create the two scripts shown in the figure and run the application to see the result.

Scratch
Sprite1
Animation
Sprite2
Script for Sprite1
when clicked
set size to 100 %
forever
repeat 25
change size by -4
repeat 25
change size by 4
Script for Sprite2
when clicked
point in direction 90
forever
turn 5 degrees

Joke.sb2 6. Open the application *Joke.sb2*, shown below. Finish the scripts for the Boy and the Girl sprites to tell any joke you want.

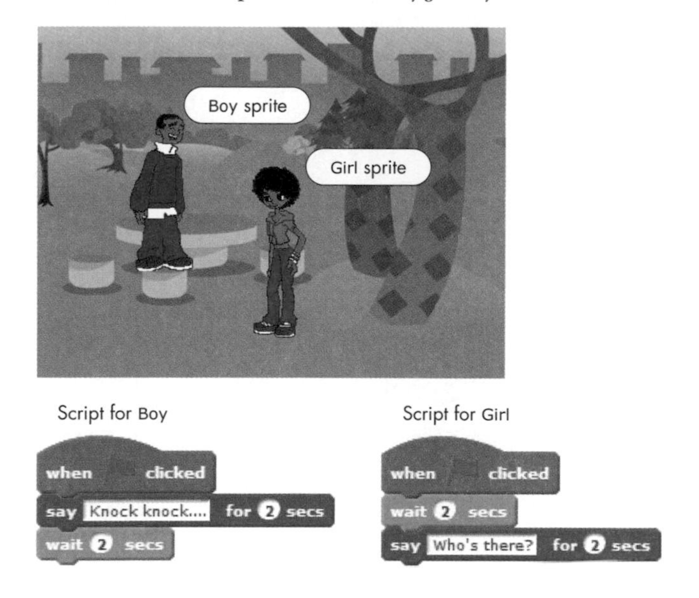
Boy sprite
Girl sprite
Script for Boy
when clicked
say Knock knock.... for 2 secs
wait 2 secs
Script for Girl
when clicked
wait 2 secs
say Who's there? for 2 secs

Nature.sb2

7. Open *Nature.sb2*. The application contains three sprites, as illustrated below. Animate the scene using both motion and sound. Here are some suggestions:

   a. The Bird sprite has two costumes that create a flying effect. Create a script to fly the Bird across the Stage and play the Bird sound at random times.

   b. The Duck sprite has 12 costumes that show the Duck plucking a fish out of the water and eating it. Create a script to move the Duck across the Stage and play the Duck sound at random times.

   c. The Seal sprite has four costumes that show the Seal playing with the ball. Create a script to have the Seal play around and make the SeaLion sound at random times.

4

PROCEDURES

This chapter explains how you can take a "divide and conquer" approach to programming. Rather than build your programs as one big piece, you'll be able to write separate procedures that you then put together. Using procedures will make your programs both easier to write and easier to test and debug. In this chapter, you'll learn how to:

- Use message broadcasting to coordinate the behavior of many sprites
- Use message broadcasting to implement procedures
- Use the "build your own block" feature of Scratch 2
- Use structured programming techniques

Most of the applications we've developed so far contain only one sprite, but most applications require multiple sprites that work together. An animated story, for example, might have several characters as well as different backgrounds. We need a way to synchronize the sprites' assigned jobs.

In this chapter, we'll use Scratch's message-broadcasting mechanism to coordinate work among several sprites (this was the only way to implement procedures in the previous version of Scratch). We'll then discuss how to use Scratch 2's "custom blocks" feature to structure large programs as smaller, more manageable pieces called *procedures*. A procedure is a sequence of commands that performs a specific function. For example, we can create procedures that cause sprites to draw shapes, perform complex computations, process user input, sequence musical notes, manage games, and do many other things. Once created, these procedures can serve as building blocks for constructing all sorts of useful applications.

Message Broadcasting and Receiving

So how does the broadcast system in Scratch work in practice? Any sprite can broadcast a message (you can call this message anything you like) using the **broadcast** or **broadcast and wait** blocks (from the *Events* palette) shown in Figure 4-1. This broadcast triggers all scripts in all sprites (including the broadcasting sprite itself) that begin with a matching **when I receive** trigger block. All sprites hear the broadcast, but they'll only act on it if they have a corresponding **when I receive** block.

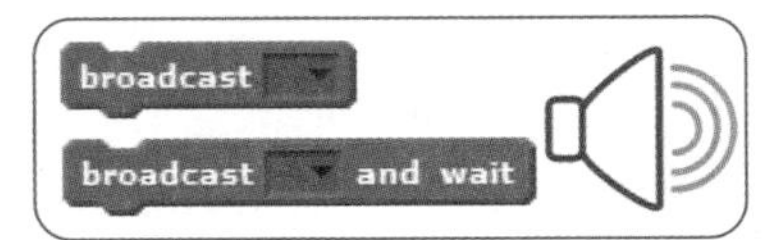

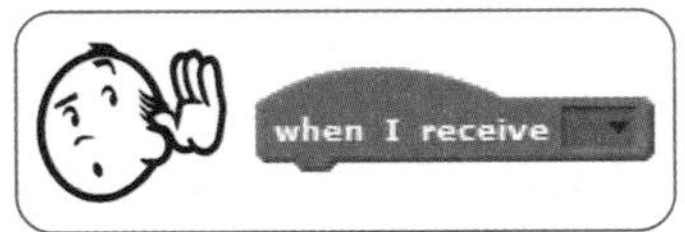

Figure 4-1: You can use the message-broadcasting and receiving blocks to coordinate the work of multiple sprites.

Consider Figure 4-2. It shows four sprites: starfish, cat, frog, and bat. The starfish broadcasts the jump message, and that broadcast is sent to all sprites, including itself. In response to this message, both the cat and the frog will execute their jump scripts. Notice how each sprite jumps in its own way, executing a different script. The bat also receives the jump message, but it does not act on it because it was not told what to do when it receives this message. The cat in this figure knows how to walk and jump, the frog can only jump, and the bat was taught only to fly.

The **broadcast and wait** command works like the **broadcast** command, but it waits until all message recipients have finished executing their corresponding **when I receive** blocks before continuing.

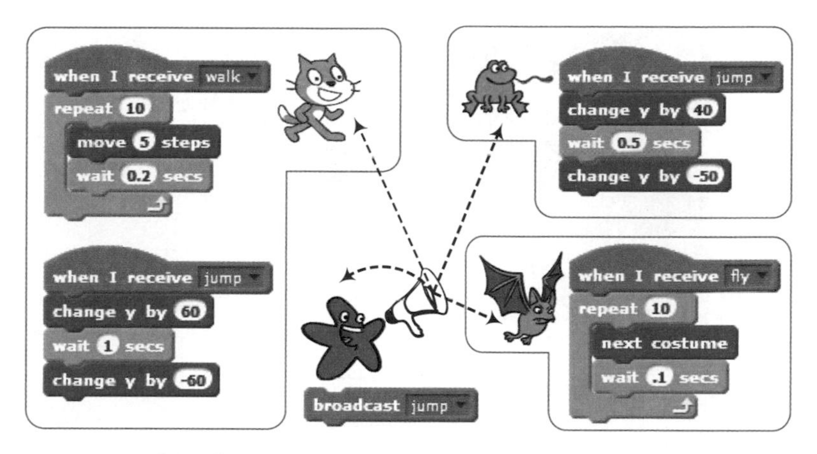

Figure 4-2: A broadcast message is received by all sprites, even by the sprite that sent the broadcast.

Sending and Receiving Broadcasts

SquareApp.sb2

To demonstrate how message broadcasting and receiving work, let's create a simple application that draws randomly colored squares. When the user clicks the left mouse button on the Stage, the Stage will detect this event (using its **when this sprite clicked** block) and broadcast a message that you'll call `Square` (you can choose a different name if you want). When the only sprite in this application receives this message, it will move to the current mouse position and draw a square. Follow these steps to create the application:

1. Start Scratch and then select **New** from the File menu to start a new application. Feel free to change the cat's costume to anything you like.
2. Add the **when I receive** block (from the *Events* palette) to the Scripts Area of the sprite. Click the down arrow in this block and select **new message...** from the drop-down menu. In the dialog that appears, type `Square` and click **OK**. The name of the block should change to **when I receive Square**.
3. Complete the script as shown in Figure 4-3. The sprite first lifts its pen and moves to the current mouse position, indicated by the **mouse x** and **mouse y** blocks (from the *Sensing* palette). It then picks a random pen color, lowers its pen, and draws a square.

The sprite is now ready to handle the `Square` message when it is received. The script in Figure 4-3 can be called a *message handler* since its job is to handle (or process) a broadcast message.

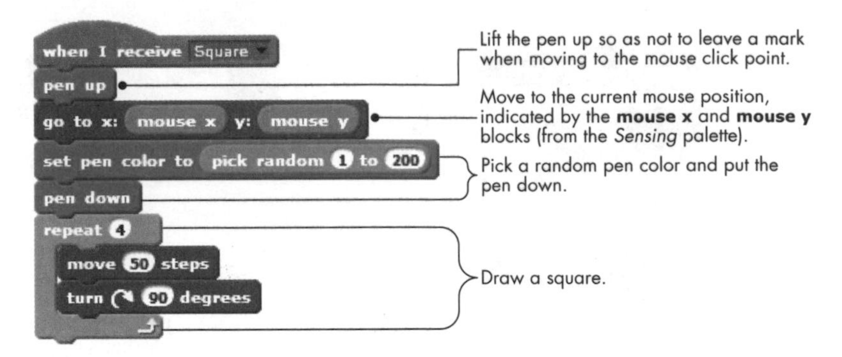
when I receive Square
pen up
go to x: mouse x y: mouse y
set pen color to pick random 1 to 200
pen down
repeat 4
move 50 steps
turn 90 degrees
Lift the pen up so as not to leave a mark when moving to the mouse click point.
Move to the current mouse position, indicated by the mouse x and mouse y blocks (from the Sensing palette).
Pick a random pen color and put the pen down.
Draw a square.

Figure 4-3: The Square *message handler*

Now, let's go to the Stage and add the code to broadcast the Square message in response to a mouse click. Click the Stage in the Sprite List and add the two scripts shown in Figure 4-4. The first script clears any pen marks from the Stage when the green flag is clicked. The second script, which is triggered when the user clicks the mouse on the Stage, uses the **broadcast** block to tell the sprite that it is time to draw.

when clicked
clear
when this sprite clicked
broadcast Square
When the green flag is clicked, clear the Stage. When the user clicks the mouse on the Stage, broadcast a message named Square.

Figure 4-4: The two scripts for the Stage in the Square *drawing application*

The application is now complete. To test it, just click the mouse on the Stage. It should respond by drawing a square in response to each mouse click.

Message Broadcasting to Coordinate Multiple Sprites

Flowers.sb2

To see multiple sprites respond to the same broadcast message, let's create an application that draws several flowers on the Stage in response to a mouse click. The Flowers application contains five sprites (named Flower1 through Flower5) that are responsible for drawing five flowers on the Stage. Each sprite has its own costume, as shown in Figure 4-5. Note how the background of each costume is transparent. Note also the location of the center of rotation for each costume (marked with the crossed lines).

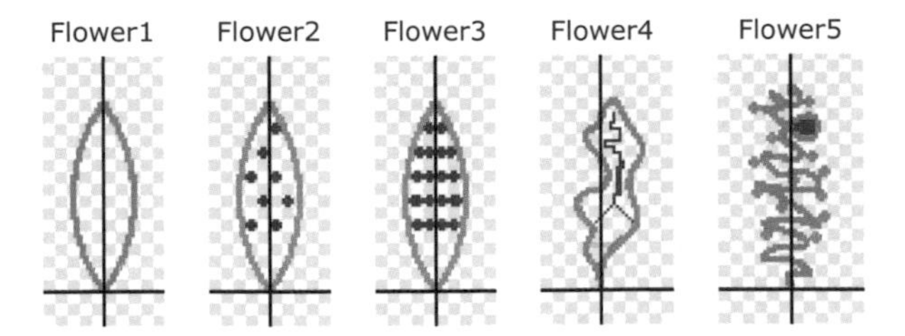
Flower1
Flower2
Flower3
Flower4
Flower5

Figure 4-5: Flowers uses these five petal sprites (as shown in the Paint Editor).

When a sprite receives a message to draw its flower, it will stamp multiple rotated copies of its costume on the Stage, as illustrated in Figure 4-6. The figure also shows sample outputs from the flower-drawing script we'll explore next.

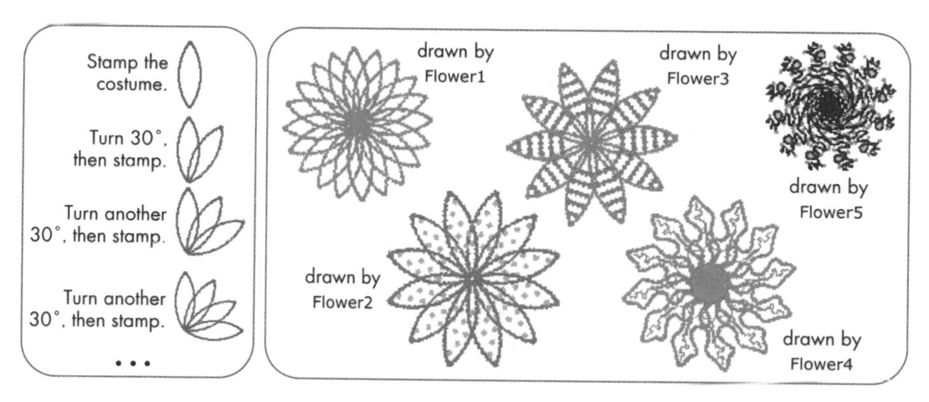

Figure 4-6: The Flowers application's drawing process (left) and some possible flowers (right)

When you click the mouse on the Stage, the Stage detects the mouse click using the **when this sprite clicked** block. In response, it clears its background and broadcasts a message called Draw. All five sprites respond to this message by executing a script similar to the one shown in Figure 4-7.

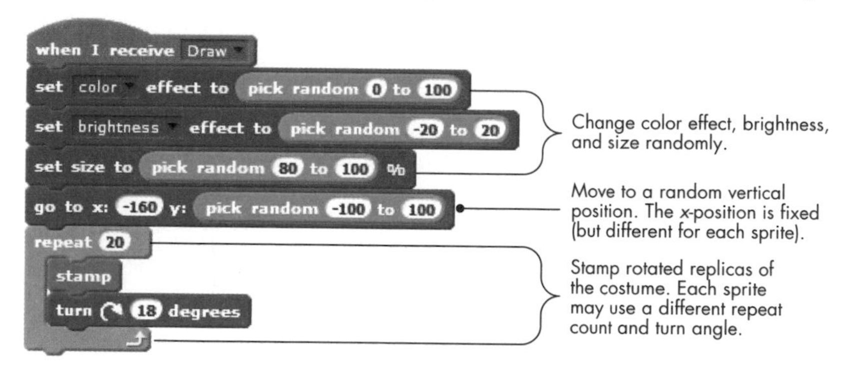

Figure 4-7: The basic script used by each of the five sprites

The script starts by assigning random values to the color effect, brightness effect, and size to change the appearance of the drawn flower. It then moves to a random vertical position on the Stage and draws a flower by stamping rotated replicas of its costume.

Open this application (named *Flowers.sb2*) and run it to see how it works. Despite its simplicity, its output is intriguing. I encourage you to design different costumes to create different types of flowers. Change the costumes' centers to discover even more interesting flower designs.

Now that you understand how message broadcasting and receiving work, we'll move on to introduce structured programming as a way to manage the complexity of large programs.

Creating Large Programs in Small Steps

The scripts that you've written up to this point are relatively short and simple. Eventually, you'll write longer, more complex scripts that contain hundreds of blocks, and understanding and maintaining them will become a real challenge.

An approach known as *structured programming* was developed in the mid-1960s to simplify the process of writing, understanding, and maintaining computer programs. Instead of having you write a single large program, this approach calls for dividing the program into smaller pieces, each of which solves one part of the overall task.

Consider, for example, the process of baking a cake. You may not think about the individual steps as you bake, but the process follows a precise recipe that lists the necessary steps. The recipe might include instructions like (1) mix 4 eggs, 2 oz of flour, and 1 cup of water; (2) put the mixture in a pan; (3) put the pan in the oven; (4) bake for 1 hour at 350°F; and so on. In essence, the recipe breaks down the problem of baking a cake into distinct logical steps.

Similarly, when you design a solution for your programming problem, it helps to break the problem down into manageable, "mind-sized" bites. This approach helps you maintain a clear view of the whole program and the relationships between its component parts.

Consider Figure 4-8, which shows a long script that draws a shape on the Stage. You'll see that you can divide this script into smaller logical blocks by function. The first six blocks, for example, initialize the sprite. The first **repeat** block draws a square, the second draws a triangle, and so on. Using the structured programming approach, we can group related blocks together under a representative name to form procedures.

Once we write these procedures, we can call them in a certain sequence to solve our programming problem. Figure 4-8 also shows how the separate procedures are put together to achieve the same function as the original script. Clearly, the script that uses procedures (right) is more modular and easier to understand than the original (left).

Procedures can also help you avoid writing the same code twice. If a set of commands is executed in several places in a program, you can write a procedure that performs these commands and use it instead. This strategy to avoid duplicating code is referred to as *code reuse*. Note, for example, how the **Draw square** procedure was reused in Figure 4-8.

Using procedures enables you to apply the "divide-and-conquer" strategy to solve complex problems. You divide a large and complex problem into subproblems and then conquer these simpler problems individually, testing each one in isolation. After solving all the subproblems in isolation, you put these pieces together in a way that solves the original problem. This is similar to our cake-baking strategy: Our recipe divided the problem into well-defined steps, and we executed these steps in the correct order to build the final product (our cake).

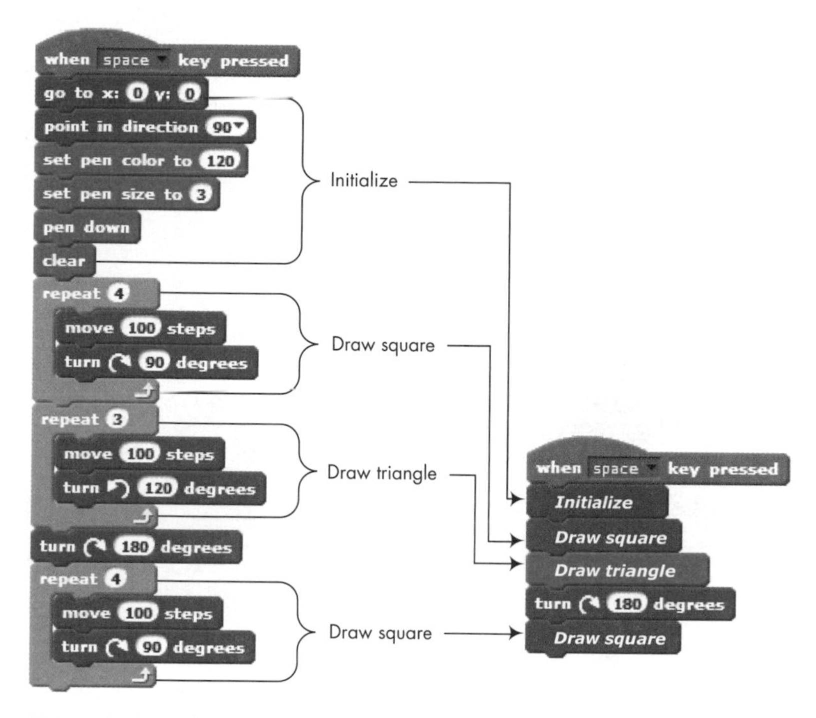

Figure 4-8: Breaking a large script into logical parts that each complete one function

At this point, you might ask, "How do we create these procedures?" Before Scratch 2, you couldn't build the **Initialize** block shown in Figure 4-8 and then call it from your script. The only way to emulate procedures and add some structure to a program was through Scratch's *message-broadcasting* mechanism. This has changed in Scratch 2, which added the powerful "custom blocks" feature.

In this section, we'll demonstrate the old way of doing things, because that's what you'll see in scripts created in an older version of Scratch. However, the build-your-own-block feature will be explained in the next section, and it will be used consistently throughout the rest of the book.

Since sprites receive their own broadcast messages, we can implement procedures by having a sprite broadcast a message to itself and perform the desired task under the **when I receive** trigger block. We can use the **broadcast and wait** block to ensure that our procedures are called in the correct sequence, thus adding structure and modularity to our programs. Confused? Let's see it in action.

Creating Procedures with Message Broadcasting

Flowers2.sb2

We'll explore how procedures work and how they can improve your code by re-creating the Flowers program from earlier.

Open the file *Flowers2.sb2*, which contains the new version of the program. The script for the Stage is the same as before (the Stage broadcasts a Draw message when it detects a mouse click), but this time, our program uses only one sprite instead of five. This sprite has five costumes, leaf1 through leaf5, and will call a procedure to draw a flower for each costume. Since we have a single sprite, we only need one copy of the drawing code (not the five duplicate scripts we had in our first version). This makes the program smaller and the code easier to understand. When the sprite in this application receives the Draw message, it executes the script shown in Figure 4-9.

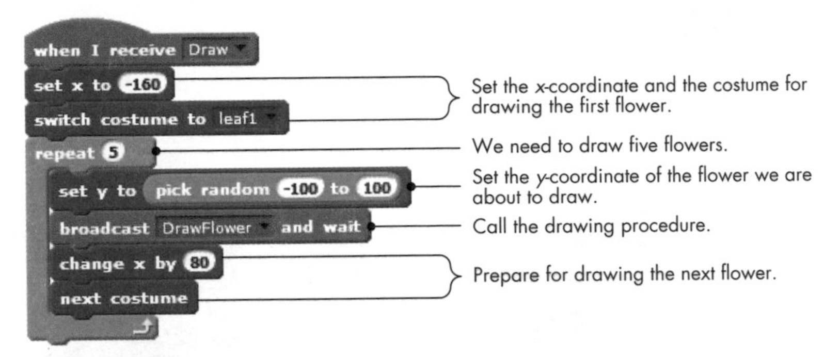

Figure 4-9: When the sprite receives the Draw *message, it calls* DrawFlower *five times (in a loop) to draw five flowers.*

The script sets the *x*-coordinate and the costume for drawing the first flower and then enters a loop to draw five flowers. On each pass, the loop sets the *y*-coordinate for the flower and calls DrawFlower by broadcasting a message to itself. This call halts the script's execution until DrawFlower is done. When this happens, the Draw script resumes execution, adjusting the *x*-coordinate and changing the costume in preparation for drawing the next flower.

NOTE *You can name a procedure anything you like, but I recommend selecting a name that reflects that procedure's purpose. This is especially helpful when you revisit a program that you wrote months ago. For example, if you want to show players how many points they have in a game, you might create a procedure named* ShowScore*. Naming this procedure* Mary *or* Alfred *certainly won't remind you (or anyone else reading your program) what the procedure does.*

The DrawFlower procedure is shown in Figure 4-10. It sets random values for the color effect, brightness, and sprite size before stamping rotated versions of the current costume to draw a flower.

While the first version of the program contained five sprites and five repeated scripts, the second version achieves the same result using a single sprite that calls one procedure for drawing all five flowers. Open *Flowers.sb2* and *Flowers2.sb2* in two tabs of your browser and compare them. Isn't the new version much simpler to follow? Using procedures lets you make smaller programs that are easier to understand and maintain. This will become more beneficial as you write programs to perform more complex tasks.

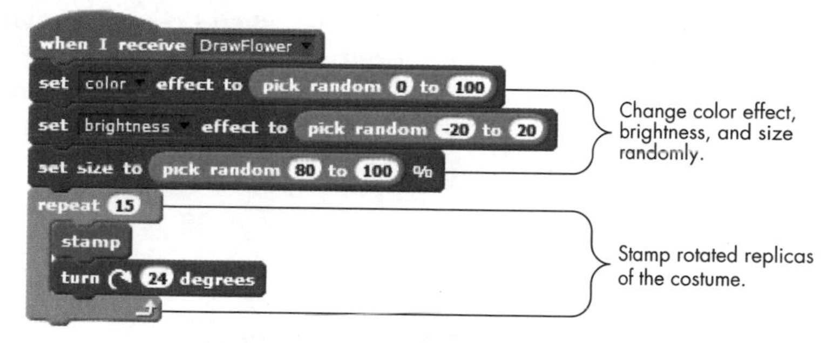

Figure 4-10: The DrawFlower *procedure*

Building Your Own Block

As of Scratch 2, you can also create your own custom blocks. After you make a custom block, it should appear in the *More Blocks* palette, where you can use it as you would any other Scratch block.

To show you how to create and use these blocks, we'll modify the Flowers2 program we discussed in the last section to use a custom block for the DrawFlower procedure. The following steps will guide you through creating this new version of the application.

1. First, open the *Flowers2.sb2* file that you looked at in the previous section. Select **File ▸ Download to your computer** from the File menu and save the file as *Flowers3.sb2*. You can pick a different name if you prefer.
2. Click the thumbnail of the Flower sprite to select it. Then select the *More Blocks* palette and click **Make a Block**. You should see the dialog shown in Figure 4-11 (left). Type DrawFlower for the block's name and click **OK**. A new function block called **DrawFlower** should appear under the *More Blocks* palette, and a **define DrawFlower** block should appear in the Scripts Area as shown in the figure (right).

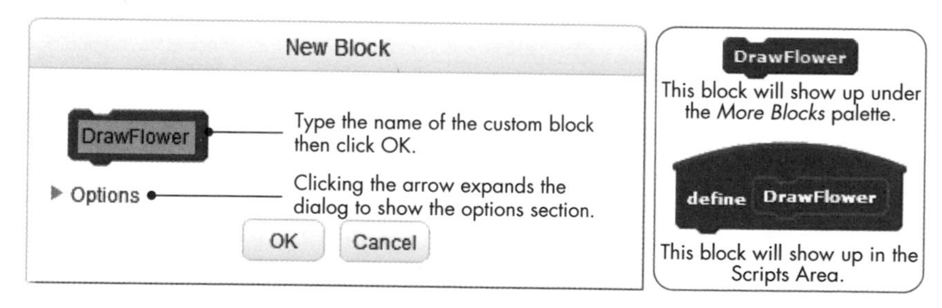

Figure 4-11: The New Block dialog and the blocks that appear after creating the **DrawFlower** *custom block*

3. Detach the script connected to the **when I receive DrawFlower** block and connect it to the **define DrawFlower** block, as shown in Figure 4-12. This results in a new procedure, called **DrawFlower**, that is implemented as a custom block. Delete the **when I receive DrawFlower** block because it is no longer needed.

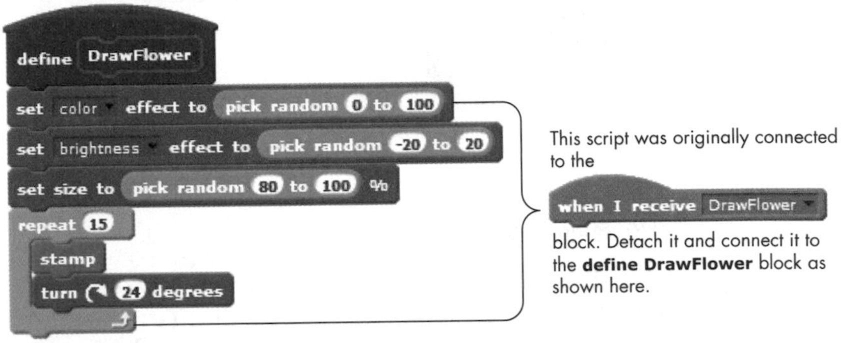

```
define DrawFlower
set color effect to (pick random 0 to 100)
set brightness effect to (pick random -20 to 20)
set size to (pick random 80 to 100) %
repeat 15
    stamp
    turn ↻ 24 degrees
```

This script was originally connected to the **when I receive DrawFlower** block. Detach it and connect it to the **define DrawFlower** block as shown here.

Figure 4-12: The **DrawFlower** *procedure implemented as a custom block*

4. Now that we've created a **DrawFlower** procedure, we just need to call it from the Draw message handler. Modify the Draw message handler as shown in Figure 4-13. Note that we only replaced the **broadcast DrawFlower and wait** block with our new **DrawFlower** custom block.

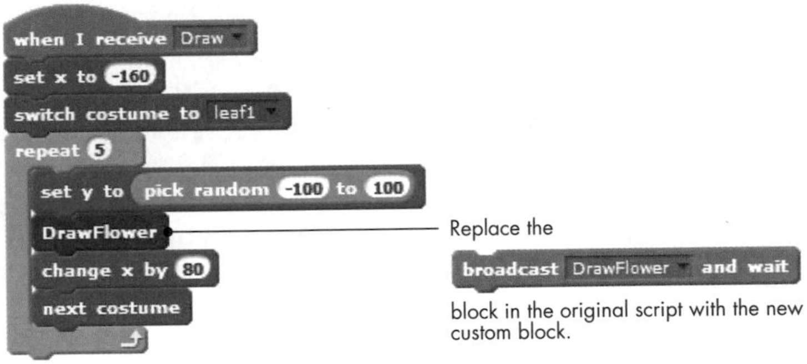

```
when I receive Draw
set x to -160
switch costume to leaf1
repeat 5
    set y to (pick random -100 to 100)
    DrawFlower
    change x by 80
    next costume
```

Replace the **broadcast DrawFlower and wait** block in the original script with the new custom block.

Figure 4-13: Calling **DrawFlower** *from the* Draw *message handler*

The program is now complete, and you can test it. Click the mouse on the Stage to verify that the program still works as before. See "Running Without Screen Refresh" on page 77 to learn how you can speed up the execution of this program.

Now that you know the basics behind custom blocks, you can take them a step further by making blocks that can accept inputs.

RUNNING WITHOUT SCREEN REFRESH

Implementing the **DrawFlower** procedure with custom blocks brings up another feature that can shorten the execution time of the drawing script. To demonstrate, perform the following:

1. Right-click the **DrawFlower** block under the *More Blocks* palette and select **edit** from the pop-up menu. This should bring up the dialog from Figure 4-11, except that the title will be *Edit Block* instead of *New Block*.
2. Click the arrow next to Options, check the **Run without screen refresh** box and click **OK** (see Figure 4-15).
3. Now, click the mouse on the Stage and see what happens. Instead of seeing the individual rotating and stamping steps as the five flowers are drawn, you should see them appear on the Stage *almost* at once. Here is an explanation of what's happening.

The **DrawFlower** procedure contains many blocks that change a sprite's appearance, including **set color**, **set brightness**, **set size**, and **stamp**. After executing such a block, Scratch normally pauses for a while to *refresh* (that is, redraw) the screen. This is why we were able to see the drawing progress when the application ran before.

If you select the Run without screen refresh option, the blocks will run without pausing to refresh the screen, allowing the procedure to run much faster. The screen will refresh after Scratch executes the entire procedure.

In addition to speeding up a procedure, the Run without screen refresh option helps to prevent the flickering that repeated redrawing can cause.

Passing Parameters to Custom Blocks

Let's start by creating a custom block named **Square**, which draws a square whose side length is 100 pixels, as shown in Figure 4-14.

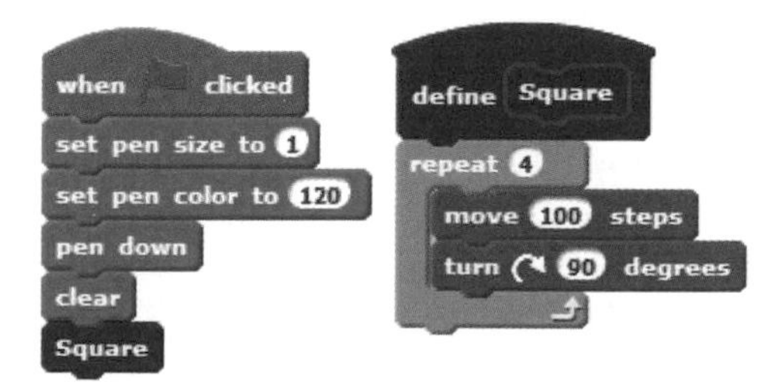

Figure 4-14: A **Square** *procedure that draws a fixed-size square*

The **Square** procedure has limited capabilities, because the drawn square size is fixed once and for all. What if you want to draw squares with different side lengths, such as 50, 75, or 200? You could define several custom blocks named **Square50**, **Square75**, and **Square200**, but creating multiple blocks that do essentially the same thing is, in most cases, a bad idea; if you need to make a change, then you have to track down all the copies and change those as well. A better solution is to have a single **Square** block that allows the user to specify the desired side length when calling it.

You've actually been applying this concept since Chapter 1. For example, Scratch provides a single **move** block that allows you to specify how many steps a sprite will move by entering that number in a parameter slot. That way, Scratch doesn't have to provide a new block for every possible move distance.

What we need to do, therefore, is add a parameter slot to our **Square** block where the user can enter the side length. Figure 4-15 illustrates how to modify the **Square** block.

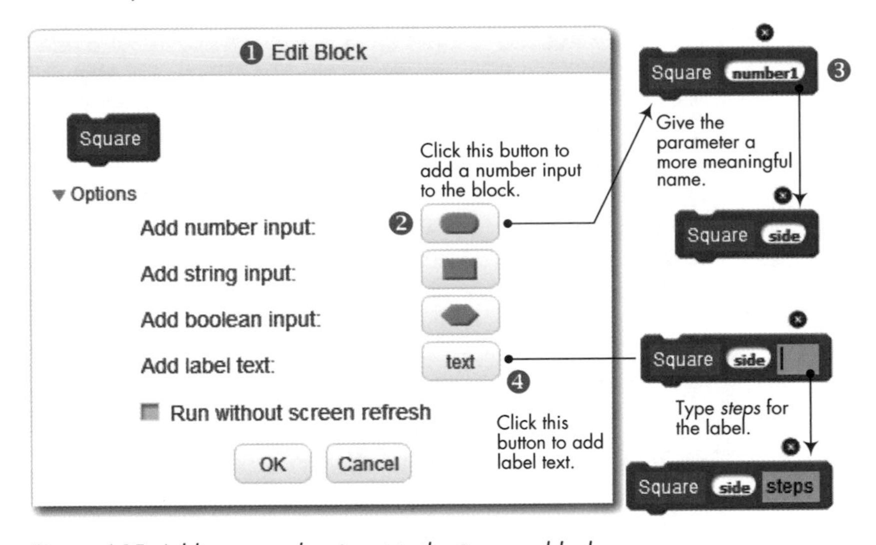

Figure 4-15: Adding a number input to the **Square** *block*

First, right-click the **Square** block in the *More Blocks* palette (or the **define Square** block in the Scripts Area) and select **edit** from the pop-up menu to bring up the Edit Block dialog ❶. Click the small arrow next to Options to expand the dialog and see the available options.

We want our **Square** block to accept the desired side length of a square, which is a number, so click **Add number input** ❷ to add a number slot to the block. A number slot named number1 should be added to the **Square** block.

To indicate that the new slot is intended to carry the side length of the square, change the default name from number1 to something meaningful ❸, such as side, length, or sideLength. (Again, although Scratch doesn't care what label you use, you do! Pick a name that reflects the meaning of the parameter.) Let's use the name side for this example.

Technically, that's all what we need to do to add a number slot to our procedure. If we click OK, we'll have a **Square** block that takes a number as input. We could drag this block into our scripts and specify the desired length in the parameter slot, as in **Square 50**. But how would a user know what the number passed to **Square** means? Does it mean an area of 50, a diagonal of 50, a side length is 50, or something else?

Imagine if Scratch's **glide** block were designed like this:

How would you know that the first slot represents time (in seconds) and the second and third slots represent the *x*- and *y*-coordinates of the target glide point? The Scratch designers made the **glide** block easier to understand and use by adding labels to these slots as follows:

Let's do the same thing for our **Square** block by adding text that describes the meaning (or usage) of the parameter slot. Click **Add label text** ❹, as shown in Figure 4-15, to add a label after the side parameter. Type **steps** for the label text and click **OK**.

Now, if you examine the definition of the **Square** procedure in the Scripts Area, you'll see a small block (named side) added to its header, as illustrated in Figure 4-16 (left). The **move** block still has the fixed number 100 inside it, but all we need to do now is drag the side block from the header of the **Square** method and drop it over the parameter slot of the **move** block to replace the number 100, as shown in Figure 4-16 (right).

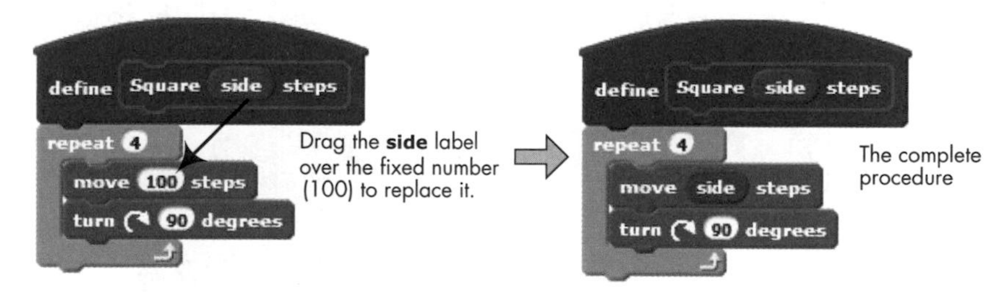

Figure 4-16: Modifying the **Square** *procedure to use the* side *parameter*

The label, side, that appears in the header of the **Square** procedure is called a *parameter*. You can think of a parameter as a named placeholder. We wanted our **Square** procedure to be able to draw squares of any size, so instead of hard-coding a fixed number inside our procedure, we used a general parameter named side. Users will specify the exact value of side when they call the **Square** procedure. Let's illustrate this point by modifying the script in Figure 4-14 to use the new version of our **Square** procedure. The required changes are illustrated in Figure 4-17.

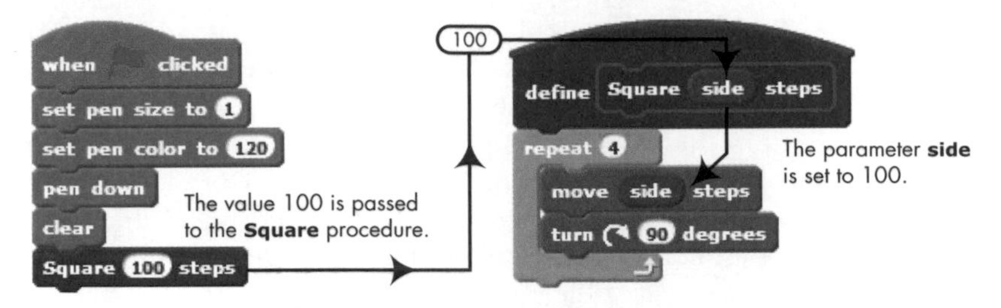

Figure 4-17: Calling the **Square** *procedure with* side *set to 100*

Here, the number 100 (called an *argument*) is passed to the **Square** procedure. When **Square** is executed, its side parameter is set to 100, and this value is used to replace all occurrences of the side block inside the procedure. As you can see, the ability to specify different arguments to a procedure is a powerful feature that adds a lot of flexibility to our programs.

We can enhance our **Square** procedure even further by making it accept the square's color as a second parameter, as shown in Figure 4-18. Here, we added a second input parameter, called clrNum (short for color number), which indicates the desired color of the square. The procedure now sets the pen color to the value specified by clrNum before executing the drawing loop. Edit the **Square** block to implement the changes shown in the figure.

PARAMETERS VS. ARGUMENTS

Although many programmers use the terms *parameter* and *argument* interchangeably, the two terms are in fact different. To clarify, consider the **Average** procedure shown below, which computes the average of two numbers.

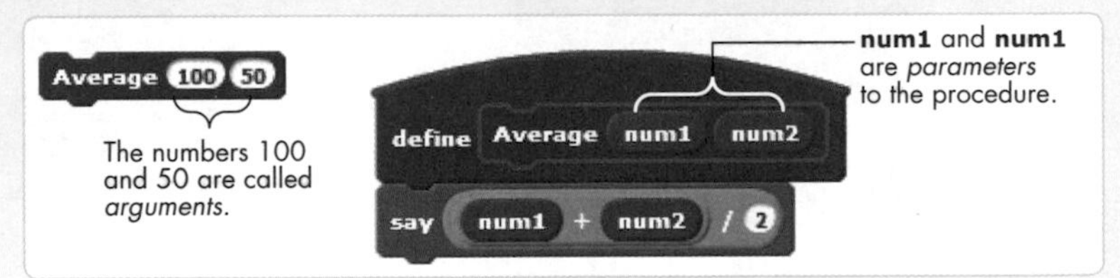

As defined, this procedure has two parameters named num1 and num2. A *parameter* defines an input to a procedure. You'd call this procedure with the block shown at the left and specify some values or expressions inside the available slots. The values 100 and 50 in the above example are called *arguments* of the procedure.

Of course, the number of arguments in the procedure call must match the number of parameters in the procedure's definition. When you call **Average**, the parameters num1 and num2 receive the values 100 and 50, respectively, because arguments and parameters are matched by position.

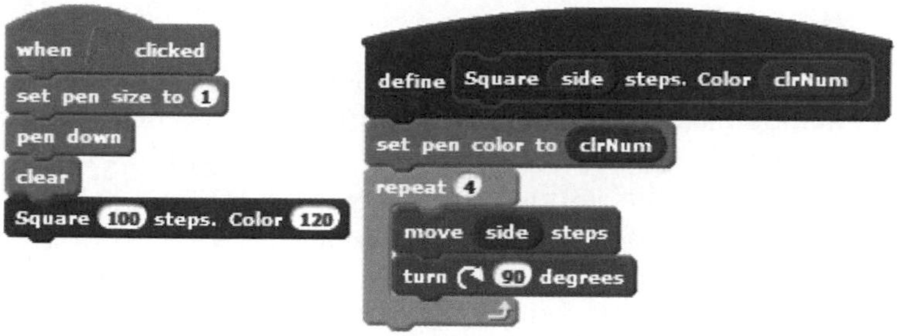

```
when [flag] clicked
set pen size to (1)
pen down
clear
Square (100) steps. Color (120)
```

```
define Square (side) steps. Color (clrNum)
set pen color to (clrNum)
repeat (4)
    move (side) steps
    turn ↻ (90) degrees
```

Figure 4-18: This version of **Square** *takes the desired color as a second parameter.*

> **TRY IT OUT 4-1**
>
> What about the thickness of the square's border? Modify the **Square** procedure to take a third parameter, called penSize, that specifies the size of the pen to be used in drawing the square.

Let's conclude this section with some useful tips for dealing with custom blocks:

- Custom blocks can't be shared among sprites. If you create a custom block for, let's say, Sprite1, then only Sprite1 can use that block. Similarly, a custom block defined for the Stage can only be called by scripts that belong to the Stage.
- Give your parameters meaningful names that indicate what they're used for.
- To delete a custom block, just drag its **define** block (that is, the hat block) from the Scripts Area and drop it over the Palettes area. You can only delete a **define** block if your project doesn't contain any stack blocks associated with it, so remove all uses of a custom block from your scripts before trying to delete it.
- To delete a parameter of a custom block, click the parameter's name in the Edit Block dialog and then click the small *X* icon that appears above the parameter's slot.
- In addition to number inputs, you can also add string and Boolean parameters. We'll talk more about data types when we discuss variables in the next chapter.

Now, you might wonder: Can a procedure call another procedure? In the next section, you'll learn about how to use nested procedure calls to extend the power and usefulness of existing procedures.

Using Nested Procedures

As we noted earlier, a procedure should be designed to perform a single, well-defined task. To execute multiple tasks, it is perfectly legal—and in many cases desirable—to have one procedure call another as part of its execution path. Nesting procedures this way gives you great flexibility in structuring and organizing your programs.

RotatedSquares.sb2

To see this in action, let's start with the **Square** procedure we wrote in the previous section (see Figure 4-17). Now, we'll create a new procedure, called **Squares**, that draws four stretched squares, as illustrated in Figure 4-19. It does so by calling the **Square** procedure four times. Each call uses a different argument, and the output is four squares that share a corner.

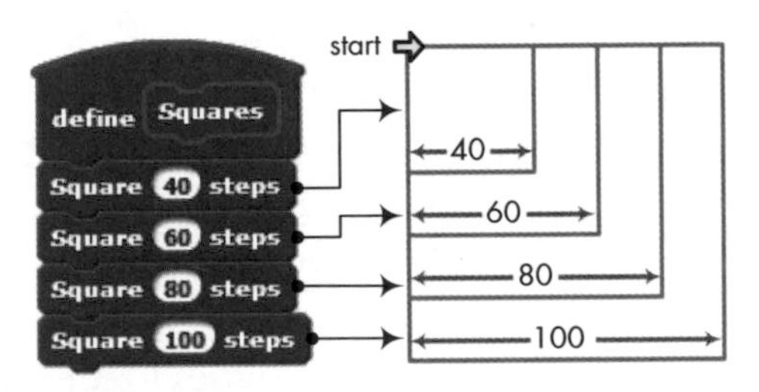

Figure 4-19: The **Squares** *procedure and its output*

We can now use **Squares** to create some interesting art. Figure 4-20 shows another procedure, called **RotatedSquares**, which calls the **Squares** procedure several times, turning the shapes by some angle after each call.

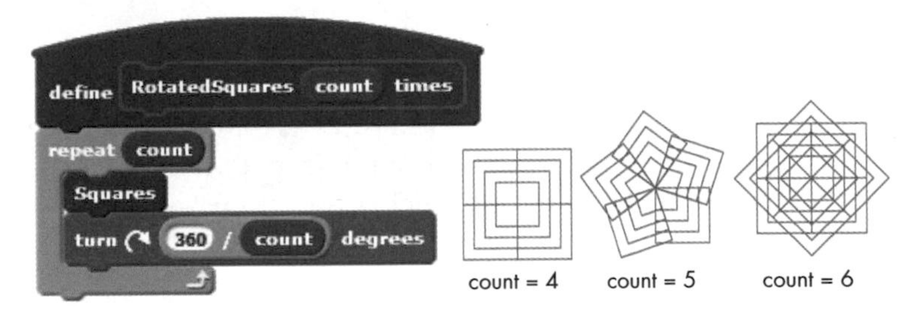

Figure 4-20: The **RotatedSquares** *procedure and some possible outputs*

In this procedure, the count parameter is used twice: once to determine the number of repetitions and again to calculate the turn angle after calling **Squares**. Setting count to 5, for example, will result in repeating the square pattern of Figure 4-20 five times with a 72° (that is, 360° / 5) right turn after each call. Experiment with different values to discover new patterns.

Checkers.sb2

Let's work out another example that demonstrates the power of nested procedures: We'll start with the **Square** procedure of Figure 4-16 and end up with a checkerboard.

Create a new procedure (called **Row**) that draws a single row of squares, as illustrated in Figure 4-21. Note that the number of squares to draw is specified as a parameter. To keep things simple, we've fixed the size of the individual squares at 20 steps instead of defining the size as a second parameter to the **Row** procedure.

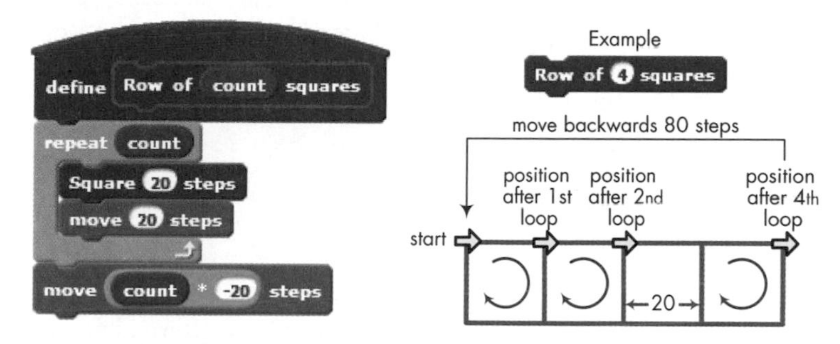

*Figure 4-21: The **Row** procedure*

Figure 4-21 also illustrates the result of calling **Row** with an argument of 4, which makes the procedure call **Square 20 steps** four times in a loop. The sprite's position is adjusted after drawing each square to set the initial position for the next square. After drawing the four squares, the last command returns the sprite to its initial position.

To draw another row of squares below the one shown in Figure 4-21, we just need to move the sprite down 20 steps and then call the **Row** procedure again. We can repeat this to draw as many rows as we want. Our **Checkers** procedure, shown in Figure 4-22, does just that.

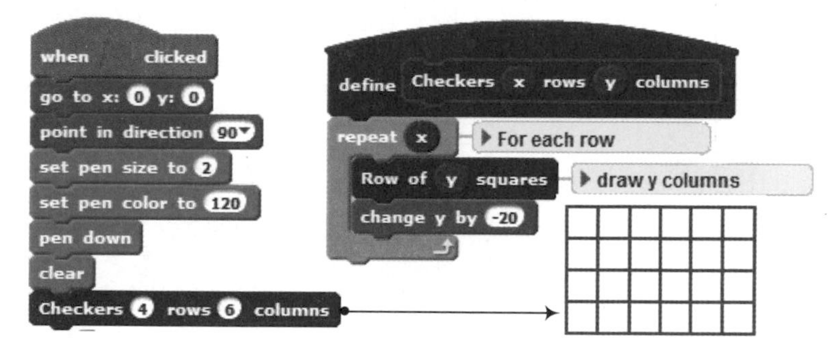

*Figure 4-22: The **Checkers** procedure and its output*

This procedure takes two parameters: the number of rows and the number of columns for the desired checkerboard. After drawing each row, the procedure moves the sprite down 20 steps to prepare to draw the next row of squares.

The examples presented in this section show how procedures can help you divide a program into smaller, more manageable pieces. Once you've written and tested your procedures, you can use them as building blocks for more complex procedures without worrying much about the low-level implementation details. You can then focus on the important task of putting together the whole application using these procedures as building blocks.

> **TRY IT OUT 4-2**
>
> What do you think will happen if you set the initial direction to 0° (up) instead of 90° (right)? Will the script work? If not, how could you fix it? Make this change and run the script to test your answer.

Working with Procedures

Now that you know why it's important to break your program down into smaller parts and tackle them one at a time, let's discuss how to perform this division. Every problem is different, and there is no "one size fits all" solution—but that's what makes this a fun puzzle!

In this section, we'll first explore the *top-down process* of dividing a large program into modular pieces with a clear logical structure. We'll then discuss another way of building complex programs: the *bottom-up process* of combining existing procedures. Figure 4-23 shows a high-level view of these two approaches.

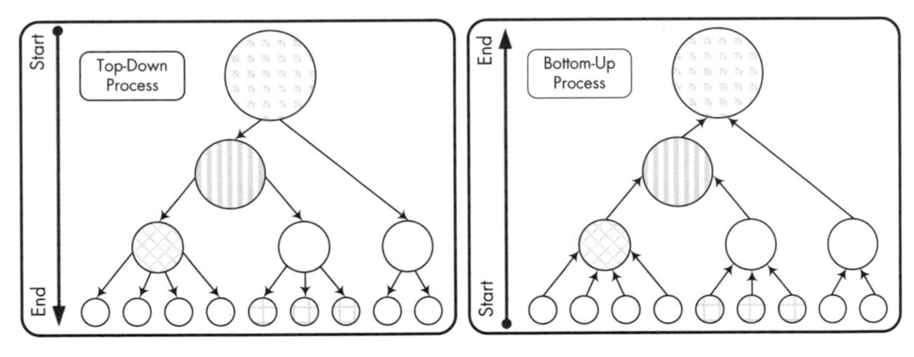

Figure 4-23: Illustrating top-down (left) and bottom-up (right) approaches

In both diagrams, the problem we want to solve is at the top, and the individual steps that build our solution are at the bottom. You can start from whichever level makes sense to you.

Breaking Programs Down into Procedures

The first step in solving any programming problem is to fully understand the problem. After that, you can plan a general solution and divide it into major tasks. There is no right or wrong way to go about dividing up any particular program, and with experience, you will get better at deciding what "major" means. Working from the general solution down to its specifics ensures that, at least, the overall logic of the program is correct.

House.sb2

To demonstrate this problem-solving strategy, let's consider how we would draw a house similar to that shown in Figure 4-24.

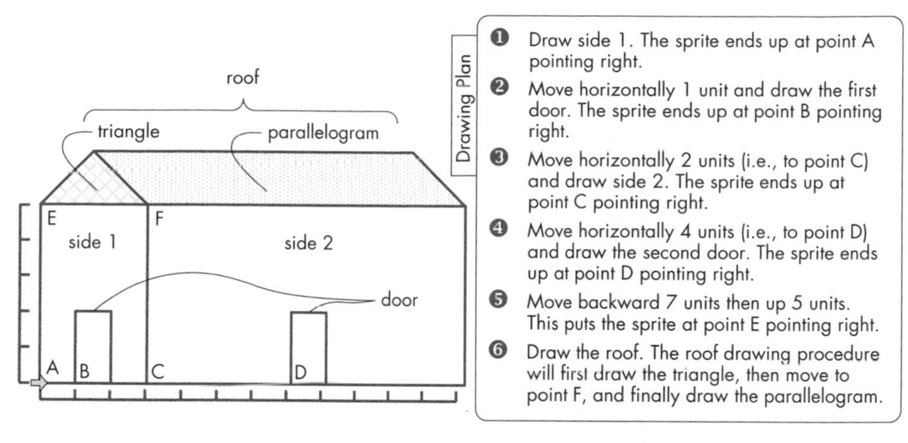

roof
triangle
parallelogram
E
F
side 1
side 2
door
A
B
C
D
Drawing Plan
❶ Draw side 1. The sprite ends up at point A pointing right.
❷ Move horizontally 1 unit and draw the first door. The sprite ends up at point B pointing right.
❸ Move horizontally 2 units (i.e., to point C) and draw side 2. The sprite ends up at point C pointing right.
❹ Move horizontally 4 units (i.e., to point D) and draw the second door. The sprite ends up at point D pointing right.
❺ Move backward 7 units then up 5 units. This puts the sprite at point E pointing right.
❻ Draw the roof. The roof drawing procedure will first draw the triangle, then move to point F, and finally draw the parallelogram.

Figure 4-24: We can draw this house by dividing the task into several smaller pieces and handling each piece individually.

On one hand, working on this simple problem allows us to focus on the solution strategy without getting bogged down in a lot of detail. On the other hand, despite its apparent simplicity, the problem lends itself to many different solutions. Here are some possibilities:

- We can view the house as made up of straight lines. In this case, drawing each line is a major task.
- We can view the house as made up of six independent shapes: side 1, side 2, two doors, a triangle, and a parallelogram. Drawing each shape constitutes a major task.
- Since the two doors are identical, we can define one major task for drawing a door and invoke that task twice.
- We can view the triangle and the parallelogram at the top of the house as one unit, the roof. In this case, one major task is to draw the roof.
- We can view side 1 and its door as one unit, the front side. In this case, one major task is to draw the front side.

There are many other possibilities, but that's enough to illustrate the point. The idea is to group tasks into small, understandable pieces that you can deal with and then focus on one piece at a time. If you find similar pieces, try to come up with a common solution and apply it to all those pieces.

With that in mind, our plan for drawing the house is also outlined in Figure 4-24. This plan assumes that the sprite starts facing right at point A. All we need to do is create a script that matches the steps outlined in the plan. We'll write a procedure (called **Side1**) to draw the left side of the house as specified in step 1. We will also write three procedures (called **Door**, **Side2**, and **Roof**) to draw the two doors, the right side of the house, and the roof (as specified in steps 2, 3, 4, and 6), and we will connect all these procedures with appropriate motion commands.

Our **House** procedure is shown in Figure 4-25 alongside the drawing steps that correspond to each procedure call. The procedure takes a single parameter (called **scale**) that specifies the unit length (that is, a scaling factor) for drawing the house. Note how the **Door** procedure was reused twice. Note also that the **Roof** procedure is responsible for drawing the entire roof, and that it may contain different sub-procedures for drawing the individual components of the roof.

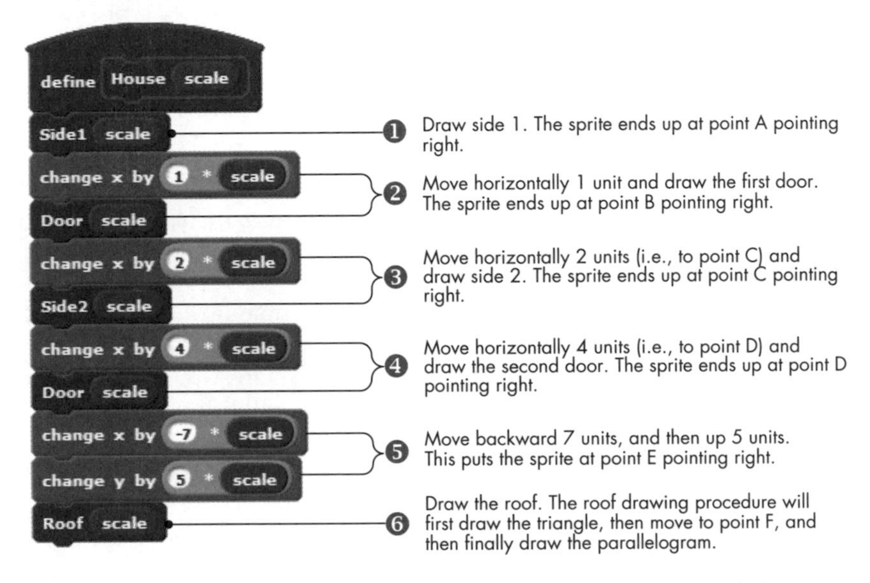

define House scale
Side1 scale
change x by 1 * scale
Door scale
change x by 2 * scale
Side2 scale
change x by 4 * scale
Door scale
change x by -7 * scale
change y by 5 * scale
Roof scale
1 Draw side 1. The sprite ends up at point A pointing right.
2 Move horizontally 1 unit and draw the first door. The sprite ends up at point B pointing right.
3 Move horizontally 2 units (i.e., to point C) and draw side 2. The sprite ends up at point C pointing right.
4 Move horizontally 4 units (i.e., to point D) and draw the second door. The sprite ends up at point D pointing right.
5 Move backward 7 units, and then up 5 units. This puts the sprite at point E pointing right.
6 Draw the roof. The roof drawing procedure will first draw the triangle, then move to point F, and then finally draw the parallelogram.

Figure 4-25: The **House** *procedure. Note how the major tasks align with the drawing plan.*

The individual procedures for drawing the house are shown in Figure 4-26. These procedures draw simple geometric shapes using the same techniques you learned in Chapter 2.

The **Side1**, **Door**, and **Side2** procedures draw 3×5, 1×2, and 9×5 rectangles (scaled by the factor scale), respectively. The **Roof** procedure has two sub-procedures (named **Triangle** and **Parallelogram**) for drawing the two parts of the roof. Note that the scaling factor scale was used consistently in all these procedures. This allows us to draw larger or smaller houses by calling the **House** procedure with a different argument.

TRY IT OUT 4-3

Did you notice that the **Side1**, **Door**, and **Side2** procedures use almost identical code? Create a new procedure named **Rectangle** that takes the length, width, and scale as parameters and draws a rectangle of the specified dimensions. Modify the **Side1**, **Door**, and **Side2** procedures to call the new **Rectangle** procedure.

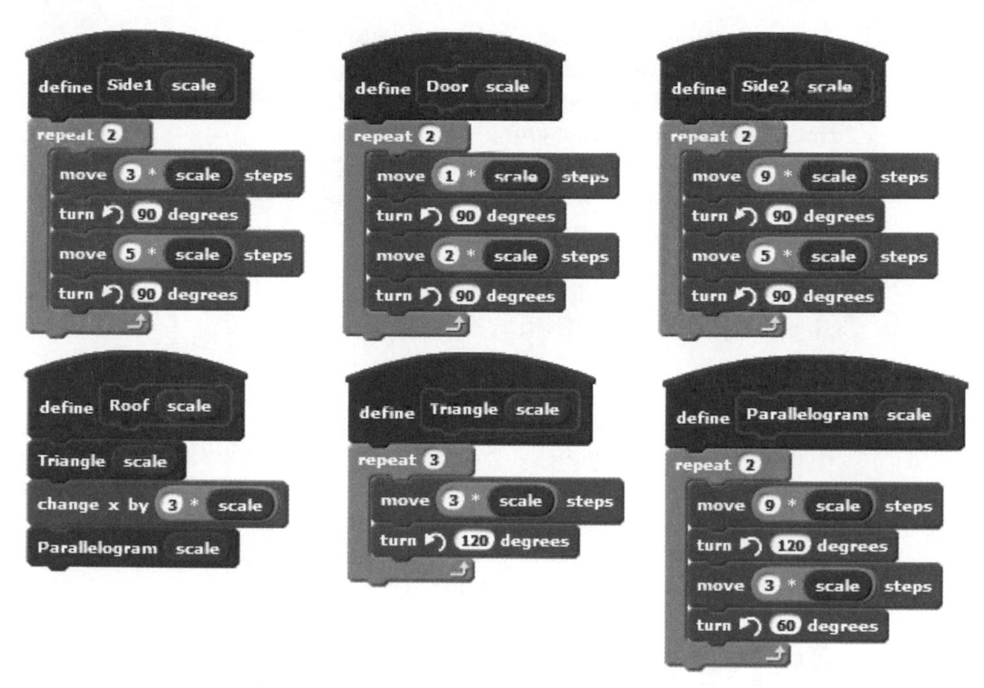

Figure 4-26: Procedures for drawing the house in Figure 4-24

Building Up with Procedures

FlowerFlake.sb2

Another way to deal with a large problem is to focus on the smaller details first. If you solve a large problem's smaller pieces (or find solutions that already exist), you can then assemble the results from the bottom up to reach a total solution.

To demonstrate this problem-solving technique, let's start with a simple procedure (called **Leaf**) that draws a single leaf as shown in Figure 4-27. The procedure contains a **repeat** loop that runs twice to draw the two halves of the leaf. Each half is drawn as a series of 15 short line segments with a 6° turn angle between them. This is similar to the method of drawing polygons we used in Chapter 2.

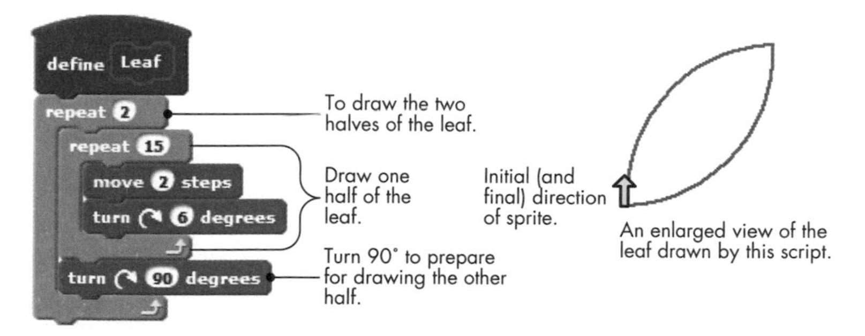

Figure 4-27: The **Leaf** *procedure and its output*

Using this procedure as a starting point, we can now draw a slightly more complex shape that contains five leaves. Our new procedure, called **Leaves**, and its output are shown in Figure 4-28. As you can see, we only had to call the **Leaf** procedure in a **repeat** loop with an appropriate turn angle in between.

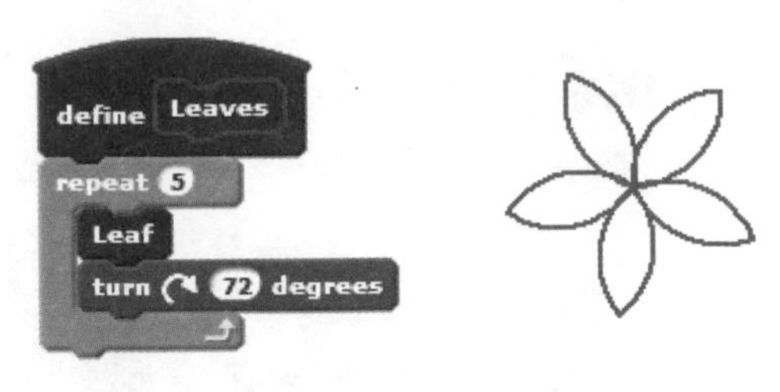

Figure 4-28: The **Leaves** *procedure calls the* **Leaf** *procedure five times with 72° turn angle between each call.*

We can now use **Leaf** and **Leaves** to build up something that is even more complex: a branch with leaves on it. Our **Branch** procedure and its output are illustrated in Figure 4-29. The sprite moves forward 40 steps, draws a single leaf (by calling the **Leaf** procedure), moves an additional 50 steps forward, draws five leaves (by calling the **Leaves** procedure), and finally returns to its starting position.

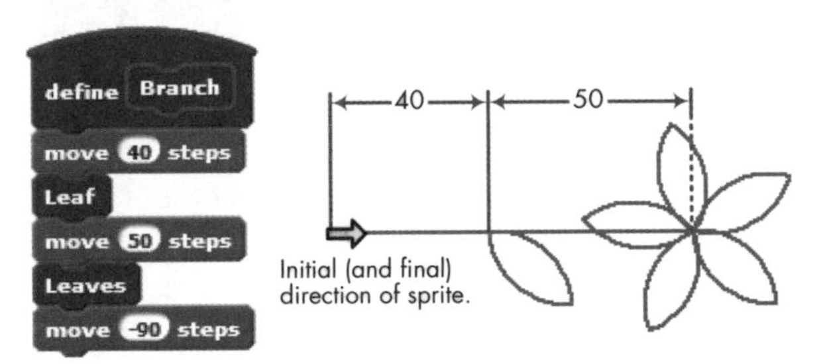

Figure 4-29: The **Branch** *procedure and its output*

Let's take this up another notch. How about using the **Branch** procedure to create a complex drawing of a flower? Our new procedure, called **Flower**, and its output are shown in Figure 4-30. The procedure simply calls the **Branch** procedure six times in a loop with 60° turn angle in between.

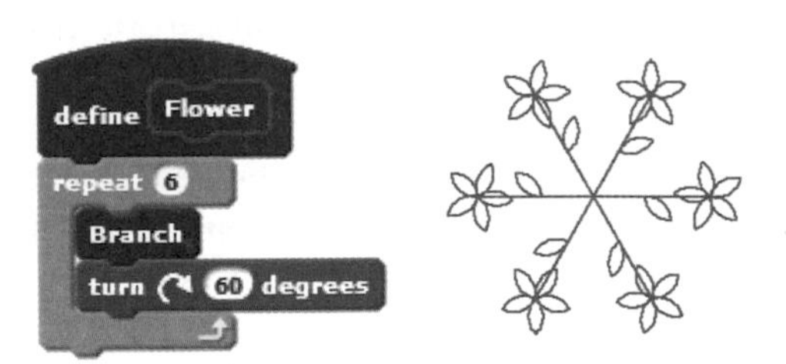

Figure 4-30: The **Flower** *procedure and its output*

We can keep going on and on, but the idea should now be clear. We started with a simple procedure called **Leaf** and used it in a new procedure (called **Leaves**) to create a complex pattern. The **Branch** procedure relied on these two procedures to create something more complicated. The **Flower** procedure then used **Branch** to draw an even more complex pattern. If we wanted to, we could create a procedure that draws an entire tree of flowers and yet another to draw a garden full of trees.

The point to take away from this example is that, regardless of the complexity of the problem we are trying to solve, we can always build the solution by gluing together a number of smaller, more manageable pieces. Using this problem-solving technique, we start with short procedures that solve very simple problems and then use them to create more sophisticated procedures.

Summary

In this chapter, we introduced a number of fundamental concepts that will be used extensively in the remainder of this book. First, we explained the concept of message broadcasting for intersprite communication and synchronization. After that, we introduced structured programming and discussed how to use message broadcasting to implement procedures. We then demonstrated the build-your-own-block feature of Scratch 2.0 and explained how to pass arguments to procedures to make the procedures more flexible. We went over several examples that demonstrated dividing a large problem into smaller, more manageable pieces and explained how to use procedures as the basic building blocks for creating large programs. Last, we examined a bottom-up problem-solving technique, in which we put together known solutions to smaller pieces of a problem to solve the big problem.

In the next chapter, you'll learn about the most important concept in any programming language: *variables*. This introduction to variables will be an essential next step in becoming a proficient programmer.

Problems

1. Write different procedures to draw each letter of your name. Name each procedure for the letter that it draws. Then write a script that calls these procedures so you can draw your name on the Stage.
2. Create the program shown below, run it, and explain how it works.

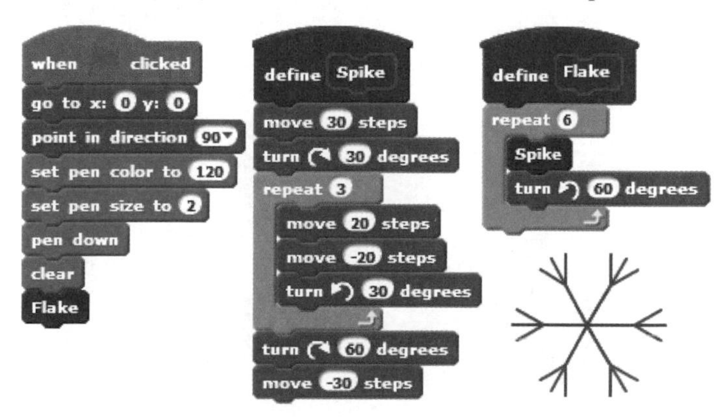

3. Write a procedure that converts degrees Celsius to degrees Fahrenheit as shown below. Have the script round the answer to the nearest integer. Test your procedure for different temperatures. (Hint: $°F = (9 / 5) \times °C + 32$.)

4. Write a procedure to create the house shown on the right. Start by writing small procedures that draw small parts of the house (for example, door, roof, windows, and so on). Then combine these procedures to create the entire house.

5. Write a procedure to compute the area of a circle ($A = \pi r^2$) given its radius, as shown below. Use $\pi = 3.14$.

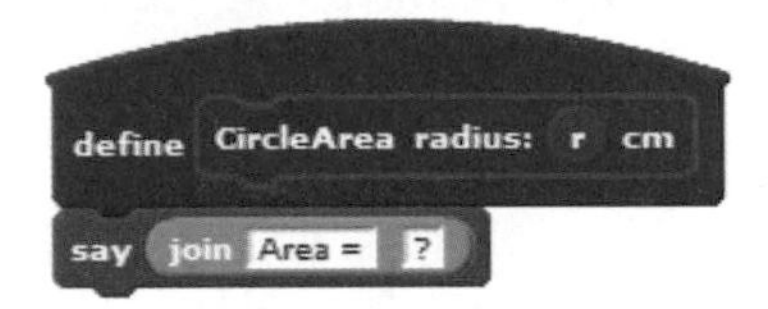

PressureUnderWater_NoSolution.sb2

6. In this exercise, you'll simulate the pressure experienced by fish under water. Assume that the pressure P (in atmospheres) felt by a fish is related to its depth d (in meters from the surface) by the relation: $P = 0.1d + 1$. *PressureUnderWater_NoSolution.sb2* contains a partial implementation of this simulation. Finish the script so that the fish says the pressure it feels while swimming, as illustrated below:

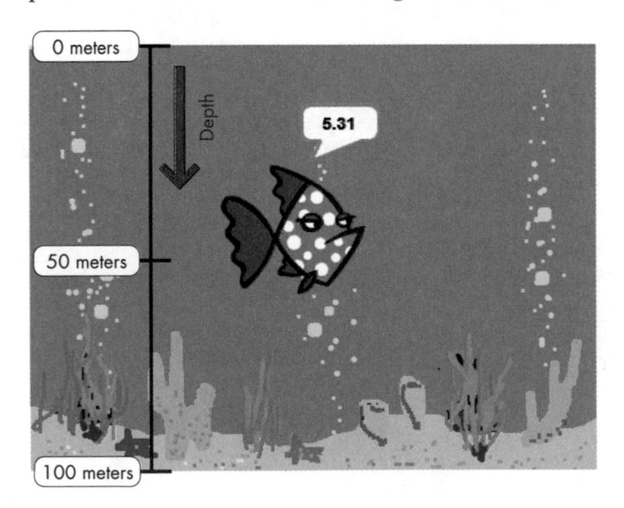

5

VARIABLES

This chapter explains how to create scripts that can read in and remember values. When you use variables, you can write applications that interact with users and respond to their input. Here's what we'll cover in this chapter:

- The data types supported by Scratch
- How to create variables and manipulate them
- How to obtain input from users and write interactive programs

Though the scripts you wrote in the last four chapters helped you learn important Scratch programming skills, they lacked many key elements of a large-scale application. More complex programs can remember values and decide to take an action based on certain conditions. This chapter will address the first of these two deficiencies, and decision making will be covered in the next chapter.

As you may have learned by now, scripts process and manipulate different types of data during their execution. These data can be input to command blocks (for example, the number 10 in the **move 10 steps** command and the "Hello!" string in the **say Hello!** command) or output from function blocks (like **mouse x, y position** and **pick random**), or data can be entered by the user in response to the **ask and wait** command. For more complex programs, you'll often need to store and modify data to accomplish certain tasks. Data management in Scratch can be done using *variables* and *lists*. This chapter will explore variables in detail. Lists will be explored in Chapter 9.

This chapter begins with an overview of the data types supported in Scratch. It continues with an introduction to variables and a discussion of how to create and use them in your programs. Variable monitors will then be explained and used in several interesting applications. After mastering the basic concepts, you'll learn how to use the **ask and wait** command to get inputs from the user.

Data Types in Scratch

Many computer programs manipulate different kinds of data, including numbers, text, images, and so on, to produce useful information. This is an important programming task, so you'll need to know the data types and operations supported in Scratch. Scratch has built-in support for three data types that you can use in blocks: Booleans, numbers, and strings.

A *Boolean* can have only one of two values: true or false. You can use this data type to test one or more conditions and, based on the result, have your program choose a different execution path. We'll discuss Booleans in detail in the next chapter.

A *number* variable can hold both integers and decimal values. Scratch doesn't distinguish between the two; they're both classified as "numbers." You can round decimal numbers to the nearest whole number using the **round** block from the *Operators* palette. You can also use the **floor of** (or **ceiling of**) functions, available from the **sqrt of** block in the *Operators* palette, to get an integer from a specified decimal number. For example, **floor of 3.9** is 3 and **ceiling of 3.1** is 4.

A *string* is a sequence of characters, which can include letters (both upper- and lowercase), numbers (0 to 9), and other symbols that you can type on your keyboard (+, –, &, @, and so on). You'd use a string data type to store names, addresses, book titles, and so on.

What's in the Shape?

Have you noticed that Scratch blocks and their parameter slots each have particular geometric shapes? For example, the parameter slot in the **move 10 steps** block is a rectangle with rounded corners, while the one in the **say Hello!** block is a rectangle with sharp corners. The shape of the parameter slot is related to the data type it accepts. Try entering your name (or any other text) in the **move 10 steps** block; you'll find that Scratch allows you to enter only numbers into the rounded-rectangle slot.

Similarly, the shape of a function block indicates the data type it returns. The meanings of the different shapes are illustrated in Figure 5-1.

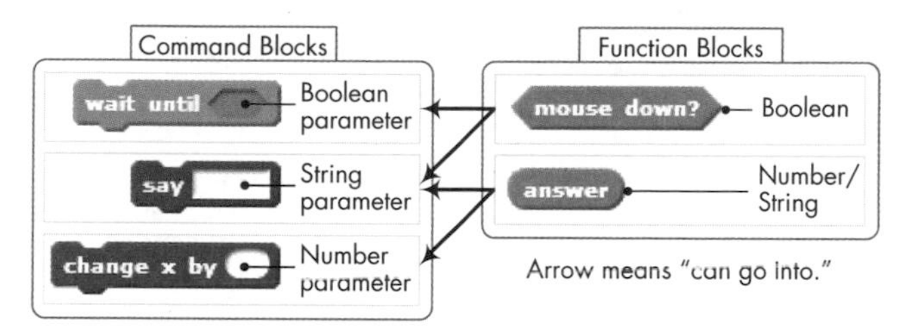

Figure 5-1: What the shapes of command and function blocks mean

Parameter slots have three shapes (hexagon, rectangle, and rounded rectangle), while function blocks have only two shapes (hexagon and rounded rectangle). Each shape is associated with a particular data type, though you should note that a rounded-rectangle function block can report either a number or a string.

Hexagon and rounded-rectangle slots take only function blocks of the same shape, while a rectangular slot will accept any function block. The good news is that Scratch prevents you from mismatching types, so you don't have to memorize this rule. Try dragging a hexagon-shaped block into a rounded-rectangle slot; you won't be able to drop it there because the types are incompatible.

Automatic Data Type Conversion

As I mentioned above, a number parameter slot only accepts a rounded-rectangle function block. All of the rounded-rectangle function blocks you've dealt with so far—including **x position**, **y position**, **direction**, **costume #**, **size**, **volume**, **tempo**, and so on—report numbers. Therefore, using them inside a number slot (like the **move 10 steps** block) isn't a problem. However, some rounded-rectangle function blocks, such as the **answer** block from the *Sensing* palette or the **join** block from the *Operators* palette, can hold either a number or a string. This brings up an important question: What happens if we, for example, insert an **answer** block containing a string into a number slot? Fortunately, Scratch automatically tries to convert between data types as needed, as illustrated in Figure 5-2.

In this example, the user enters `125` in response to the Enter a number prompt. The user's input is saved in the **answer** function block. When this input is passed to the **say** command, it is automatically converted to a string. When the same answer is passed to the addition operation (which expects a number), it is converted to the number 125. When the addition operation is performed, the result (25 + 125 = 150) is converted back to a string, and "150" is passed to the **say** block. Scratch automatically attempts to take care of these conversions for you.

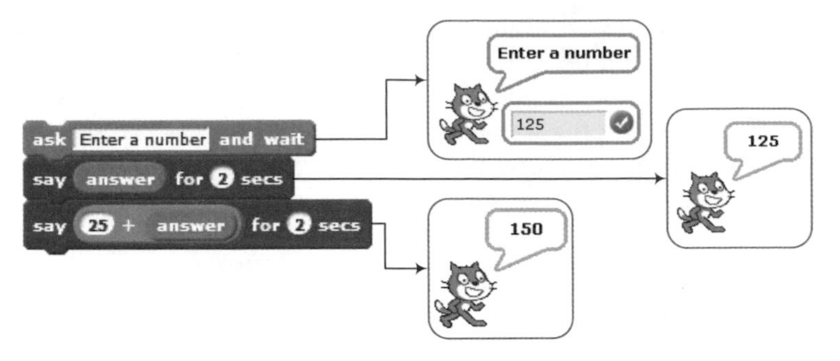

Figure 5-2: Scratch automatically converts between data types based on context.

Understanding the data types available in Scratch, the operations permitted on these types, and how Scratch converts between them will help you understand why things work the way they do. In the next section, you'll learn about variables and how to use them to store and manipulate data in your programs.

Introduction to Variables

Let's say we want to create a software version of the game Whac-a-Mole. The original game has a flat surface with several holes. The player uses a mallet to smack moles as they pop out of these holes. In our version, a sprite appears at a random location on the Stage, stays visible for a short time, and disappears. It waits a bit, and then appears again at a different location. The player needs to click on the sprite as soon as it appears. Every time he clicks on the sprite, he gains one point. The question for you as a programmer is, how do you keep track of the player's score? Welcome to the world of variables!

In this section, I'll introduce variables, one of the most important elements of any programming language. You'll learn how to create variables in Scratch and how to use them to remember (or store) different types of data. You'll also explore the available blocks for setting and changing the values of variables in your programs.

What Is a Variable?

A *variable* is a named area of computer memory. You can think of it as a box that stores data, including numbers and text, for a program to access as needed. In Figure 5-3, for example, we depict a variable named side whose current value is 50.

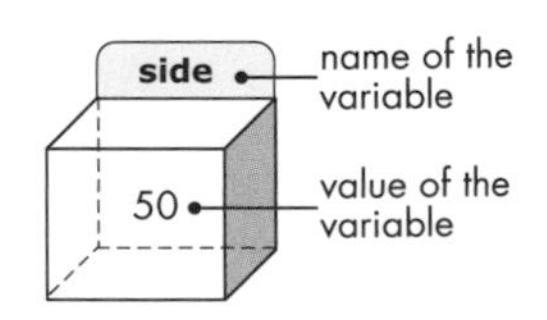

Figure 5-3: A variable is like a named box that contains some value.

When you create a variable, your program sets aside enough memory to hold the value of the variable and tags the allocated memory with that variable's name. After creating a variable, you can use its name in your program to refer to the value it represents. For example, if we have a box (that is, a variable) named side that contains the number 50, we can construct a command such as **move (3*side) steps**. When Scratch executes this command, it will locate the box named side in computer memory, grab its contents (in this case, the number 50), and use that value to replace the side label inside the **move (3*side) steps** block. As a result, the sprite will move 150 (that is, 3 × 50) steps.

In our Whac-a-Mole game, we need a way to remember the player's score. To do that, we can reserve some space in the computer's memory (like a box) to store the score. We also need to give that box a unique label, let's say score, which will let us find it whenever we need to know or change what's inside.

When the game starts, we'll tell Scratch to "set score to 0," and Scratch will look for the box labeled score and put the value 0 inside it. We'll also tell Scratch to "increase score by 1" any time the player clicks on the sprite. In response to the first click, Scratch will look inside the score box again, find our 0, add 1 to it, and put the result (which is 1) back in the box. The next time the player clicks on the sprite, Scratch will again follow our "increase score by 1" command to increment score and store the resulting value of 2 in the box.

You'll see the actual Scratch blocks for these operations in a moment. For now, notice that the value of score changes throughout the program. This is why we call it a *variable*—its value varies.

One important use of variables is to store the intermediary results of evaluating an algebraic expression. This is similar to the way you do mental math. For example, if you were asked to find 2 + 4 + 5 + 7, you might start by adding 2 + 4 and memorizing the answer (6). You'd then add 5 to the previous answer (which is stored in your memory) and memorize the new answer, which is 11. Finally, you'd add 7 to the previous result to get the final answer of 18.

To illustrate how variables can be used for temporary storage, let's say that you want to write a program to compute the following expression:

$$\frac{(1/5)+(5/7)}{(7/8)-(2/3)}$$

You could evaluate the whole thing with one command, but cramming everything into one statement makes it hard to read, as shown below:

```
say 1 / 5 + 5 / 7 / 7 / 8 - 2 / 3
```

Another way to write the program is to evaluate the numerator and denominator individually and then use the **say** block to display the result of their division. We can do that by creating two variables called num (for numerator) and den (for denominator) and setting their values as shown in Figure 5-4.

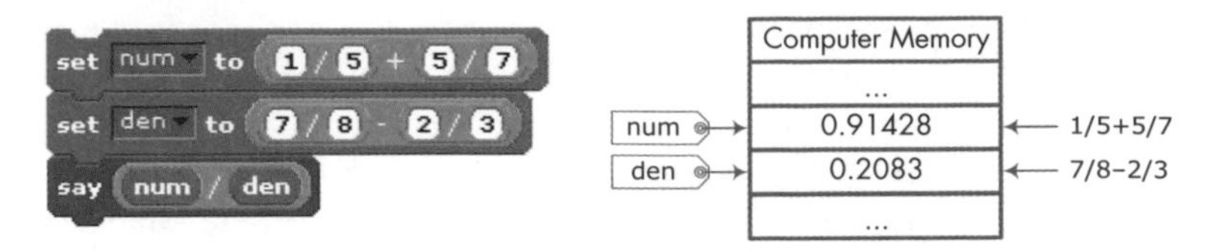

*Figure 5-4: Two variables (*num *and* den*) hold the value of the expression's numerator and denominator, respectively.*

Take a look at how our variables are arranged in computer memory. Here, num is like a tag referring to the location in memory where the result of evaluating (1 / 5 + 5 / 7) is stored. Similarly, den refers to where (7 / 8 – 2 / 3) is stored. When the **say** command is executed, Scratch grabs the contents of memory labeled num and den. It then divides the two numbers and passes the result to the **say** command for display.

We could break this expression down even further by evaluating each fraction individually before displaying the result of the total expression, as shown in Figure 5-5.

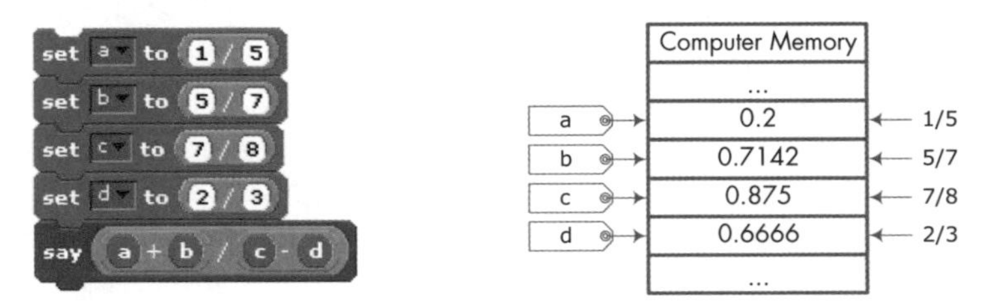

*Figure 5-5: Using four variables (*a*,* b*,* c*, and* d*) to hold the four fractions in the expression*

Here, we use four variables (named a, b, c, and d) to hold the four fractions in our mathematical expression. The figure also depicts the memory allocation; this time, you can see four variables and their contents.

Although these three programs give the same answer, each implementation follows a different style. The first program puts everything in one statement, which is tough to read. The third program breaks things down to a greater level of detail, but that can be hard to read, too. The second solution breaks the expression down to a reasonable level and uses variables to both make the program easier to understand and clearly show the major parts of the expression (the numerator and the denominator). As Goldilocks would say, this one is just right.

This simple example demonstrates how a problem can have multiple solutions. Sometimes you might be concerned about a program's speed or size, and other times your goal might be readability. Since this is an introductory programming book, the scripts in this book are written to emphasize readability.

Now that you understand what variables are and why you'd want to use them, let's make some variables and take our Scratch applications a step further.

Creating and Using Variables

DiceSimulator_NoCode.sb2

In this section, we'll explore how to create and use variables through a simple application that simulates rolling a pair of dice and displays their sum, as illustrated in Figure 5-6.

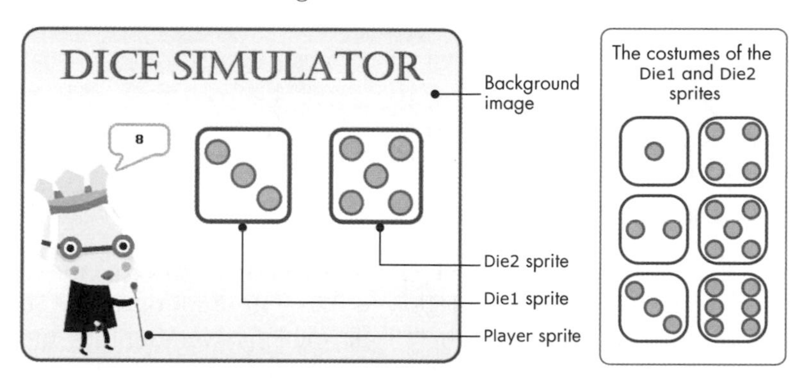

Figure 5-6: The user interface of the dice simulator

Our dice simulator contains three sprites: Player, Die1, and Die2. The Player sprite manages the simulation. When the green flag icon is pressed, this sprite generates two random numbers between 1 and 6 and saves those values in two variables named rand1 and rand2, respectively. It then broadcasts a message to the other two sprites (Die1 and Die2) to show the randomly generated values; Die1 will show the value of rand1, and Die2 will show rand2. After that, the Player sprite adds rand1 to rand2 and displays the sum using the **say** block.

Let's build this application from the ground up. Open the file *DiceSimulator_NoCode.sb2*. This file contains the background image for the Stage as well as the three sprites used in the application. We'll create all the scripts we need one at a time.

First, click the thumbnail of the Player sprite to select it. Select the *Data* palette and click **Make a Variable**, as shown in Figure 5-7 (left). In the dialog that appears, as shown in Figure 5-7 (right), type the name of the variable and select its scope. A variable's *scope* determines which sprites can write to (or change the value of) that variable, as I will explain in more detail in the next section. For this example, enter rand1 for the variable's name and select the **For all sprites** option for the variable's scope. Click **OK** when done.

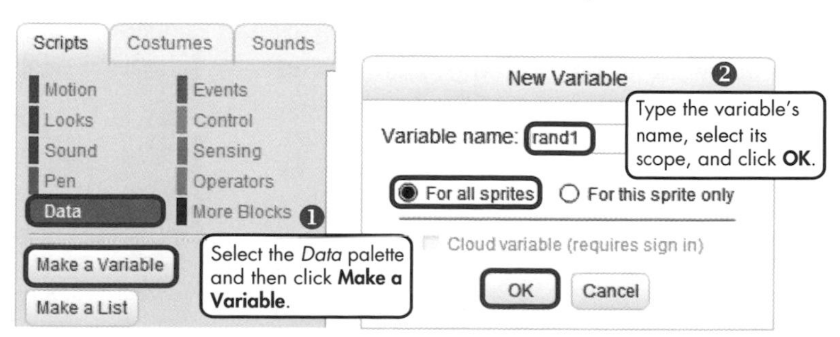

Figure 5-7: Creating a variable, naming it, and specifying its scope

After you create the variable, several new blocks related to it will appear in the *Data* palette, as illustrated in Figure 5-8.

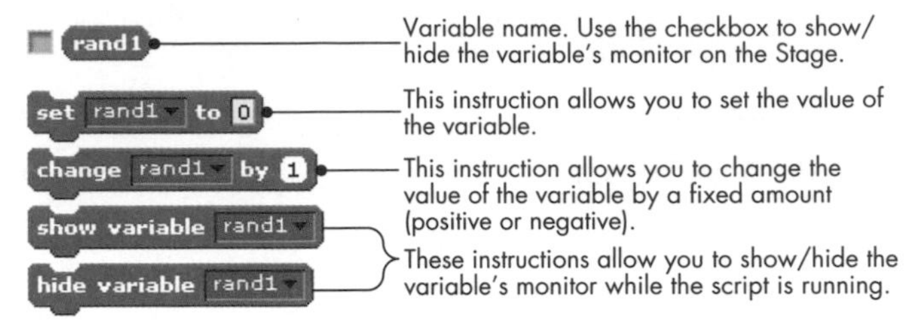

rand1
set rand1 to 0
change rand1 by 1
show variable rand1
hide variable rand1
Variable name. Use the checkbox to show/hide the variable's monitor on the Stage.
This instruction allows you to set the value of the variable.
This instruction allows you to change the value of the variable by a fixed amount (positive or negative).
These instructions allow you to show/hide the variable's monitor while the script is running.

Figure 5-8: The new blocks that appear when you create the rand1 *variable*

You can use these blocks to set a variable to a specific value, change it by a fixed amount, and show (or hide) its monitor on the Stage. A variable's *monitor*, as you'll learn in "Displaying Variable Monitors" on page 106, displays the current value stored in that variable.

NAMING VARIABLES

Over the years, people have come up with different ways to name the variables in their programs. One popular convention is to start the name with a lowercase letter and capitalize the first letter of each additional word, such as in sideLength, firstName, and interestRate.

Although Scratch allows variable names to start with numbers and contain white spaces (for example, 123Side or side length), most programming languages don't, so I recommend that you avoid these unusual names for your variables. And while you can name a variable anything you want, I highly recommend using descriptive and meaningful names. Single-letter variables like w and z should be kept to a minimum unless their meaning is very clear. On the other hand, names that are too long can make your script harder to read.

Also, note that variable names in Scratch are case sensitive, meaning that side, SIDE, and siDE are all unique variables. To avoid confusion, try not to use variables in the same script whose names differ only in case.

Repeat the procedure I outlined above to create another variable, named rand2. The *Data* palette should now contain a second variable block (named rand2), and the down arrows on the blocks of Figure 5-8 should let you choose between rand1 and rand2. Now that we've created the two variables, we can build the script for the Player sprite. The complete script is shown in Figure 5-9.

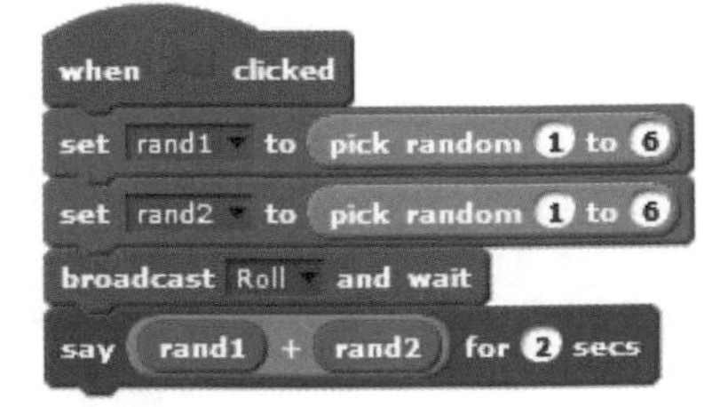

when clicked
set rand1 to pick random 1 to 6
set rand2 to pick random 1 to 6
broadcast Roll and wait
say rand1 + rand2 for 2 secs

Figure 5-9: The script for the Player *sprite*

The first command sets rand1 to a random number between 1 and 6. Think back to our box analogy: This command causes the sprite to find the box labeled rand1 and put the generated random number inside it. The second command assigns rand2 another random value between 1 and 6. Next, the script broadcasts a message called Roll to the other two sprites (Die1 and Die2) to notify them that they need to switch their costumes as specified by rand1 and rand2. Once the Die1 and Die2 sprites have finished their job, the script resumes and displays the sum of the numbers on the faces of the dice using the **say** block. Let's look at the Roll message handler for the Die1 sprite, shown in Figure 5-10.

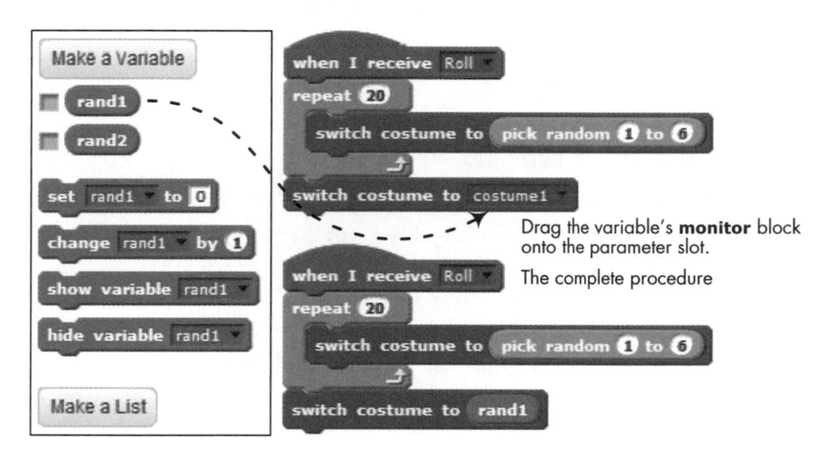

Figure 5-10: To use a variable in a command block, just drag that variable over the parameter slot of that block.

After creating the script shown at the top right of the figure, drag the rand1 block from the *Data* palette to the parameter slot of the **switch to costume** block to form the complete script (bottom right). In this script, the **repeat** block changes the costume of the die randomly 20 times to simulate rolling the die (you can change this number if you want). After that, the die sets its costume to the number specified by rand1. Recall that each die has six costumes that correspond to numbers 1 through 6 in order. That means if rand1 were 5, the last **switch to costume** command would display the costume that has five dots in it.

Now, we can create the script for the Die2 sprite, which should be nearly identical to the one we made for Die1. Since Die2 changes its costume based on rand2, all you need to do is duplicate the Die1 script for Die2 and replace rand1 with rand2.

Our dice simulator is now complete, so let's test it out. Click the green flag icon to see the simulation in action. If the application doesn't work, examine the file *DiceSimulator.sb2*, which contains the correct implementation of the program.

TRY IT OUT 5-1

Select the Player sprite and create a new variable called sum. Set the scope for this variable to For this sprite only. Modify the last block of the Player script to use this new variable, like this:

```
set sum to (rand1 + rand2)
say sum for 2 secs
```

Now select the Die1 (or Die2) sprite and look under the *Data* palette. Can you explain why you don't see the sum variable there?

The Scope of Variables

Another important concept related to variables is *scope*. The scope of a variable determines which sprites can write to (or change the value of) that variable.

ScopeDemo.sb2

You can specify the scope of a variable when you create it by selecting one of the two options you saw in Figure 5-7. Choosing For this sprite only creates a variable that can be changed only by the sprite that owns it. Other sprites can still read and use the variable's value, but they can't write to it. The example shown in Figure 5-11 illustrates this point.

Figure 5-11: Only the Cat *sprite can write to* count.

In this figure, the Cat sprite has a variable, named count, with the scope For this sprite only. The Penguin sprite can read count with the **x position of Penguin** block from the *Sensing* palette. When you select Cat as the second parameter of this block, the first parameter will let you choose an attribute of the Cat sprite, including one of its variables.

Scratch, however, doesn't provide a block that allows the Penguin sprite to change the count variable. This way, the Penguin sprite can't tamper with count and cause undesirable effects for scripts run by the Cat sprite. It's good practice to use the For this sprite only scope for variables that should only be updated by a single sprite.

Variables created with the For this sprite only scope are said to have *local scope*, and they can be called *local variables*. Different sprites can use the same name for their local variables without any conflict. For example, if

DATA TYPE OF A VARIABLE

At this point, you might wonder, "How does Scratch know the data type of a variable?" The answer is, it doesn't! When you create a variable, Scratch has no idea whether you intend to use that variable to store to a number, a string, or a Boolean. Any variable can hold a value of any data type. For example, all of the following commands are valid in Scratch.

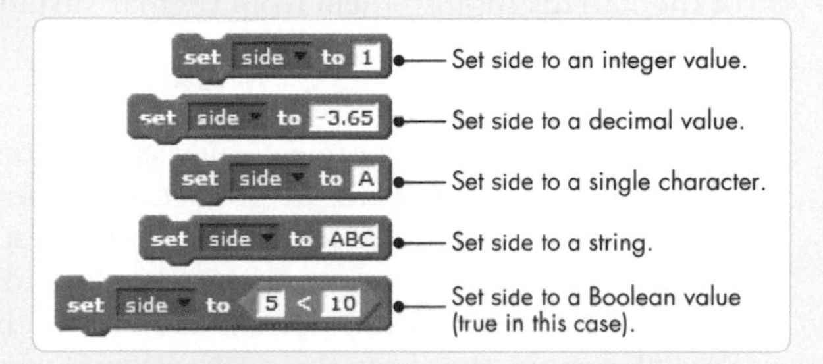
set side to 1
Set side to an integer value.
set side to -3.65
Set side to a decimal value.
set side to A
Set side to a single character.
set side to ABC
Set side to a string.
set side to 5 < 10
Set side to a Boolean value (true in this case).

It's up to you to store the correct values in your variables. As I described earlier in this chapter, however, Scratch will try to convert between data types depending on the context. To see what happens when you store an incorrect data type in a variable, consider these two examples:

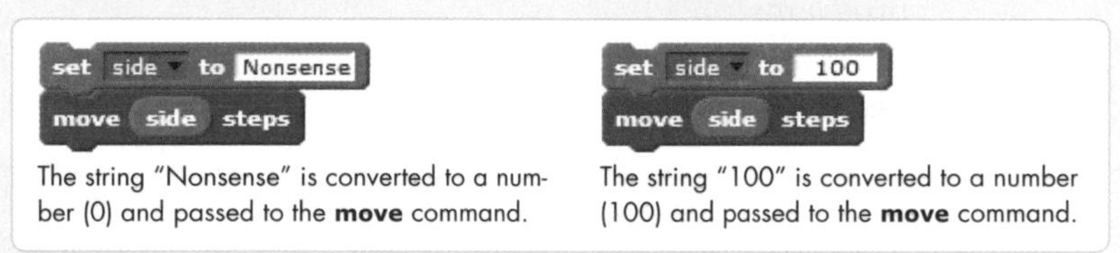
set side to Nonsense
move side steps
set side to 100
move side steps

The string "Nonsense" is converted to a number (0) and passed to the **move** command.

The string "100" is converted to a number (100) and passed to the **move** command.

Since the **move** command expects a number parameter, Scratch will automatically try to convert the value stored in the side variable to a number before passing it to the **move** command. In the first script (left), Scratch can't convert the string "Nonsense" to a number. Rather than showing an error message, Scratch will silently set the result of the conversion to 0 and pass this value to the **move** command. As a result, the sprite won't move. On the other hand, in the second script (right), Scratch ignores the whitespace in the string and passes the resulting number to the **move** block, so the sprite moves 100 steps forward. Note that if the target block had expected a string instead of a number, Scratch would have passed the string as it was, whitespace included.

you have two car sprites in a racing game, each might have a local variable named speed that determines the car's speed of motion on the Stage. Each car sprite can change its speed variable independently of the other. This means that if you set the speed of the first car to 10 and the speed of the second to 20, the second car should move faster than the first.

Variables with the scope For all sprites, on the other hand, can be read and changed by any sprite in your application. These variables, often called *global variables*, are useful for intersprite communication and synchronization. For example, if a game has three buttons that allow the user to select a level to play, you can create a global variable named gameLevel and have each button sprite set this variable to a different number when clicked. Then you can easily find out the user's choice by examining gameLevel.

Selecting the For all sprites option also enables the Cloud variable checkbox in Figure 5-7. This feature allows you to store your variables on Scratch's server (in the cloud). Blocks for cloud variables have a small square in front of them to distinguish them from regular variables, like this:

☐ score

Anyone who views a project you've shared on the Scratch website can read the cloud variables in the project. For example, if you share a game, you can use a cloud variable to track the highest score recorded among all the players. The score cloud variable should update almost immediately for everyone interacting with your game. Because these variables are stored on Scratch servers, they keep their value even if you exit your browser. Cloud variables make it easy to create surveys and other projects that store numbers over time.

Now that you understand scope, it's time to learn about updating variables—and then use that knowledge to create more interesting programs.

Changing Variables

Scratch provides two command blocks that allow you to alter variables. The **set to** command directly assigns a new value to a variable, regardless of its current contents. The **change by** command, on the other hand, is used to change the value of a variable by a specified amount relative to its current value. The three scripts in Figure 5-12 demonstrate how you could use these commands in different ways to achieve the same outcome.

Figure 5-12: Three methods for changing the value of a variable

All three scripts in the figure start by setting the values of two variables, sum and delta, to 0 and 5, respectively. The first script uses the **change** command to change the value of sum by the value of delta (that is, from 0 to 5). The second script uses the **set** command to add the current value of sum to the value of delta (0 + 5) and store the result (5) back into sum. The third script achieves the same result with the aid of a temporary variable named temp. It adds the value of sum to delta, stores the result in temp, and finally copies the value of temp into sum.

After executing any of the scripts in Figure 5-12, sum will contain the number 5, making these scripts functionally equivalent. Note that the method used in the second script is a common programming practice, and I recommend that you study it for a moment to become comfortable with it. Now let's see the **change** command in action.

Spider Web

SpiderWeb.sb2

We can create a spider web by drawing several hexagons of increasing size, as shown in Figure 5-13. The **Triangle** procedure draws an equilateral triangle with a variable side length, while the **Hexagon** procedure calls **Triangle** six times with a 60° (that is, 360° / 6) right turn after each call. The figure clearly shows how the hexagon is made up of the six triangles.

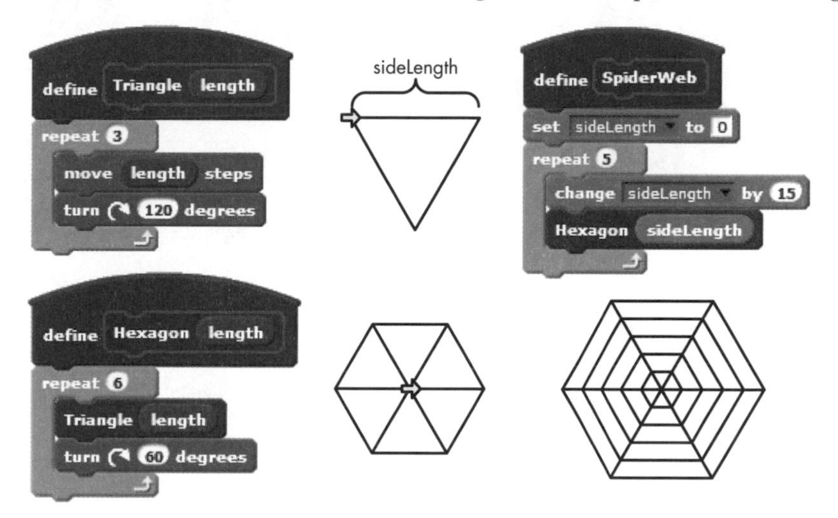

Figure 5-13: Creating a spider web by drawing several hexagons of increasing size

The **SpiderWeb** procedure simply calls **Hexagon** repeatedly with a different value of the sideLength variable each time. This results in the concentric (that is, having the same center) hexagons you see in the figure. Note how the **change** command is used to set the value of sideLength inside the **repeat** loop. Reproduce the **SpiderWeb** procedure, run it, and see how it works.

Pinwheel

Pinwheel.sb2

This example is similar to the previous one except that this time, we'll use a variable to control the number of triangular repetitions. The resulting procedure (called **Pins**) is shown in Figure 5-14. The **Pinwheel** procedure in the same figure works like the **SpiderWeb** procedure above, but we also change the pen's color each time through the loop for a fun rainbow effect. Some outputs of the **Pinwheel** procedure for different pin counts are shown in the figure. Experiment with this procedure to see what else you can create.

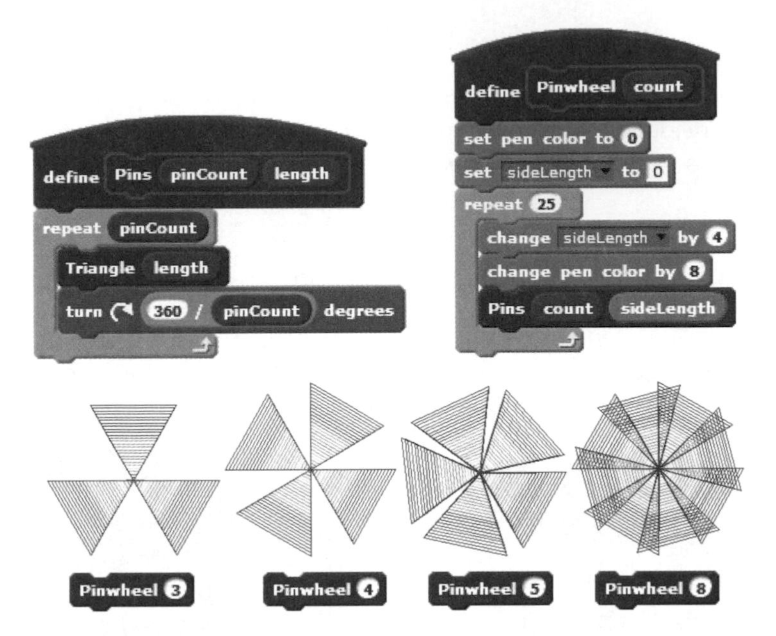

Figure 5-14: Creating a pinwheel by rotating an equilateral triangle several times

Now that we've explored the fundamentals of variables, you might wonder what happens to variables when you duplicate a sprite. Does the duplicate share the parent sprite's variables, or does it have its own copies? Do clones have access to global variables? We'll answer these questions in the next section.

> **TRY IT OUT 5-2**
>
> Alter the Pinwheel program to hide the sprite. This should make it easier for you to watch the drawing without the sprite getting in the way.

Variables in Clones

Every sprite has a list of properties associated with it, including its current *x*-position, *y*-position, direction, and so on. You can imagine that list as a backpack holding the current values of the sprite's attributes, as illustrated in Figure 5-15. When you create a variable for a sprite with a scope of For this sprite only, that variable gets added to the sprite's backpack.

When you clone a sprite, the clone inherits copies of the parent sprite's attributes, including its variables. An inherited property starts out identical to the parent's property at the time the clone is created. But after that, if the clone's attributes and variables change, those changes don't affect the parent. Subsequent changes to the parent sprite don't affect the clone's properties, either.

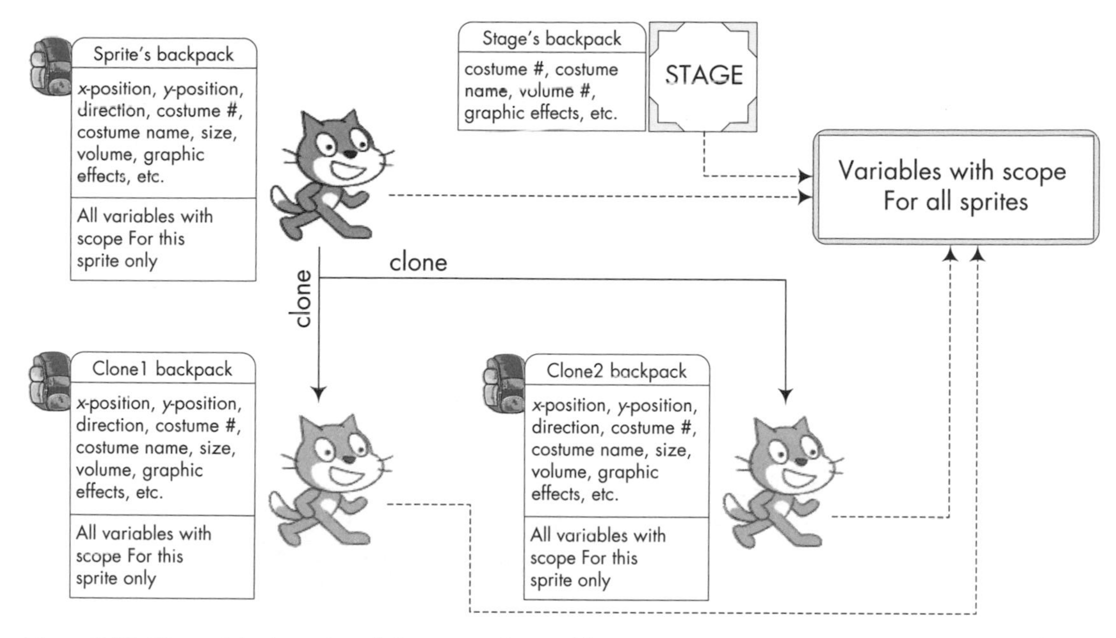

Figure 5-15: Clones inherit copies of their parent's variables

To illustrate, let's say the parent sprite owns a variable named speed whose current value is 10. When you clone the parent, the new sprite will also have a variable named speed with the value 10. After that, if the parent sprite changes speed to 20, the value of speed in the clone will stay at 10.

CloneIDs.sb2

You can use this concept to distinguish between clones in your applications. For example, let's look at the program in Figure 5-16.

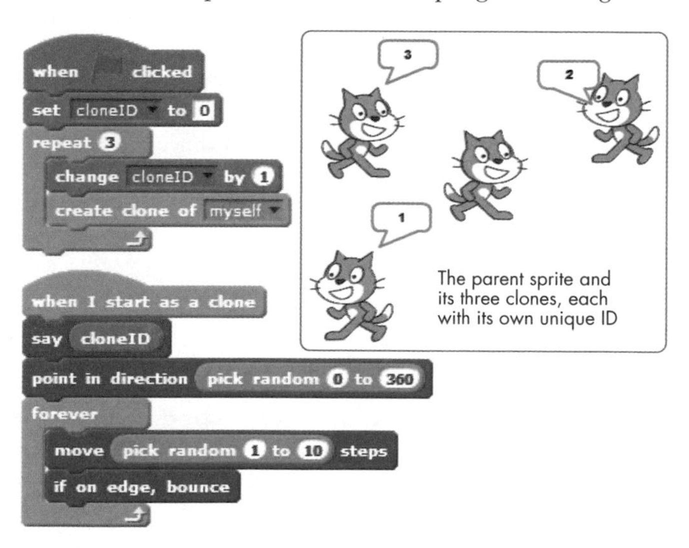

Figure 5-16: Using variables to distinguish between clones

The parent sprite in this example owns a variable named cloneID. When the green flag is clicked, it starts a loop to create three clones, and it sets cloneID to a different value (1, 2, or 3 in this case) before creating a clone. Each clone comes to life with its own copy of cloneID initialized to a different value. You could now use an **if** block, which we'll study in depth in the next chapter, to check for the clone's ID and have it perform a corresponding action.

ClonesAndGlobalVars.sb2

Now, let's discuss how clones can interact with global variables. Recall from Figure 5-15 that variables with scope For all sprites can be read and written by the Stage and all sprites, including clones. As an example, the program in Figure 5-17 uses this fact to detect when all clones of the parent sprite have disappeared.

```
when green flag clicked
set numClones to 5
repeat 5
    create clone of myself
wait until numClones = 0
say Game Over!
```

```
when I start as a clone
wait pick random 0 to 10 secs
set x to pick random -200 to 200
set y to pick random -150 to 150
say Hello! for 2 secs
change numClones by -1
delete this clone
```

Figure 5-17: Using a global variable to track when clones are deleted

In this script, the parent sprite sets the global variable numClones to 5 and creates five clones. It then waits for numClones to become 0 before announcing the end of the game. The clones appear at random times and locations on the Stage, say "Hello!" for two seconds, and then disappear. Before a clone is deleted, it decreases numClones by 1. When all five clones are gone, numClones reaches 0, the main script stops waiting, and the original sprite says "Game Over!"

In the following section, you'll learn about variables' monitors, which allow you to see, and even change, the current values stored in variables. The ability to view and change a variable on the Stage will open the door to creating totally new kinds of applications.

Displaying Variable Monitors

You'll often find yourself wanting to see the current value stored in a variable. For example, when one of your scripts doesn't work as expected, you might want to track some of its variables to see if they change correctly. Using variable monitors can help you with this debugging task.

You can display a Scratch variable on the Stage as a *variable monitor*. Checking or unchecking the box next to a variable's name allows you to show or hide a variable's monitor on the Stage, as illustrated in Figure 5-18. You can also control a monitor's visibility from within your script with the **show variable** and **hide variable** commands.

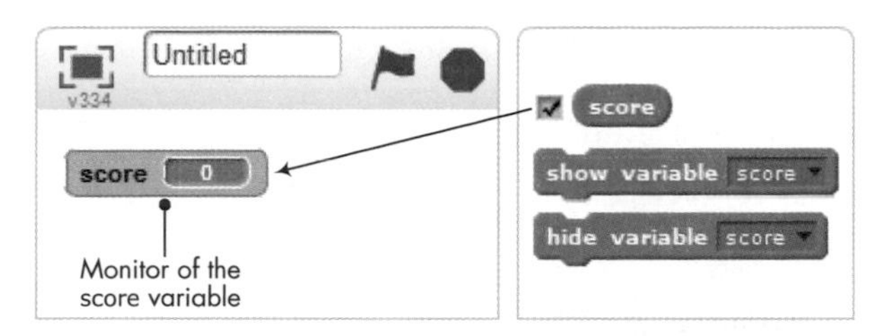

Figure 5-18: Show a variable's monitor by checking the box next to its name.

Monitors can be used as readouts or controls, which display or allow you to change a variable's contents, respectively. Double-click the monitor's box on the Stage to choose a normal readout (the default state), large readout, or slider control. When you choose to display a slider, you can set its range by right-clicking the slider and selecting the set slider min and max option from the pop-up menu, as shown in Figure 5-19.

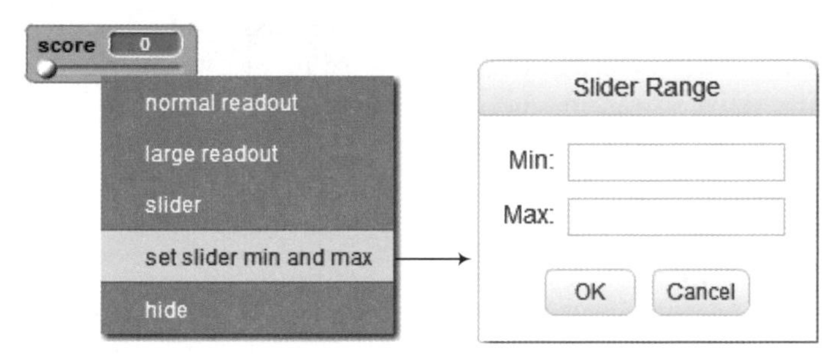

Figure 5-19: Setting the minimum and maximum values for a monitor in slider mode

StageColor.sb2

Using a slider allows you to change the value of a variable while a script is running, which is a convenient way for users to interact with your application. You can see a simple example of using the slider control in Figure 5-20.

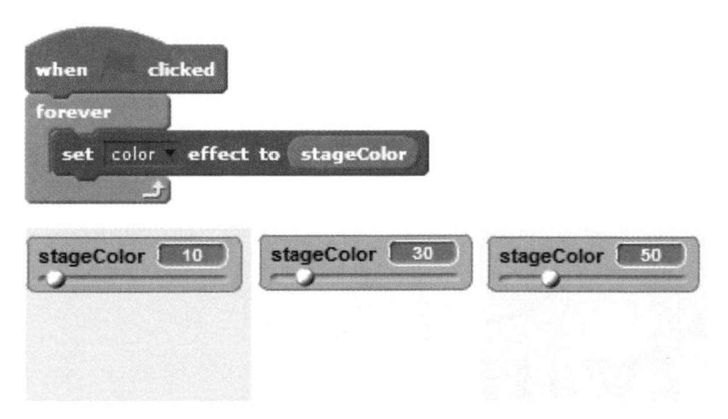

Figure 5-20: Adjusting Stage color with a slider

In this example, dragging the slider's handle changes the value of the stageColor variable, which is a parameter in the **set color effect to** command. Assuming this script belongs to the Stage, dragging the slider should change the Stage's background color.

NOTE *A variable's monitor also indicates its scope. If a variable belongs to one sprite, its monitor should show the sprite name before the variable name. For example, the monitor* **Cat speed 0** *indicates that* speed *belongs to* Cat. *If the* speed *variable were a global variable, its monitor would only say* **speed 0**. *The difference between the two cases is illustrated in the following figure.*

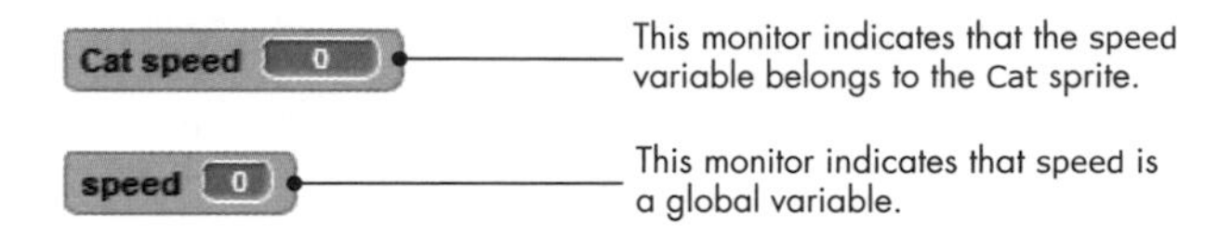

Cat speed 0
This monitor indicates that the speed variable belongs to the Cat sprite.
speed 0
This monitor indicates that speed is a global variable.

Using Variable Monitors in Applications

Now that you know the basics behind variable monitors, I'll show you some ways you could use them to add some extra functionality to your Scratch applications.

The ability to use monitors as both displays and controls opens the door for a wide range of applications, including games, simulations, and interactive programs. Let's explore some examples that make use of monitors in the following subsections.

Simulating Ohm's Law

OhmsLaw.sb2

Our first example is a simulation of Ohm's law. When a voltage (*V*) is applied across a resistor (*R*), a current (*I*) will flow through that resistor. According to Ohm's law, the amount of current is given by this equation:

$$Current\left(I\right) = \frac{Voltage\left(V\right)}{Resistance\left(R\right)}$$

Our application allows the user to change the values of *V* and *R* using slider controls. Then it calculates and displays the corresponding value of the current, *I*. The user interface for this application is shown in Figure 5-21.

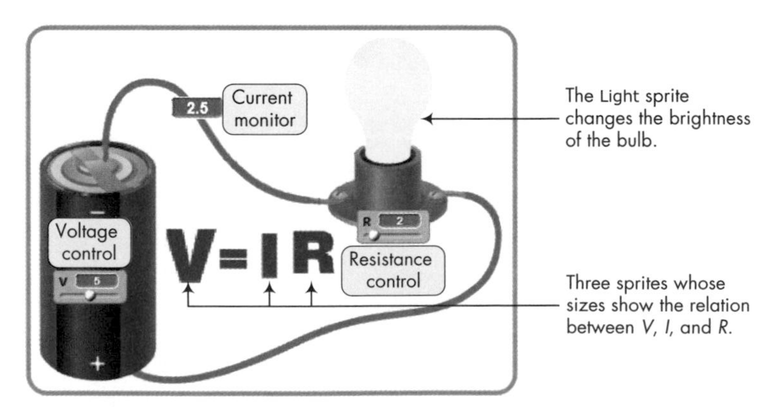

Figure 5-21: User interface for the Ohm's law application

The slider for the battery voltage (*V*) has a range of [0, 10], and the slider for the resistor (*R*) has a range of [1, 10]. When the user changes *V* or *R* with the sliders, the application calculates the corresponding value of the current (*I*) that flows in the circuit. The brightness of the bulb changes in proportion to the value of the current passing through it: The higher the current, the brighter the light bulb. The sizes of the *V*, *I*, and *R* letters in the figure also change to indicate the relative values of these quantities.

In total, the application has five sprites (named Volt, Current, Resistance, Equal, and Light) and three variables (named V, I, and R). Everything else you see in Figure 5-21 (the battery, wires, socket, and so on) is part of the Stage's backdrop image. The main script that drives the application, which belongs to the Stage, is shown Figure 5-22.

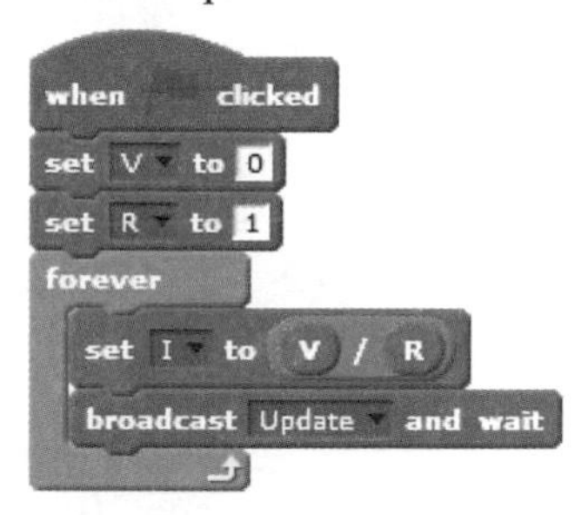

Figure 5-22: Main script of Ohm's law application

The script initializes the values of V and R and then enters an infinite loop. On each pass through the loop, it calculates I using the present values of V and R, which are set by the user through the slider controls. It then broadcasts a message to the other sprites in the application to update their appearance in relation to the calculated values. Figure 5-23 shows the response of the Volt, Current, Resistance, and Light sprites (which show the letters *V*, *I*, *R*, and the light bulb, respectively) when they receive the Update message.

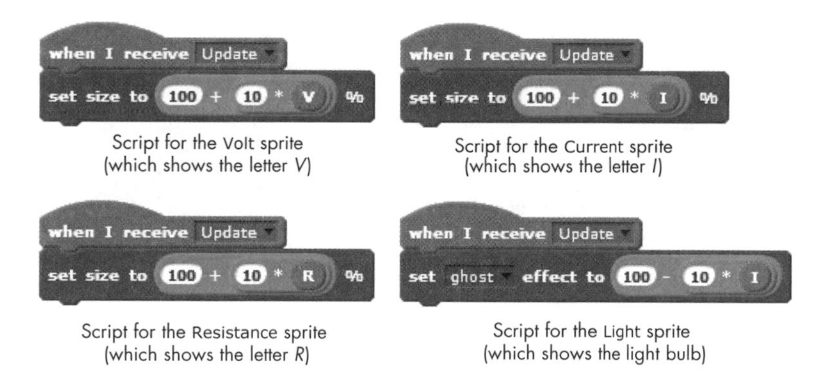

Figure 5-23: Scripts triggered in response to the Update message

When the Update broadcast is received, the Volt, Current, and Resistance sprites change their size (from 100 percent to 200 percent of their original size) in relation to the current values of their respective variables. The Light sprite executes the **set ghost effect to** command to change its transparency level in proportion to the value of I. This gives the light bulb a realistic visual effect that simulates an actual bulb.

> **TRY IT OUT 5-3**
>
> Open the Ohm's law simulator to run it, and study the scripts to understand how it works. What do you think would happen if you added the command **change color effect by 25** at the end of the script for the Light sprite? Implement this change to check your answer. What are some ways you could enhance this application?

Demonstrating a Series Circuit

SeriesCircuit.sb2

Our second example simulates a circuit that contains a battery and three resistors connected in series. The user can change the battery voltage as well as the resistor values using the sliders. The current that flows through the resistors and the voltages across the three resistors are shown using large display readouts. You can see the interface for the application in Figure 5-24. (Note that the color bands on the resistors do not represent the actual values of the resistors.)

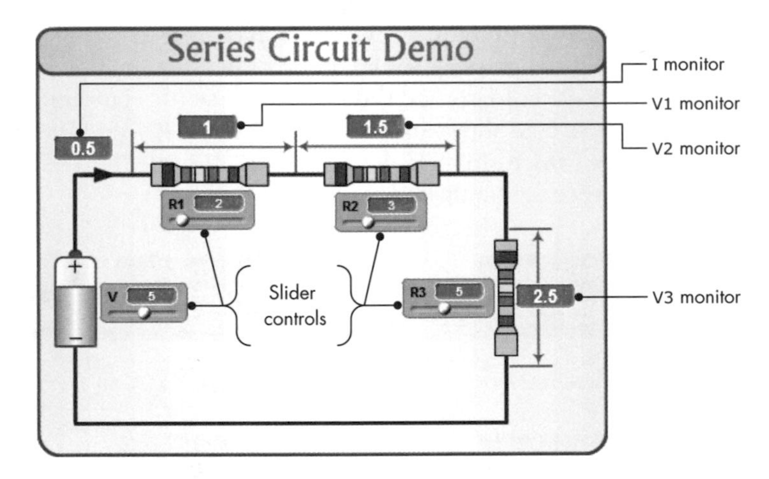

Figure 5-24: An application that demonstrates a series circuit

The equations that govern the operation of this circuit are shown below. We can calculate the current that flows in the circuit by dividing the battery voltage, *V*, by the sum of the three resistances. After that, the voltage across each resistor is calculated by multiplying the current by the value of that resistor:

$$\text{Total Resistance: } R_{tot} = R_1 + R_2 + R_3$$
$$\text{Current through the circuit: } I = V \div R_{tot}$$
$$\text{Voltage across } R_1\text{: } V_1 = I \times R_1$$
$$\text{Voltage across } R_2\text{: } V_2 = I \times R_2$$
$$\text{Voltage across } R_3\text{: } V_3 = I \times R_3$$

This application has no sprites, but when the green flag is clicked, the script shown in Figure 5-25, which belongs to the Stage, is executed.

```
when [green flag] clicked
forever
    set Rtot to (R1 + (R2 + R3))
    set I to (V / Rtot)
    set V1 to (I * R1)
    set V2 to (I * R2)
    set V3 to (I * R3)
```

Figure 5-25: Script that runs when the green flag is clicked

This script takes care of the math for us and displays the results in the readouts on the Stage. Note that while the slider controls for resistors R2 and R3 can change from 0 to 10, the minimum value for R1 was intentionally set to 1. This ensures that Rtot is always greater than 0 and lets us avoid dividing by 0 when calculating the value of the current.

Most of the work for this application went into designing the interface (that is, the background of the Stage). After that, all we had to do was to position the displays and sliders at the right locations on the Stage.

TRY IT OUT 5-4

SeriesCircuitWithSwitch.sb2

Open the series circuit simulator application and run it. Experiment with different values of R1, R2, R3, and V. Watch the calculated values of V1, V2, and V3 as you drag the slider controls. What is the relationship between the voltage sum (V1 + V2 + V3) and the battery voltage? What does this tell you about the voltage relation in series circuits? You can make an interesting enhancement to the application by adding an image of a switch that opens or closes the circuit, as shown below. When the switch is open, no current will flow in the circuit. Try to implement this change using the hints given below.

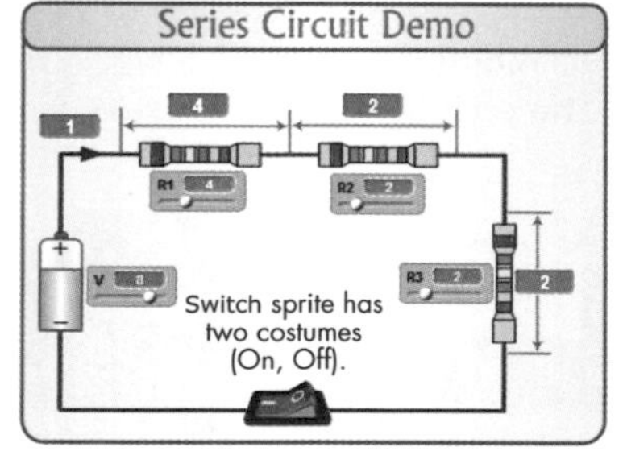

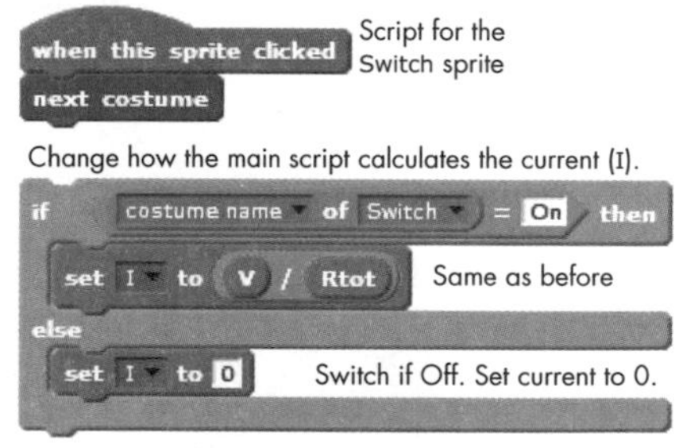

Visualizing a Sphere's Volume and Surface Area

Sphere.sb2

Our third example is an interactive application for calculating the volume and surface area of a sphere. The user changes the sphere's diameter by clicking some buttons on the user interface, and the application automatically calculates and displays the corresponding volume and surface area.

To make the application more appealing, the size of the sphere displayed on the Stage is also changed in proportion to the selected diameter. The user interface for the application is illustrated in Figure 5-26.

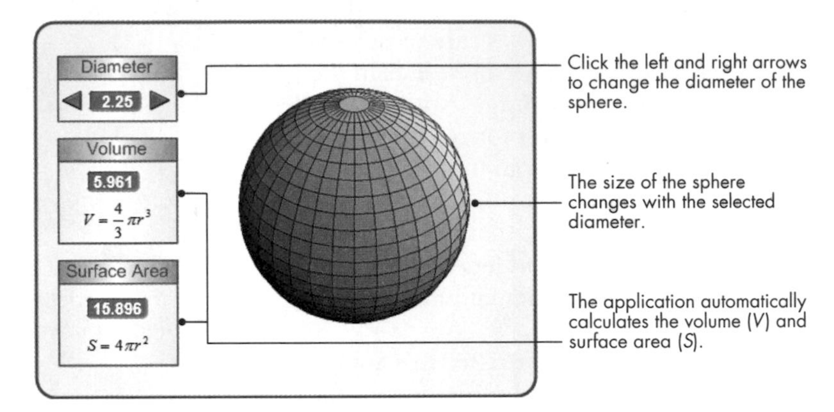

Figure 5-26: User interface for the sphere application

The application contains three sprites: the two arrow buttons (named Up and Down) and the sphere image (named Sphere). The scripts associated with the two buttons broadcast a message to indicate that they have been clicked, as shown in Figure 5-27.

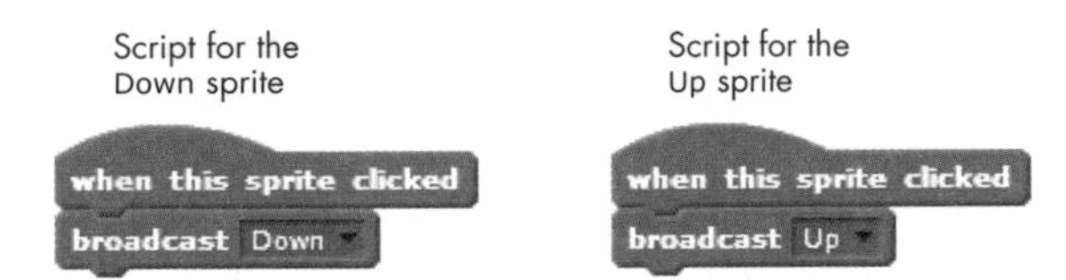

Figure 5-27: Scripts for the Up *and* Down *sprites*

The Sphere sprite has nine costumes that represent spheres with diameters 1, 1.25, 1.5, 1.75, ... , 3. When this sprite receives the Up or Down broadcast messages, it executes the scripts shown in Figure 5-28.

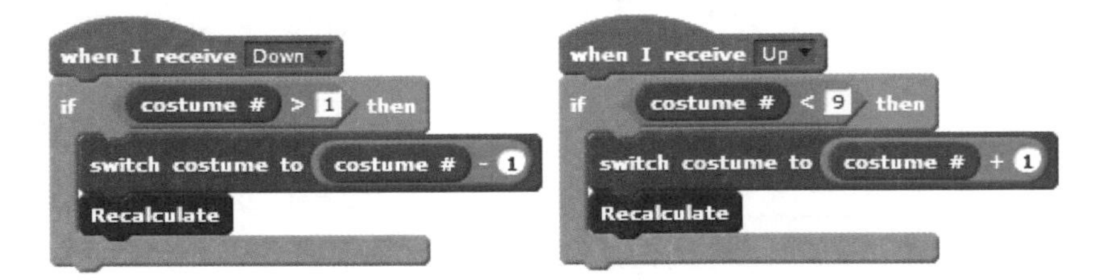

Figure 5-28: Scripts triggered by the Up *and* Down *messages*

The sprite switches its costume and then calls the **Recalculate** procedure to update the volume and surface area calculations. Note that these scripts use the value of the current costume to determine whether the sphere has reached its highest or lowest size, thus ensuring valid responses to the Up and Down buttons. I'll say more about the **if** block in the next chapter, but for now, let's discuss the sphere's **Recalculate** procedure, shown in Figure 5-29.

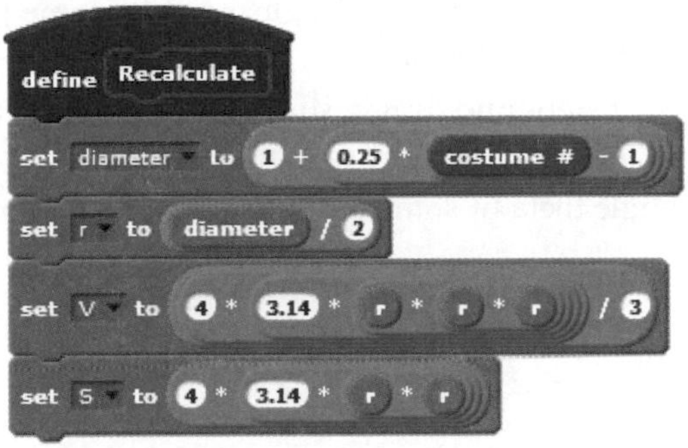

Figure 5-29: **Recalculate** *procedure*

First, the value of the diameter variable is set according to this formula:

$$diameter = 1 + 0.25 \times (costume\ number - 1)$$

Since the costume number ranges from 1 to 9, the corresponding values of the diameter variable will be 1, 1.25, 1.50, ... , 2.75, 3, which is what we intended.

The script finds the radius, r, by dividing the diameter by 2. It then calculates the volume and the surface area of the sphere using the formulas shown in Figure 5-26. The computed values will show up automatically on the corresponding monitors on the Stage.

TRY IT OUT 5-5

Open the application and run it. Study the scripts to understand how the application works. Add a script to the Sphere sprite so it rotates and changes color as the application runs. As another exercise, modify the original program to use a single costume for the Sphere sprite and use the **change size by** block to change the sphere's size. The scaled image won't look as nice, but otherwise, the application should perform identically.

Drawing an n-Leaved Rose

N-LeavedRose.sb2

In this example, we'll create an application that draws a rose with multiple leaves on the Stage. The rose-drawing process can be broken down into the following steps:

1. Start at the origin of the Stage.
2. Point the sprite in some direction. By convention, the Greek letter θ (pronounced *theta*) represents an angle, so we'll name the variable for the sprite's direction theta.
3. Move the sprite r steps and draw a single point on the Stage. After that, lift the pen up and return to the origin.
4. Change the angle theta by some amount (we'll use 1°) and repeat steps 2–4.

The relation between the distance r and the angle theta is given by

$$r = a \times \cos(n \times \theta)$$

where a is a real number and n is an integer. This equation produces a rose whose size and number of leaves are controlled by a and n, respectively. This equation also involves the cosine trigonometric function (*cos*), which you'll find as a reporter block in the *Operators* palette (check the **sqrt** block). Given the values of a and n, all we have to do is choose different values for theta, calculate the corresponding values of r, and mark the resulting points on the Stage. The user interface for this example is shown in Figure 5-30.

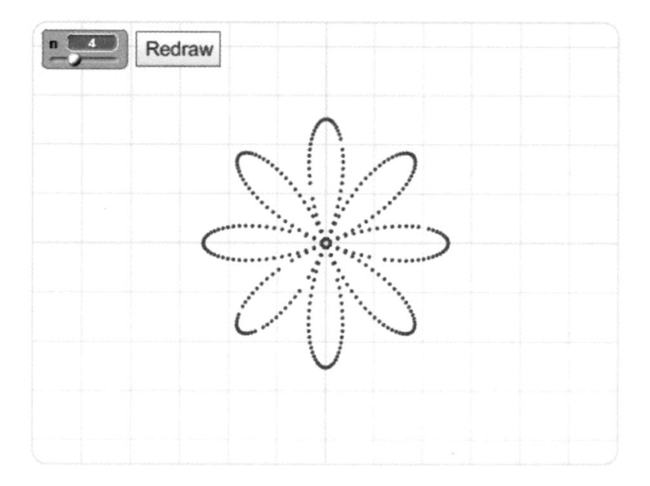

Figure 5-30: User interface for the n-leaved rose application

The application contains two sprites: The first sprite has the Redraw button costume, and the second sprite (called Painter) is a hidden sprite that draws the rose. The user controls the number of desired leaves by changing n with the slider control and then clicks the Redraw button to draw the rose. When the user clicks that button, the button sprite simply broadcasts a Redraw message. When the Painter sprite receives this message, it executes the script shown in Figure 5-31.

```
when I receive Redraw
go to x: 0 y: 0
set pen color to 120
set pen size to 3
pen up
clear
set a to 100
Rose

define Rose
set theta to 0
repeat 360
    pen up
    go to x: 0 y: 0
    point in direction theta
    move (a * (cos of (n * theta))) steps
    pen down
    change theta by 1
```

*Figure 5-31: The **Redraw** procedure for drawing an n-leaved rose on the Stage*

The script first sets the pen's color and size and clears the previous pen marks from the Stage. It then sets the variable a to 100 and calls the **Rose** procedure, which will run through a loop 360 times to draw the rose on the Stage. On each pass of the loop, the procedure points in the direction theta, moves r steps, and draws a pen mark at that location. It then increments theta by 1° to prepare for the next pass of the **repeat** loop.

Figure 5-32 shows some of the roses created for different values of n. Can you figure out the relation between the value of n and the number of leaves?

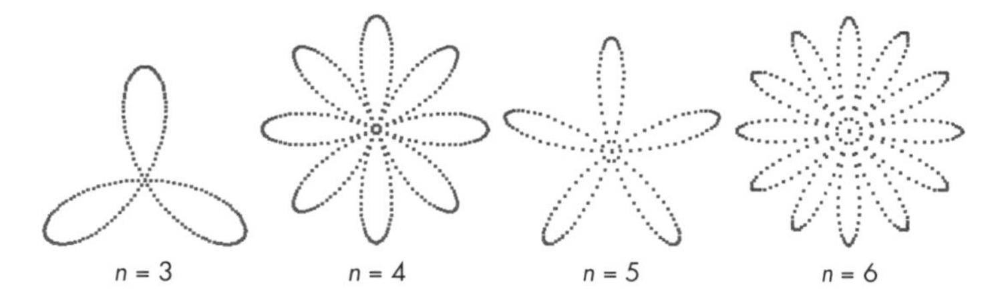

*Figure 5-32: Some roses created by the **Rose** procedure*

TRY IT OUT 5-6

Open the application and run it. Change the value of n to see what else you can create with the **Rose** procedure. Add another slider to the application to allow the user to change the value of a and modify the scripts as needed. You can also modify the **Rose** procedure to take a as a parameter. (See "Passing Parameters to Custom Blocks" on page 77 for a refresher on how to add parameters to procedures.)

Modeling Sunflower Seed Distribution

Sunflower.sb2

Biologists and mathematicians have studied the arrangement of leaves on the stems of plants extensively. Let's delve into botany a bit ourselves by examining a geometric model for representing flowers with spiral seed patterns. In particular, we'll program two equations that model the distribution of seeds in a sunflower. To draw the *n*th seed of the sunflower, we'll follow these steps:

1. Point the sprite in the direction of $n \times 137.5°$.
2. Move a distance $r = c\sqrt{n}$, where c is a constant scaling factor (set to 5 in our example).
3. Draw a point on the Stage at the final location.

We'll repeat these steps for each seed we want to draw. For the first seed, we set $n = 1$; for the second seed, we set $n = 2$; and so on. Using angles other than 137.5° in the first step will result in different arrangements of seeds. If you're curious about these equations and want to learn more about sunflower seed patterns, check out *The Algorithmic Beauty of Plants* by Przemyslaw Prusinkiewicz and Aristid Lindenmayer (Springer-Verlag, 2004), specifically Chapter 4, which you'll find on the book's website, *http://algorithmicbotany.org/papers/#abop.*

Our application will generate patterns similar to the ones described in that work, and you can see some of those patterns in Figure 5-33.

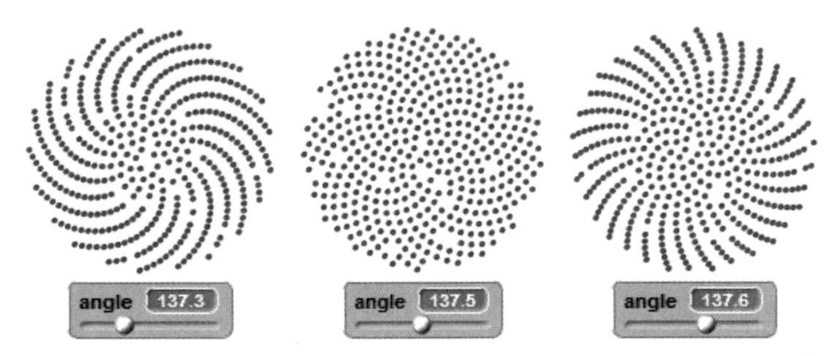

Figure 5-33: Some sunflower patterns generated using different angles

The interface for this example contains a slider control to change the value of the angle from 137° to 138° in increments of 0.01° and a button labeled `Redraw`. When the user clicks that button, it broadcasts a message to the `Painter` sprite, which executes the scripts shown in Figure 5-34.

The **Sunflower** procedure executes a loop that draws 420 seeds, though you can change this number if you like. On every iteration of the loop, the procedure goes to the location of the *n*th seed (by calculating the seed's angle ❶ and moving $c\sqrt{n}$ ❷ steps) and draws a pen mark at that location. The procedure then increments `n`, which represents the seed number, to prepare to draw the next seed.

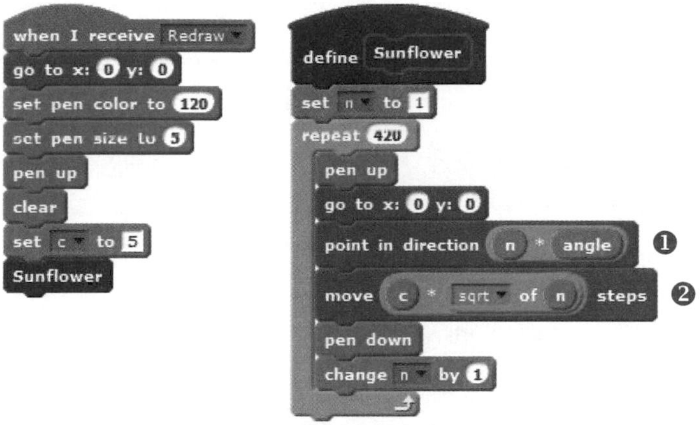

```
when I receive Redraw
go to x: 0 y: 0
set pen color to 120
set pen size to 5
pen up
clear
set c to 5
Sunflower
```

```
define Sunflower
set n to 1
repeat 420
    pen up
    go to x: 0 y: 0
    point in direction (n * angle)        ❶
    move (c * sqrt of n) steps            ❷
    pen down
    change n by 1
```

Figure 5-34: The scripts for the Painter *sprite*

The scripts I've presented in this section are just a few samples of the amazing applications we can create by using variables and monitors. Letting the user interact with our applications through the slider control is just the start of a new breed of interactive applications. In the following section, you'll learn to create scripts that directly prompt users for input.

TRY IT OUT 5-7

Open the application and run it. Change the value of the angle to see what else you can create with the **Sunflower** procedure. Study the procedure to understand how it works and then come up with some ways to enhance it.

Getting Input from Users

GettingUserInput.sb2

Imagine that you want to create a game that tutors children in basic arithmetic. Your game would probably have a sprite that displays an addition problem and asks the player to enter an answer. How would you read the player's input to see whether the answer was correct?

Scratch's *Sensing* palette provides one command block, **ask and wait**, that you can use to read user input. This block takes a single parameter that specifies a string to show to the user, usually in the form of a question. As illustrated in Figure 5-35, the execution of this block produces slightly different outputs depending on the visibility state of the sprite (that is, whether the sprite is shown or hidden). The output shown in Figure 5-35 (right) also appears when the **ask and wait** command is called from a script that is owned by the Stage.

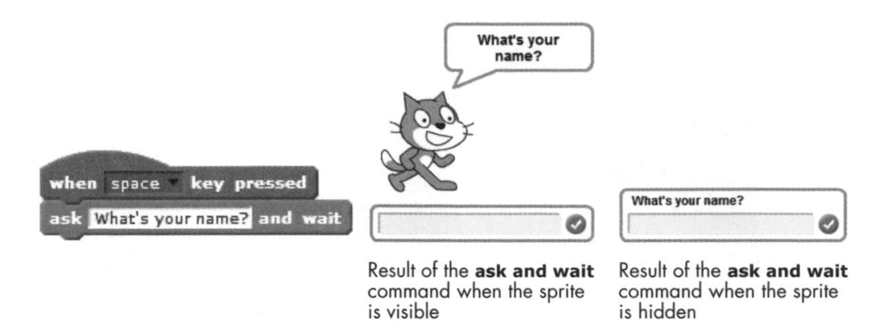

Figure 5-35: The **ask and wait** *block may produce different outputs depending on whether the sprite that executes it is shown or hidden.*

After executing the **ask and wait** command, the calling script waits for the user to press the ENTER key or click the check mark at the right side of the input box. When this happens, Scratch stores the user's input in the **answer** block and continues execution at the command immediately after the **ask and wait** block. To see this command block in action, take a look at the following examples illustrating how to use it.

Reading a Number

AskAndWait .sb2

The script of Figure 5-36 asks the user for her age, waits for an answer, and tells the user how old she will be in 10 years.

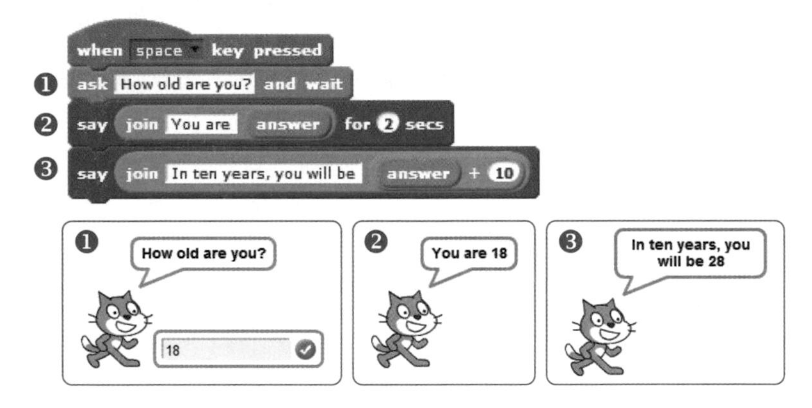

Figure 5-36: A script that accepts the user's age as input

The figure shows the output of the program when the user types 18 and presses ENTER on the keyboard. Notice that the program uses the **join** block (from the *Operators* palette) to concatenate (that is, connect) two strings.

Reading Characters

AskAndWait2 .sb2

The script of Figure 5-37 asks the user for his initials and then constructs and displays a greeting based on the user's response.

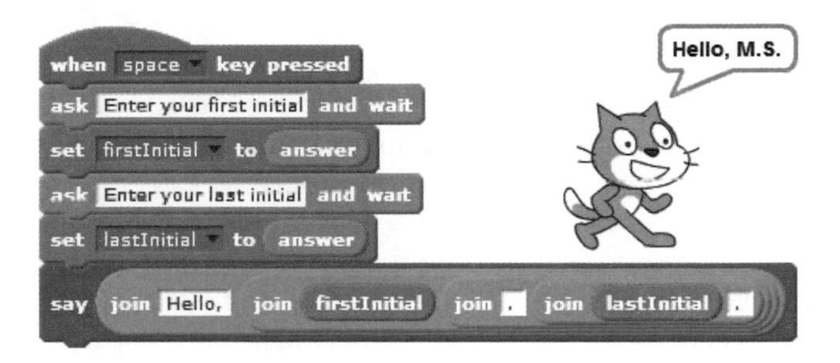

Figure 5-37: A script that uses two variables to read in and store the user's initials

The program uses two variables (firstInitial and lastInitial) to save the values entered by the user. You can see the final output of the program when the user enters the letters M and S at the two prompts, respectively. Notice that the program uses nested **join** blocks to construct the greeting. You can use this technique to create all sorts of strings and display customized messages in your applications.

Performing Arithmetic Operations

AskAndWait3.sb2

The script of Figure 5-38 asks the user to input two numbers. It then computes the product of these two numbers and shows the answer in a voice bubble using the **say** command. As in the previous example, the script uses two variables (num1 and num2) to store the values entered by the user.

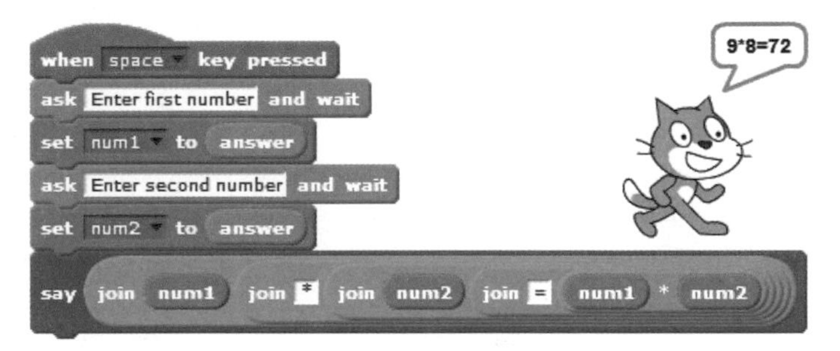

Figure 5-38: Computing a value based on user input

The figure shows the output when the user enters 9 and 8, respectively, in response to the two prompts. Again, notice that I've nested the **join** blocks to construct the output string.

The examples I've presented in this section demonstrate several ways to use the **ask and wait** block to write scripts that take in user input and solve a variety of problems. You can, for example, write a program to find the roots of a quadratic equation of the form $ax^2 + bx + c = 0$ for any values of a, b, and c entered by the user. You could then use this program to check your own answer to the equation. I hope this will give you some ideas of how to use this powerful block to solve any math problem that may arise.

Summary

Variables are one of the most important concepts in programming. A variable is the name of an area in computer memory where we can store a single value, such as a number or a string.

In this chapter, you learned the basic data types supported in Scratch and the operations permitted on these types. You then learned how to create variables and use them to store a piece of data.

You also implemented several practical applications that used variables to demonstrate different features. You explored variables' monitors and used them to create different kinds of interactive programs. Finally, you learned how to use the **ask and wait** block to prompt the user for some input and process the user's responses in your program.

In the next chapter, you'll learn more about the Boolean data type and the fundamental role it plays in decision making. You'll also learn about the **if** and the **if/else** blocks and use them to add another level of intelligence to your Scratch programs. So roll up your sleeves and get ready for another exciting chapter!

Problems

1. Create a script that implements the following instructions:
   - Set the speed variable to 60 (mph).
   - Set the time variable to 2.5 (hours).
   - Calculate the distance traveled and save the answer in the distance variable.
   - Display the calculated distance, with an appropriate message, to the user
2. What is the output of each of the scripts shown below? Reproduce these scripts and run them to test your answer.

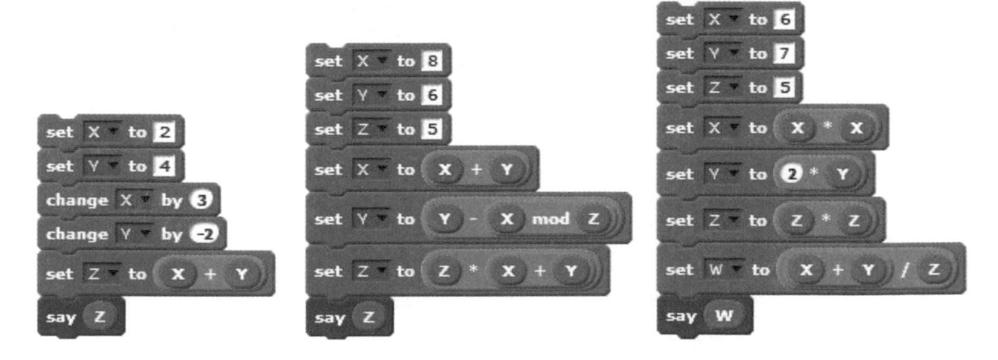

3. What are the values of X and Y at the end of each iteration of the repeat loop in the script to the right? Reproduce the script and run it to check your answer.

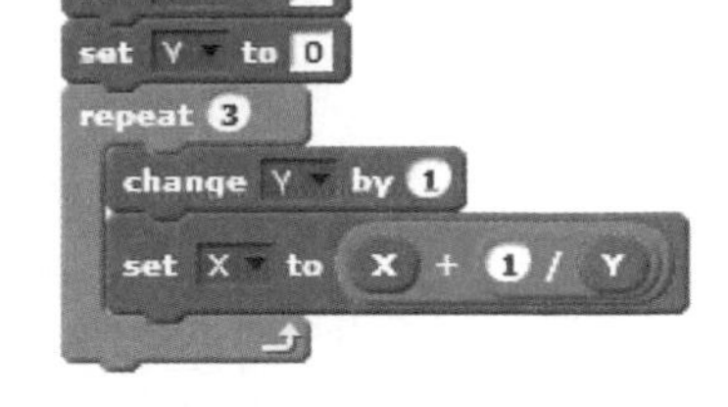

4. Let x and y be two variables. Create function blocks equivalent to the following statements:
   - Add 5 to x and store the result in y.
   - Multiply x by 3 and store the result in y.
   - Divide x by 10 and store the result in y.
   - Subtract 4 from x and store the result in y.
   - Square x, add y to the result, and store the result back in x.
   - Set x equal to twice the value of y plus three times the cube of y.
   - Set x equal to minus the square of y.
   - Set x equal to the result of dividing the sum of x and y by the product of x and y.
5. Write a program that asks that user to enter an article, a noun, and a verb. The program then creates a sentence of the form *article noun verb*.
6. Write a program that asks the user to enter a temperature in degrees Celsius. The program will convert the temperature to degrees Fahrenheit and display the result to the user with an appropriate message. (Hint: $F° = (1.8 \times C°) + 32$.)
7. When a current I flows through a resistance R, the power P dissipated by the resistance is $I^2 \times R$. Write a program that reads I and R and calculates P.
8. Write a program that reads the lengths of the two sides of a right triangle and calculates the length of the hypotenuse.
9. Write a program that prompts the user to enter the length (L), width (W), and height (H) of a box. The program will then compute and display the volume and surface area of the box. (Hint: $Volume = L \times W \times H$; $Surface\ area = 2\times[(L \times W) + (L \times H) + (H \times W)]$.)
10. The equivalent resistance R of three resistors (R_1, R_2, and R_3) connected in parallel is given by this equation:

$$1/R = 1/R_1 + 1/R_2 + 1/R_3$$

Write a program that reads the values of R_1, R_2, and R_3 and calculates R.

Whac-a-Mole.sb2

11. Complete the Whac-a-Mole game introduced earlier in the chapter. The file *Whac-a-Mole.sb2* contains a partial implementation of this program. When the green flag is clicked, the provided script starts a loop that moves the Cat sprite randomly over the holes. Add two scripts (one for the Cat and the other for the Stage) to change the values of the two variables (hits and misses) appropriately. Try adding some sound effects to make the game more fun! You could also add a condition that ends the game after a timer or the number of misses reaches a certain value.

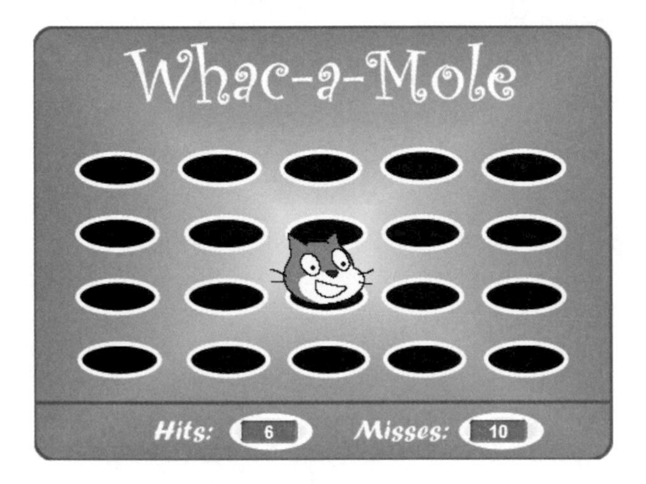

6

MAKING DECISIONS

This chapter will teach you the Scratch tools you need to write programs that can compare values, evaluate logical expressions, and make decisions based on the results. We'll also go through several useful example applications. Here's what you'll learn along the way:

- Basic problem-solving techniques
- How to use the **if** and **if/else** blocks to choose among alternative actions
- How to construct logical expressions to evaluate given conditions
- The flow of control in branching statements

The programs we have written so far follow a simple execution model. They start with the first instruction, execute it, move on to the next instruction, and so on until they reach the end of the program. The command blocks of these programs are executed in sequence, without any skipping or jumping.

In many programming situations, however, you may want to alter this sequential flow of program execution. If you were writing an application to tutor children in basic arithmetic, you'd want to execute certain blocks to reward correct answers and a completely different set of blocks for wrong answers (to reveal the right answer or offer another chance, for example). Your script can decide what to do next by comparing the student's input with the correct answer. This is the basis of all decision-making tasks.

In this chapter, we'll explore the decision-making commands available in Scratch and write several programs that use these commands to test inputs and perform different actions.

First, I'll introduce you to Scratch's comparison operators and show how you can use them to compare numbers, letters, and strings. Then, I'll introduce the **if** and **if/else** blocks and explain their key role in decision making. You'll also learn how to test multiple conditions using nested **if** and **if/else** blocks and write a menu-driven program to put these blocks into action. After that, I'll introduce logical operators as an alternative way to test multiple conditions. In the last section, we'll write several interesting programs based on all of the concepts you've learned so far.

Comparison Operators

You make decisions every day, and each decision normally leads you to perform certain actions. You may think, for example, "If that car is less than $2,000, I'll buy it." You then ask about the car's price and decide whether or not you want to buy it.

You can make decisions in Scratch, too. Using *comparison operators*, you can compare the values of two variables or expressions to determine whether one is greater than, less than, or equal to the other. Comparison operators are also called *relational operators* because they test the relationship between two values. The three relational operators supported in Scratch are shown in Table 6-1.

Table 6-1: Relational Operators in Scratch

Operator	Meaning	Example
(>)	greater than	(price > 2000) Is price greater than 2,000?
(<)	less than	(price < 2000) Is price less than 2,000?
(=)	equal to	(price = 2000) Is price equal to 2,000?

BOOLEANS IN THE REAL WORLD

The word *Boolean* is used in honor of George Boole, a 19th-century British mathematician who invented a system of logic based on just two values: 1 and 0 (or True and False). Boolean algebra eventually became the basis for modern-day computer science.

In real life, we use Boolean expressions all the time to make decisions. Computers also use them to determine which branch of a program to follow. A robotic arm may be programmed to inspect moving parts on an assembly line and move each part to Bin 1 if goodQuality = true, or Bin 2 if goodQuality = false. Home security systems are usually programmed to sound an alarm if the wrong code is entered (correctCode = false) or deactivate when we enter the correct code (correctCode = true). A remote server may grant or deny access when you swipe your credit card at a department store based on whether your card was valid (true) or invalid (false). One computer in your vehicle will automatically deploy the air airbags when it decides that a collision has occurred (collision = true). Your cell phone may display a warning icon when the battery is low (batteryLow = true) and remove the icon when the battery's charge is acceptable (batteryLow = false).

These are just few examples of how computers cause different actions to be taken by checking the results of Boolean conditions.

Note that the blocks in Table 6-1 all have a hexagonal shape. As you might recall from Chapter 5, that means the result of evaluating one of these blocks is a *Boolean* value, which can be either true or false. For this reason, these expressions are also called *Boolean expressions.*

For example, the expression **price < 2000** tests whether the value of the variable price is less than 2,000. If price is less than 2,000, the block returns (or evaluates to) true; otherwise, it returns false. You can use this expression to construct your decision condition in the form, "If (**price < 2000**), then buy the car."

Before we look at the **if** block, which allows you to implement such a test, let's go over a simple example that illustrates how Boolean expressions are evaluated in Scratch.

Evaluating Boolean Expressions

Let's say that we set two variables, x and y, as follows: x = 5, and y = 10. Table 6-2 shows some examples that use Scratch's relational blocks.

These examples reveal several important points about relational operators. First, we can use them to compare both individual variables (such as x, y) and complete expressions (such as 2 * x and x + 6). Second, the result of a comparison is always true or false (that is, a Boolean value). Third, the **x = y** block doesn't mean "Set x equal to y." Instead, it asks, "Is x equal to y?" So when the statement **set z to (x = y)** is executed, the value of x is still 5.

Table 6-2: Sample Relational Block Uses

Statement	Meaning	z (output)	Explanation
set z to (x < y)	z = is(5 < 10)?	z = true	because 5 is less than 10
set z to (x > y)	z = is(5 > 10)?	z = false	because 5 is not more than 10
set z to (x = y)	z = is(5 = 10)?	z = false	because 5 is not equal to 10
set z to (y > 2 * x)	z = is(10 > 2*5)?	z = false	because 10 is not more than 10
set z to (x = 5)	z = is(5 = 5)?	z = true	because 5 is equal to 5
set z to (y < x + 6)	z = is(10 < 5 + 6)?	z = true	because 10 is less than 11

Comparing Letters and Strings

Let's think about a game in which the player tries to guess a one-letter secret code between *A* and *Z*. The game reads the player's guess, compares it with the secret code, and instructs the player to refine his guess based on the alphabetical order of letters. If the secret letter were *G*, for example, and the player entered a *B*, the game should say something like "After B" to tell the player that the secret code comes after the letter *B* in the alphabet. How can you compare the correct letter with the player's input to decide what message to display?

Fortunately, the relational operators in Scratch can also compare letters. As illustrated in Figure 6-1, Scratch compares letters based on their alphabetical order. Since the letter *A* comes before the letter *B* in the alphabet, the expression **A < B** returns true. It is important to note, however, that these comparisons are not case sensitive; capital letter *A* is the same as small letter *a*. Thus, the expression **A = a** also returns true.

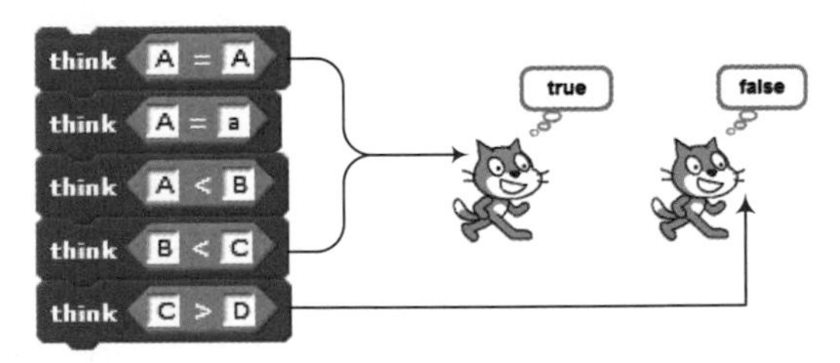

Figure 6-1: Using relational operators to compare letters

Knowing this information, you can test the player's guess using the following set of conditionals:

```
IF (answer = secretCode), then say Correct
IF (answer > secretCode), then say Before <answer>
IF (answer < secretCode), then say After <answer>
```

A *conditional* is a statement of the form, "If the condition is true, then take this action." In the next section, I'll teach you how to implement conditionals in Scratch, but let's explore relational operators a bit further with our code-guessing game first.

What if the secret code contains more than one letter? For example, the player might need to guess the name of an animal. Can you still use Scratch's relational operators to do the comparison? Luckily, the short answer is yes: You can use Scratch's relational operators to compare strings. But how does Scratch process a comparison like **elephant > mouse**? The examples in Figure 6-2 illustrate the result of comparing strings.

Figure 6-2: Using relational operators to compare ❶ identical strings, ❷ strings that differ only in case, ❸ one string to another that contains extra spaces, and ❹ strings that vary according to the dictionary order of their letters

A careful study of Figure 6-2 shows the following:

- Scratch compares strings irrespective of their case. The strings "HELLO" and "hello" in ❷, for example, are considered equal.
- Scratch counts white spaces in its comparison. The string " HELLO ", which starts and ends with a single space, is not the same as the string "HELLO" ❸.
- When comparing the strings "ABC" and "ABD", as in ❹, Scratch first considers the first character in the two strings. Since they are the same (the letter *A* in this case), Scratch examines the second character in both strings. Since this character is also the same in the two strings, Scratch moves on to examining the third character. Since the letter *C* is less than the letter *D* (that is, *C* comes before *D* in the alphabet), Scratch considers the first string to be less than the second string.

Knowing this, it shouldn't surprise you when the expression **elephant > mouse** evaluates to false, even though actual elephants are much larger than mice. According to Scratch's string comparison rules, the string "elephant" is less than the string "mouse" because the letter *e* (the first letter in elephant) comes before the letter *m* (the first letter in mouse) in the alphabet.

Comparing and sorting strings based on the alphabetical order of their characters is used in many real-life situations, including ordering directory listings, books on bookshelves, words in dictionaries, and so on. The word *elephant* comes before the word *mouse* in the dictionary, and string comparison in Scratch gives an answer based on this order.

Now that you understand what relational operators are and how Scratch uses these operators to compare numbers and strings, it's time to learn about conditional blocks.

Decision Structures

Scratch's *Control* palette contains two blocks that allow you to make decisions and control actions in your programs: the **if** block and the **if/else** block. Using these blocks, you can ask a question and take a course of action based on the answer. In this section, we'll discuss these two blocks in detail, talk about flags, and learn to test multiple conditions with nested **if** blocks. I'll then introduce menu-driven applications and explain how nested **if** blocks can aid in their implementation.

The if Block

The **if** block is a decision structure that gives you the ability to specify whether a set of commands should (or should not) be executed based on the result of a test condition. The structure of the **if** block and its corresponding flowchart are shown in Figure 6-3.

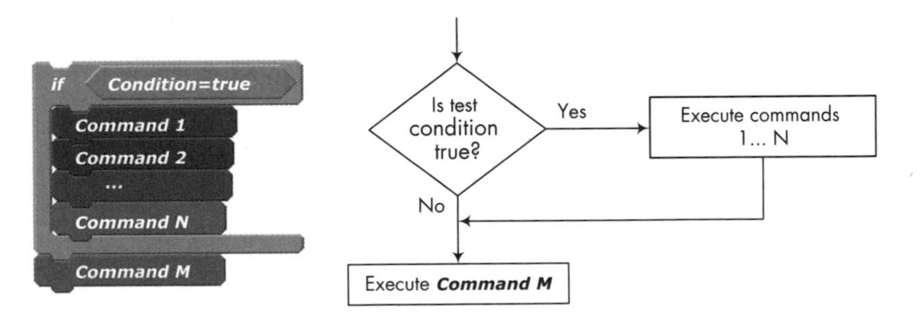

Figure 6-3: Structure of the **if** *block*

In Figure 6-3, the diamond shape represents a decision block that gives a yes/no (or true/false) answer to a question. If the test condition in the *header* of the **if** block is true, the program executes the commands listed inside the *body* before moving on to the command that follows the **if** block (***Command M*** in the figure). If the test condition is false, the program skips those commands and moves directly to ***Command M***.

To see the **if** block in action, create the script shown in Figure 6-4 and run it. The script runs a **forever** loop that moves a sprite around the stage, changes its color, and makes it bounce off the edges of the Stage.

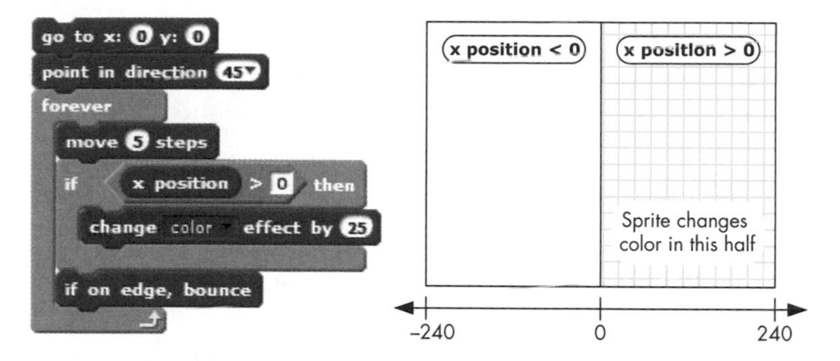

Figure 6-4: This script causes the sprite to change its color only when it is moving in the right half of the Stage.

The **forever** loop in our script contains an **if** block that checks the sprite's *x*-position after every **move** command. If the *x*-position is greater than zero, the sprite should change its color. When you run this script, you'll notice that the sprite changes its color only when it is moving in the right half of the Stage. This is because the **change color effect by 25** block is executed only when the **x position > 0** condition is true.

Using Variables as Flags

Let's say that you are developing a space adventure game where the goal is to destroy a fleet of attacking warships. The player, who is the captain, maneuvers a starship with the arrow keys on the keyboard and fires missiles by pressing the spacebar. If the player's starship gets hit by enemy fire a certain number of times, the ship loses its ability to attack. At this point, pressing the spacebar should not fire any more missiles, and the captain has to adopt a defense strategy to avoid taking any more hits. Clearly, when the spacebar is pressed, your program needs to check the state of the starship's attack system to decide whether or not the player can fire.

Checks of this nature are normally performed using *flags*, which are variables you use to indicate whether or not an event of interest has happened. You could use any two values to describe the event's status, but it's common practice to use 0 (or false) to indicate that the event hasn't occurred and 1 (or true) to indicate that it has.

In your space shooter game, you can use a flag named canFire to indicate the state of the starship. A value of 1 means that the starship can fire missiles, and a value of 0 means that it can't. Based on this, your spacebar event handler may be coded as shown in Figure 6-5.

Figure 6-5: Using a flag for condition execution

At the start of the game, you'd initialize the value of the canFire flag to 1 to indicate that the starship is capable of firing missiles. When the starship gets hit by a certain amount of enemy fire, you'd set the **canFire** flag to 0 to indicate that the attack system has become dysfunctional; at that point, pressing the spacebar won't fire any more missiles.

Although you can name your flags anything you want, I recommend using names that reflect their true/false nature. Table 6-3 shows some examples of flags you might use in the space shooter game.

Table 6-3: Some Examples of Using Flags

Example	Meaning and Possible Course of Action
set gameStarted to 0	Game has not started yet. Ignore all keyboard inputs.
set gameStarted to 1	Game has started. Start processing user input.
set gameOver to 0	Game is not over yet. Show remaining time.
set gameOver to 1	Game is over. Hide the remaining time display.
set fireDetected to 0	The starship is not hit by enemy's fire. Alarm sound is off.
set fireDetected to 1	The starship has been hit by a missile. Play the alarm sound.

Now that you know how to use the **if** block and flags, let's talk about another conditional block, one that will let you execute one block of code when a certain condition is true and another if that condition is false.

The if/else Block

Imagine that you are creating a game to teach basic math to elementary students. The game presents an addition problem and then asks the student to enter an answer. The student should receive one point for a correct answer and lose one point for an incorrect answer. You can perform this task using two **if** statements:

```
If the answer is correct, add one point to score
If the answer is incorrect, subtract one point from score
```

You could also simplify this logic—and make the code more efficient—by combining the two **if** statements into one **if/else** statement as follows:

```
If the answer is correct
    add one point to score
Else
    subtract one point from score
```

The specified condition is tested. If the condition is true, the commands in the **if** part of the block are executed. If the condition is false, however, the commands under **else** will execute instead. The program will only execute one of the two groups of commands in the **if/else** block. Those alternative paths through the program are also called *branches*. The structure of the **if/else** block and its corresponding flowchart are shown in Figure 6-6.

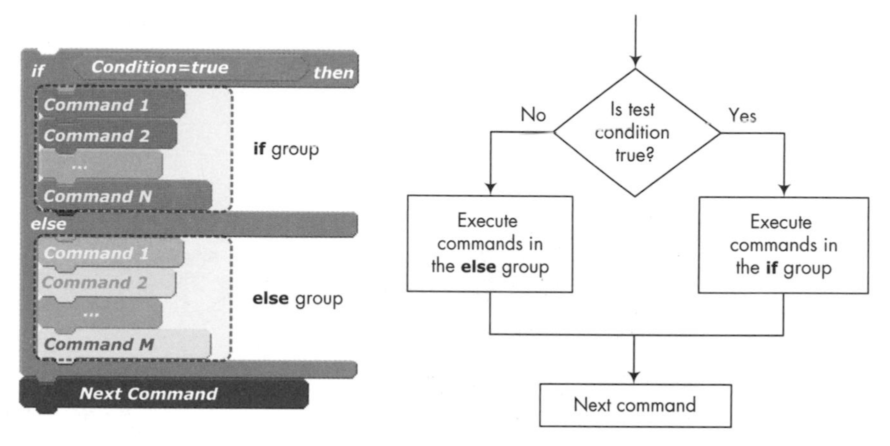

Figure 6-6: Structure of the **if/else** *block*

You might use the **if/else** structure when you want to decide where to eat lunch. If you have enough money, you'll go to a fancy restaurant; otherwise, you'll settle for more casual food. Let's call the money in your wallet availableCash. When you open your wallet, you're checking the condition **availableCash > $20**. If the result is true (you have more than $20), you'll go to a place with white tablecloths, and if not, you'll head to the nearest burger joint.

One simple script that illustrates using the **if/else** block is shown in Figure 6-7. This example uses the *modulus operator* (**mod**), which returns the remainder of a division operation, to determine whether a number entered by the user is even or odd. (Remember that an even number has a remainder of zero when divided by two.)

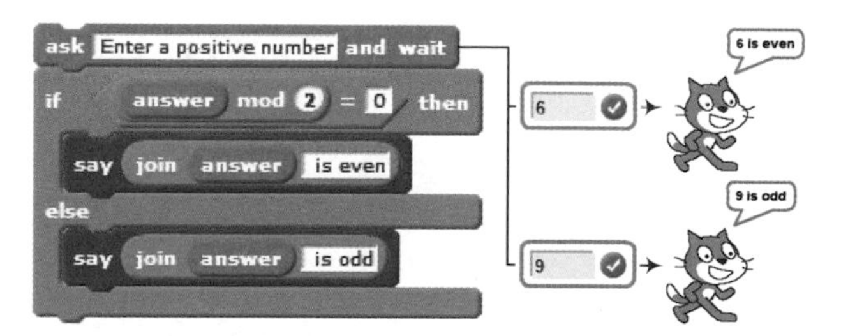

Figure 6-7: This script finds out whether the number the user entered is even or odd.

Figure 6-7 shows two sample outputs for when the user enters 6 and 9, respectively, in response to the **ask** command. Can you explain how this script works?

Nested if and if/else Blocks

If you want to test more than one condition before taking an action, you can nest multiple **if** (or **if/else**) blocks inside each other to perform the required test. Consider for example the script shown in Figure 6-8, which determines whether a student should receive a scholarship. To qualify, the student must have: (1) a grade point average (GPA) higher than 3.8 and (2) a grade above 92 percent in math.

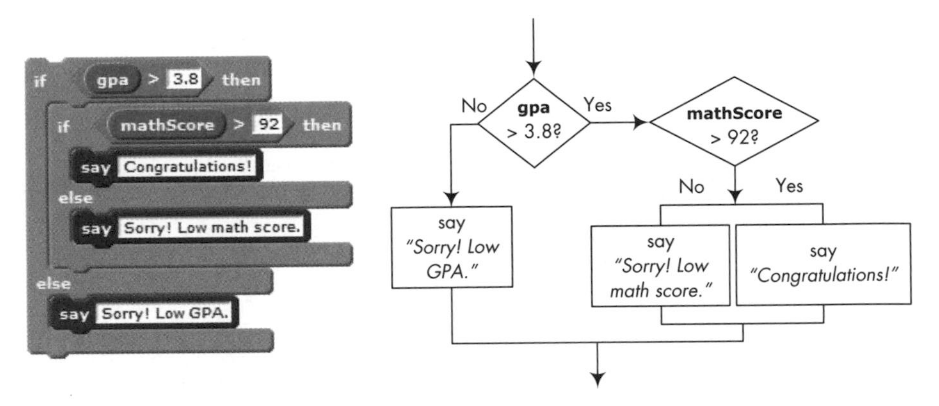

Figure 6-8: You can use nested **if/else** *blocks to test multiple conditions.*

First, the expression **gpa > 3.8** is tested. If this expression is false, we don't need to check the other condition because the student doesn't meet the scholarship criteria. If the expression **gpa > 3.8** is true, however, we need to test the second condition. This is done with the nested **if/else** block, which tests the condition **mathScore > 92**. If this second condition is also true, the student gets the scholarship. Otherwise, the student does not qualify, and an appropriate message explaining the reason is displayed.

Menu-Driven Programs

AreaCalculator .sb2

Next, we'll explore a typical use of nested **if** blocks. In particular, you'll learn how to write programs that present the user with choices and act on the user's selection.

When you start up some programs, they display a list (or menu) of available options and wait for you to make a selection. Sometimes, you'll interact with these programs by entering a number that corresponds to your desired option. Such programs may use a sequence of nested **if/else** blocks to determine the user's selection and act appropriately. To see how nested **if/else** blocks work, we'll discuss an application, shown in Figure 6-9, that calculates the area of different geometric shapes.

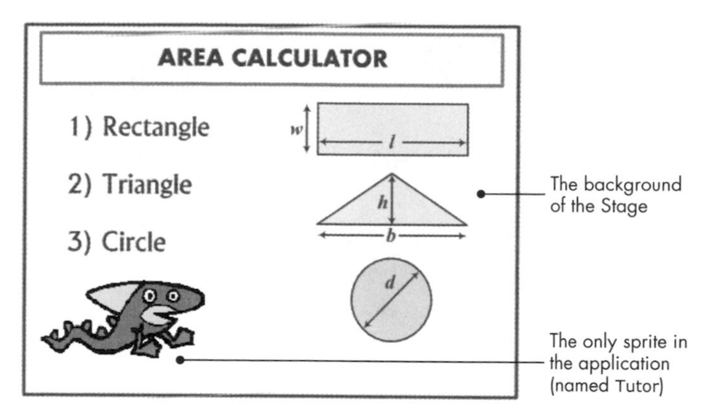

Figure 6-9: User interface for the area calculator program

The user interface for this application contains the Stage's background image, which shows the available options (the numbers 1, 2, or 3), and the Tutor sprite, which asks the user for a choice, performs the calculation, and displays the result. The main script, shown in Figure 6-10, starts when the green flag icon is clicked.

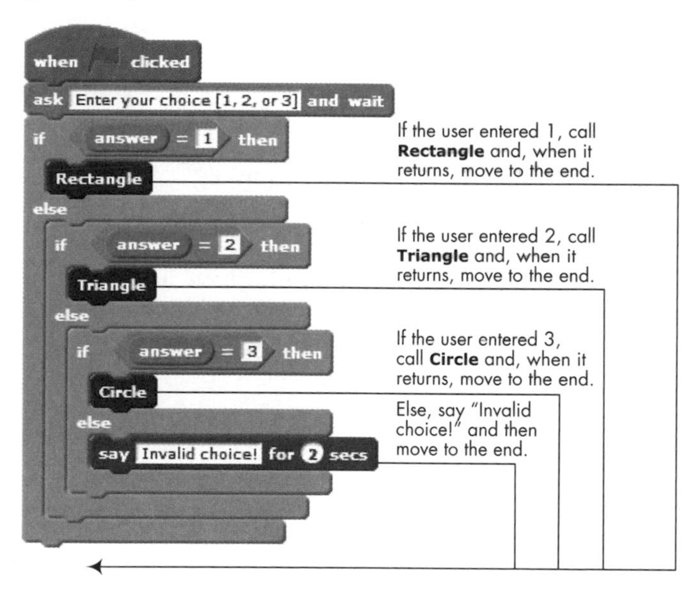

Figure 6-10: The main script of the Tutor *sprite*

After asking the user to enter a choice, the Tutor sprite waits for the user's input and uses three **if/else** blocks to process it. If the user entered a valid choice (that is, 1, 2, or 3), the script calls the appropriate procedure to calculate the area of the indicated shape. Otherwise, the script invokes the **say** command to inform the user that the choice entered is invalid. The procedures for calculating the areas of the three shapes are shown in Figure 6-11.

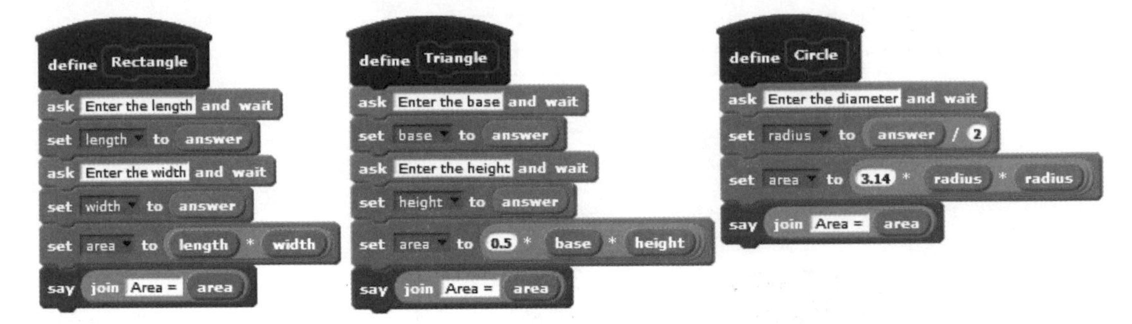

Figure 6-11: Procedures for the area calculator program

Each procedure asks the user to enter the dimensions for its corresponding shape, calculates the area, and displays the result. For example, the **Rectangle** procedure asks the user to enter the length and width of the rectangle and saves the answers in the length and width variables, respectively. It then computes the area by multiplying the length by the width and displays the answer. The other two procedures work similarly.

Logical Operators

In the previous section, you learned how to use nested **if** and **if/else** blocks to test multiple conditions, but you can also do that with *logical operators*. Using logical operators, you can combine two or more relational expressions to produce a single true/false result. For example, the logical expression (x > 5) and (x < 10) is made up of two logical expressions (x > 5 and x < 10) that are combined using the logical operator **and**. We can think of x > 5 and x < 10 as the two operands of the **and** operator; the result of this operator is true only if both operands are true. Table 6-4 lists the three logical operators available in Scratch with a brief explanation of their meaning.

Table 6-4: Logical Operators

Operator	Meaning
and	The result is true only if the two expressions are true.
or	The result is true if either of the two expressions is true.
not	The result is true if the expression is false.

Now that you've seen a brief overview of each operator, let's explore how they work in more detail, one at a time.

The and Operator

The **and** operator takes two expressions as parameters. If both expressions are true, the **and** operator returns true; otherwise, it returns false. The truth table for **and**, which lists the output of the operator for all possible combinations of inputs, is shown in Table 6-5.

Table 6-5: Truth Table for the and Operator

X	Y	X and Y
true	true	true
true	false	false
false	true	false
false	false	false

As an example of using the **and** operator, let's say we're creating a game in which the player gets 200 bonus points when the score reaches 100 in the first level. The game level is tracked by a variable named level, and the score is tracked using a variable named score. Figure 6-12 shows how these conditions can be tested using nested **if** blocks ❶ or with the **and** operator ❷.

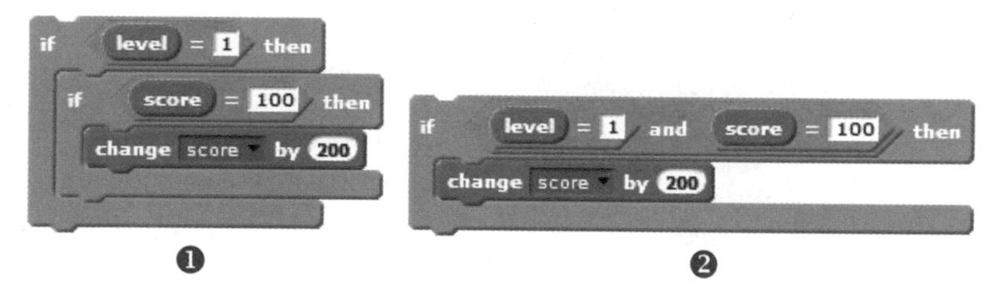

Figure 6-12: Checking multiple conditions using nested **if** *blocks and the* **and** *operator*

In both cases, the bonus points are added only when both conditions are true. As you can see, the **and** operator provides a more concise way for performing the same test. The command(s) inside the **if** block in Figure 6-12 ❷ will be executed only if level equals 1 and score equals 100. If either condition is false, the entire test evaluates to false, and the **change score by 200** block will not be executed.

The or Operator

The **or** operator also takes two expressions as parameters. If either expression is true, the **or** operator returns true. It returns false only when the two expressions are both false. The truth table for the **or** operator is given in Table 6-6.

Table 6-6: Truth Table for the or Operator

X	Y	X or Y
true	true	true
true	false	true
false	true	true
false	false	false

To demonstrate the use of the **or** operator, let's assume that players of a certain game have a limited time to reach the next level. They also start with a given amount of energy that depletes as they navigate the current level. The game ends if the player fails to reach the next level in the allowable time or if the player depletes all the allotted energy before reaching the next level. The remaining time is tracked by a variable named timeLeft, and the player's current energy level is tracked by a variable named energyLevel. Figure 6-13 shows how the game end condition can be tested using nested **if/else** blocks ❶ and the **or** operator ❷.

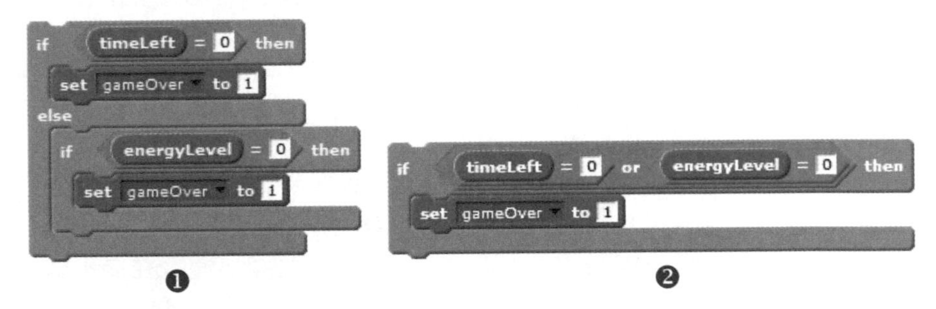

Figure 6-13: Checking multiple conditions using nested **if** *blocks and with the* **or** *operator*

Note again that the **or** operator provides a more concise way to test multiple conditions. The command(s) inside the **if** block in Figure 6-13 ❷ will be executed if timeLeft or energyLevel is 0. If both of these two conditions are false, the entire test evaluates to false, and the gameOver flag will not be set to 1.

The not Operator

The **not** operator takes only one expression as input. The result of the operator is true if the expression is false and false if the expression is true. The truth table for this operator is given in Table 6-7.

Table 6-7: Truth Table for the not Operator

X	not X
true	false
false	true

Going back to our hypothetical game from earlier, let's say the player can't progress to the next level if the score isn't more than 100 points. This would be a good place to use the **not** operator, as shown in Figure 6-14. You can read this block of code as, "If score is not greater than 100, do the command(s) inside the **if** block."

Figure 6-14: Example of using the not *operator*

In effect, if the value of the score variable is 100 or lower, the test expression evaluates to true, and the **say** command will execute. Note that the expression **not (score > 100)** is equivalent to **(score ≤ 100)**.

Using Logical Operators to Check Numeric Ranges

When you need to validate data entered by a user or filter out bad inputs, you can use logical operators to determine whether a number is inside (or outside) a numeric range. Table 6-8 shows some examples of numerical ranges.

Table 6-8: Expressing Numerical Ranges

Expression	Value
(x > 10) and (x < 20)	Evaluates to true if the value of **x** is greater than 10 and less than 20.
(x < 10) or (x > 20)	Evaluates to true if the value of **x** is less than 10 or greater than 20.
(x < 10) and (x > 20)	Always false. **x** can't be both less than 10 and greater than 20.

Although Scratch does not have built-in support for ≥ (greater than or equal to) and ≤ (less than or equal to) operators, you can use logical operators to implement these tests. Let's say, for example, that you need to test the condition **x ≥ 10** in your program. The solution set for this inequality is shown in Figure 6-15 ❶. The filled circle in the figure means that the number 10 is included in the solution set.

One way to test this condition is shown in Figure 6-15 ❷. The figure shows the solution set for **x < 10**, where the nonfilled circle means that the corresponding point is not in the solution set. As you can see from the figure, the *complementary* solution (that is, "*x* is not less than 10") is equivalent to **x ≥ 10**. Another way to perform the inequality test is shown in Figure 6-15 ❸. Clearly, if **x ≥ 10**, then either *x* is greater than 10 or *x* is equal to 10.

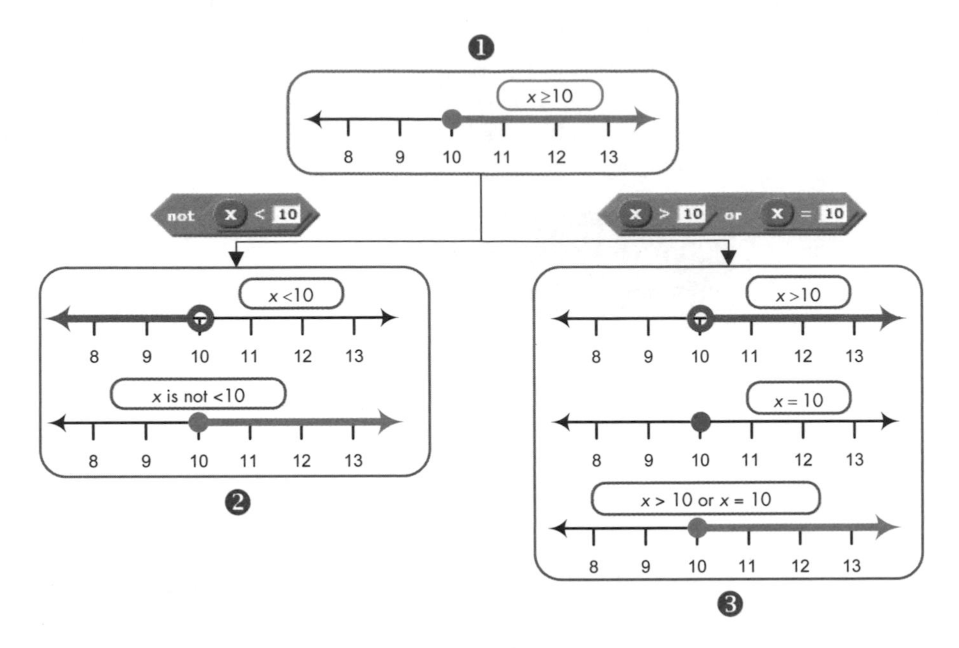

Figure 6-15: Two ways to implement the inequality **x ≥ 10**

The examples provided in Table 6-9 demonstrate how to use Scratch's relational and logical operators to express inequalities that contain the ≥ and the ≤ operators.

Table 6-9: Examples of Testing Inequalities

Expression	Implementation Using Logical Operators
$x \geq 10$	not x < 10
$x \geq 10$	x > 10 or x = 10
$x \leq 10$	not x > 10
$x \leq 10$	x < 10 or x = 10
$10 \leq x \leq 20$	not x < 10 and not x > 20
$10 \leq x \leq 20$	x > 10 and x < 20 or x = 10 or x = 20

We've explored several Scratch concepts in this chapter so far, including comparisons, conditional statements, and logical operators. Now, let's use that knowledge to create some fun and useful applications.

COMPARING DECIMAL NUMBERS

Special care must be taken when using the equal operator to compare decimal numbers. Because of the way these numbers are stored inside the computer, the comparison may sometimes be imprecise. Consider the command blocks shown here:

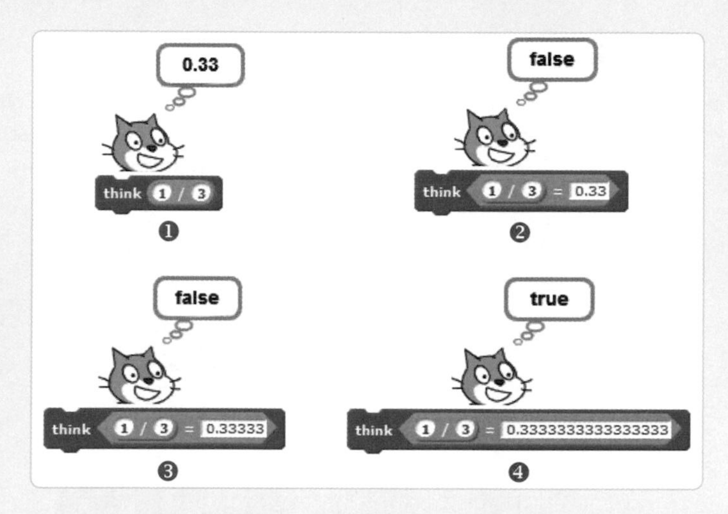

The result of dividing 1 by 3 is 0.3333... with the sequence of 3s repeating forever. Since the computer uses a fixed amount of space to store the result, the fraction 1/3 cannot be exactly stored by the computer. Although Scratch tells you that the result of the division is 0.33 at ❶, the actual result is saved internally with much higher precision. Therefore, the results of the first two comparisons in the figure (❷ and ❸) evaluate to false.

Depending on your programming situation, you may be able to prevent this type of error by using one of the following approaches:

- Use the less than (<) and greater than (>) operators instead of the equals operator (=) when possible.
- Use the **round** block to round the two numbers you need to compare, and then compare the rounded numbers for equality.
- Test the absolute difference between the two values you are comparing. For example, instead of testing if *x* equals *y*, we can check to see if the absolute difference between *x* and *y* is within an acceptable tolerance by using a block similar to this one:

Depending on the accuracy of the numbers and the method of calculating these numbers, this method may be sufficient for your purpose.

Scratch Projects

The new commands you've learned in this chapter should allow you to create a wide range of useful Scratch applications, and hopefully the projects I present in this section will give you some ideas for your own projects. I encourage you try out these applications, understand how they work, and then think of ways to enhance them.

Guess My Coordinates

GuessMy Coordinates.sb2

In this section, we'll develop an interactive game that can be used to test anyone's knowledge of the Cartesian coordinate system. The game contains a single sprite (called `Star`) that represents a random point on the Stage (see Figure 6-16).

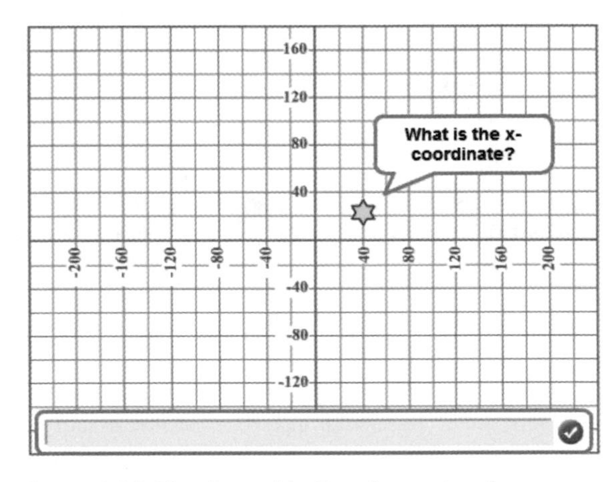

Figure 6-16: The Guess My Coordinates interface

Each time you run the game, the sprite moves to a different location on the Stage and asks the user to guess its *x*- and *y*-coordinates. The game checks the user's answers and provides an appropriate feedback message. The main script for the `Star` sprite is shown in Figure 6-17.

This script uses two variables, `X` and `Y`, to hold the random coordinates of the sprite. I'll explain how each numbered section from Figure 6-17 works below.

1. The `X` variable is assigned a random value from the set {–220, –200, –180, ... , 220}. This is achieved by first selecting a random integer between –11 and 11 and multiplying the result by 20. Similarly, the `Y` variable is assigned a random value from the set {–160, –140, –120, ... , 160}. The selected `X` and `Y` values ensure that the resulting point is located on one of the grid intersection points of Figure 6-16. The sprite is then moved to the location specified by `X` and `Y`.

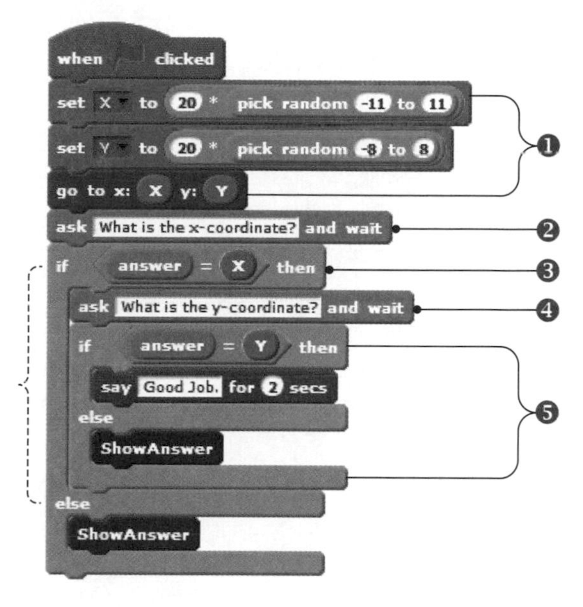

Figure 6-17: Script for the Guess My Coordinates game

2. The script asks the user to enter the *x*-coordinate of the sprite and waits for an answer.
3. If the answer is correct, the script moves to step 4. Otherwise, it will call the **ShowAnswer** procedure to display the correct coordinates of the point.
4. When the user enters the correct value for the *x*-coordinate, the script prompts the user to enter the *y*-coordinate of the sprite and waits for an answer.
5. If the user answers correctly, the script displays the message "Good Job." Otherwise, it calls **ShowAnswer** to display the correct coordinates.

The **ShowAnswer** procedure is shown in Figure 6-18. The point variable is first constructed to have a string of the form (X,Y) using the **join** operator. The procedure then uses the **say** command to show the correct answer to the user.

Figure 6-18: The **ShowAnswer** *procedure*

> **TRY IT OUT 6-1**
>
> Enhance this guessing game with some fun modifications. For example, you could make the game play music when someone wins, trigger a buzz for a wrong answer, run automatically (without having to press the green flag each time), or keep track of the number of correct answers to display the player's score.

Triangle Classification Game

Triangle Classification.sb2

As Figure 6-19 illustrates, a triangle can be classified as scalene, isosceles, or equilateral based on the lengths of its sides. In this section, you'll explore a game that quizzes players on these concepts.

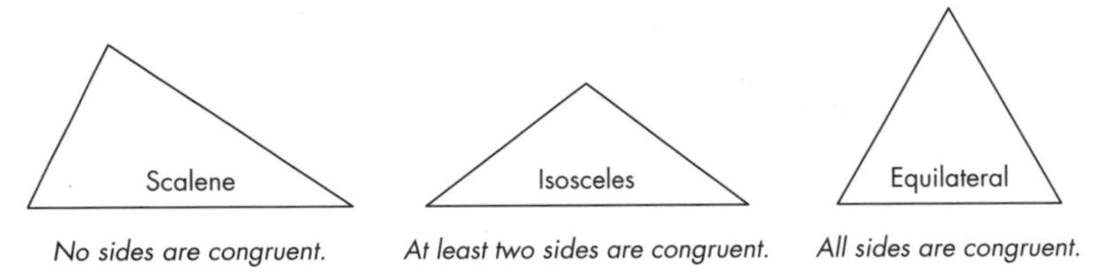

Figure 6-19: Classifying a triangle based on its sides

The game draws a triangle on the Stage and asks the player to classify that triangle as one of the three types. The user interface for this game is illustrated in Figure 6-20.

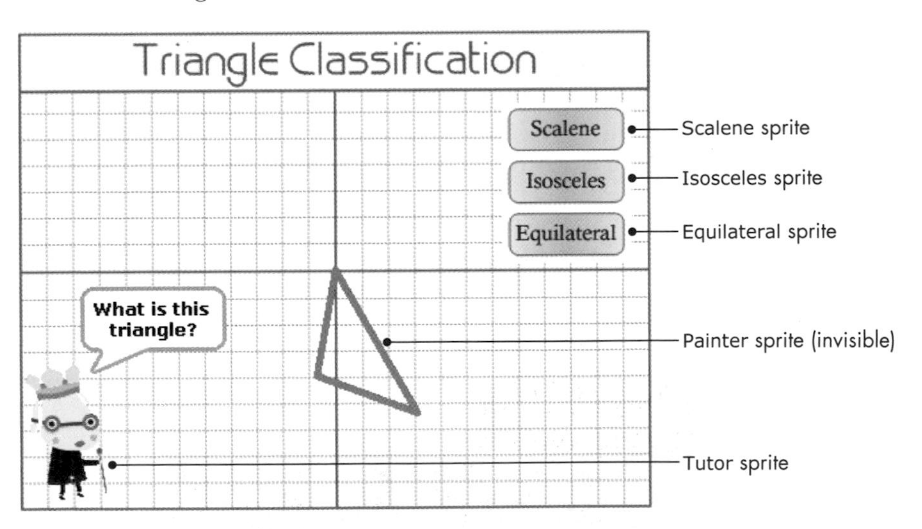

Figure 6-20: User interface for the triangle classification game

Figure 6-20 shows that this game contains five sprites. Three sprites (named Scalene, Isosceles, and Equilateral) represent the buttons the user clicks to select an answer, and the invisible Painter sprite draws the triangle on the Stage.

NOTE *I made the* Painter *sprite invisible by unchecking its Show checkbox in the sprite info area. If you prefer to control the sprite's visibility from the script, you can add a* **hide** *block to explicitly hide the sprite when the game starts.*

The Tutor sprite is the game's main driver; it determines the type of triangle to draw for each run and checks the user's answer. The scripts for the Tutor sprite are shown in Figure 6-21.

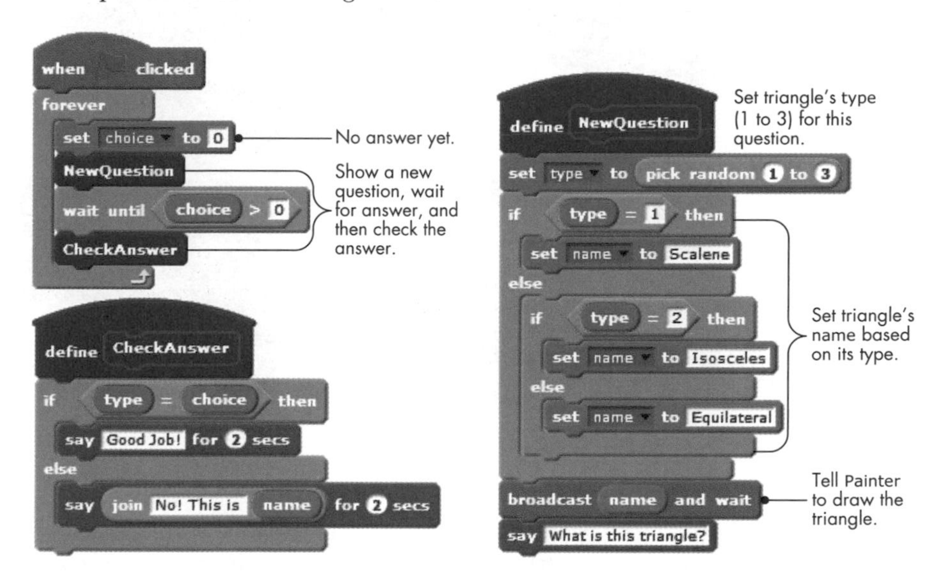

Figure 6-21: Scripts for the Tutor *sprite. The main driver script (top left) calls* **NewQuestion** *(right) and* **CheckAnswer** *(bottom left).*

When the green flag icon is clicked to start the game, the main script enters an infinite loop. On each pass of the loop, the script sets choice to 0 (to indicate that the player hasn't answered yet), draws a different triangle, and waits for an answer. The choice variable should change when the user clicks any of the three answer buttons. When the user clicks a button to classify the triangle, the script checks the answer and provides appropriate feedback. Let's look at each step in more detail.

The **NewQuestion** procedure starts by randomly setting type—which determines the type of the triangle to be drawn on the Stage—to 1, 2, or 3. The script then uses two **if/else** blocks to set the value of the name variable based on the value of type. The name variable serves two purposes: (1) it specifies which broadcast message to send so the Painter sprite knows what to draw (note how the **broadcast and wait** block uses name), and

(2) it is used in the **CheckAnswer** procedure to create the user's feedback message. When the Painter sprite finishes drawing, the **NewQuestion** procedure prompts the user for an answer with the **say** command.

When the Painter sprite receives the broadcast message, it draws the corresponding triangle on the Stage. To make the game more exciting, the Painter sprite uses random values for the triangle's size, orientation, and color, as shown in Figure 6-22.

```
when I receive Isosceles
Setup
move side steps
turn ↺ 10 * pick random 3 to 11 degrees
move side steps
go to x: 0 y: 0

when I receive Scalene
Setup
move side steps
turn ↺ 10 * pick random 3 to 9 degrees
move side + 40 steps
go to x: 0 y: 0

when I receive Equilateral
Setup
repeat 3
  move side steps
  turn ↺ 120 degrees

define Setup
go to x: 0 y: 0
point in direction 10 * pick random 0 to 18
set side to pick random 30 to 70
set pen color to pick random 1 to 200
set pen size to 5
pen down
clear
```

Figure 6-22: Scripts for the Painter *sprite*

After asking the user to classify the drawn triangle, the main script uses the **wait until** block (from the *Control* Palette) to pause until **choice > 0** becomes true. The three button sprites will change choice when they are clicked. The Scalene button sets choice to 1, the Isosceles button sets choice to 2, and the Equilateral button sets choice to 3 (see Figure 6-23).

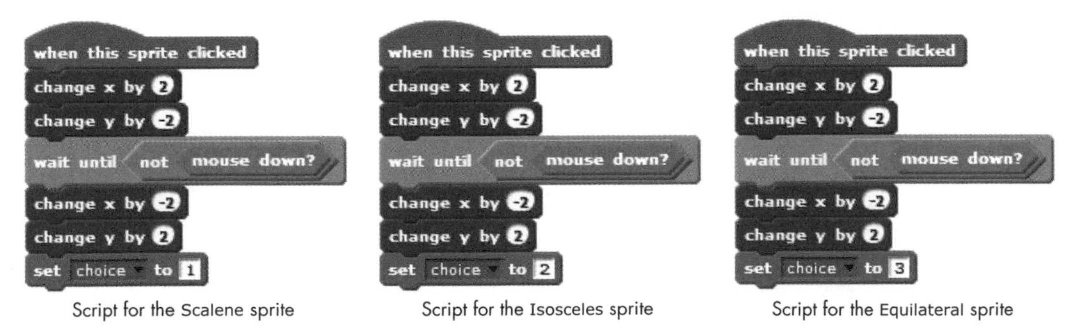

Figure 6-23: Scripts for the three button sprites

When a button is pressed, its sprite moves a little bit down and to the right to give the visual effect of a button press. When the mouse is released, the sprite returns to its original position and sets the value of the variable choice to indicate that the user clicked that button. Note that each sprite sets choice to a different number. The blocks for moving the buttons in these scripts are not strictly necessary and can be removed if desired.

Once the user chooses a triangle type, choice becomes greater than zero, and the main script calls the **CheckAnswer** procedure. This procedure compares the type variable (which specified the type of the drawn triangle) with the value of the choice variable. If the two variables have the same value, then the user's answer was correct. Otherwise, the user's answer was wrong, and the script will say the correct classification.

TRY IT OUT 6-2

Open this game and play it a few times. Once you understand how it works, try adding some extra functions. Here are a few ideas:

- Make the game keep score. It could add a point for each correct answer and deduct a point for each incorrect answer.
- Give the user an option to quit the game.
- Define a criterion for ending the game. For example, you could set the main repeat loop to run 20 times instead of forever. You could also stop the game after five incorrect answers.
- Have something exciting happen while the game is running. For example, you might create a variable named specialNumber and assign it a random value at the start of the game. When the number of correct answers matches specialNumber, the game could give the user bonus points, play music, or even tell a joke.
- Bring the buttons to life with graphics effects. For example, if you add the script shown below to each button, the buttons will change color when the mouse hovers over them.

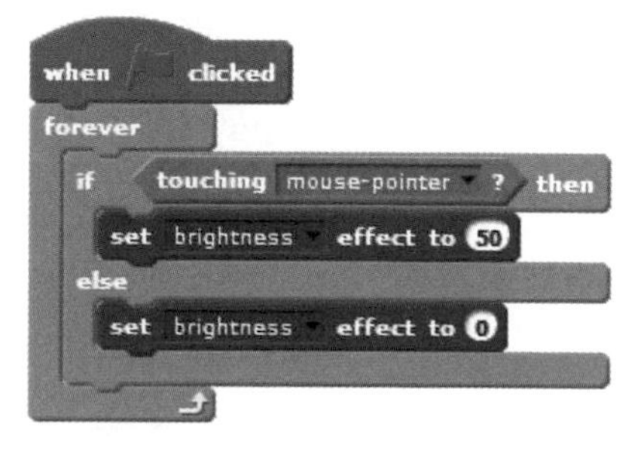

Line Follower

LineFollower.sb2

Can we make a sprite follow (or trace) a path on the Stage, like the one shown in Figure 6-24, all by itself? The answer is yes, and in this section, we'll write a program to do it. If you look closely at the sprite in the figure, you'll notice that we painted the nose and the two ears of the cat with different colors. The figure also shows an enlarged view of the cat's head.

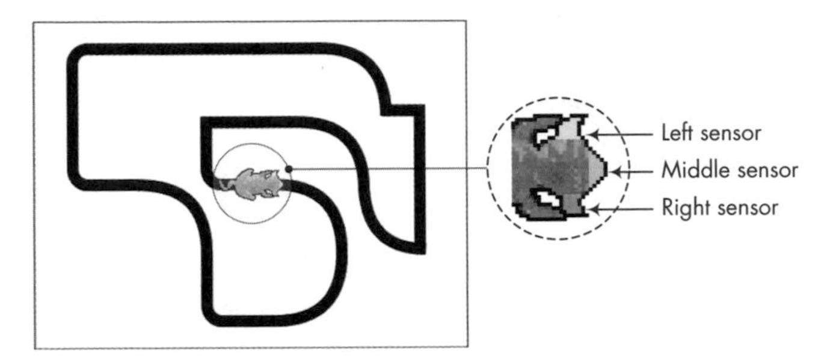

Figure 6-24: Sample path for a sprite to follow

The plan is to use the cat's nose and ears as color sensors for detecting the black line underneath. Our algorithm for tracing the black line uses the following *heuristics* (rules based primarily on logical reasoning and trial-and-error experimentation):

- If the nose of the cat (pink color) is touching the line, move forward.
- If the left ear of the cat (yellow color) is touching the line, turn counterclockwise and move forward at a reduced speed.
- If the right ear of the cat (green color) is touching the line, turn clockwise and move forward at a reduced speed.

Of course, the exact speed (movement steps) and turning angles can be different for different routes and have to be determined by experimentation. A script that implements the above algorithm and causes the sprite to follow the line is shown in Figure 6-25.

The script in Figure 6-25 uses a new block: **color is touching?** (from the *Sensing* palette). This block checks whether a color on the sprite (specified in the first color square) is touching another color (specified in the second color square). If the specified color on the sprite is touching the other color, the block returns true; otherwise, it returns false. The color in a color square can be chosen by clicking on the color square and then clicking anywhere in the Scratch project to pick the desired color.

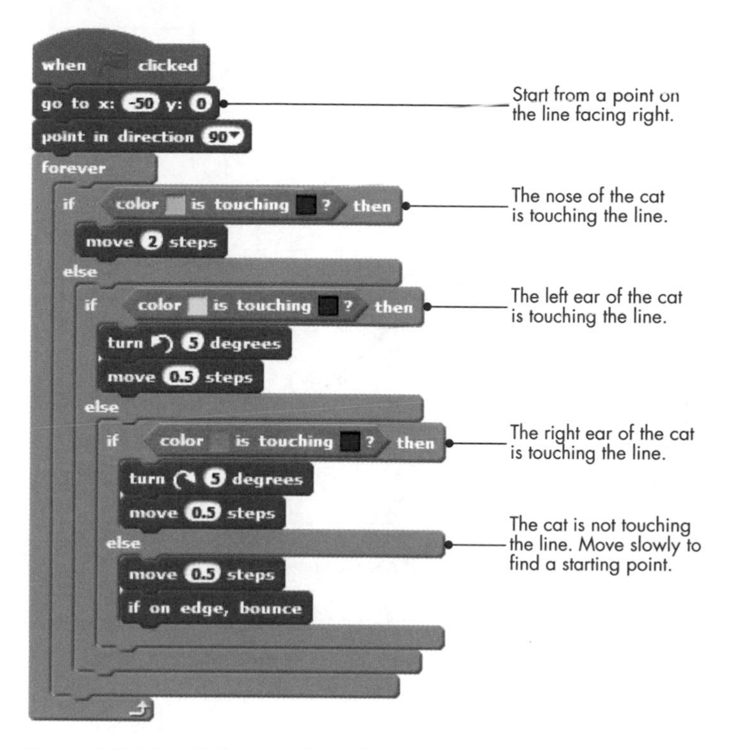
when clicked
go to x: -50 y: 0
point in direction 90
forever
if color is touching ? then
move 2 steps
else
if color is touching ? then
turn 5 degrees
move 0.5 steps
else
if color is touching ? then
turn 5 degrees
move 0.5 steps
else
move 0.5 steps
if on edge, bounce
Start from a point on the line facing right.
The nose of the cat is touching the line.
The left ear of the cat is touching the line.
The right ear of the cat is touching the line.
The cat is not touching the line. Move slowly to find a starting point.

Figure 6-25: Line-following algorithm

TRY IT OUT 6-3

Open the application and run it to see how it works. Experiment with the given values to make the sprite finish the track in the fastest possible time. One reviewer completed the track in 11 seconds. Can you beat the record? Create other tracks and see if this simple algorithm still works.

Equation of a Line

EquationOfALine.sb2

The equation of a line joining two points $P = (x_1, y_1)$ and $Q = (x_2, y_2)$ is $y = mx + b$, where $m = (y_2 - y_1) / (x_2 - x_1)$ is the slope of the line and b is the y-intercept. A vertical line has an equation of the form $x = k$, and a horizontal line has an equation of the form $y = k$, where k is a constant. In this section, we'll develop an application that finds the equation of the line that joins two points in the Cartesian plane. The user interface for the application is shown in Figure 6-26.

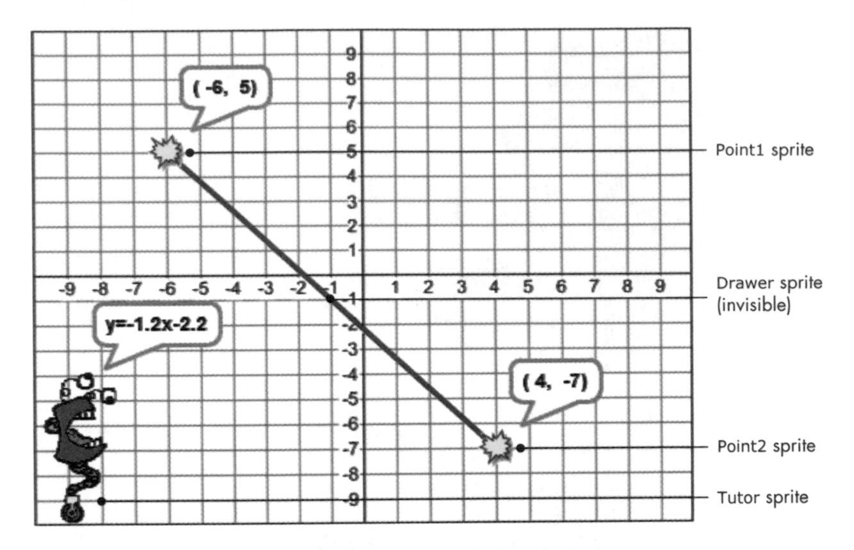

Figure 6-26: User interface for the equation-finder application

The user drags the two sprites representing the end points of the line onto the Stage, and the application automatically displays the equation of the resulting line. The application contains four sprites: Point1 and Point2 are used to mark the two end points of the line; Drawer is a hidden sprite that draws a straight line between the two points; and Tutor is responsible for computing and displaying the equation of the line.

The scripts for Point1 and Point2 are very similar. They contain some logic (not shown here) that restricts the sprites' locations to the intersection points of the grid. Essentially, when the user drags the Point1 sprite, it updates the variables that hold its coordinates (named X1 and Y1) and broadcasts Redraw. Similarly, when the user drags the Point2 sprite, it updates the variables that hold its coordinates (named X2 and Y2) and broadcasts the same message. All four variables (X1, X2, Y1, and Y2) can only take integer values in the range –9 to 9. You can find the details of these scripts in the file *EquationOfALine.sb2*. Let's now take a look at the scripts for the Drawer sprite, shown in Figure 6-27.

```
when clicked
set pen color to
set pen size to 4
pen down
clear
hide
```

```
when I receive Redraw
go to Point1
clear
go to Point2
```

Figure 6-27: Scripts for the Drawer *sprite*

When the game starts, this sprite sets its pen's size and color and gets ready to draw. When it receives the Redraw message, it moves to the Point1 sprite, clears the Stage, and then moves to the Point2 sprite. The result is a straight line that connects Point1 and Point2.

The Tutor sprite also executes a script when it receives the Redraw message, as shown in Figure 6-28.

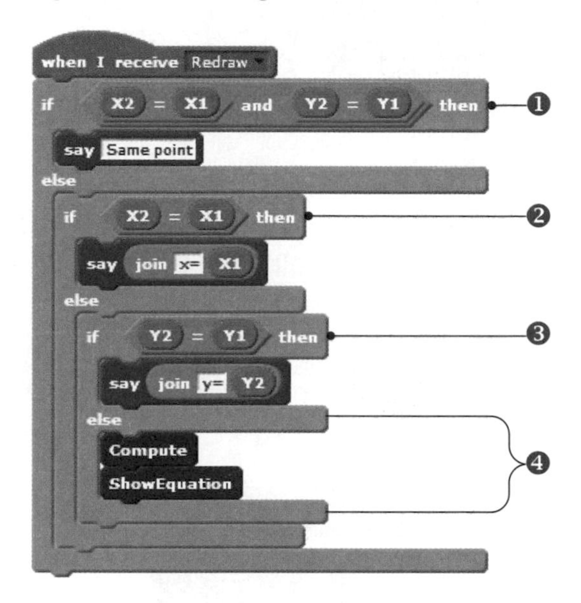

Figure 6-28: Redraw *message handler for the* Tutor *sprite*

The script performs the following checks:

- If the coordinates of Point1 and Point2 are the same, there is no line to process. The script simply says "Same point."
- If the two points are different but their *x*-coordinates are the same, then we have a vertical line. The script displays an equation of the form $x = constant$.
- If the two points are different but their *y*-coordinates are the same, then we have a horizontal line. The script displays an equation of the form $y = constant$.
- Otherwise, the two points form a straight line whose equation has the form $y = mx + b$. The script first calls the **Compute** procedure to find the slope and the *y*-intercept of the line. Then it calls **ShowEquation** to put the equation in a proper format and show it to the user.

The **Compute** procedure is shown in Figure 6-29. It computes the slope (m) and the *y*-intercept (b) and then rounds these values to the nearest hundredth.

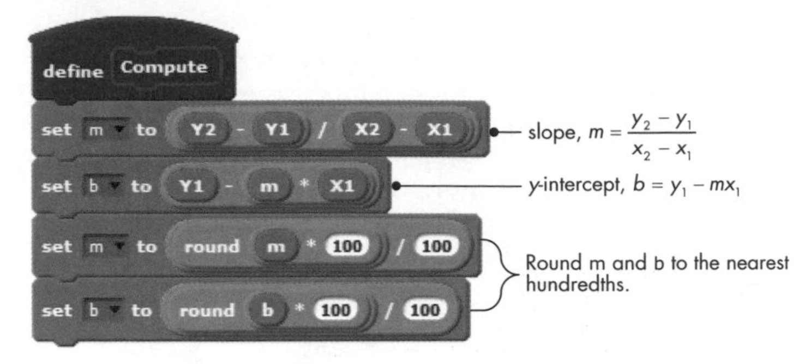

Figure 6-29: The **Compute** *procedure*

The **ShowEquation** procedure is shown in Figure 6-30. It uses two variables (term1 and term2) and two subprocedures to properly format the equation for display.

Figure 6-30: The **ShowEquation** *procedure*

The **ShowEquation** procedure considers the following special cases while formatting the line equation:

- If the slope is 1, term1 will be set to x (instead of $1x$).
- If the slope is –1, term1 will be set to $-x$ (instead of $-1x$).
- term2 is formed using the proper sign (plus or minus) of the y-intercept.
- If the y-intercept is 0, the equation will have the form $y = mx$.

TRY IT OUT 6-4

Open the application and run it. Drag the two points to different locations on the Stage and check the displayed equation. To enhance this application, try adding a script to move Tutor sprite out of the way if it overlaps with the coordinates displayed by the Point1 and Point2 sprites.

Other Applications

GuessMy Number.sb2

Now let's discuss some games you'll find in the extra resources for this book (download the extra resources from *http://nostarch.com/learnscratch/*). The supplementary material contains two classic games that you can explore on your own. The first is a "guess my number" game. The application secretly selects an integer at random between 1 and 100 and prompts the player to guess that number. The application then tells the player whether the guess was higher or lower than the secret number by displaying "too high" or "too low," respectively. The player has six chances to guess the secret number. A correct guess wins the game; otherwise, it's a loss.

RockPaper.sb2

The second game allows the user to play Rock, Paper, Scissors against the computer. The player makes a selection by clicking one of three buttons that represent rock, paper, or scissors. The computer makes a random selection. The winner is selected according to the following rules: Paper beats (wraps) rock, rock beats (breaks) scissors, and scissors beat (cut) paper.

Summary

In this chapter, you learned about the comparison operators in Scratch and used them to compare numbers, characters, and strings. After that, you learned about the **if** and **if/else** blocks and used them to make decisions and control actions in several programs. You also learned how to use nested **if** and **if/else** blocks for testing multiple conditions and applied this technique to develop a menu-driven application. You also learned about logical operators as an alternative, and more concise, way to test multiple conditions. Finally, you explored several complete applications that demonstrated decision-making structures in action.

The next chapter will take you deeper into the *Control* palette, showing you the various repetition structures available in Scratch and teaching you how to use them to write even more powerful programs.

Problems

1. What is the value of W after executing each command in this script?

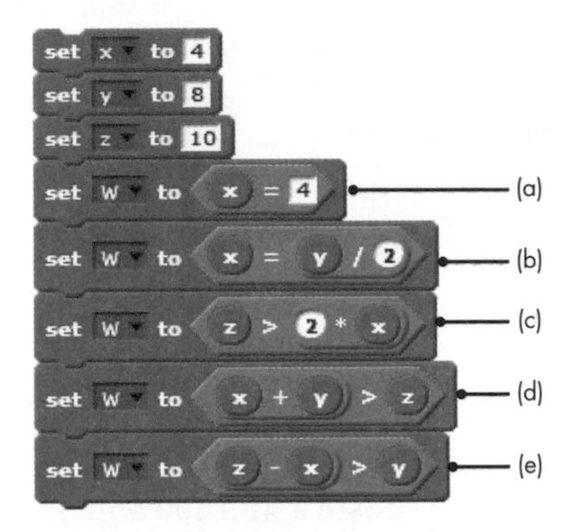

2. Express each of the following statements using an **if** block:
   a. If x divided by y is 5, then set x to 100.
   b. If x times y is 5, then set x to 1.
   c. If x is less than y, then double the value of x.
   d. If x is greater than y, then increment the value of x by 1.
3. Write a program that prompts the user to enter five test scores between 1 and 10. The program will then count the number of scores that are greater than 7.
4. Express each of the following statements using an **if/else** block:
   a. If x times y is 8, then set x to 1; otherwise, set x to 2.
   b. If x is less than y, then double the value of x; otherwise, increment x by 1.
   c. If x is greater than y, then increment both by 1; otherwise, decrement both by 1.
5. Trace through the script on the right for each of the following cases to find the output of each:
   a. x = –1, y = –1, z = –1
   b. x = 1, y = 1, z = 0
   c. x = 1, y = –1, z = 1
   d. x = 1, y = –1, z = –1

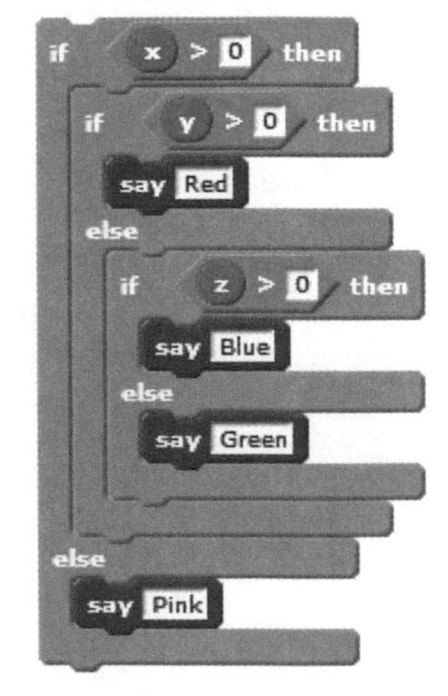

6. Write a program that asks the user to enter three numbers. The program will then determine and print the largest of the three numbers.
7. A company sells five different products whose retail prices are shown in the following table. Write a program that asks the user to enter the product number and the quantity sold. The program will then calculate and display the total retail value.

Product Number	Retail Price
1	$2.95
2	$4.99
3	$5.49
4	$7.80
5	$8.85

8. Construct a logical expression to represent each of the following conditions:
   a. score is greater than 90 and less than 95.
   b. answer is either y or yes.
   c. answer is an even number between 1 and 10.
   d. answer is an odd number between 1 and 10.
   e. answer is between 1 and 5 but not equal to 4.
   f. answer is between 1 and 100 and divisible by 3.
9. The *triangle inequality theorem* states that the sum of the lengths of any two sides of a triangle is greater than the length of the third side. Write a program that gets three numbers from the user and determines whether they could represent the sides of a triangle.
10. The *Pythagorean theorem* states that if a and b are the lengths of the legs of a right triangle and c is the length of the hypotenuse (the longest side), then $a^2 + b^2 = c^2$. Write a program that gets three numbers from the user and determines whether they could represent the sides of a right triangle.

7

REPETITION: A DEEPER EXPLORATION OF LOOPS

You've seen some of Scratch's repetition structures before, but this chapter covers them in greater detail. It's time to discuss new blocks that create loops, nested loops, and recursion. By the end of this chapter, we'll have explored the following programming concepts:

- Repetition structures to execute statements repeatedly
- How to validate user input
- Counter-controlled and event-controlled loops
- Procedures that can call themselves with recursion

Although most people find repetitive tasks boring, computers seem to like nothing more. *Repetition structures*, better known as *loops*, are programming commands that tell a computer to repeatedly execute a statement or a sequence of statements. The simplest kind of loop is a *definite loop*, which repeats a sequence of statements a specific number of times. These loops are also called *counter-controlled loops* or *counted loops*. Other types of loops continue to repeat until some condition occurs; these are called *condition-controlled loops* or *indefinite loops*. Another loop, called an *infinite loop*, repeats forever.

In this chapter, you'll learn about the different repetition structures available in Scratch. I'll explain both counter-controlled and condition-controlled loops in detail, and I'll introduce you to the **stop** block, which you can use to end infinite loops. You'll learn how to use loops to validate user input, as well.

The chapter also discusses *nested loops* (loops that contain other loops) and shows several examples of their use. We'll also talk about *recursion*—a procedure calling itself—as another way to achieve repetition. At last, we'll develop a number of interesting applications that use both loops and conditionals, and we'll look at incorporating loops into practical programs.

More Loop Blocks in Scratch

As you learned in Chapter 2, loop blocks allow you to repeat a command or a set of commands in a program. Scratch supports the three repetition blocks shown in Figure 7-1.

Figure 7-1: Scratch's repeat blocks

You've already used two of these blocks, the **repeat** and the **forever** blocks, in many examples throughout this book. In this section, we'll examine the third kind of loop block—the **repeat until** block—and explain some of the technical terms associated with loops in general.

Each repetition of a loop is called an *iteration*, and the word *count* is often used to describe the number of times a loop repeats. The **repeat** block, which you are very familiar with, is a counter-controlled loop because it repeats its commands a specific number of times. We usually use this loop when we know the number of repetitions the loop will need to execute, as when we want to draw a polygon with a known number of sides.

On the other hand, the **repeat until** block is a condition-controlled loop. The statements inside this block are repeated based on the truth or falsity of its test expression. We use this block when we don't know in advance how many times the loop will need to repeat and want the repetition to continue until some condition is met. You can say, for example, "Repeat the **ask** command until the user enters a positive number." Or, "Repeat firing missiles until the player's energy level drops below a certain value." The following sections explain condition-controlled loops in more detail.

The repeat until Block

Let's say you are developing a game that presents the player with an elementary math question. If the player's answer is incorrect, the game asks the same question again to give the player another chance. In other words, the game asks the same question *until* the player enters the correct answer. Clearly, the **repeat** block is inappropriate for this task because you don't know in advance how many times it will take the player to enter the right answer; the first try might be a winner, or it may take 100 tries. The **repeat until** block can help you in scenarios like this one. The structure of the **repeat until** block is illustrated in Figure 7-2.

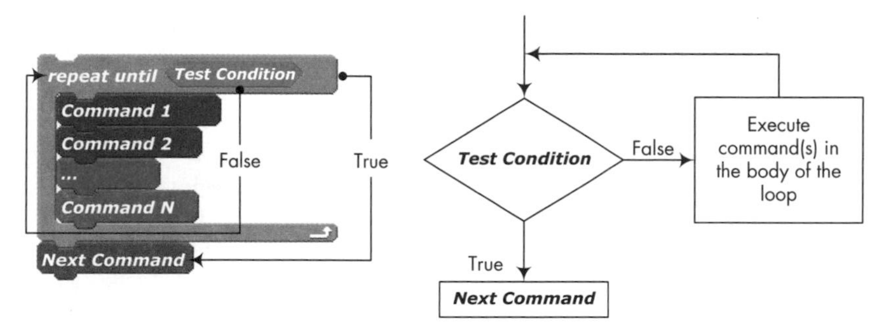

Figure 7-2: The **repeat until** *block allows you to execute a series of instructions repeatedly until some condition is true.*

This block contains a Boolean expression whose value is tested at the entry of the loop. If the expression is false, the commands inside the loop are executed. When the last command in the loop is executed, the loop starts over, and the expression is tested again. If the expression is still false, the commands inside the loop are executed again. This cycle repeats *until* the test expression becomes true. When that happens, the commands inside the loop are skipped, and the program moves to the command that immediately follows the loop.

Note that if the test condition is already true before the program runs the loop the first time, the commands in the loop won't be executed. Also, the **repeat until** block won't terminate unless a command (either inside the loop or in some other active part of the program) causes the test condition to become true. If the result of the test condition never becomes true, we get into an infinite loop.

Figure 7-3 shows a practical example of using the **repeat until** block. In this example, as long as the Player sprite is more than 100 steps away from the Guard sprite, the Guard sprite will continue to move in its current direction (horizontally in this case), bouncing when it touches the left or the right edge of the Stage. If the distance between the two sprites becomes less than 100, the **repeat until** block will terminate, and the Guard sprite will start to chase the Player sprite. The code for the chase is not shown in the figure. The **distance to** block is found in the *Sensing* palette.

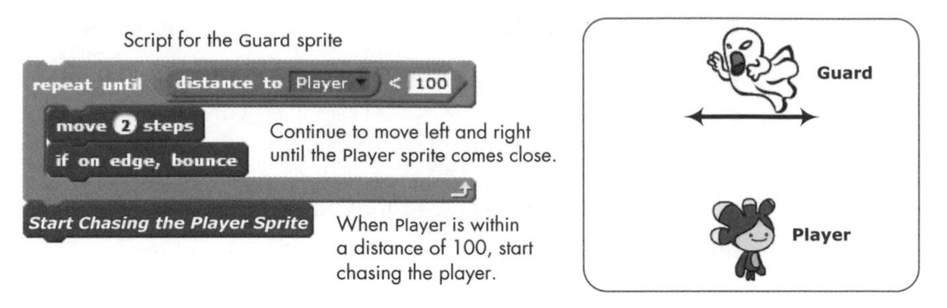

Figure 7-3: A simple example showing the **repeat until** *block in action*

Chase.sb2

TRY IT OUT 7-1

Open the application *Chase.sb2* and run it. Use the arrow keys to move the Player sprite close to the Guard to see the chase in action. How would you change the test condition to unleash the Guard sprite if the *y*-position of the Player sprite goes outside a certain range (for example, –50 to 50)? Implement this change to check your solution.

Building a forever if Block

Infinite loops are useful in a lot of programming situations. In the previous chapters, for example, you used the **forever** block to play background music, and you animated sprites by changing their costumes continuously. The **forever** block is an *unconditional infinite loop* because it doesn't have a test condition that controls the execution of the commands inside it.

You can easily change that, however, by nesting an **if** block inside a **forever** block to create a *conditional infinite loop*, as shown in Figure 7-4. The test condition of the **if** block is tested at the beginning of every iteration, and its commands only execute when the test condition is true. Note that since the **forever** block is supposed to execute forever, you can't snap command blocks after it.

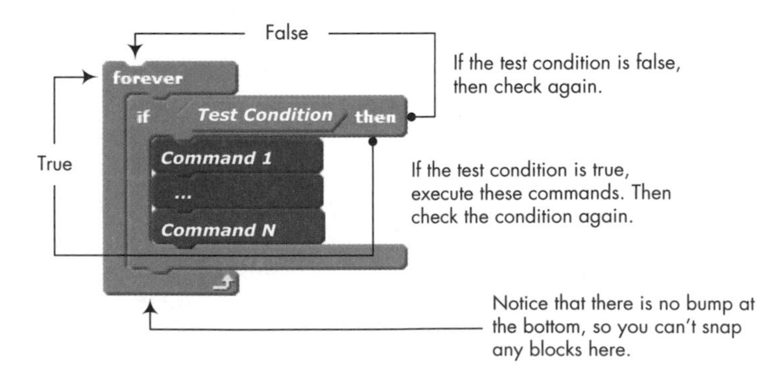

Figure 7-4: You can create a **forever/if** *loop by combining a* **forever** *block with an* **if** *block.*

The combined **forever/if** structure is frequently used to control sprite movement with the keyboard arrow keys, as demonstrated in Figure 7-5.

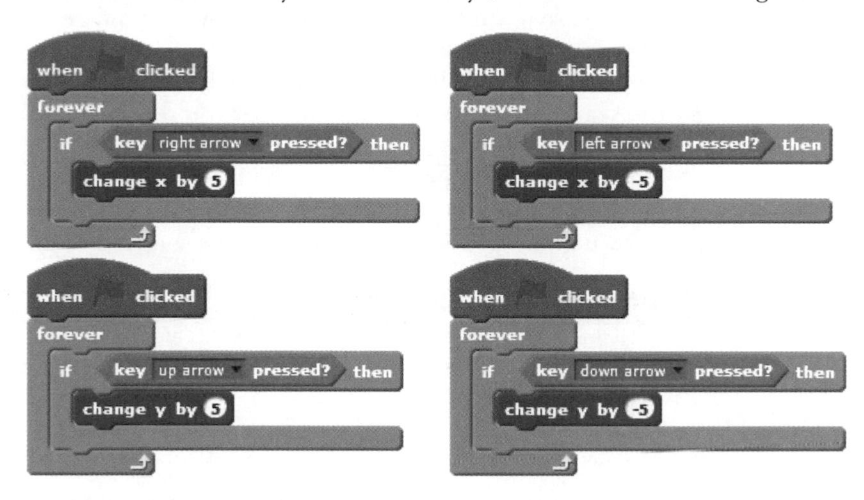

Figure 7-5: These scripts allow you to move a sprite using the keyboard arrow keys. Each script responds to one of the four keys.

ArrowKeys1.sb2

When the green flag icon is pressed, the four keyboard arrow keys (left, right, up, and down) are monitored in four independent infinite loops. When any of these keys is pressed, the corresponding loop causes a change in the *x*- or *y*-coordinate of the sprite.

Create these scripts in Scratch (or open *ArrowKeys1.sb2*) and run the program. Notice that if you press the up and right arrow keys simultaneously, the sprite will move diagonally in the northeast direction. Try other combinations of the arrow keys to see how the application responds.

TRY IT OUT 7-2

Another way to control the sprite's movement with the arrow keys is shown below. Compare this method to the one shown in Figure 7-5. Which is more responsive to keyboard strokes? How does the alternate script behave if you press two keys (for example, up and right) simultaneously? Now, try placing the four **if** blocks in Figure 7-5 together in a single **forever** loop and press two arrow keys at the same time. How does the sprite's behavior change?

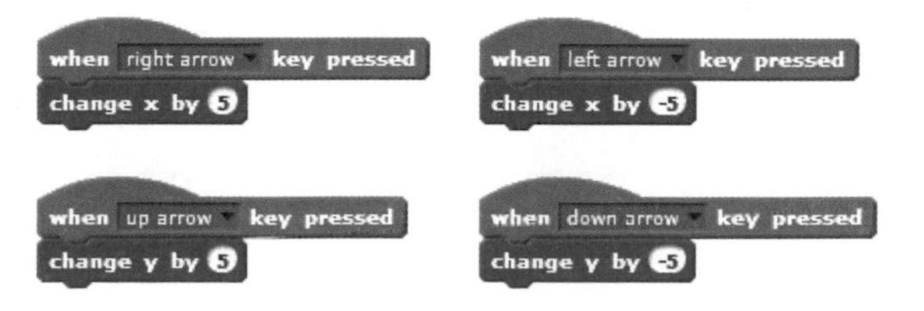

Stop Commands

Let's say you're writing a program to find the first integer less than 1,000 that is evenly divisible by 3, 5, and 7. You can write a script that checks the numbers 999, 998, 997, and so on, one by one, in a loop. You want to *stop* the search when you find the number you're looking for (945 in this example).

How can you tell Scratch to end the loop and stop the script? You can use the **stop** command (from the *Control* palette) to end active scripts. The drop-down menu provides the three options shown in Figure 7-6.

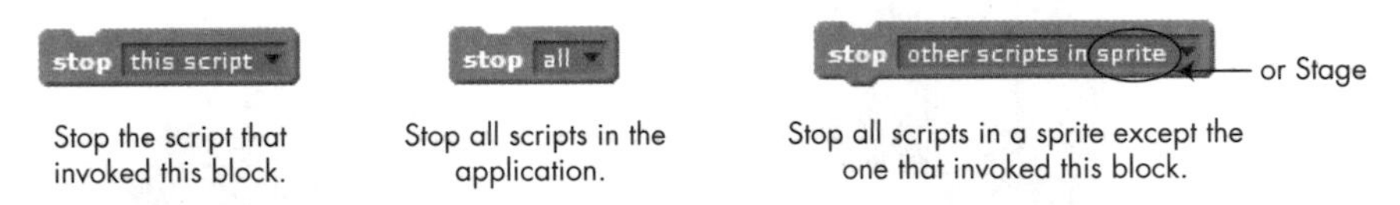
stop this script
stop all
stop other scripts in sprite
or Stage
Stop the script that invoked this block.
Stop all scripts in the application.
Stop all scripts in a sprite except the one that invoked this block.

*Figure 7-6: Using the **stop** command in Scratch*

The first option immediately terminates the script that calls it. The second option, on the other hand, stops all running scripts in your application; it is equivalent to the red stop icon located at the top of the Stage. Note that you can't snap any commands after the **stop** block when you use either of these two options.

StopDemo.sb2

The third **stop** option allows a sprite or the Stage to end all of its scripts except the one that invoked the **stop** block. This command is shaped as a stack block, so you can add blocks below it to execute after it suspends the sprite's other scripts. Let's see this command in action in a simple game, illustrated in Figure 7-7.

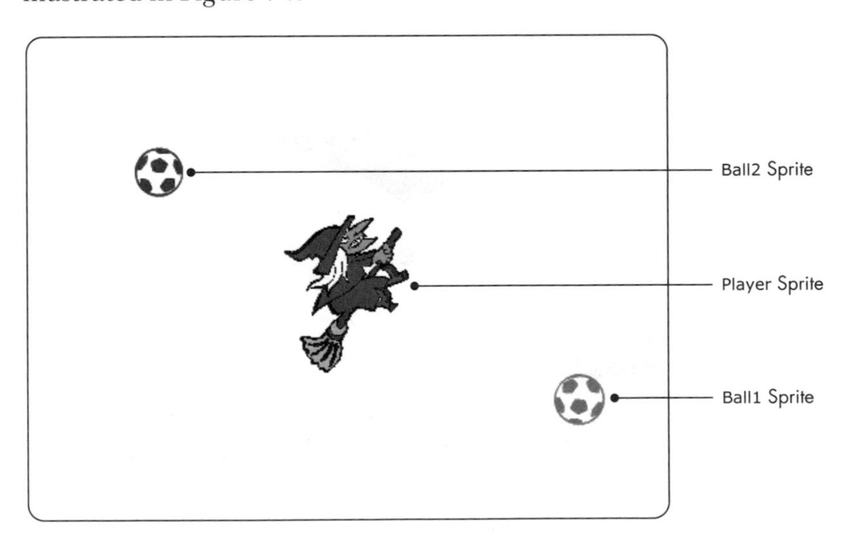
Ball2 Sprite
Player Sprite
Ball1 Sprite

Figure 7-7: In this game, the player moves the witch on the Stage while trying to avoid the two balls.

The two balls in this figure move around the Stage and chase the witch. The player moves the witch sprite with the keyboard and tries to avoid being touched by the two balls. If the red ball touches the player at any time, the game ends. If the green ball touches the player, it will stop chasing the player, but the red ball will start to move a little faster—which makes escaping it a real challenge.

The scripts for moving the witch sprite are similar to those of Figure 7-5, so I won't show them here. The scripts for the two balls are shown in Figure 7-8—let's take a look at those.

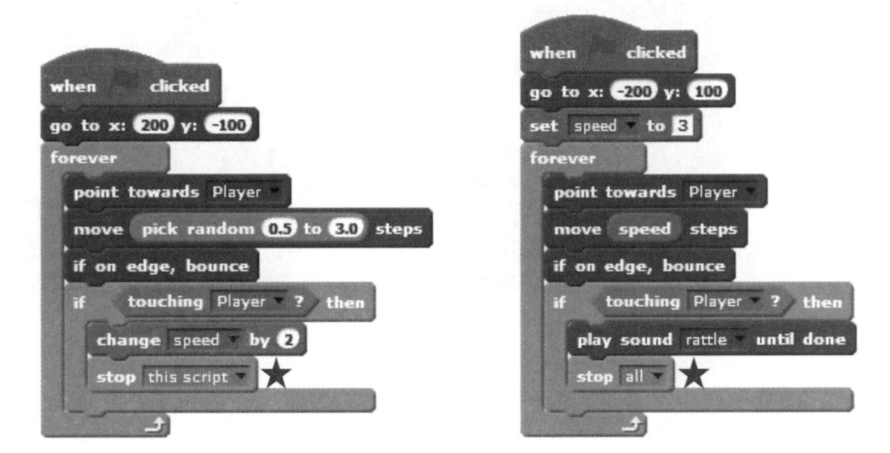

Figure 7-8: Scripts for the green ball (left) and red ball (right)

When the green ball touches the player, it increases the speed variable (which sets the movement speed of the red ball), and it invokes the **stop this script** command to terminate its script. All other scripts in the game should continue to run normally. Using the **stop this script** command works well here because we only want to speed up the red ball once. If the red ball touches the player, however, it executes the **stop all** command, which causes all running scripts in the application to stop.

TRY IT OUT 7-3

Load this game and play it to see how it works. Watch what happens to the yellow border around the two scripts of Figure 7-8 when the green and the red balls touch the Player.

You can also use the **stop** block to terminate a procedure and make it return to the caller at any point during its execution. The next section shows this concept in action.

Ending a Computational Loop

NumberSearch .sb2

Let's say that we want to find the first power of 2 that is larger than 1,000. We'll write a procedure that checks the numbers 2^1, 2^2, 2^3, 2^4, and so on, in a loop. When we find the number we need, we want the program to say the answer and stop the procedure. Figure 7-9 shows two ways to implement this approach.

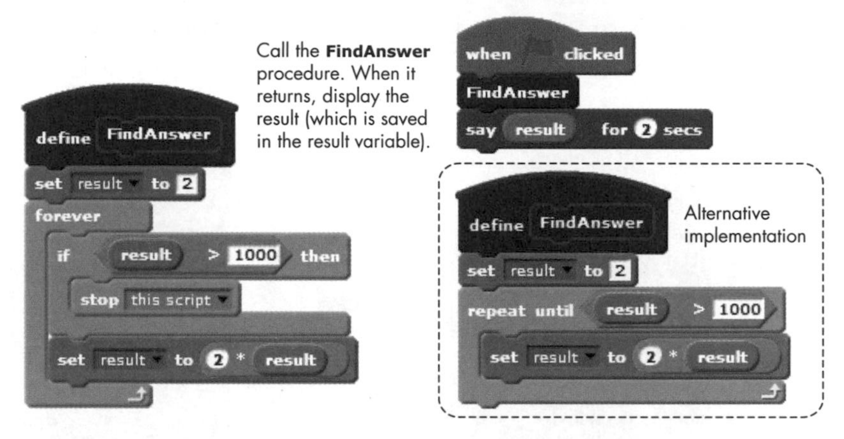

Figure 7-9: Two ways to find the first power of 2 that is larger than 1,000

The procedure on the left in Figure 7-9 initializes the result variable to 2, which is the first power of 2 to be checked, and enters an infinite loop in search for the answer. It checks the value of result in each iteration of the loop. If result is greater than 1,000, the procedure invokes the **stop this script** command to stop and return to the caller. Otherwise, the command after the **if** block (which multiplies the previous value of result by 2) executes, and the next iteration of the loop begins. If you trace through this procedure, you'll see that the **if** block finds result to be 2 in the first iteration, 4 in the second iteration, 8 in the third iteration, and so on. This continues until result exceeds 1,000; at this point, the procedure stops and returns to the caller, which displays the result using the **say** block.

Figure 7-9 (right) shows another way to implement the procedure. Here, we used a **repeat until** block that continues to loop until result becomes greater than 1,000. As in the first implementation, the loop continues to double the value of result until it exceeds 1,000. When this happens, the loop terminates naturally, and the procedure returns to the caller. Note that we did not have to use the **stop** block in this case.

The **stop** block is also useful when you need to validate input from users. You'll see an example of this practical application next.

Validating User Input

When you write an application that reads some data from the user, you should always check that the entered values are valid before starting to process the data. Repetition structures can help you with this task. If the user's input is invalid, you can use a loop to display an appropriate error message and ask the user to reenter the value.

To demonstrate, let's say that you are developing a game with two levels and you want to let the user select a level to play. The only valid entries in this case are the numbers 1 and 2. If the user enters a number other than these two numbers, you'd like to offer another chance to enter an acceptable value. One way to implement this check is shown in Figure 7-10.

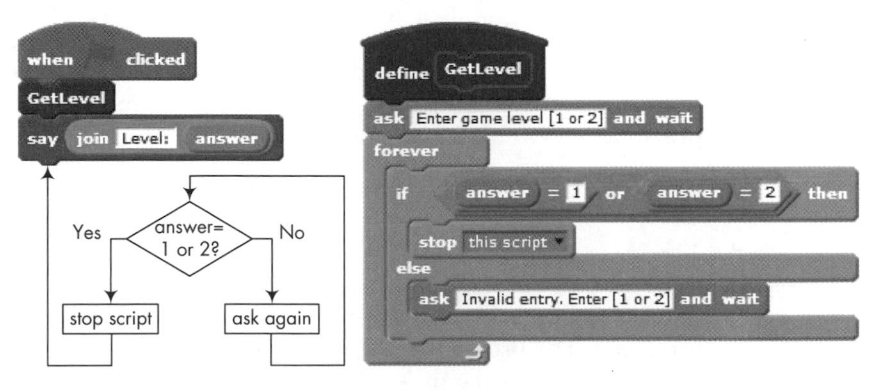

Figure 7-10: Input validation using the **forever** *block*

The **GetLevel** procedure asks the user to enter a choice and checks the answer inside a **forever** loop. If the user's answer is invalid, the loop prompts the user to reenter the level. If the user enters a valid number, the procedure calls **stop this script** to terminate the loop and end the procedure. When this happens, the main script, which has been patiently waiting for the **GetLevel** procedure to return, moves on to execute the **say** command. Figure 7-11 shows how to achieve the same task using the **repeat until** block.

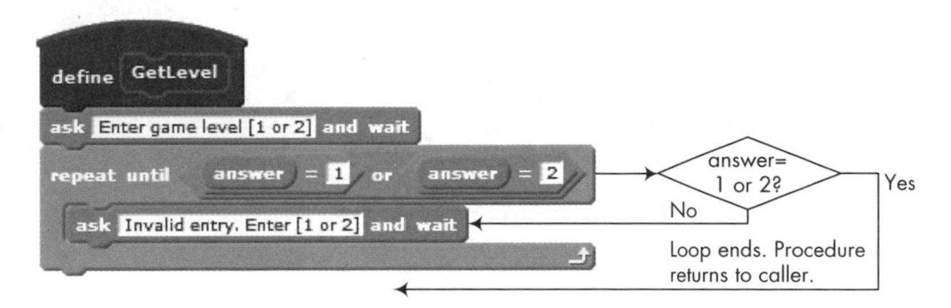

Figure 7-11: Input validation using the **repeat until** *block*

The procedure in Figure 7-11 asks the user to enter a choice and waits for the answer. If the user enters 1 or 2, the condition in the header of the **repeat until** block evaluates to true, which naturally terminates the loop and ends the procedure. On the other hand, if the user enters anything other than 1 or 2, the loop's condition evaluates to false, and the **ask** command inside the loop executes. This command waits for the user's input again, and the **repeat until** block will continue asking for input until the user enters a valid choice. Once again, note that this implementation doesn't require a **stop** block.

Counters

Sometimes, you'll need to keep track of the number of iterations a loop performs. For example, if you want to give users only three chances to enter the correct password, you'll have to count their attempts and lock them out after the third try.

You can handle such programming scenarios by using a variable (commonly referred to as the *loop counter*) that counts the number of loop iterations. Let's jump right in and explore some examples that demonstrate practical ways to use loop counters.

Check a Password

Password Check.sb2

The program in Figure 7-12 asks the user to enter a password for unlocking a laptop. The Laptop sprite has two costumes: the off image indicates that the laptop is locked, and the on image indicates that the laptop is unlocked. The user will be denied access to the laptop if an invalid password is entered three times.

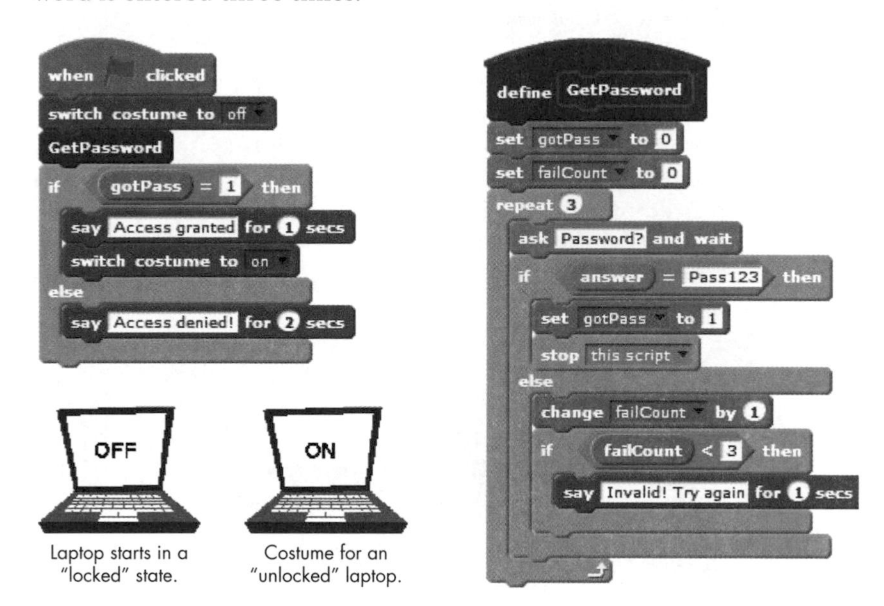

Figure 7-12: This script gives the user three chances to enter the correct password.

When the green flag is clicked, the Laptop sprite switches to the off costume and calls the **GetPassword** procedure to authenticate the user. This procedure is expected to return the password check result to the main script using the gotPass flag. When the procedure returns, the **if/else** block checks the gotPass flag to decide whether or not the user should be allowed to access the system. If gotPass was set to 1, meaning the user entered the correct password, the **if** block executes a **say** command that displays *Access* *granted* and changes the laptop's costume to the on image. Otherwise, the script displays *Access denied!* and the sprite continues to show its initial off costume.

The **GetPassword** procedure sets the gotPass flag to 0, to indicate that it hasn't received a valid password yet, and initializes the failCount variable (our loop counter) to 0. It then executes a **repeat** loop with a maximum repeat count of three. During each iteration of the loop, the user is prompted to enter a password. If the user enters the correct password (Pass123 in this example), the gotPass flag is set to 1, the procedure stops itself by invoking the **stop this script** command, and execution returns to the caller. Otherwise, if the user hasn't used up all three attempts, an error message is displayed, and the user is given another chance. If the user fails three consecutive times, the **repeat** loop automatically terminates, and the procedure returns to the caller with the value of the gotPass flag still set to 0.

TRY IT OUT 7-4

Open this application and run it. What happens if you enter paSS123 (instead of Pass123) for the password? What does this tell you about string comparison in Scratch? Try to implement the **GetPassword** procedure using a **repeat until** block.

Counting by a Constant Amount

CountingBy ConstAmount .sb2

Of course, you don't always have to increase your counters by 1 each time through a loop. The script in Figure 7-13 at ❶, for example, has a sprite count from 5 to 55 in increments of 5. The script at ❷ causes the sprite to count down from 99 to 0 in decrements of 11—in other words, 99, 88, 77, ... , 11, 0.

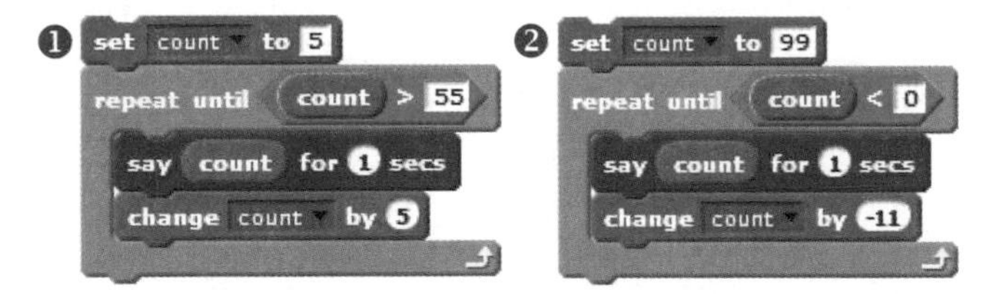

Figure 7-13: You can increment and decrement counters by amounts other than 1.

To see this counting technique in a practical application, let's say that we want to find the sum of all even integers from 2 to 20 (inclusive). (That is, we want the sum 2 + 4 + 6 + 8 + ... + 20.) The script of Figure 7-14 does exactly that.

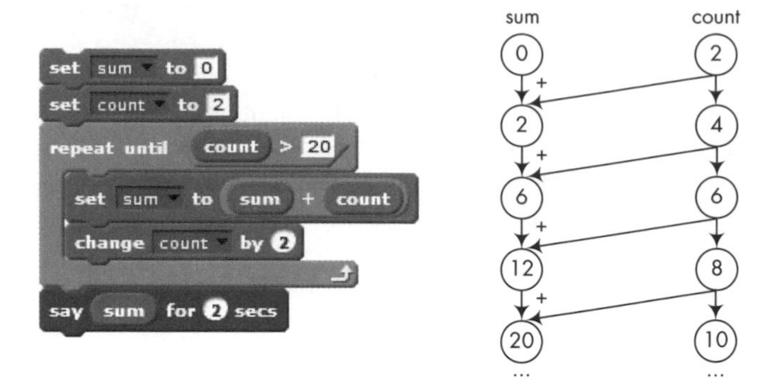

Figure 7-14: This script finds the sum of all even integers from 2 to 20.

This script starts by initializing the sum variable to 0 and the count variable to 2, and then enters a conditional loop that repeats until count exceeds 20. Each time the loop iterates, the value of count is added to the current sum and the count variable is increased by 2 to get the next even integer in the sequence. Predict the output of this script then run it to check your answer.

Non-Integer RepeatCount.sb2

NON-INTEGER REPEAT COUNT

What do you think would happen if you asked Scratch to repeat a loop 2.5 times? The three examples shown below demonstrate how Scratch handles non-integer repeat counts.

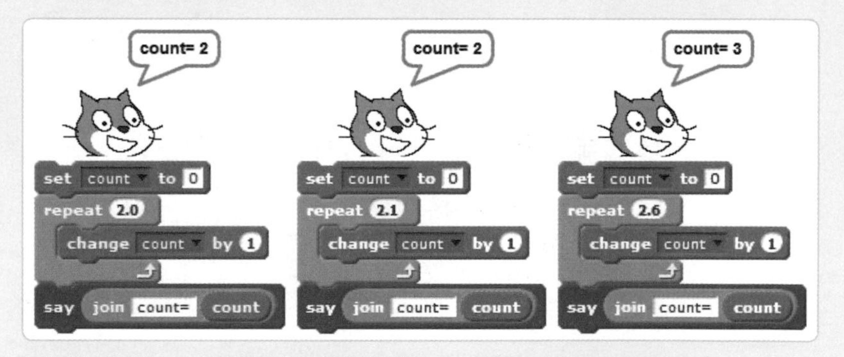

Of course, there is no such thing as "repeat 2.5 times," but Scratch doesn't prevent you from entering such values. Rather than giving an error message, Scratch automatically rounds a decimal repeat count to its nearest integer.

Revisiting Nested Loops

Back in "Rotated Squares" on page 34, we used nested loops to draw rotated squares. One loop (the *inner loop*) was responsible for drawing the square, while the other loop (the *outer loop*) controlled the number of rotations. In this section, you'll learn how to use the concept of loop counters in conjunction with nested loops to create iterations in two (or more) dimensions. This technique is an essential part of programming and, as you'll see in a moment, can be used to solve a wide range of programming problems.

To set the stage, let's say that a local restaurant offers four kinds of pizza (P1, P2, P3, and P4) and three kinds of salads (S1, S2, and S3). If you ate there, you would have 12 possible combinations to choose from; you could have P1 with any of three salad types, P2 with any of three salad types, and so on. The restaurant's owner wants to print out a menu that lists the available pizza/salad combinations along with their combined prices and calorie contents. Let's see how nested loops can be used to generate a list of all possible combinations. (I'll leave calculating the prices and calorie content as an exercise for you.)

If you think about it, you'll see that we just need two loops: one loop (the outer loop) to cycle through the pizza types and another loop (the inner loop) to cycle through the salad types. The outer loop starts with P1, while the inner loop tries S1, S2, and S3. The outer loop then moves to P2, and the inner loop again chooses S1, S2, and S3. This continues until the outer loop has passed through all four pizza types. An implementation of this idea is illustrated in Figure 7-15.

NestedLoops1.sb2

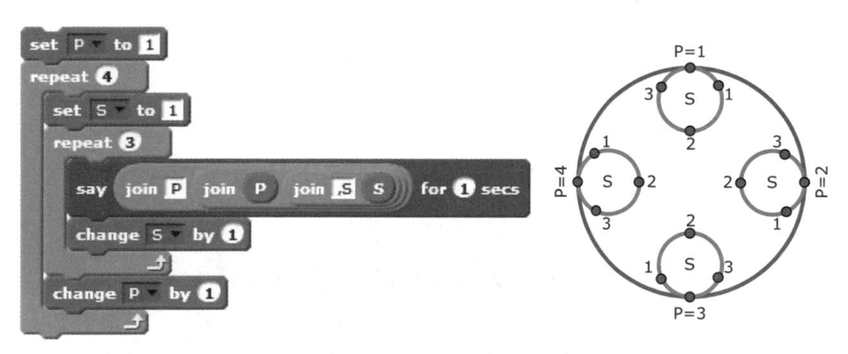

Figure 7-15: Visualizing nested loops. The variable P *controls the outer loop and the variable* S *controls the inner loop.*

The script uses two loops and two counters. The counter for the outer loop is named P, and the counter for the inner loop is named S. In the first iteration of the outer loop (where P = 1), the value of counter S is set to 1, and the inner loop repeats three times. Each time, it executes a **say** command to display the current values of P and S, and then it increments S by 1. Thus, the first iteration of the outer loop causes the sprite to say "P1,S1" and "P1,S2" and "P1,S3."

When the inner loop terminates after looping three times, P is incremented by 1, and the second iteration of the outer loop starts. The value of S is reset to 1, and the inner loop is executed again. This causes the sprite to say "P2,S1" and "P2,S2" and "P2,S3." The process continues in a similar manner, causing the sprite to say "P3,S1" and "P3,S2" and "P3,S3" and finally "P4,S1" and "P4,S2" and "P4,S3" before the script ends. Trace through this script to make sure you understand how it works.

Now that you've seen what nested loops can do, let's apply this technique to solve an interesting math problem. We want to write a program to find three positive integers n_1, n_2, and n_3 such that $n_1 + n_2 + n_3 = 25$ and $(n_1)^2 + (n_2)^2 + (n_3)^2 = 243$. Because computers are good at repetitive tasks, our plan is to try all possible combinations of numbers (a technique called *exhaustive search*) and let the computer do the hard work.

Based on our first equation, the first number, n_1, can have any value between 1 and 23 since we'll need to add two numbers to it to get 25. (You might have noticed that n_1 can't be more than 15 because $16^2 = 256$, which is greater than 243. But we'll just ignore our second equation for now and set the upper limit of the loop to 23 anyway.)

The second number, n_2, can be any value between 1 and $24 - n_1$. For example, if n_1 is 10, the maximum possible value of n_2 is 14 because n_3 must be at least 1. If we know n_1 and n_2, we can compute n_3 as $25 - (n_1 + n_2)$. Then, we'll need to check whether the sum of the squares of these three numbers is 243. If it is, we are done. Otherwise, we need to try a different combination of n_1 and n_2. You can see the finished script to find n_1, n_2, and n_3 in Figure 7-16.

NestedLoops2.sb2

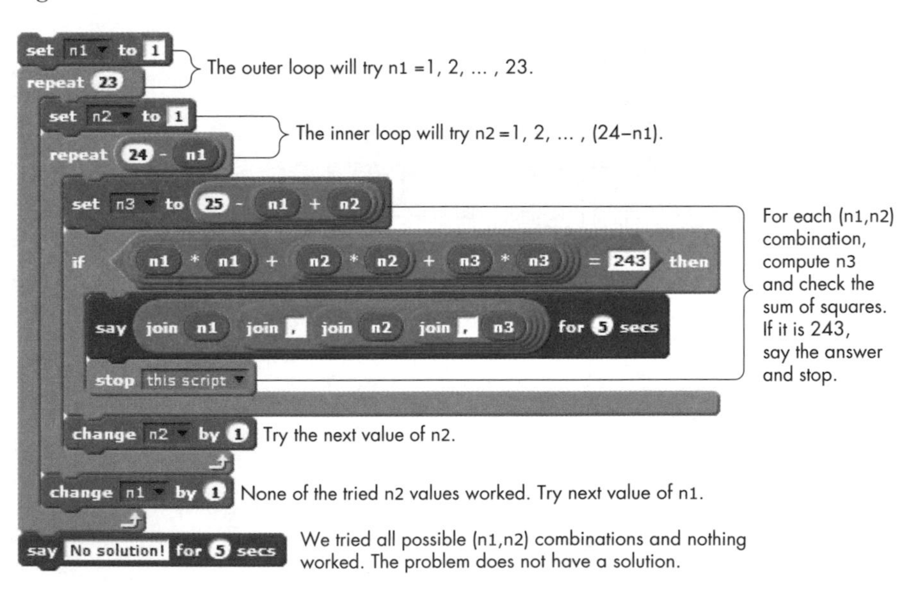

Figure 7-16: This script searches for three positive numbers whose sum is 25 and whose sum of squares is 243.

The outer loop tries all values of n1 from 1 to 23. For each value of n1, the inner loop tries all values of n2 from 1 to (24 – n1). For each combination of n1 and n2, the script sets n3 equal to 25 – (n1 + n2), and then it checks to see whether the sum of the squares of these three numbers is 243. If it is, the script says the answer and stops.

TRY IT OUT 7-5

Create the script shown in Figure 7-16 and run it to find n_1, n_2, and n_3. If you study the script carefully, you'll find that it tries some (n_1, n_2) combinations more than once. For example, the numbers (1, 2) are tested in the first iteration of the outer loop, whereas the numbers (2, 1) are tried in the second iteration. These two tests are redundant; we only need one of them. You can fix this by having the inner loop start from n_1 instead of 1. Make this change to the script and then run it to make sure it still works as expected.

Recursion: Procedures That Call Themselves

Recursion.sb2

The repetition structures introduced so far allow us to repeat a command or a set of commands through iteration. Another powerful technique that produces repetition is *recursion*. Recursion allows a procedure to either call itself directly or do so indirectly through another procedure (for example, A calls B, B calls C, then C calls A). It may not be obvious why you want to do this, but it turns out that recursion can simplify the solution of many computer science problems. Let's demonstrate this concept by considering the simple example shown in Figure 7-17.

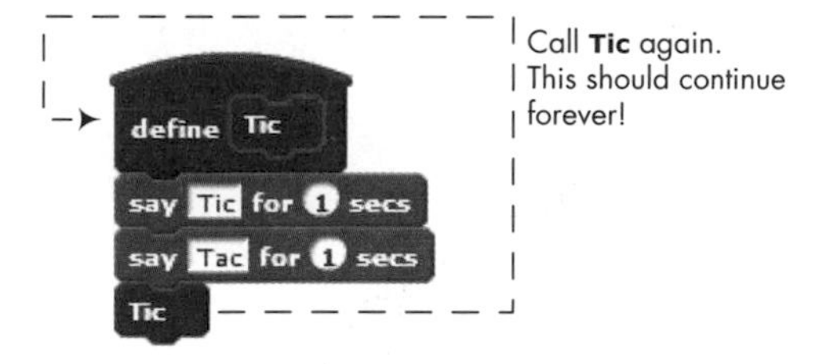

Figure 7-17: A recursive procedure

The **Tic** procedure executes two **say** commands (the first says "Tic" and the second says "Tac"), then calls itself again. The second call does the same thing, and the sprite would continue saying, "Tic Tac" forever if no outside action stopped it. Of course, the only way to stop it in this case is to click the red stop icon. Having a procedure call itself this way allowed us to repeat the two **say** commands forever without using any loop blocks. The form of recursion used in this example is called *tail recursion* because the recursive call is located at the very end of the procedure. Scratch also allows recursive calls to come before the last line, but we won't explore that type of recursion in this book.

Since infinite recursion is generally not a good idea, you must control the execution of a recursive procedure with conditionals. For example, the procedure could include an **if** block that determines whether the recursive call should be made. To demonstrate this technique, Figure 7-18 shows a recursive procedure that counts from some initial number (specified by the parameter count) down to 0.

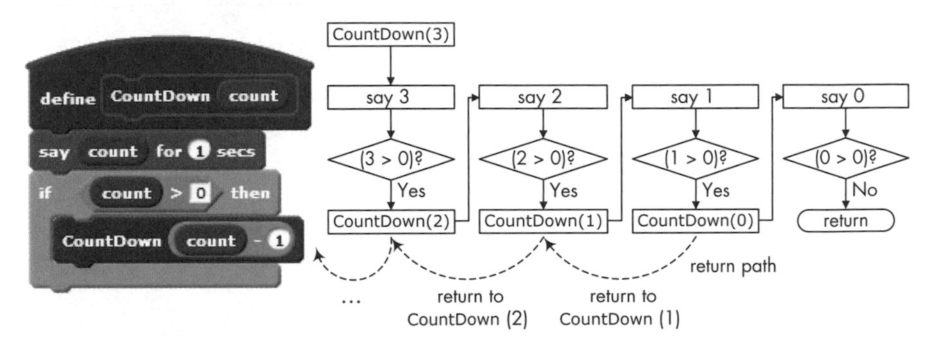

*Figure 7-18: The **if** block is used to determine whether (or not) the recursive call should be made.*

Let's walk through how **CountDown** works when it is called with an argument of three. When the procedure starts, the **say** command shows the number 3, then checks whether count is greater than 0. Since 3 is greater than 0, the procedure subtracts 1 from count to call itself with an argument of 2.

In the second call, the procedure shows the number 2 and, because 2 is greater than 0, calls itself one more time with an argument of 1. This continues until the call CountDown(0) is made. After showing the number 0 in a voice bubble, the procedure checks whether count is greater than 0. Since the expression in the header of the **if** block evaluates to false, no further recursive calls will be made, and the procedure returns. Try to follow the return path shown in Figure 7-18.

Now that we've covered the basics of tail recursion, we can apply it to more interesting applications. Let's consider, for example, the **Blade** procedure shown in Figure 7-19.

RecursionBlade .sb2

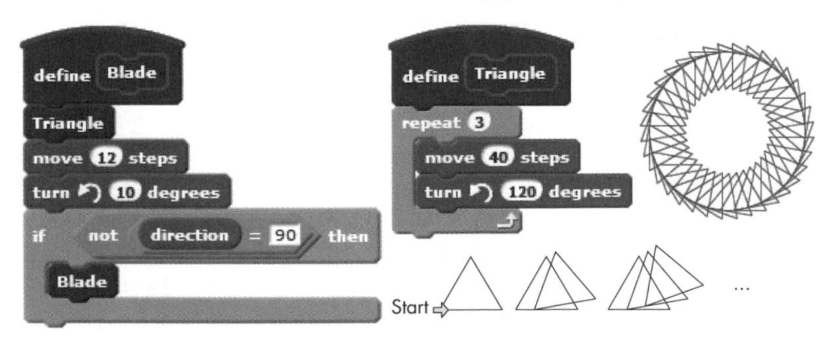

Figure 7-19: Using a sprite's direction to stop recursion

We assume that the sprite that executes this procedure starts somewhere on the Stage pointing in the direction of 90°. After drawing an equilateral triangle, the sprite moves 12 steps forward and then turns 10° counterclockwise. The procedure then checks the new direction of the sprite. If the sprite is not pointing in the direction of 90°, the procedure calls itself again to draw the next triangle in the sequence. Otherwise, the recursive call doesn't happen, and the procedure ends after drawing the saw blade shown in Figure 7-19.

For simple examples like the ones shown here, it is probably easier to use a **repeat** block to achieve the desired repetition. But as I mentioned at the start of this section, there are many problems that are easier to solve with recursion rather than iteration.

TRY IT OUT 7-6

What does the following procedure do? Implement it and call it with different arguments to check your answer.

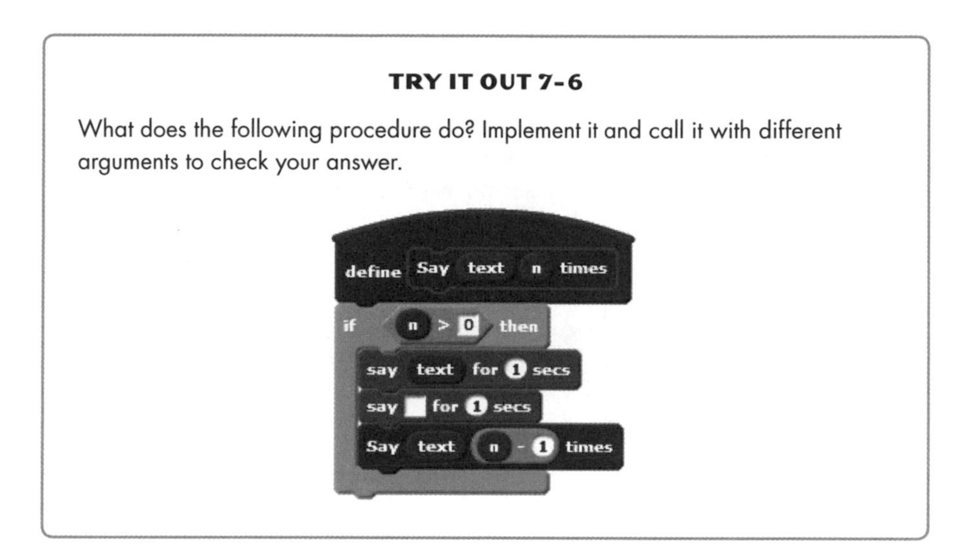

Scratch Projects

Now that you know how to use repetition to your advantage in Scratch scripts, it's time to put what we've learned in this chapter to some practical use. In this section, I'll guide you through a range of projects to help you strengthen your understanding of programming and provide you with some ideas for your own projects.

Analog Clock

AnalogClock.sb2

The **current** block from the *Sensing* palette can report the current year, month, date, day of the week, hour, minutes, or seconds, depending on what you select from the drop-down menu. Our first project will use this block to implement the analog clock shown in Figure 7-20. The application contains four sprites: the Sec, Min, and Hour sprites, which represent the three hands of the clock, and the Time sprite (a small white dot), which displays the time in digital format (see the thought bubble in the figure).

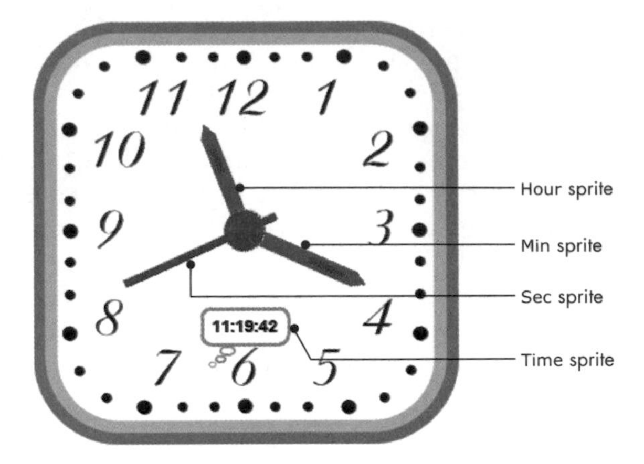

Figure 7-20: The Analog Clock application

The clock starts running when the green flag is clicked. In response, all four sprites start a **forever** loop to update their status based on the current system time. The scripts for the Sec and Min sprites are shown in Figure 7-21.

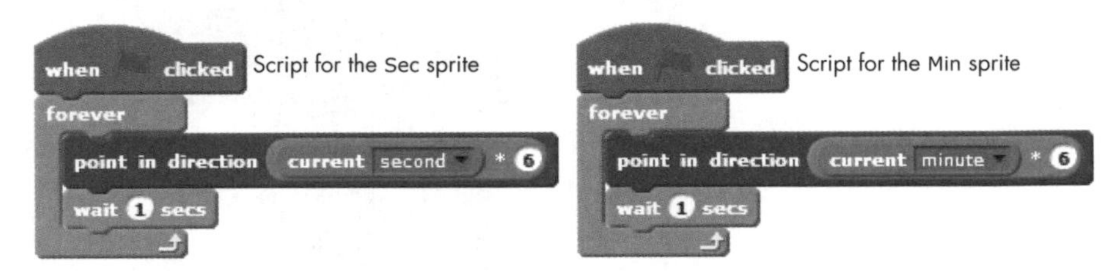

Figure 7-21: The scripts for the Sec *and* Min *sprites*

The number of seconds and minutes reported by the **current** block ranges from 0 to 59. When the system reports 0 seconds, the Sec sprite should point up (toward 0°), at 15 seconds, the Sec sprite should point right (toward 90°), and so on. Every second, the Sec hand should turn 6° (360° divided by 60 seconds) clockwise. A similar reasoning applies to the Min hand. If you watch this clock running, you'll notice the Sec hand jumping every second and the Min hand jumping every minute. Now, let's look at the script for the Hour sprite, shown in Figure 7-22.

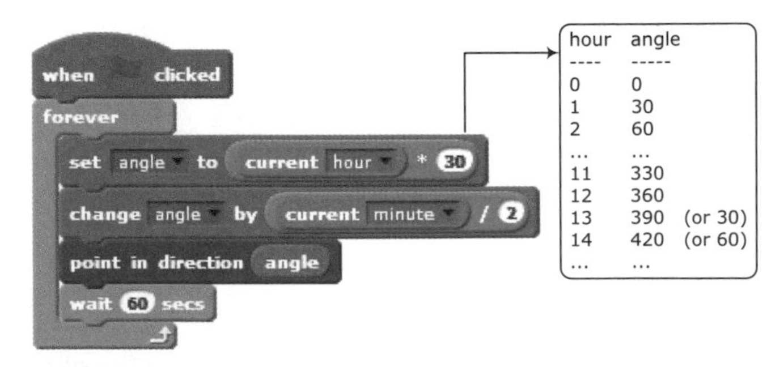

Figure 7-22: The script for the Hour *sprite*

The **current(hour)** block reports the system clock's hour as a number from 0 to 23. We need the Hour hand to point toward 0° (that is, up) for hour 0, 30° for hour one, 60° for hour two, and so on, as illustrated in the figure. Of course, if the current time is, let's say, 11:50, we don't want the Hour hand to point exactly at 11 but rather more toward 12. We can make this adjustment by taking the current minutes into account.

Since every hour (or 60 minutes) corresponds to 30° on the face of the clock, every minute is worth 2°. Therefore, every minute, we need to adjust the angle of the Hour hand by the current number of minutes divided by 2, as shown in the script.

The script for the Time sprite is trivial and isn't shown here. It uses nested **join** blocks to construct a display string of the form *hour:min:sec* and shows this string in a think bubble, as shown in Figure 7-20.

> **TRY IT OUT 7-7**
>
> Open the application and run it. Change the script for the Min sprite to make it move smoothly, instead of jumping every minute. (Hint: Use the same idea we applied to smooth the movement of the hour hand.) Also, change the script of the Time sprite to display a string of the form "3:25:00 PM" (12-hour format) instead of "15:25:00" (24-hour format). Think of other ways to enhance the application and try to implement them as well.

Bird Shooter Game

BirdShooter.sb2

Now, let's make a simple game that uses most of the blocks we introduced in this chapter. The player's goal will be to knock two birds out of the sky, and you can see the user interface in Figure 7-23.

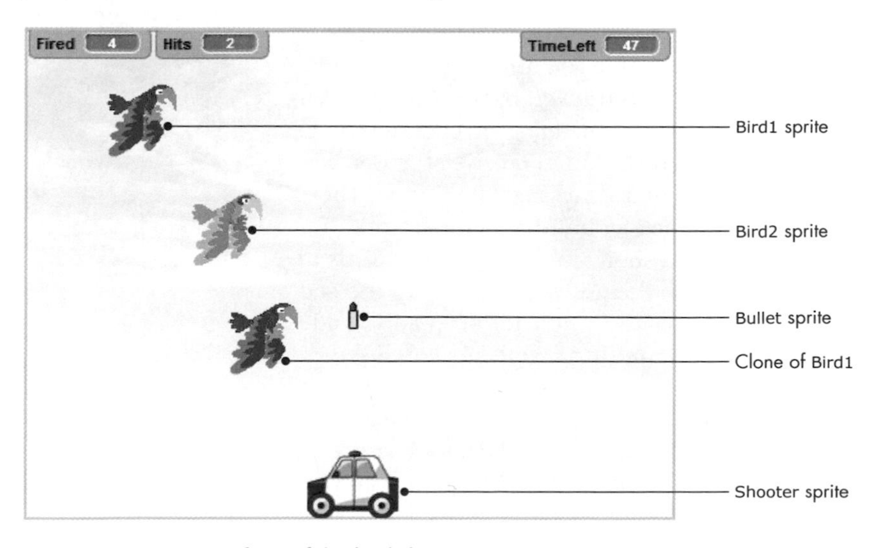

Figure 7-23: User interface of the bird shooter game

As shown, the game contains five sprites: Bird1, a clone of Bird1, Bird2, a shooter, and a bullet. The player can move the shooter horizontally using the left and right keyboard arrows. Pressing the spacebar fires a bullet into the sky. If the bullet hits Bird1 or its clone, the player gets a point. Bird2 is an endangered species, so the player isn't allowed to shoot that one; if the bullet hits that sprite, the game ends. The player has one minute to shoot as many birds as possible.

Each bird uses two costumes. When switching between these two costumes, the birds appear to be flapping their wings.

The Stage has two backgrounds named start and end. The start background is shown in Figure 7-23. The end background is identical, with the addition of the words *Game Over* to the center of the image. The scripts that belong to the Stage are shown in Figure 7-24.

```
when [flag] clicked
switch backdrop to start
reset timer
forever
  set TimeLeft to round 60 - timer
  if TimeLeft = 0 then
    broadcast GameOver and wait

when I receive GameOver
wait 0.1 secs
switch backdrop to end
stop all
```

Figure 7-24: The scripts for the Stage in the bird shooter game

When the green flag icon is pressed, the Stage switches to the start background, resets the timer, and starts a loop that updates and checks the remaining game time, which is tracked by the TimeLeft variable. When TimeLeft reaches 0 or when the Stage receives the GameOver broadcast message, it executes the GameOver handler. This script waits for a short time to allow the birds to hide themselves, switches to the end backdrop, and calls **stop all** to end any running scripts. As you'll see soon, the GameOver message will be sent by the Bullet sprite when it hits Bird2. Let's now take a look at the script for the Shooter sprite, shown in Figure 7-25.

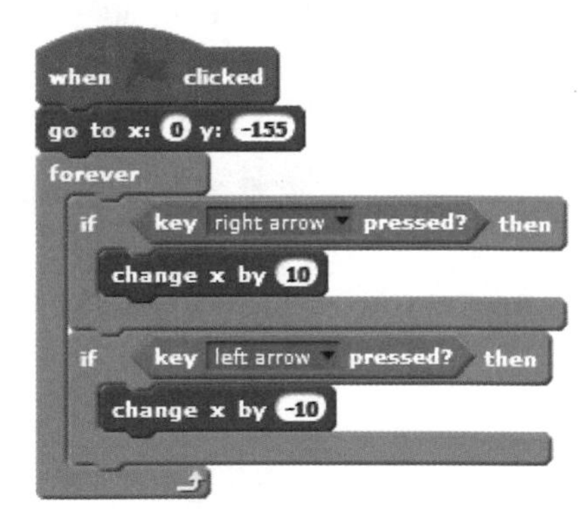
when clicked
go to x: 0 y: -155
forever
if key right arrow pressed? then
change x by 10
if key left arrow pressed? then
change x by -10

Figure 7-25: The script for the Shooter sprite

This script starts by positioning the shooter in the middle of the bottom edge of the Stage. The script then enters an infinite loop that detects whether the left or right arrow keys have been pressed and moves the shooter in the corresponding direction. Now let's move on to the scripts for `Bird1`, shown in Figure 7-26.

```
when clicked
show
create clone of myself
go to x: -240 y: 120
Start

when I start as a clone
go to x: -240 y: -40
Start

when I receive GameOver
hide

define Start
forever
  move pick random 5 to 20 steps
  if x position > 239 then
    set x to -240
  next costume
  wait 0.1 secs
```

Figure 7-26: The scripts for the `Bird1` *sprite*

When the game starts, `Bird1` clones itself, moves to left edge of the Stage, and calls the **Start** procedure. The clone also starts at the left edge of the Stage (but at a different height) and calls **Start**. This procedure uses a **forever** loop to move the bird and its clone horizontally across the Stage, from left to right with random steps. When the bird approaches the right edge of the stage, it is moved back to the left edge, as if it wraps around and reappears. The last script hides both birds when the `GameOver` message is broadcast.

The scripts for `Bird2` are very similar to those of `Bird1`, so we won't show them here. When the green flag is clicked, `Bird2` moves to the right edge of the Stage at a height of 40 and then executes a loop similar to that of the **Start** procedure of Figure 7-26. The bird simply moves from left to right, wrapping around when it reaches the right edge of the Stage. `Bird2` also responds to the `GameOver` broadcast by hiding itself.

Of course, the player can't hit any birds just by moving the shooter around, and that's where the `Bullet` sprite comes in. The main script for this sprite is shown in Figure 7-27.

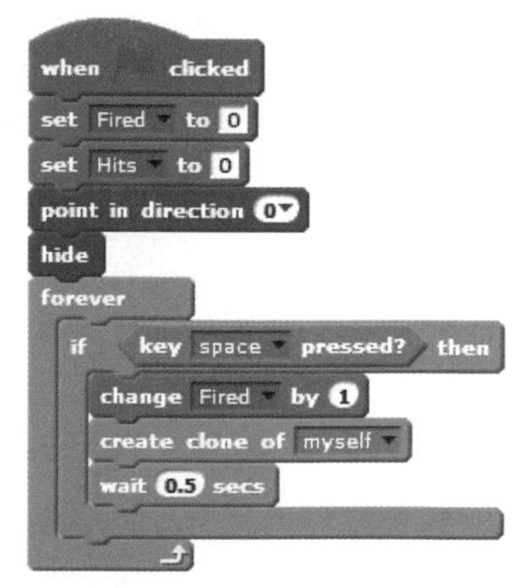

Figure 7-27: The main script of the `Bullet` *sprite*

When the green flag is clicked, this script initializes the variables Fired (the number of bullets fired) and Hits (how many birds have been hit) to 0. It then points the Bullet sprite up and hides it. After that, it enters an infinite loop to repeatedly check the status of the spacebar key. When spacebar is pressed, the script increments Fired by 1 and creates a clone of the Bullet sprite to move the bullet upward, as we'll see next. The script then waits some time to prevent the player from firing another bullet too soon. Now we're ready to study the script of the cloned bullet, shown in Figure 7-28.

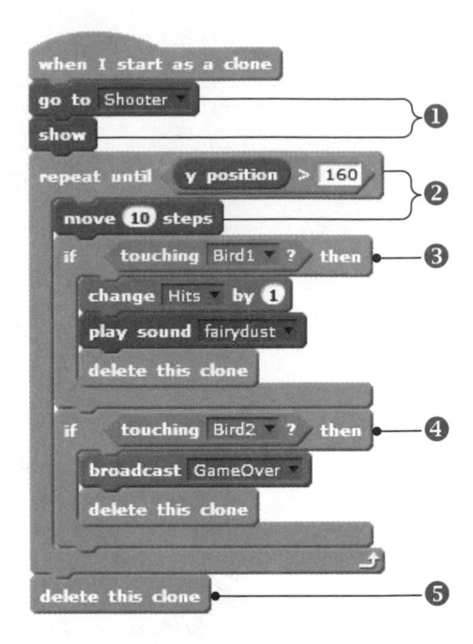

Figure 7-28: The startup handler of a cloned Bullet

First, the Bullet is moved to the center of the Shooter and is made visible ❶. The Bullet is then moved upward in increments of 10 steps using a **repeat until** block ❷. If the bullet's *y*-coordinate exceeds 160, then the Bullet has reached the upper edge of the Stage without touching any birds. In this case, the **repeat until** block exits ❺, and the clone is deleted. A hit check, however, is performed each time the bullet moves. If the bullet touches Bird1 (or its clone) ❸, the script increases the Hits variable and plays a sound to make the game more exciting. On the other hand, if the bullet touches Bird2 ❹, the script broadcasts GameOver to signal the end of the game. In both cases, the clone is deleted since it has finished its job.

The game is now fully functional, but you could add many features to it. Here are two suggestions:

- Give the player a limited number of bullets and keep score based on the number of missed shots.
- Add more birds and have them move at different speeds. Reward the player with more points for hitting faster birds.

TRY IT OUT 7-8

Open the game and play it to see how it works. Modify the game with some of the enhancements suggested above—or come up with a few of your own and implement those!

Free-Fall Simulation

FreeFall.sb2 In this section, I'll present an application that simulates the motion of a falling object. Ignoring the effects of buoyancy and air resistance, when an object at rest is dropped from some height, the distance d (in meters) fallen by the object during time t (in seconds) is given by $d = \frac{1}{2} gt^2$, where $g = 9.8\ m/s^2$ is the gravitational acceleration. The goal of this simulation is to show the position of the falling object at times 0.5 s, 1.0 s, 1.5 s, 2.0 s, and so on, until the object reaches the ground. The interface for this simulation is shown in Figure 7-29.

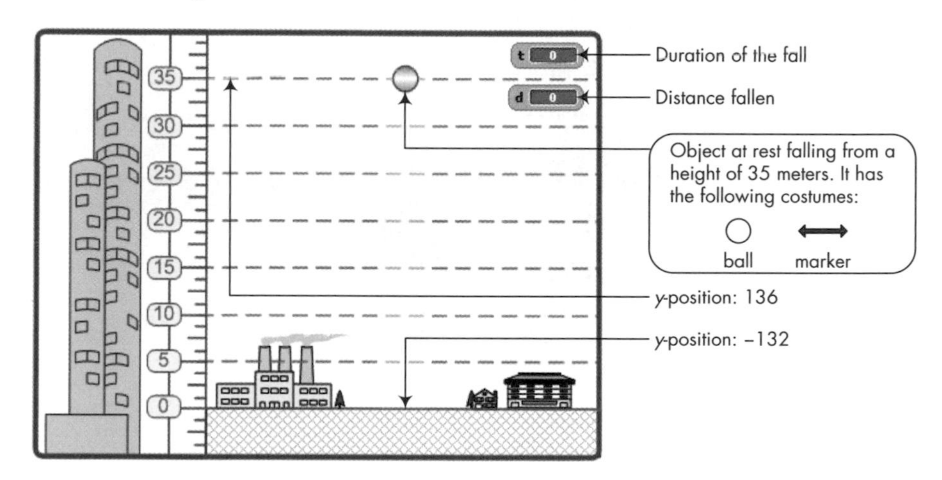

Figure 7-29: User interface for the free-fall simulation

An object at rest (the ball in the figure) will be allowed to fall from a height of 35 m. A simple substitution in the above formula shows that the object will reach the ground after $t = \sqrt{(2 \times 35)/9.8} = 2.67$ s. The application has one sprite (called Ball) that has the two costumes shown in the figure. When it is time to show the position of the falling ball, the sprite changes momentarily to the marker costume, makes a stamp, and switches back to the ball costume.

The simulation starts when the green flag is clicked. In response, the Ball sprite runs the script shown in Figure 7-30.

During initialization ❶, the sprite moves to its starting position, switches to the ball costume, clears its voice bubble from the previous run, and clears the Stage from any previous stamps. It then initializes t and counter to 0. The variable t represents the duration of the fall, and counter keeps track of the number of loop repetitions.

The script then enters an infinite loop ❷ to calculate the simulation parameters at different time intervals. It performs those calculations and updates the ball's position every 0.05 s ❸ to ensure the ball's smooth movement. Every 0.05 s, the value of the time variable t is updated, and the distance the ball has fallen (d) is calculated. The value of the counter variable is also incremented by 1.

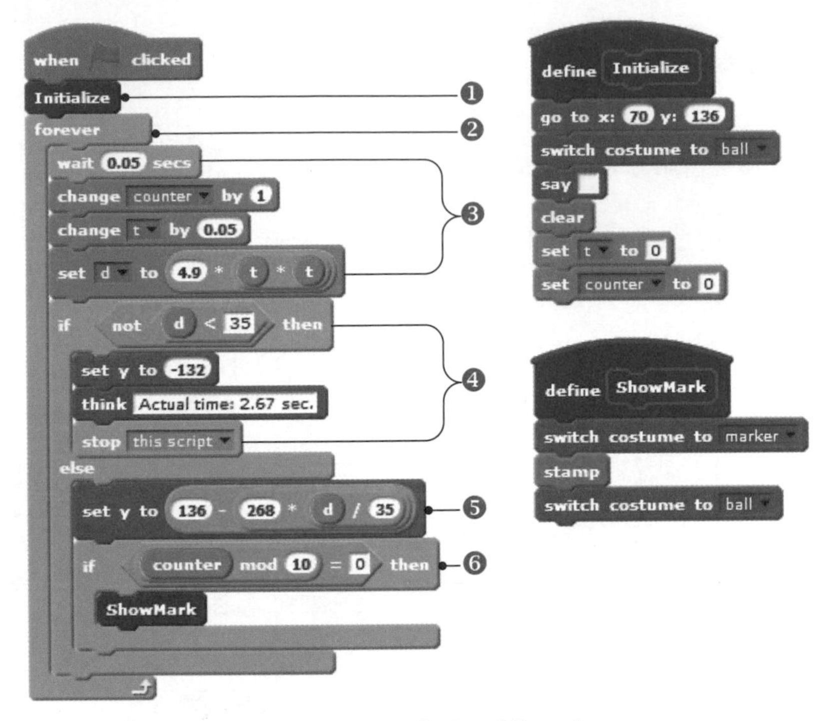

Figure 7-30: Script for the Ball *sprite in the free-fall simulation*

If the ball reaches the ground (which happens at d ≥ 35), the script sets the ball's *y*-position to that of the ground, displays the actual duration of the journey, and stops the script to end the simulation ❹.

Otherwise, the script sets the vertical position of the ball in accordance with the fallen distance ❺. Since a height of 35 m corresponds to 268 pixels on the Stage (see Figure 7-29), a distance of *d* meters corresponds to 268 * (d / 35). The final *y*-position is established by subtracting this number from the initial *y*-position, which is 136.

Since the iteration duration is 0.05 s, it takes 10 iterations to get 0.5 s. Thus, when the counter becomes 10, 20, 30, and so on, the Ball sprite switches to (and stamps) the marker costume to show the position of the falling ball at those instants ❻.

Figure 7-31 illustrates the result of running this simulation. Note how the distance fallen in each time interval increases as the object falls. Because of gravity, the ball accelerates—its velocity increases—at a rate of 9.8 m/s^2.

TRY IT OUT 7-9

Open the application and run it to understand how it works. Try converting the simulation into a game in which players drop the ball to hit a moving object on the ground. You can add a score, change the speed of the target, or even set the action on another planet (change the gravitational acceleration).

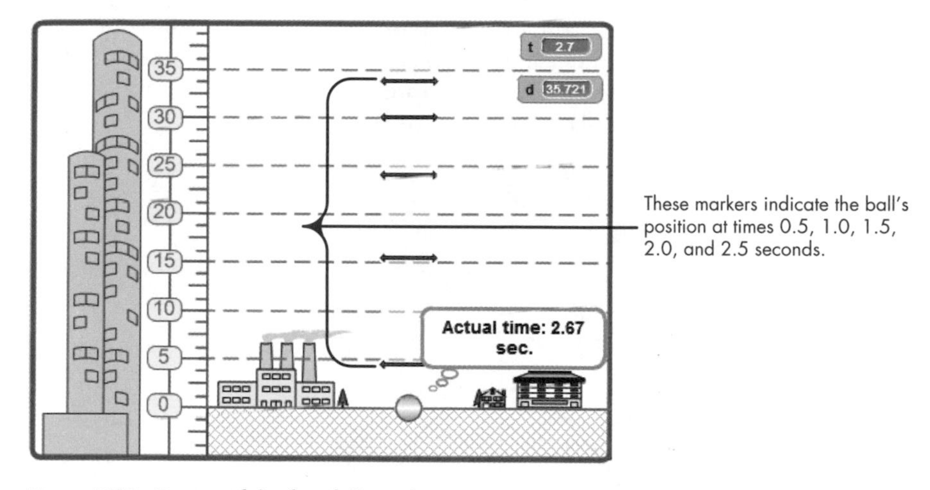

Figure 7-31: Output of the free-fall simulation

Projectile Motion Simulator

Projectile.sb2

Consider a ball fired at some initial velocity (v_0) from a cannon that points at an angle θ from the horizontal. You can analyze the ball's trajectory by resolving the velocity vector (v_0) into its horizontal and vertical components at different times. The horizontal component remains constant, but the vertical component is affected by gravity. When the motions corresponding to these two components are combined, the resulting path is a parabola. Let's examine the equations that govern projectile motion (neglecting air resistance).

The origin of our coordinate system is the point at which the ball begins its flight, so the ball's x-coordinate at any time, t, is given by $x(t) = v_{0x}t$, and the y-coordinate is $y(t) = v_{0y}t - (0.5)gt^2$, where $v_{0x} = v_0 \cos\theta$ is the x-component of v_0; $v_{0y} = v_0 \sin\theta$ is the y-component of v_0; and $g = 9.8\ \text{m/s}^2$ is the gravitational acceleration. Using these equations, we can calculate the total flight time, the maximum height, and the horizontal range of the ball. The equations for these quantities are shown in Figure 7-32.

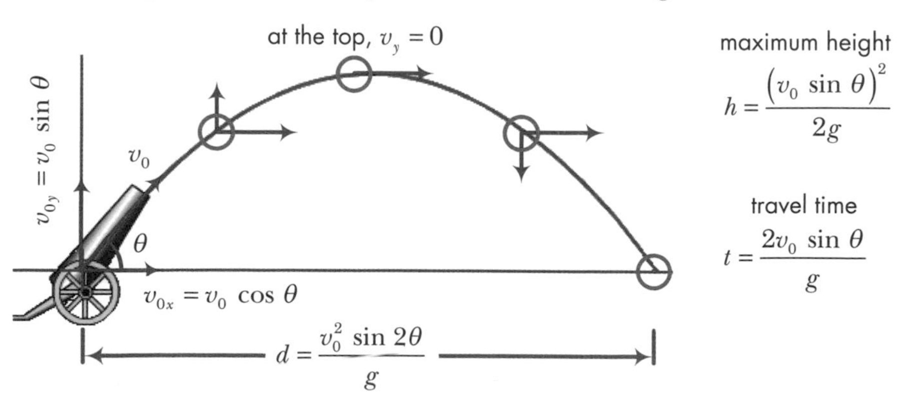

Figure 7-32: Parabolic trajectory of a ball

This information is all we need to realistically simulate the ball's motion, so let's create a Scratch program so we can see this bit of physics in action and deepen our understanding of trajectories. The user interface of the simulation is shown in Figure 7-33.

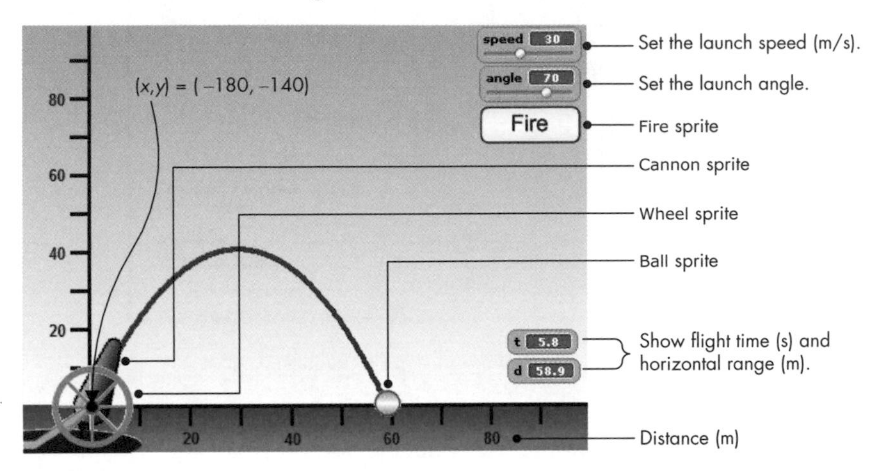

Figure 7-33: User interface for the projectile motion simulator

As shown, the application contains four sprites. The Wheel sprite provides a rotation shaft for the cannon, while the Cannon sprite, which rotates in accordance with the angle slider, provides a visual indication of the launch angle. The Fire sprite is a button that the user clicks to fire the ball, and the Ball sprite contains the main script for calculating the ball's coordinates and drawing its trajectory. The user specifies the launch angle and the initial velocity using the two slider controls, then clicks the Fire button. The Ball starts from point (–180, –140) on the Stage and draws the parabolic trajectory for the specified parameters. The two monitors at the lower-right corner of the Stage show the flight time and the horizontal range during the flight.

The simulation starts when the green flag icon is clicked. The scripts for the Cannon sprite (not shown here) point the cannon in the direction specified by the angle slider control. The user can also specify the angle by clicking and dragging the cannon. When the user clicks the Fire button, it broadcasts a Fire message, which is received and processed by the Ball sprite via the script shown in Figure 7-34.

To prepare to fire ❶, the Ball moves in front of the Cannon and the Wheel and positions itself at the launch point. It puts its pen down and clears all pen marks from the Stage. The script then calculates the horizontal (or *x*) and vertical (or *y*) components of the initial velocity (named vx and vy, respectively) and initializes the time variable (t) to 0.

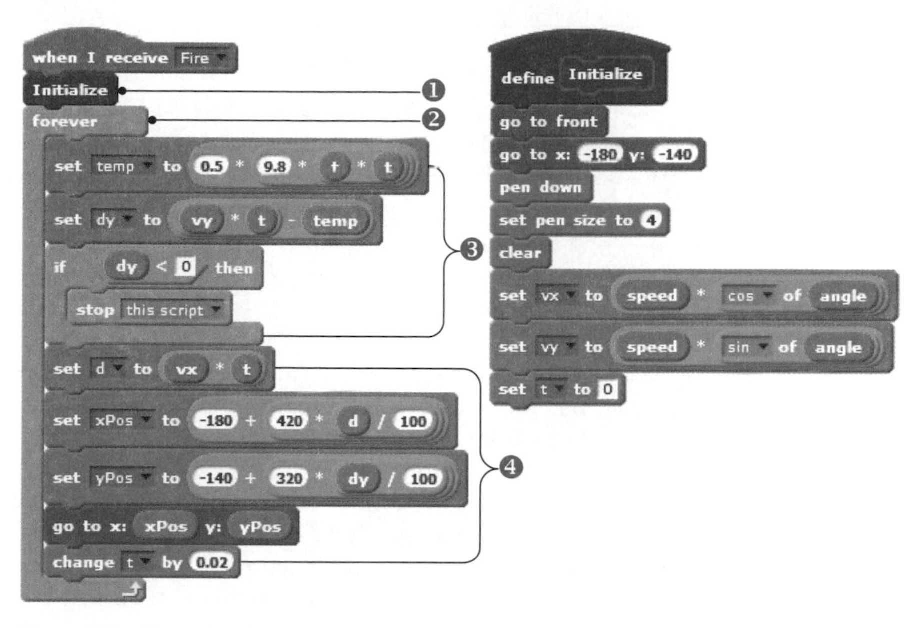

Figure 7-34: Script for the Ball *sprite*

The script then enters an infinite loop ❷, which calculates and updates the ball's position every 0.02 s. First, the vertical distance (dy) of the sprite is calculated ❸. If the calculated value is negative, then the ball has reached ground level. When this happens, the **stop this script** command is called to end the simulation.

If dy is not negative, the horizontal distance (d) is calculated ❹. The two distances (dy and d) are then scaled in accordance with the Stage's backdrop. In the vertical direction, we have 320 steps (from –140 to 180) that correspond to 100 m, and in the horizontal direction, we have 420 steps (from –180 to 240) that correspond to 100 m. This means a vertical distance of dy meters is equivalent to 320 * dy / 100 steps, and a horizontal distance of d meters is equivalent to 420 * d / 100 steps. The *x*- and *y*-coordinates of the ball are updated, and the ball is moved to its current position on its trajectory. The time variable (t) is then incremented by a small amount (0.02 s in this case), and the loop is repeated to calculate the next position of the ball.

As an example, if the ball is projected with a 70° launch angle and an initial speed of 30 m/s, as shown in Figure 7-33, the total flight time is 5.75 s, and the range is 59 m. An examination of the monitors in Figure 7-33 shows that our simulation is very accurate. We could improve the simulation by updating our calculations more often (for example, every 0.01 s instead of every 0.02 s), but that would slow down the simulation. It's necessary to adjust this parameter to achieve a good compromise between speed and accuracy.

TRY IT OUT 7-10

Open the application and run it to understand how it works. Then try converting this simulation into a game. You could, for example, show an object at a random height at the right edge of the stage and ask the player to try to hit it. If the player misses the target, the game can provide some hints on adjusting the firing angle and velocity.

Other Applications

MatchThatAmount.sb2

The extra resources for this book (available at *http://nostarch.com/learnscratch/*) contain three more games that you can explore on your own, with full explanations of each script. The first is an educational game that can be used to test the counting skills of elementary students. It shows an amount of money in pennies and asks the player to find the smallest number of coins needed to get that amount.

Orbit.sb2
MoleculesInMotion.sb2

The second application is a planetary motion simulation for a simple solar system that contains a sun and a single planet. The third application is also a simulation, this one demonstrating the dynamics of motion as a single gas molecule collides with the walls of a container.

Open up these applications, run them, and read through my explanations to understand how they work. If you feel inspired to flex your programming muscles, try modifying the scripts to make them do new things!

Summary

In this chapter, we explored different ways to repeat commands in Scratch. We first examined the various loop blocks and explained the technical terms associated with them. Then, we discussed definite and indefinite loops and the difference between counter-controlled and condition-controlled loops. We explored the **repeat until** block and the **forever if** structure and used them in several examples. I also explained Scratch's **stop** commands and how you can use them to stop infinite loops and procedures. From there, we went on to discuss using loops to validate data from user input.

You then learned how to use counters to keep track of how many iterations of a loop have passed and how to use counters with nested loops to create iterations in two or more dimensions. After that, we looked at recursion—a procedure calling itself—as another way to achieve repetition. In the last section, we developed several applications that tied these new concepts together to create practical programs.

The next chapter will expand on the topics you learned here and teach you how to use counters and loops to process strings and create a different class of interesting programs, such as a binary to decimal converter, a hangman game, and a math tutor for teaching fractions.

If you want to further explore the new concepts from this chapter, I suggest trying out some of the following problems.

Problems

1. Create an input validation loop that only accepts numbers in the range of 1 through 10.
2. Write a script that asks the user, "Are you sure you want to quit [Y, N]?" The script then checks the user's input and only accepts the letters *Y* and *N* as valid answers.
3. Write a program that calculates and displays the sum of all integers between 1 and 20.
4. Write a program that calculates and displays the sum of all odd integers between 1 and 20.
5. Write a program that displays the first 10 numbers in the following sequence (using the **say** command): 5, 9, 13, 17, 21, ...
6. What does the script on the right do? Implement the script and run it to check your answer.

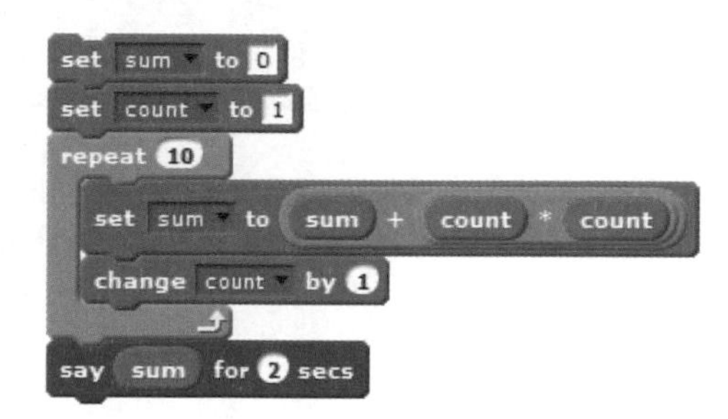

7. If the remainder of dividing a whole number (x) by another whole number (y) is 0, we say that y is a factor of x. For example, 1, 2, 4, and 8 are factors of 8. The script below finds and displays all the factors of a given number (other than the number itself). Study this script and explain how it works. What are the outputs of this script when the input numbers are 125, 324, and 419?

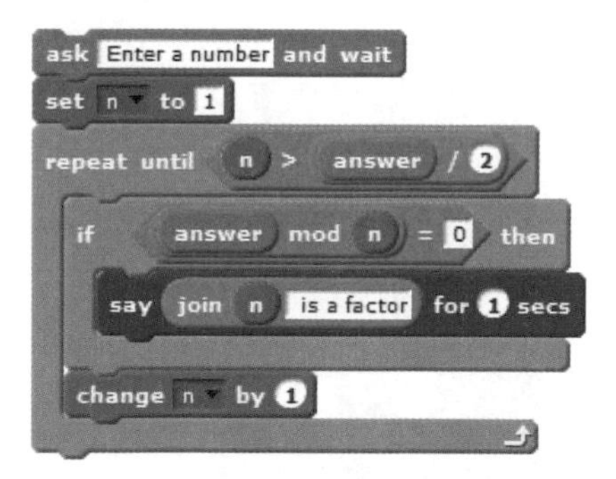

8. An integer is said to be prime if it is divisible by only 1 and itself. For example, 2, 3, 5, 7, 11 are prime numbers, but 4, 6, and 8 are not. The procedure on the next page tests whether a number is a prime number or not. Study this procedure and explain how it works. What are the outputs of this procedure for the inputs 127, 327, and 523?

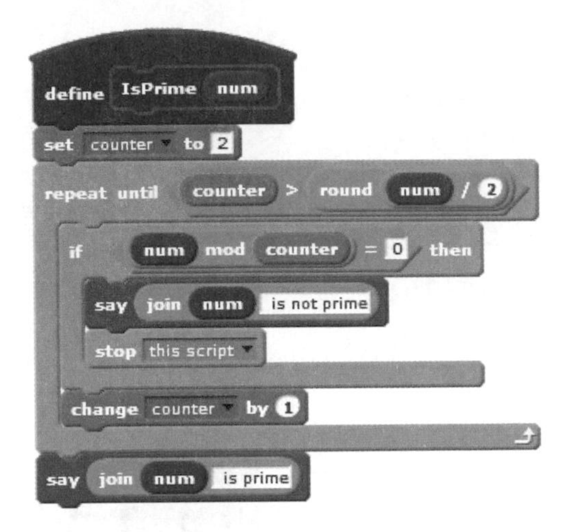

9. Although the procedure in problem 8 checks all integers up to one-half the input value, it is sufficient to set the upper limit to the square root of the input. Make this change to the procedure and test it to see if it still gives the same answers.
10. The sequence of numbers

    0, 1, 1, 2, 3, 5, 8, 13, 21, 34 ....

    is called a Fibonacci series. The first two numbers in the series are 0 and 1. Each subsequent number is then calculated as the sum of the previous two. Write a program that calculates the *n*th term of the Fibonacci series, where *n* is entered by the user.
11. Consider the following program and its generated output. Re-create the program and run it to see how it works. Change the turn angle (from 10°) and the argument in the recursive call (to **side + 1** or **side + 3**, and so on) to discover what else you can create.

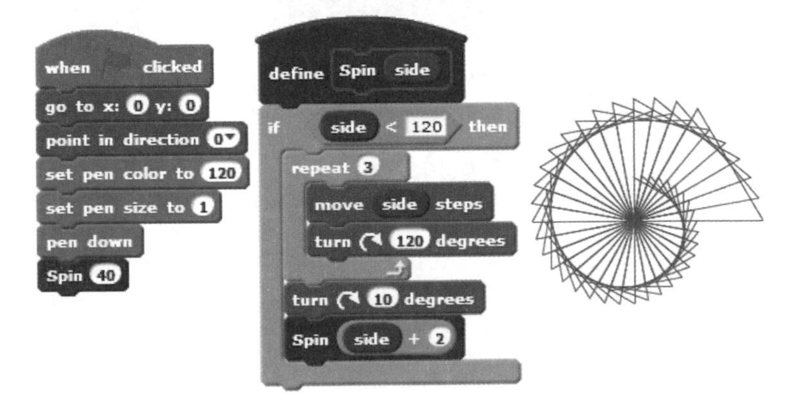

8

STRING PROCESSING

A string is a series of characters that is treated as a single unit. You can write programs to combine, compare, sort, encrypt, and otherwise manipulate strings. Here's what you'll learn in this chapter:

- How Scratch stores strings
- How to use the string manipulation blocks available in Scratch
- Several string processing techniques
- How to write interesting programs that process strings

We'll start with a detailed look at the string data type, and then we'll write procedures to manage and manipulate strings. Those procedures will remove and replace characters, insert and extract substrings, and randomize character order. After that, we'll use these procedures and apply these techniques to write some fun and practical applications.

Revisiting the String Data Type

As I mentioned in Chapter 5, Scratch has three data types: *Boolean*, *number*, and *string*. At its simplest, a string is just an ordered sequence of characters. These characters can include letters (both upper- and lowercase), digits, and other symbols that you can type on your keyboard (+, -, &, @, and so on). You can use strings in your programs to store names, addresses, phone numbers, book titles, and more.

In Scratch, the characters of a string are stored sequentially. For example, if you have a variable called name, executing the command **set name to Karen** would store the characters as illustrated in Figure 8-1.

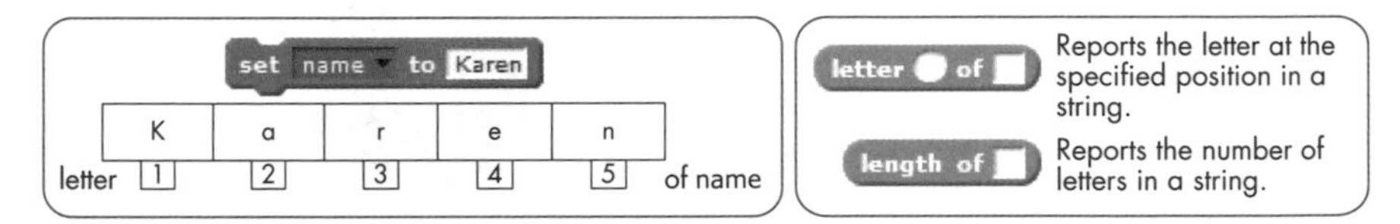

Figure 8-1: A string is stored as a sequence of characters.

You can access individual characters of a string with the **letter of** operator. For example, the block **letter 1 of name** returns the letter K, and **letter 5 of name** returns the letter n. Scratch also provides the **length of** operator, which returns the number of characters in a string. If you use these two operators with **repeat** blocks, you can count characters, examine multiple characters, and do many other useful things, as I'll demonstrate in the following subsections.

Counting Special Characters in a String

VowelCount.sb2

Our first example script, shown in Figure 8-2, counts how many vowels are in an input string. It asks the user to enter a string, and then it counts and displays the number of vowels in that string.

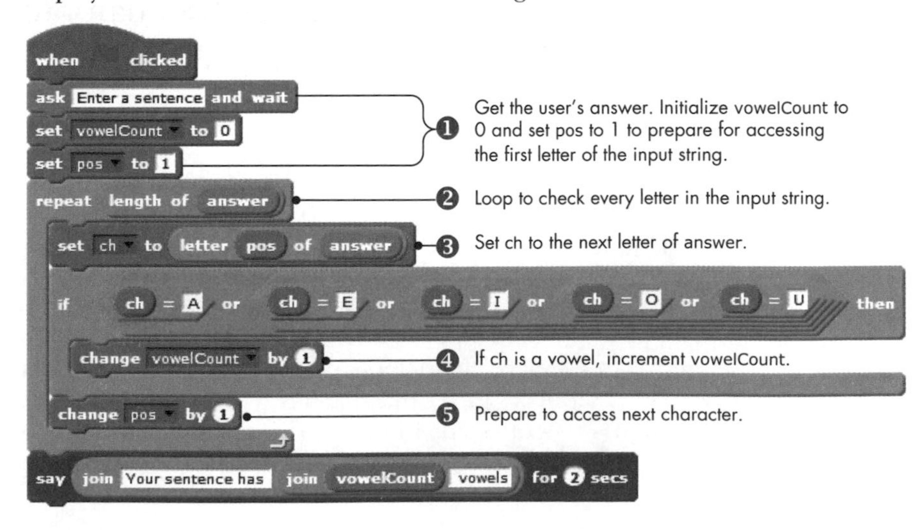

Figure 8-2: Vowel-counting program

The program checks each letter in the input string one by one and looks for vowels. Every time it finds a vowel, it increments a variable named vowelCount by 1. The script uses a variable named pos (short for *position*) to track the position of the character being checked. Let's explore this script in more detail.

First, the script asks the user to enter a sentence ❶. Scratch should save the user's string automatically in the built-in answer variable. Then it sets vowelCount to 0 (since it hasn't seen any vowels yet) and sets pos to 1 to access the first letter of the input string.

Next, a **repeat** loop ❷ checks every letter in the input string. The **length of** operator reports the number of characters in the input string, which is how many times the loop should repeat.

On each pass, the loop uses ch (short for character) to check one character of the input string ❸. In the first iteration of the loop, ch is set to the first letter of **answer**. The second iteration sets ch to the second letter, and so on, until the loop reaches the end of the string. The pos variable is used to access the desired character.

The **if** block then checks whether the examined character is a vowel ❹. If the character is a vowel, whether capital or lowercase, vowelCount is increased by 1.

After checking one character, the loop increments pos by 1 ❺ and starts over to read the next character. When all the letters in the input string have been checked, the loop terminates, and the program displays the number of vowels it counted using the **say** block.

The techniques used in this example will be applied many times in the rest of this chapter. Load the script *VowelCount.sb2*, run it several times, and make sure you understand it thoroughly.

Comparing String Characters

Palindrome.sb2

Our second example checks whether an integer entered by the user is a palindrome. A *palindrome* is a number (or text string) that reads the same backward and forward. For example, 1234321 and 1122332211 are palindromes. Likewise, Racecar, Hannah, and Bob are a few text palindromes. To illustrate our palindrome-testing algorithm, let's say that the input number is 12344321, as illustrated in Figure 8-3.

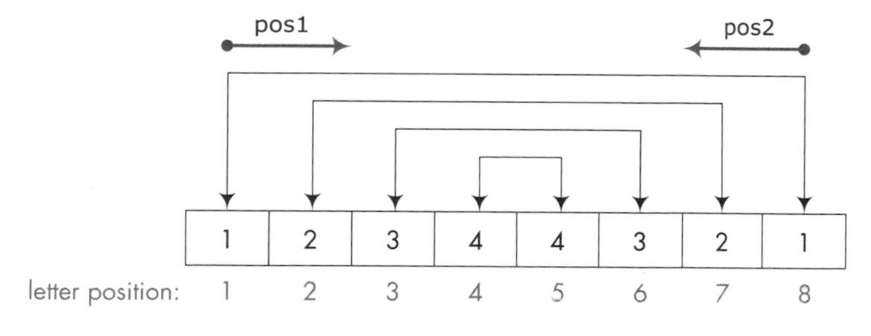

Figure 8-3: Using two variables to check whether or not a number is a palindrome

To check whether the number is a palindrome, we need to compare the first and eighth digits, the second and seventh digits, the third and sixth digits, and so on. If any comparison produces a false result (meaning that the two digits are not equal), then the number is not a palindrome. A program that implements this palindrome test algorithm is shown in Figure 8-4.

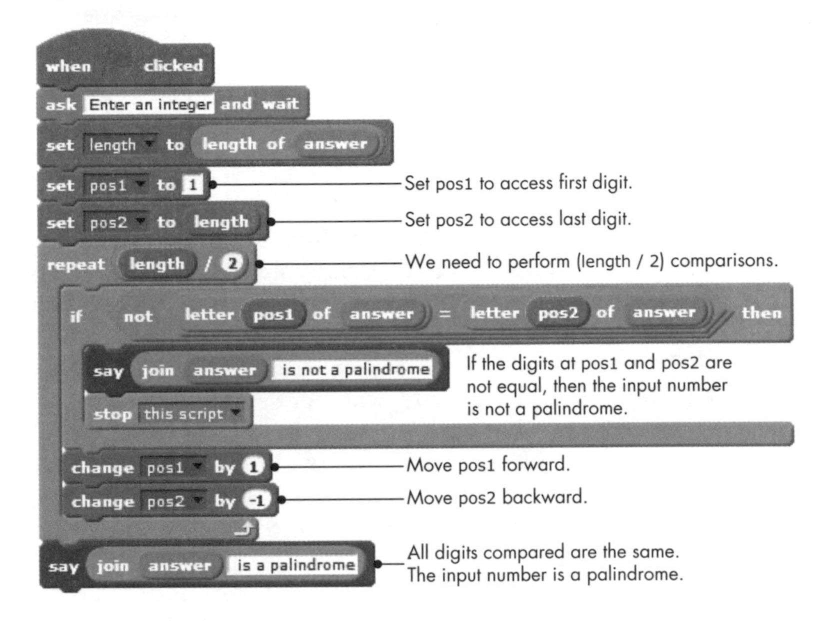

Figure 8-4: This program tests whether an integer input by the user is a palindrome.

The script accesses the digits to be compared with two variables (pos1 and pos2 in Figure 8-3) that move in opposite directions. The first variable (pos1) starts at the first digit and moves forward, while the second variable (pos2) starts at the last digit and moves backward. The number of required comparisons is at most one-half the digits in the input number. With an input of 12344321, we need at most four comparisons because the input number has eight digits. (The same logic applies if the input integer has an odd number of digits, since the digit in the middle of the number need not be compared.) Once the program determines whether or not the user's number is a palindrome, it displays a message with the result.

Palindrome.sb2

TRY IT OUT 8-1

Load *Palindrome.sb2* and run it to understand how it works. Because of the way Scratch handles decimal repeat counts, if the input number has an odd number of digits, the script performs one extra comparison of the two digits that surround the middle digit. Try to fix the program to perform the correct number of repeats when the input number has an odd number of digits.

In the next section, we'll explore some of the most common operations on strings and see some strategies for writing string manipulation procedures in Scratch.

String Manipulation Examples

The **letter of** operator only lets you read the individual characters of a string. If you want to insert characters into (or remove characters from) a string, you have to do all the work yourself.

In Scratch, you can't alter the characters in a string, so the only way to change a string is to create a new one. For example, if you want to capitalize the first letter in the string "jack", you need to create a new string that contains the letter *J* followed by the rest of the letters, *ack*. The idea is to use the **letter of** operator to read the letters of the original string and append theses letters to the new string, as needed, using the **join** operator.

In this section, we'll develop some simple applications that demonstrate common string manipulation techniques.

Igpay Atinlay

PigLatin.sb2

What if our sprites could speak a secret language? In this section, we'll teach them a coded language called *pig latin*. Our rules for creating pig latin words will be simple. To convert a word into pig latin, move the first letter to the end and add the letters *ay*. So, the word *talk* becomes *alktay*, *fun* becomes *unfay*, and so on. Now that you know the rules, can you tell what the title of this section originally said?

The strategy we'll use to convert a word into pig latin is illustrated in Figure 8-5, using the word *scratch*.

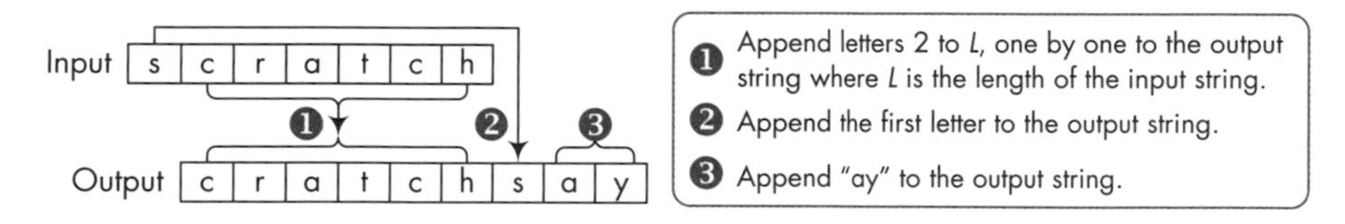

Figure 8-5: How to translate an English word into pig latin

We'll first append all the letters (except the first), one by one, from the input word to the output word ❶. We then add the first letter in the input word to the output ❷, followed by *ay* ❸. Our **PigLatin** procedure that implements these steps is shown in Figure 8-6.

The procedure uses three variables to create our coded words. The variable outWord holds the output string as it's assembled. A counter called pos (for position) tells the script which character from the original string to append to outWord. Finally, a variable named ch holds one character from the input string. The procedure takes the word you want to translate into pig latin as a parameter, named word.

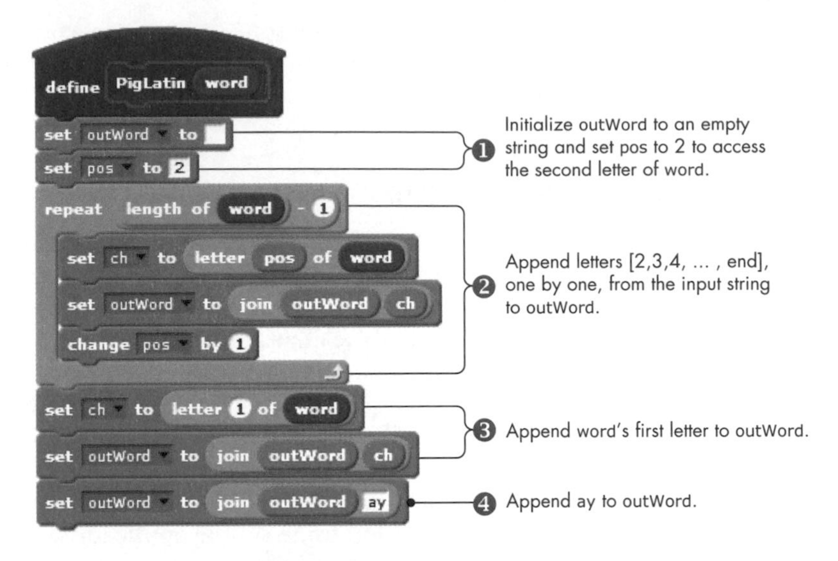

Figure 8-6: The **PigLatin** *procedure*

First, the procedure creates an empty string for outWord and sets pos to 2 ❶. (An *empty string* is string that does not contain any characters; its length is 0.) The procedure then uses a **repeat** block to append all letters but the first from the input string (word) to the output string (outWord) ❷. We skipped the first character, so the repeat count is one less than the length of the input string. For each loop iteration, one character of word is appended to outWord. At the end of the loop, the first letter of word is appended to outWord ❸, along with the letters ay ❹.

PigLatin.sb2

TRY IT OUT 8-2

Load *PigLatin.sb2* and run it to test this procedure. The application asks for an input word and then says its pig latin translation. Modify it to translate a phrase, like "Would you like some juice?" into pig latin. (Hint: Call **PigLatin** for each word to assemble the output phrase.) As another challenge, write a procedure that takes a pig latin word as input and shows its original English word.

Fix My Spelling

FixMySpelling .sb2

In this section, we'll develop a simple game that generates misspelled words and asks the player to enter the correct spelling. The game will create misspelled words by inserting a random letter at a random position in an English word. Of course, there could be more than one correct spelling of misspelled simple words. For example, if the original word is *wall* and the game produces *mwall*, either *mall* or *wall* would be correct. To keep our game simple, we'll ignore that possibility and insist on a particular spelling for the correct answer.

First, let's make a general procedure to insert characters at a specific position in a string. This procedure, called **Insert**, takes three parameters: the input word (strIn), the string (or character) to insert (strAdd), and the position where you want those new characters (charPos). The procedure generates a new string (strOut) with strAdd inserted into strIn at the correct position, as illustrated in the example of Figure 8-7.

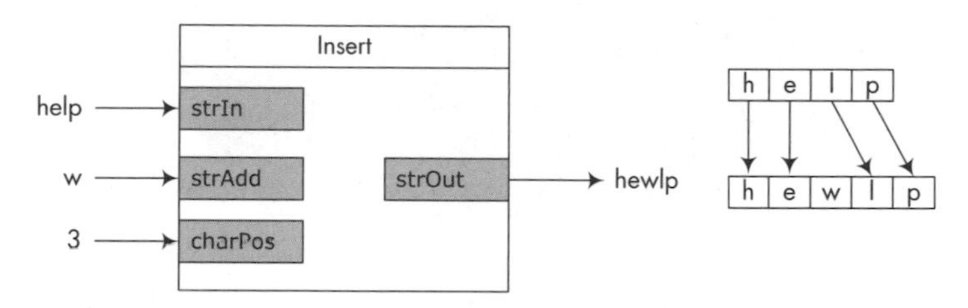

Figure 8-7: Illustrating the **Insert** *procedure*

We'll add the characters from strIn, one by one, into strOut. When we reach charPos, we'll just add the character(s) from strAdd to strOut before appending the letter at charPos from strIn. The complete procedure is shown in Figure 8-8.

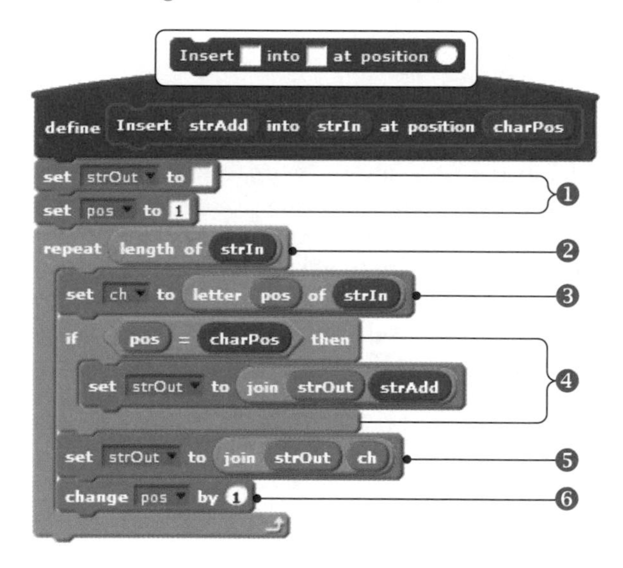

Figure 8-8: The **Insert** *procedure*

First, the procedure initializes strOut to an empty string and sets pos to 1 to access the first letter of the input string ❶. It then starts a **repeat** loop to append the letters of strIn, one by one, to strOut ❷. Each iteration grabs the next letter of strIn and places it in the ch variable ❸. If the position of the current character matches charPos, the procedure appends strAdd to strOut ❹. In all cases, ch is appended to strOut ❺, and pos is incremented to access the next letter of strIn ❻.

Now that we have our **Insert** procedure, let's look at the main script of the game, shown in Figure 8-9.

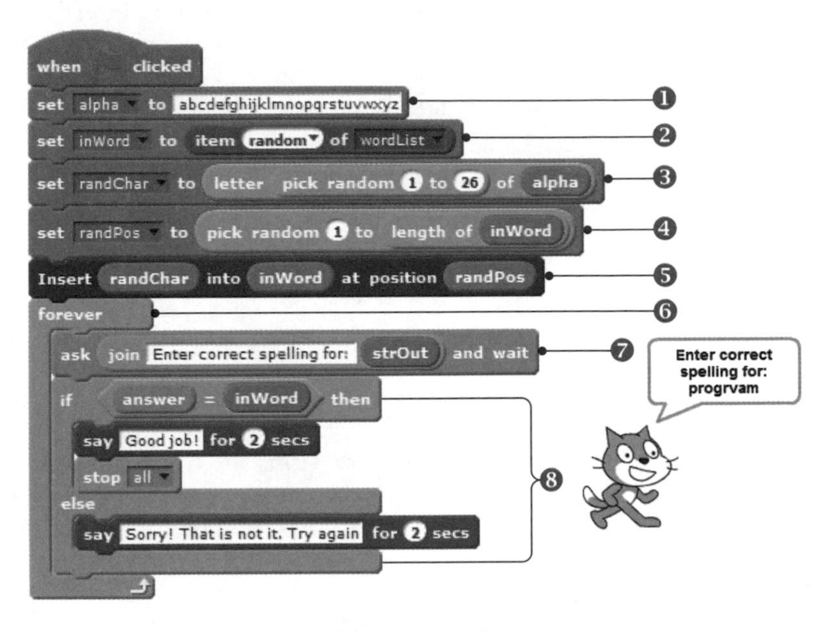

Figure 8-9: The main script for the Fix My Spelling game

The alpha string contains all the letters of the alphabet. It will provide the random letter to insert into the word we want to misspell ❶. The script randomly picks a word from a premade list and saves that word as inWord ❷. You'll learn more about lists in the next chapter; for now, just think of this list as a word bank. The script then selects a random letter (randChar) from alpha ❸ and a random position (randPos) to place this letter into inWord ❹. The script then calls our **Insert** procedure to create the misspelled word (strOut) ❺. After that, the script starts a loop to get the player's answer ❻. Inside the loop, the script asks the player to enter the correct spelling ❼, and it uses an **if/else** block to check the answer ❽. If the player's answer matches the original word (inWord), the game ends; otherwise, the player has to try again.

FixMySpelling .sb2

TRY IT OUT 8-3

Load *FixMySpelling.sb2* and play it several times to understand how it works. Can you modify the game such that the corrupt word contains two additional letters instead of just one?

Unscramble

Unscramble.sb2

Our last example presents another word game that is a little more challenging to play. We'll start with an English word, scramble its letters, and ask the player to guess the original word.

Let's start by creating a procedure that rearranges the characters of a given string in random order. The caller sets the input string (strIn), and the procedure, named **Randomize**, modifies it so that its characters are shuffled around, as illustrated in Figure 8-10.

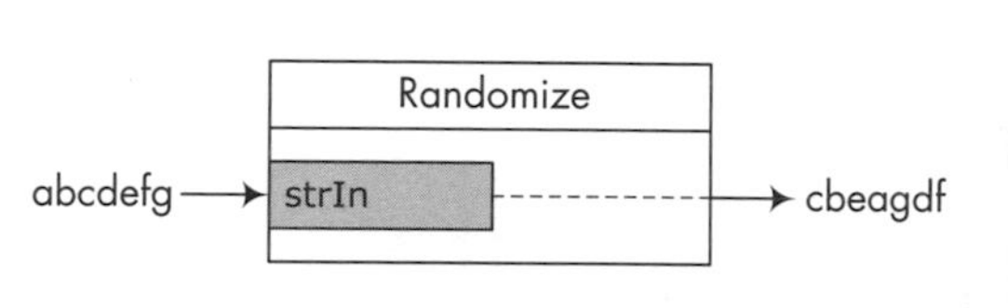

Step	Pick random	Append to str1	Remove from strIn
1	3	c	abdefg
2	2	cb	adefg
3	1	cba	defg
4	2	cbae	dfg
...	...	...	...

Figure 8-10: Illustrating the **Randomize** *procedure*

We'll pick a random letter from strIn and append that letter to a *temporary string*, str1. (This temporary string, which starts off empty, is where we'll store the scrambled word as we build it.) We'll then remove that letter from strIn so we don't reuse it and repeat the whole process until strIn is empty. The **Randomize** procedure implements these steps as shown in Figure 8-11.

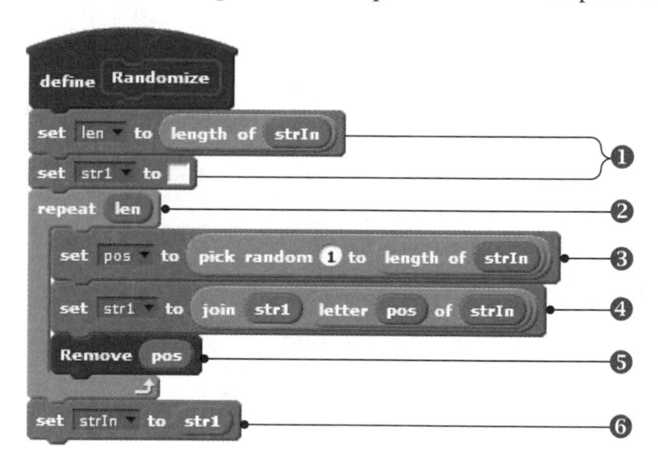

Figure 8-11: The **Randomize** *procedure*

First, **Randomize** sets len to the length of the input string, strIn, and empties the temporary string, str1 ❶. The procedure then starts a **repeat** loop to assemble the scrambled word ❷. The repeat count equals the length of the input string. For each loop iteration, we pick a random position in strIn ❸ and append that letter to str1 ❹. Note that we used **length of** in step ❸ because strIn and its length will change inside the loop. After that, we call a procedure named **Remove** to delete the character we just used from strIn ❺. When the loop finishes shuffling letters around, strIn is set to the scrambled word (str1) ❻.

The **Remove** procedure, which lets us avoid adding the same letter to our scrambled word twice, is shown in Figure 8-12. It removes a character from strIn at the position you specify with the charPos parameter.

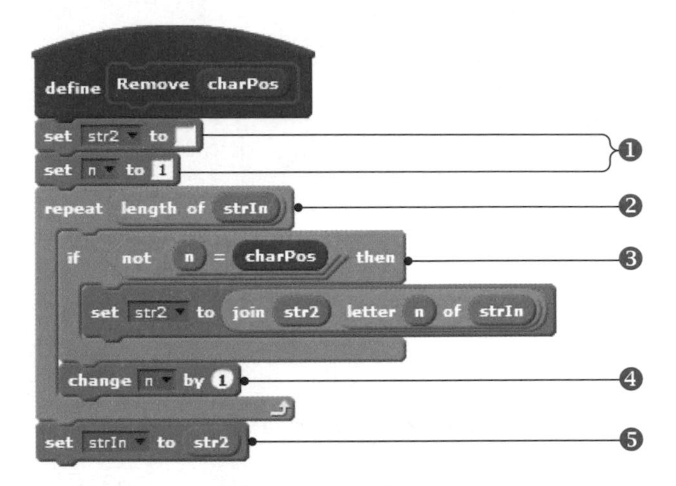

Figure 8-12: The ***Remove*** *procedure*

This procedure uses another temporary string, named str2, to build the new string we want to create. It starts by emptying str2 and setting a loop counter, n, to 1 to access the first character of strIn ❶. The procedure then starts a **repeat** loop to assemble the output string ❷. If we don't want to delete the current character, we append it to str2 ❸. The loop counter is then incremented to access the next letter of strIn ❹. When the procedure finishes, strIn is set to the new word (str2) ❺.

Now we are ready to explore the main script of the game, shown in Figure 8-13.

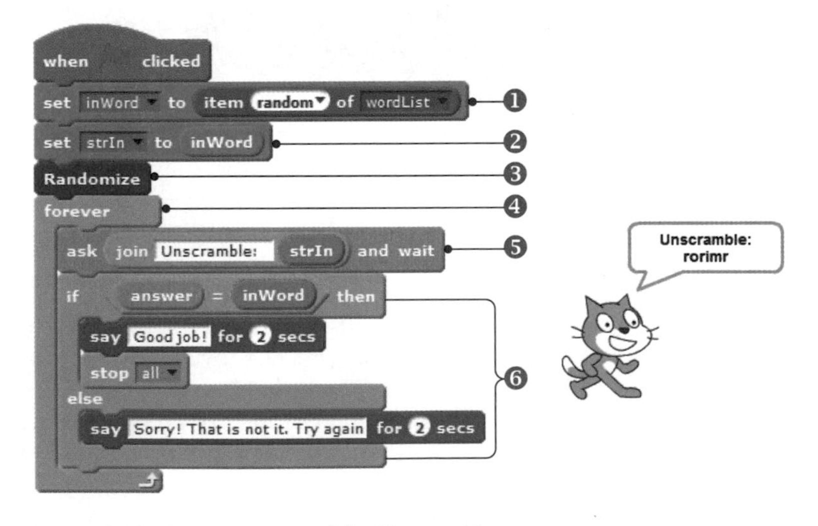

Figure 8-13: The main script of the Unscramble game

The script selects a word randomly from a list and saves that word in inWord ❶. It then sets strIn equal to inWord ❷ and calls **Randomize** to shuffle the characters of strIn ❸. After that, the script starts a loop to get the player's answer ❹. Inside the loop, the script asks the player to enter the unscrambled word ❺ and uses an **if/else** block to check that answer ❻. This part is identical to what we did in the Fix My Spelling game in the previous section.

The previous examples were just a small set of the different operations you can do on strings. Try using the same techniques to change strings in your own projects!

In the rest of this chapter, we'll explore some programs that use strings to solve interesting problems.

Scratch Projects

The procedures you just saw demonstrated the basics of processing strings. In this section, we'll apply what we've learned to write several practical applications. Along the way, you'll learn some new programming tricks that you can use in your own creations.

Shoot

Shoot.sb2

This game is intended to teach the concept of relative motion in a fun and engaging way. The object of the game is to estimate the turn angle and moving distance between two objects on the Stage. The user interface for the game is illustrated in Figure 8-14.

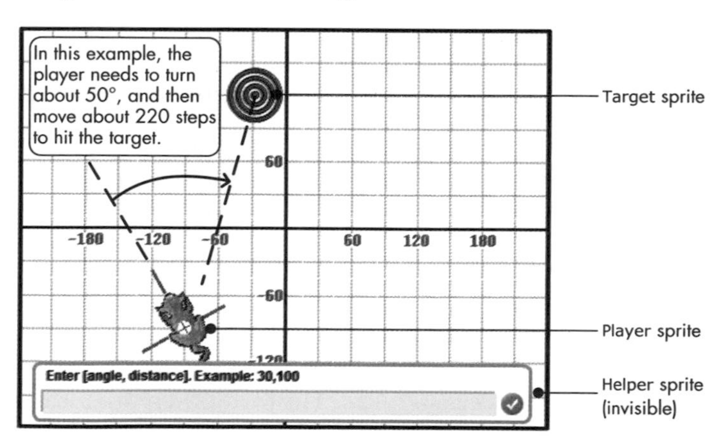

Figure 8-14: The user interface of the Shoot game

When the game starts, it positions the Player and the Target sprites at random locations on the Stage. Next it prompts the player to estimate the turn angle and the distance the Player sprite would need to move to hit the Target. The Player sprite is then moved according to the numbers entered by the player. If the sprite stops within a certain radius of the Target, the player wins the game. Otherwise, the Player sprite returns to its initial position, and the player can try again. When the green flag icon is clicked to start the game, the Player sprite runs the script shown in Figure 8-15.

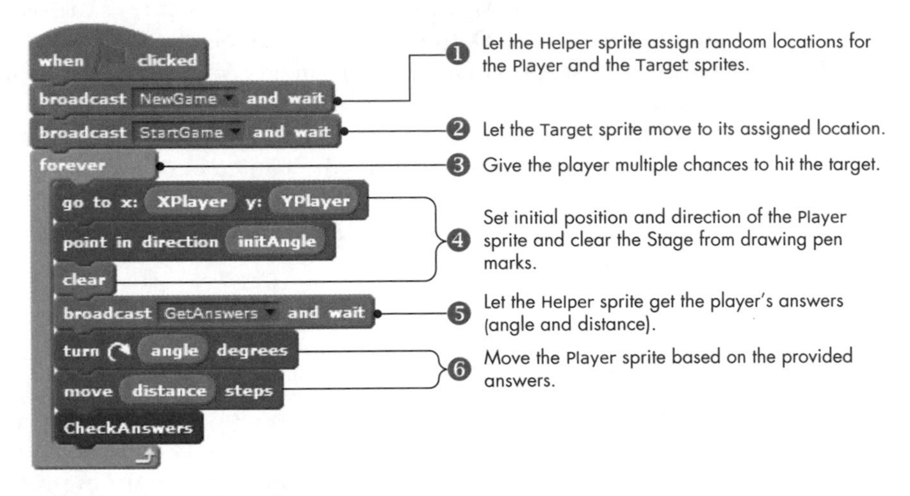

Figure 8-15: The Player *sprite script that runs when the green flag icon is clicked*

The script broadcasts NewGame to instruct the Helper sprite to assign new locations for the Player and the Target sprites ❶. The Helper sprite runs a simple procedure (not shown) that updates the following five variables with random numbers that will keep Player and Target visible (and separated by a certain distance) on the Stage:

XPlayer and YPlayer	The *x*- and *y*-coordinates of the Player sprite
XTarget and YTarget	The *x*- and *y*-coordinates of the Target sprite
initAngle	The initial direction of the Player sprite

Once the script has new positions for Player and Target, it broadcasts StartGame to move the Target sprite to its new location ❷. (The script for the Target sprite is not shown here.) Then the script enters an infinite loop to give the player multiple chances to hit the target ❸. The loop will be terminated by a **stop all** command (in the **CheckAnswers** procedure) when the player hits the target.

Each loop iteration sets the initial position and direction of the Player sprite and clears all pen marks from the Stage ❹ to delete the trace left behind from the previous guess. The script then broadcasts GetAnswers ❺, and in response, the Helper sprite prompts the player to enter an answer, as shown in Figure 8-16. The Helper sprite then splits the answer into two parts (before and after the comma) and updates angle and distance accordingly. Follow along with the comments on Figure 8-16 to see how this script works.

The Player sprite is then moved, with its pen down, as directed by the player ❻. This leaves a visual trace of the movement route that the player can use to refine his or her estimate for the next round.

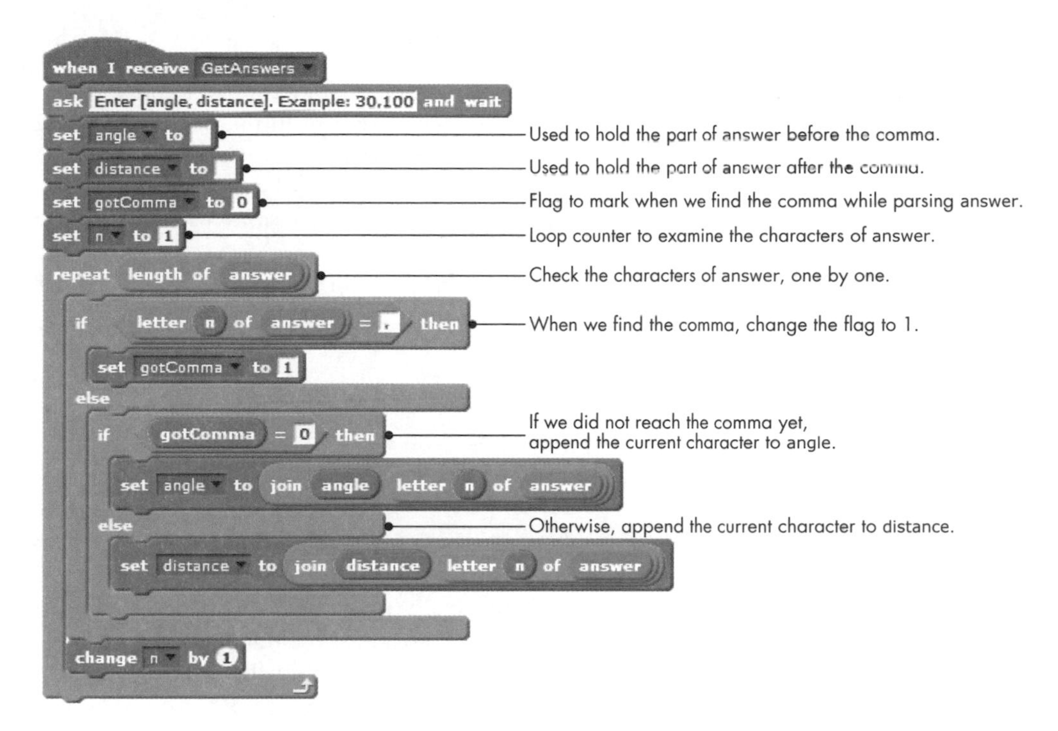

Figure 8-16: The GetAnswers *script*

Finally, the Player sprite executes the **CheckAnswers** procedure to see whether it is close enough to the target. The game ends only if the Player sprite comes within a very close distance of the target. Figure 8-17 shows how the Player sprite checks its distance from the target.

The Player sprite uses the **distance to** block to check how close it is to the Target sprite. If the distance is less than 20 steps, the game considers this a hit and says, "You won!" Otherwise, the shooting trial is considered a miss, the **forever** loop starts again, and the player gets another chance.

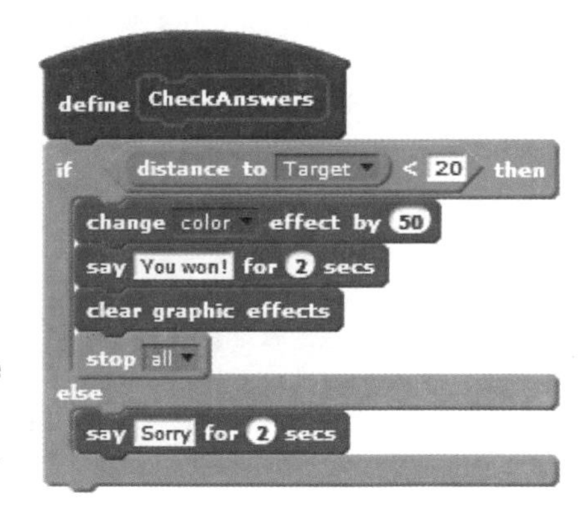

Figure 8-17: The **CheckAnswers** *procedure of the* Player *sprite.*

TRY IT OUT 8-4

Modify the Shoot game to keep track of the number of times it takes the player to hit the target and assign the player a score accordingly.

Binary to Decimal Converter

BinaryToDecimal .sb2

Binary (base-2) numbers have only two possible digits: 0 and 1. Most computers operate and communicate with binary numbers. Humans, however, prefer to work with numbers in the decimal (base-10) system. In this section, you'll develop an application that converts binary numbers to their decimal equivalents. Later, you could use it as a game to test your ability to perform such conversions.

Let's first discuss how to convert from binary to decimal. Figure 8-18 shows an example using the binary number 10011011.

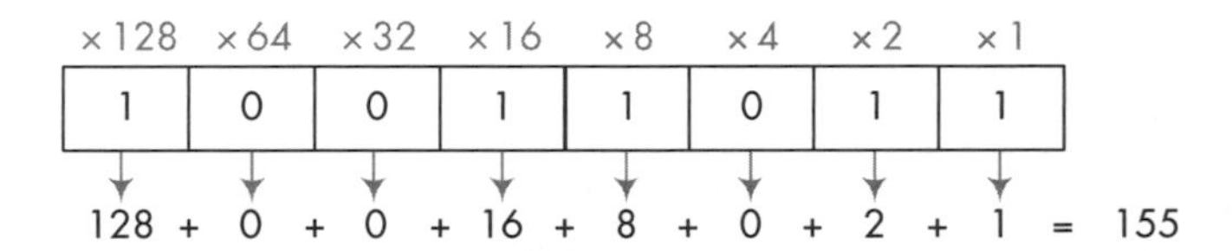

Figure 8-18: Converting a binary number to a decimal number

All we have to do is multiply each binary digit by its corresponding positional value and add the resulting products. *Positional values* correspond to increasing powers of the base from right to left, with the first position having a power of 0. Since binary is base 2, the rightmost digit has a positional value of $2^0 = 1$, so you'd multiply the digit by 1. You'd multiply the next digit by $2^1 = 2$, the next by $2^2 = 4$, and so on.

Figure 8-19 illustrates the user interface of the binary-to-decimal conversion application. The program asks the user to input an 8-bit binary number. It then shows the input number on the Stage with the Bit sprite, which uses two costumes to represent 0 and 1. The program also computes the equivalent decimal number, and the Driver sprite, which has a computer costume, displays that value to the user.

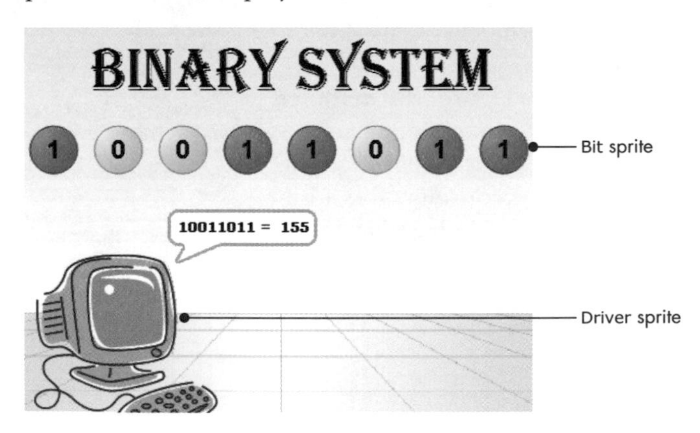

Figure 8-19: Binary-to-decimal conversion program

TRY IT OUT 8-5

To check your understanding, practice the following binary-to-decimal conversions: (a) 1010100, (b) 1101001, and (c) 1100001.

The program starts when the green flag icon is clicked. This event is trapped by the Driver sprite, which executes the script shown and described in Figure 8-20.

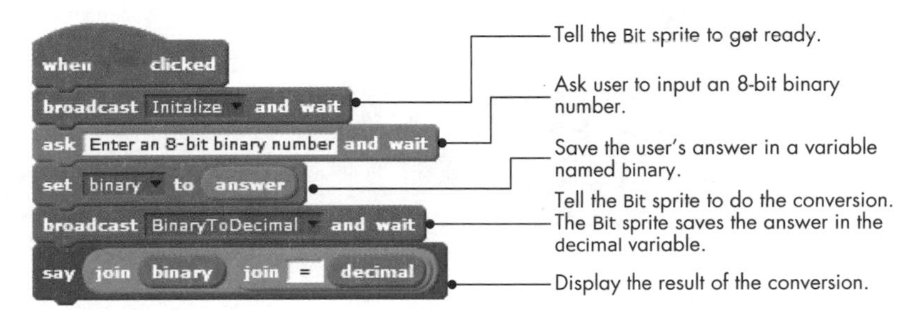

Figure 8-20: The script for the Driver *sprite*

This script prepares the Stage and asks the user to input a binary number so the Bit sprite can begin a new round of conversion. When the Bit sprite completes its work, the Driver sprite shows the user the decimal value, which is computed and stored by the Bit sprite in a shared variable named decimal.

The script that the Bit sprite runs in response to the Initialize message is illustrated in Figure 8-21.

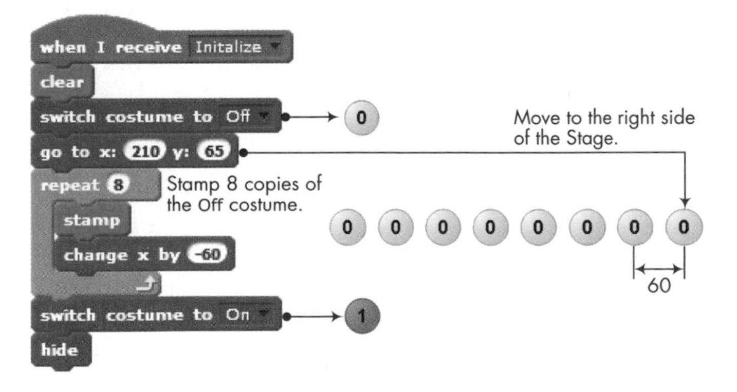

Figure 8-21: The Initialize *script for the* Bit *sprite*

This script draws a bit pattern representing eight zeros on the Stage. As you'll see in a moment, wherever a binary 1 appears in the user's input string, the script should stamp a costume of digit 1 over the corresponding bit. When the user enters the binary number to be converted, the Bit sprite should receive the BinaryToDecimal message and execute the script shown in Figure 8-22.

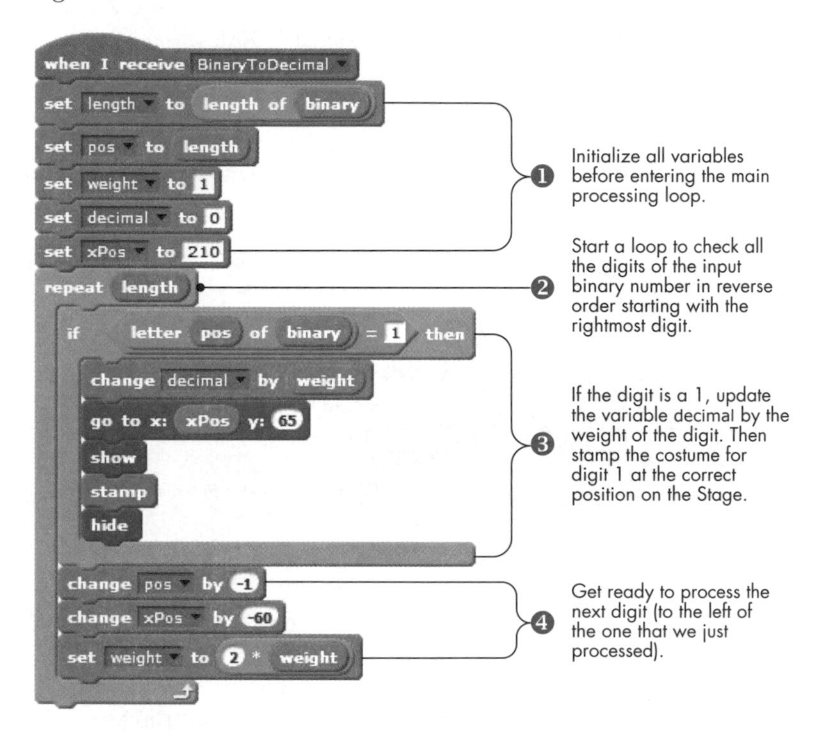
when I receive BinaryToDecimal
set length to length of binary
set pos to length
set weight to 1
set decimal to 0
set xPos to 210
repeat length
if letter pos of binary = 1 then
change decimal by weight
go to x: xPos y: 65
show
stamp
hide
change pos by -1
change xPos by -60
set weight to 2 * weight
❶ Initialize all variables before entering the main processing loop.
❷ Start a loop to check all the digits of the input binary number in reverse order starting with the rightmost digit.
❸ If the digit is a 1, update the variable decimal by the weight of the digit. Then stamp the costume for digit 1 at the correct position on the Stage.
❹ Get ready to process the next digit (to the left of the one that we just processed).

Figure 8-22: The BinaryToDecimal *script for the* Bit *sprite*

First, the conversion procedure initializes all of the variables it will use ❶:

- length is the number of bits in the user's binary number.
- pos points to the rightmost digit of the input number.
- weight starts at the positional value of the rightmost binary digit.
- decimal is set to 0 but will hold the result of the conversion at the end.
- xPos begins at the *x*-coordinate of the image of the rightmost binary digit.

Inside the repeat loop ❷, the procedure checks each digit to see whether it is a 1 or a 0. If the loop finds a 1 ❸, it adds the current value of weight to decimal and stamps the digit-1 costume on top of the digit-0 image.

At the end of the loop, the script updates several variables before moving to the next iteration:

- pos is updated to point to the digit to the left of the one we just processed.
- xPos is aligned with the center of the image of the next digit, just in case we need to stamp a new image.
- weight is multiplied by 2, which means it will take on the values 1, 2, 4, 8, 16, and so on as the loop iterates.

TRY IT OUT 8-6

Make the Driver sprite validate the number entered by the user before broadcasting the BinaryToDecimal message to the Bit sprite. You should verify that (1) the number entered by the user is a binary number (that is, it only contains ones and zeros) and (2) the length of the input is at most eight digits.

Hangman

Hangman.sb2

In this section, we'll write a classic Hangman game. Figure 8-23 shows the game in action.

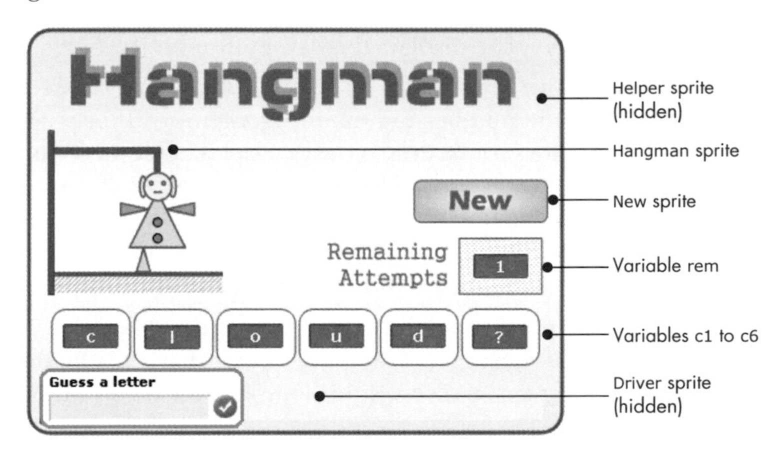

Figure 8-23: The user interface for the Hangman game

The program randomly selects a secret six-letter word and shows one question mark for each letter. The player has eight chances to guess the letters in the word. If the player guesses a letter correctly, the program shows all occurrences of that letter in the secret word. Otherwise, the program shows a new part of a hanging figure (the head, body, left arm, and so on). After eight wrong guesses, the program finishes the figure, and the player loses the game. If the player guesses the secret word in eight attempts or fewer, the result is victory. This application has the following four sprites:

Driver This sprite hides itself when the game starts, prompts the player to enter guesses, and processes the player's answers. When the game ends, the sprite shows one of the following two costumes:

Good job! You won. | Sorry! You lost.

Hangman This sprite displays the evolving image of the hangman. It has a total of nine costumes, each one showing an additional part of the hangman's body, as depicted in Figure 8-24.

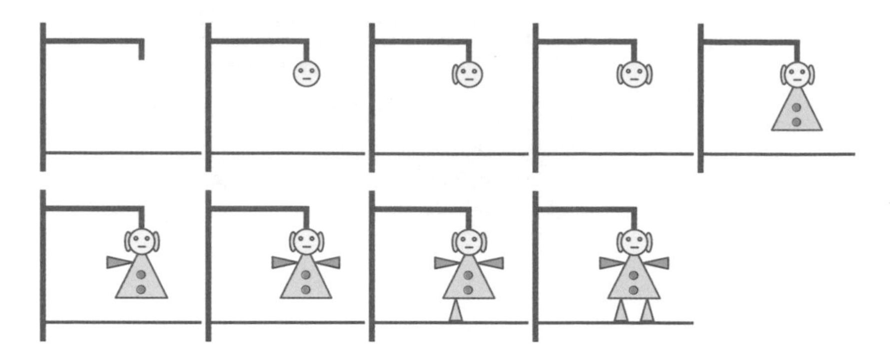

Figure 8-24: The nine costumes of the Hangman *sprite*

New This sprite displays the New button on the Stage.

Helper This invisible sprite displays the letters guessed by the player as well as the number of remaining attempts. It uses seven variables with monitors configured as large displays and positioned at the correct locations on the Stage. Using a different sprite to update the display separates the game logic from the user interface. You can, for example, change this sprite to show more fancy letters on the Stage without affecting the rest of the application.

When the player presses the New sprite (the New button), it broadcasts a NewGame message to alert the Driver sprite that a new game has started. When the Driver sprite receives this message, it executes the script shown in Figure 8-25.

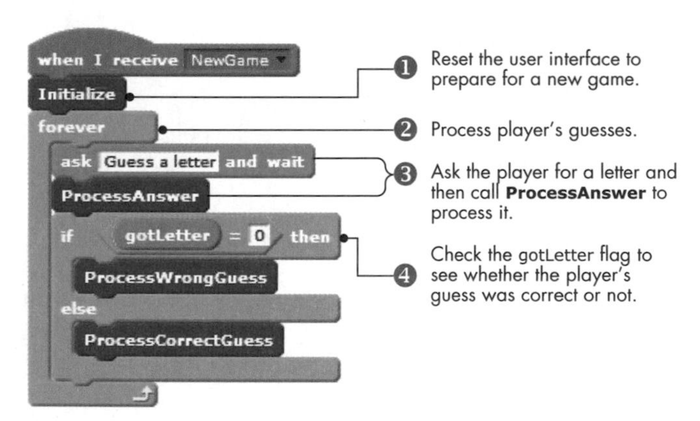

when I receive NewGame
Initialize
forever
ask Guess a letter and wait
ProcessAnswer
if gotLetter = 0 then
ProcessWrongGuess
else
ProcessCorrectGuess
1 Reset the user interface to prepare for a new game.
2 Process player's guesses.
3 Ask the player for a letter and then call ProcessAnswer to process it.
4 Check the gotLetter flag to see whether the player's guess was correct or not.

Figure 8-25: The NewGame *script of the* Driver *sprite*

The script resets the game's user interface ❶ and starts a loop ❷ to read in letter guesses. Another procedure called by the Driver sprite will terminate this loop via a **stop all** block when the game's end condition is detected.

In each iteration of the loop, the Driver sprite asks the player to guess a letter and waits for input ❸. When the player enters a guess, the script calls **ProcessAnswer**, which will update a flag (named gotLetter) to indicate whether the letter was right or wrong.

When **ProcessAnswer** returns, the script checks the gotLetter flag ❹ and acts based on whether the player's guess was correct or not. I'll explain the procedures called by NewGame next, starting with the scripts in Figure 8-26.

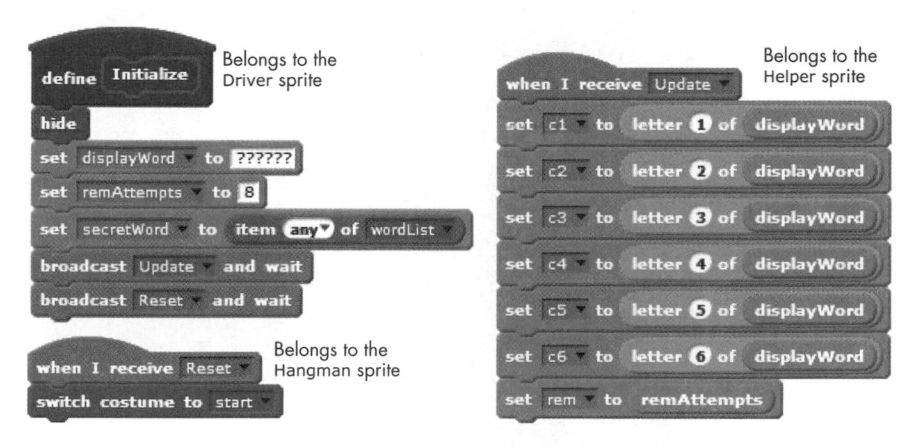

Figure 8-26: Scripts triggered from the **Initialize** *procedure*

During initialization, the Driver sprite hides itself, initializes displayWord to a string with six question marks, and sets remAttempts (how many guesses the player has left) to 8. It then selects the secretWord from a predefined list of six-letter words. Next the procedure broadcasts Update so the Helper sprite will assign its variables (whose monitors are visible on the Stage) to the correct values. The last instruction broadcasts the Reset message to the Hangman sprite. When the Hangman sprite receives this message, it switches to its start costume, which shows an empty gallows.

Now let's consider a simple example to help us understand what the **ProcessAnswer** procedure does (see Figure 8-27). Assume the secret word is *across* and that this is the first round of the game (which means that displayWord is "??????"). If the player's first guess is r, **ProcessAnswer** should set gotLetter to 1 to indicate a correct guess, set displayWord to "??r???" to show the letter's position, and set qmarkCount (the number of question marks in the updated display string) to 5. When qmarkCount reaches 0, the player has guessed all the letters in the secret word. **ProcessAnswer** belongs to the Driver sprite, and you can see the full script in Figure 8-27 (left).

ProcessAnswer starts by resetting both the gotLetter flag and qmarkCount to 0. It will increase qmarkCount by 1 for every unknown letter in the secret word. The temporary variable, temp, which is used to construct the display string after every guess, is initialized to an empty string. The pos variable is used as a loop counter.

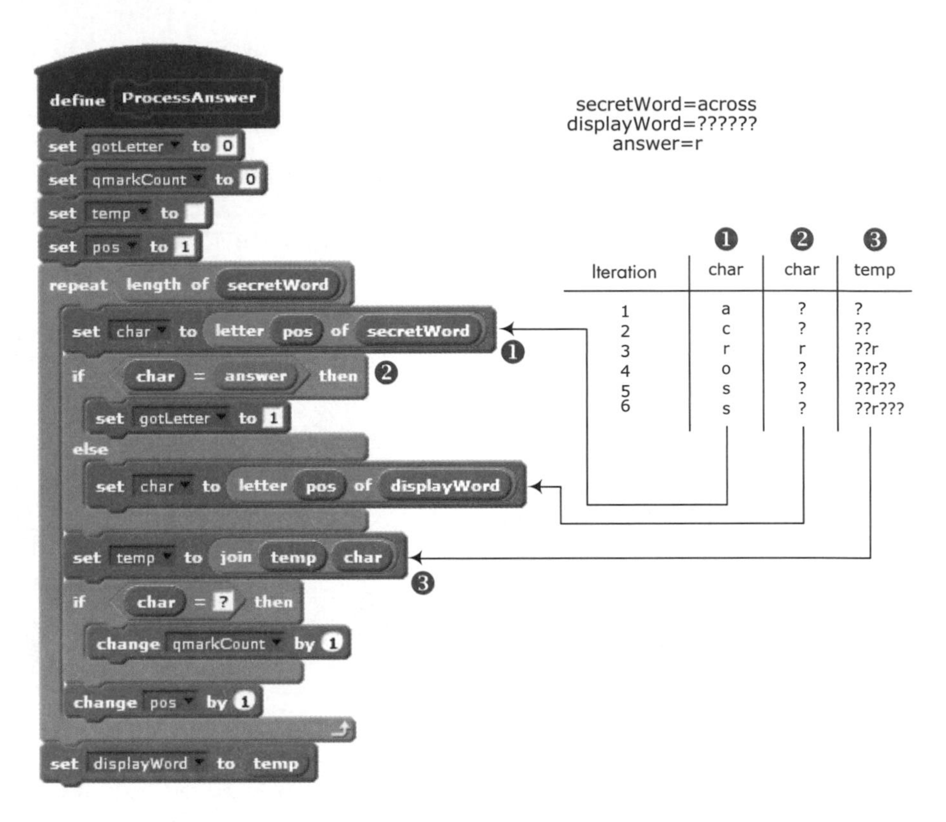

Figure 8-27: The **ProcessAnswer** *procedure*

The loop examines each letter of secretWord, using pos as an index. If the examined letter (saved in char) equals the guessed letter (saved in Scratch's built-in answer variable), the gotLetter flag is set to 1. Otherwise, the char variable is set to the letter at the corresponding position in the displayWord variable. Either way, the script adds char to the end of temp, as illustrated in Figure 8-27 (right).

When the loop terminates, the displayWord variable will contain the six letters to be displayed on the Stage, taking the user's most recent guess into account. The loop also tracks the number of question marks in the display string. If there are none, then the user has successfully guessed the secret word.

When **ProcessAnswer** returns, the NewGame message handler checks gotLetter to see whether the player guessed correctly. If not, it will call **ProcessWrongGuess**, shown in Figure 8-28.

This procedure broadcasts WrongGuess to notify the Hangman sprite to show its next costume, and then it decrements the number of remaining guesses by 1. If the user is out of guesses, the script reveals the secret word and ends the game. Otherwise, it broadcasts an Update message to show how many trials the player has left.

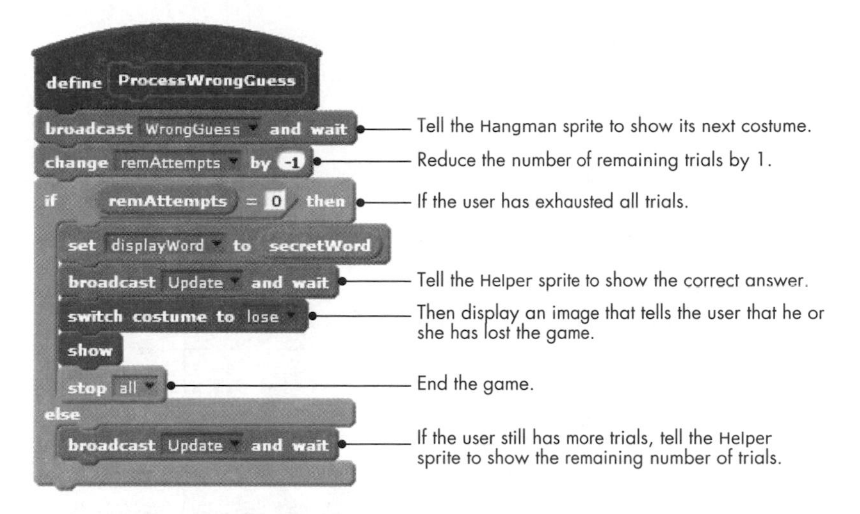
define ProcessWrongGuess
broadcast WrongGuess and wait
change remAttempts by -1
if remAttempts = 0 then
set displayWord to secretWord
broadcast Update and wait
switch costume to lose
show
stop all
else
broadcast Update and wait
Tell the Hangman sprite to show its next costume.
Reduce the number of remaining trials by 1.
If the user has exhausted all trials.
Tell the Helper sprite to show the correct answer.
Then display an image that tells the user that he or she has lost the game.
End the game.
If the user still has more trials, tell the Helper sprite to show the remaining number of trials.

Figure 8-28: The **ProcessWrongGuess** *procedure*

If the player's letter was correct, the **ProcessCorrectGuess** shown in Figure 8-29 should be called instead of **ProcessWrongGuess**.

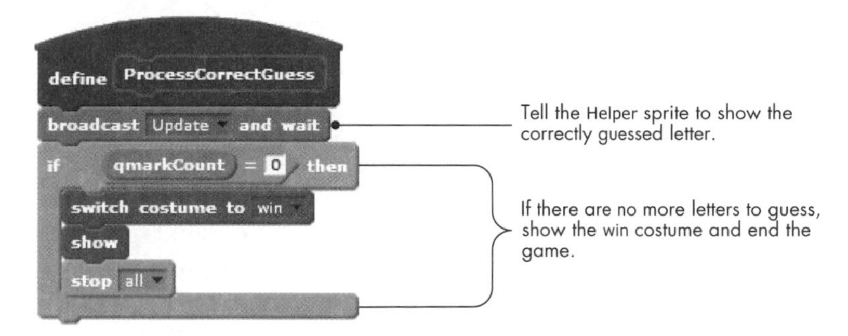
define ProcessCorrectGuess
broadcast Update and wait
if qmarkCount = 0 then
switch costume to win
show
stop all
Tell the Helper sprite to show the correctly guessed letter.
If there are no more letters to guess, show the win costume and end the game.

Figure 8-29: The **ProcessCorrectGuess** *procedure*

ProcessCorrectGuess broadcasts Update to show the letter the player guessed correctly. It then checks the value of qmarkCount. If qmarkCount is 0, the player has guessed all of the letters correctly, so the Driver sprite shows its win costume and ends the game.

TRY IT OUT 8-7

The Hangman program doesn't validate the user input; you could enter a non-alphabetic character or even an entire word. Modify the program so that it rejects any invalid input by the user.

Fraction Tutor

FractionTutor.sb2

For our last example, we'll present an educational game for teaching fractions. The interface for this game is shown in Figure 8-30. The player can select an operation (+, –, ×, or ÷) and click the New button to create a new problem. When the player enters an answer and clicks the Check button, the Teacher sprite (image of a woman) checks that answer and provides an appropriate feedback message.

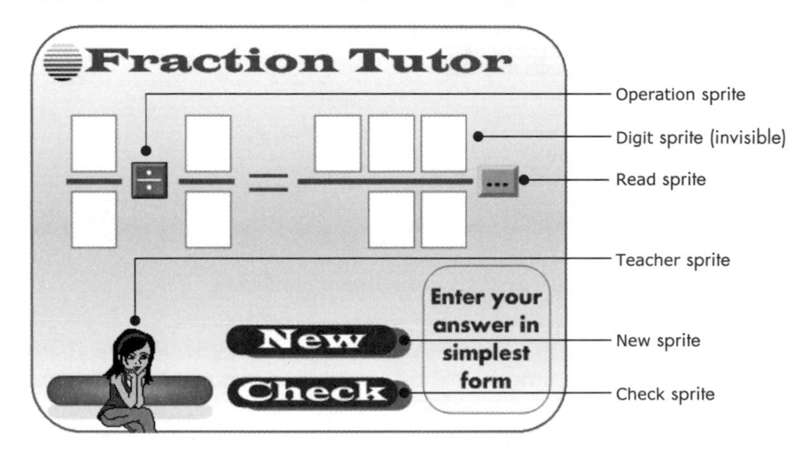

Figure 8-30: The user interface for the Fraction Tutor application

The application contains six sprites. Operation allows the player to choose a mathematical operation. Read shows the answer entry button, New shows the New button, and Check shows the Check button. The Teacher sprite checks the player's answer, and an invisible sprite named Digit stamps the numbers that correspond to the current problem on the Stage.

When the player clicks the New sprite (the New button), it executes the script shown in Figure 8-31. The script assigns random values between 1 and 9 to the numerator and denominator of both operands, which are represented by the four variables num1, den1, num2, and den2. It then broadcasts a NewProblem message to tell the Digit sprite to stamp these numbers on the Stage.

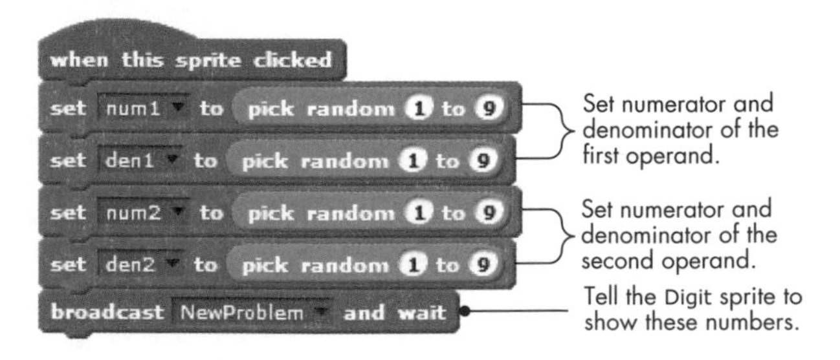

Figure 8-31: The script for the New sprite

The Digit sprite has 12 costumes (named d1 through d12), as shown in Figure 8-32 (right). When this sprite receives the NewProblem broadcast, it stamps costumes representing the numerators and denominators of the two operands. Figure 8-32 also shows the procedure that does the actual stamping.

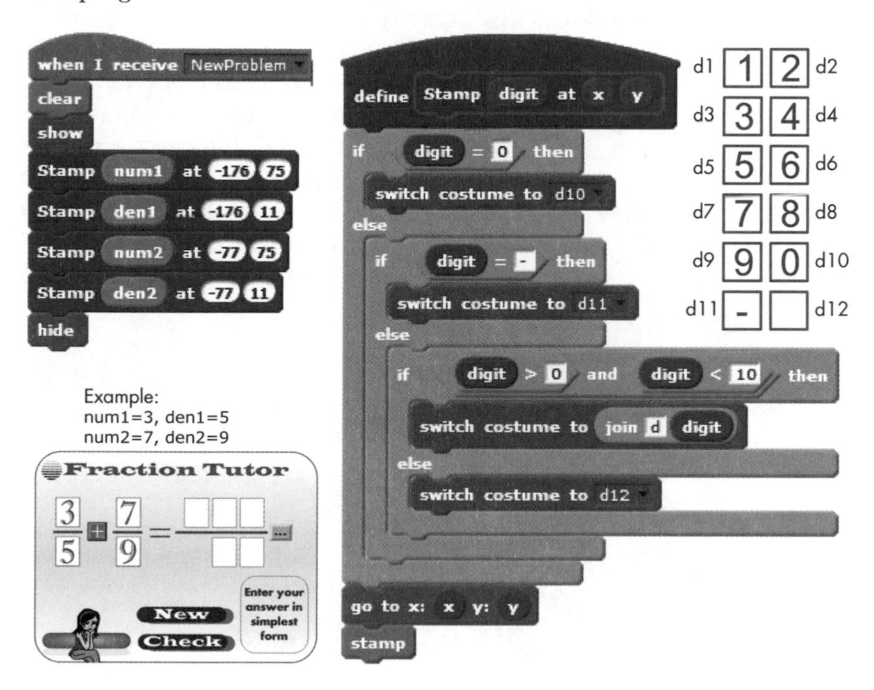

Figure 8-32: The function of the Digit *sprite*

The procedure uses nested **if/else** blocks to determine which costume corresponds to the digit to be stamped. Note how the costume name for digits 1 through 9 is formed using the **join** operator. After switching to the correct costume, the Digit sprite moves to the specified (*x*,*y*) position and stamps the image of the costume at that location.

When the new problem is shown, the user can click the Read button to enter an answer. The script associated with this button is illustrated in Figure 8-33. The part of the script that parses the player's answer into two tokens (numerator and denominator) is similar to the one presented in Figure 8-16 for extracting the angle and distance from answer in the Shoot game and, therefore, is not shown here. Check the *FractionTutor.sb2* file for the complete procedure.

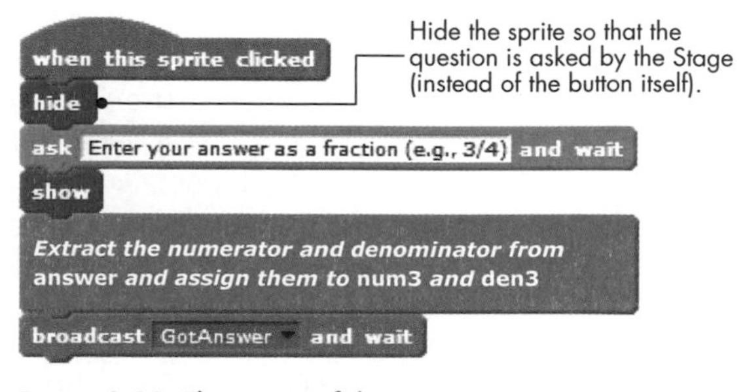

Figure 8-33: The script of the Read *sprite*

First, the user is asked to enter an answer in fraction form (for example, 3/5 or –7/8). The script then extracts the numerator and the denominator of the answer string (which are separated by the division sign) and assigns them to the num3 and den3 variables, respectively. For example, if the user enters –23/15, num3 will be set to –23 and den3 will be set to 15. After that, the script broadcasts a GotAnswer message to tell the Digit sprite to show the user's answer on the Stage. When the Digit sprite receives this message, it stamps the digits of num3 and den3 at the correct positions on the Stage in the same way it displayed the numerators and denominators of the two operands. You can check the file *FractionTutor.sb2* for the details.

After entering an answer, the user can click the Check button to see if the answer is correct. The script for the Check sprite broadcasts a CheckAnswer message to inform the other sprites of the user's request. This message is trapped and processed by the Teacher sprite, which will execute the script shown in Figure 8-34.

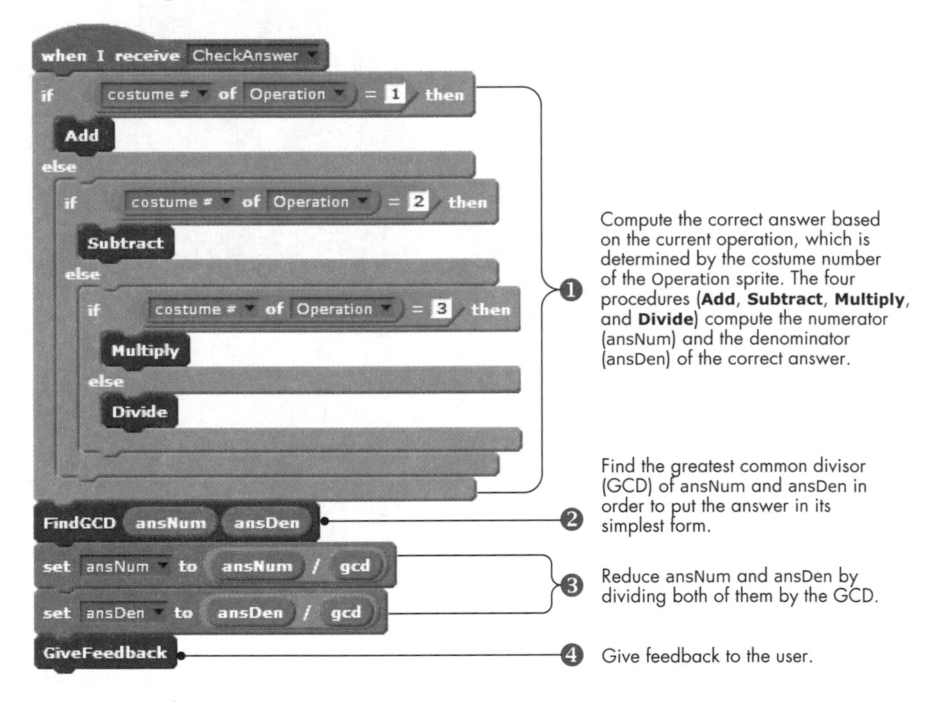

Figure 8-34: The CheckAnswer *script*

The current costume of the Operation sprite tells which operation procedure (**Add**, **Subtract**, **Multiply**, or **Divide**) to execute ❶. The operations take num1, den1, num2, and den2 as inputs and set the values of ansNum and ansDen, which represent the numerator and denominator of the correct answer, respectively. The four procedures are shown in Figure 8-35.

After finding the answer, CheckAnswer needs to put it in its simplest form. For example, 2/4 should be simplified to 1/2. To perform this reduction, the script first finds the greatest common divisor (GCD), also known as the greatest common factor, of the numerator and denominator ❷. (We'll look at this procedure in a moment.)

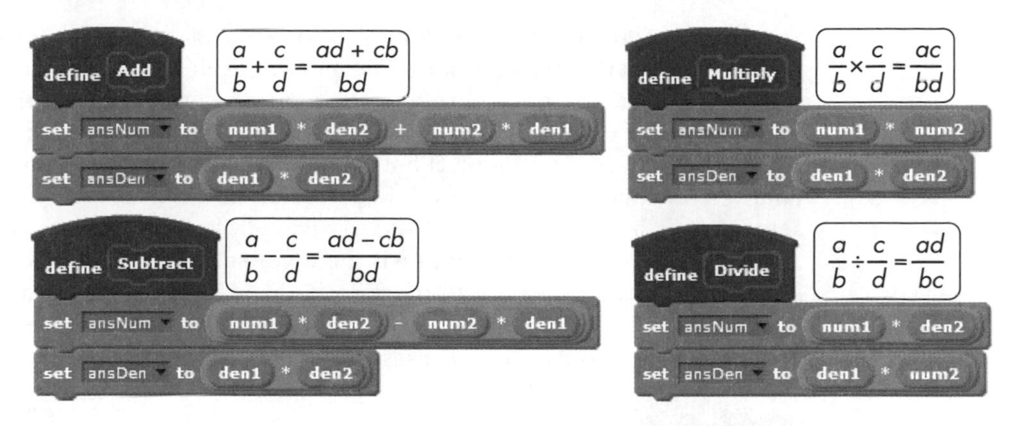

Figure 8-35: The **Add**, **Subtract**, **Multiply**, *and* **Divide** *procedures of the* Teacher *sprite*

After finding the GCD, the script divides ansNum and ansDen by that value ❸ and calls **GiveFeedback** ❹ to display whether or not the user's answer was correct.

Now let's look more closely at the details of these procedures, starting with the four operation procedures shown in Figure 8-35.

These procedures compute the result of performing an operation of the form

$$\frac{num1}{den1}[+,-,\times,\div]\frac{num2}{den2}=\frac{ansNum}{ansDen}$$

and store the result in two variables (ansNum and ansDen) corresponding to the answer's numerator and denominator, respectively.

Let's now move on to the **FindGCD** procedure, shown in Figure 8-36.

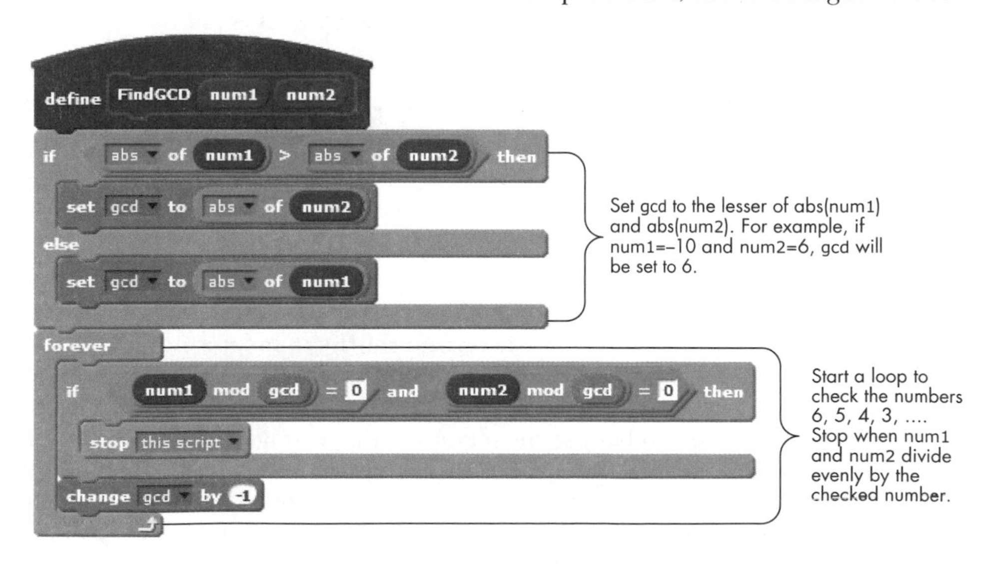

Figure 8-36: The **FindGCD** *procedure of the* Teacher *sprite*

Let's trace the operation of **FindGCD** when num1 = –10 and num2 = 6. We need to find the largest positive integer that divides num1 and num2 without a remainder. The procedure starts by setting gcd, the result, to the lesser absolute value of the two numbers, –6 in our example. A loop then tests the numbers 6, 5, 4, and so on, until both num1 and num2 divide evenly by the checked number. This is the result we are after. In this example, gcd will be set to 2 since both numbers (–10 and 6) divide by 2 without a remainder.

The last procedure to examine is the **GiveFeedback** procedure, which compares the user's answer with the correct answer and displays an appropriate message, as shown in Figure 8-37. The figure also shows some examples that demonstrate the different cases of the **if/else** structure.

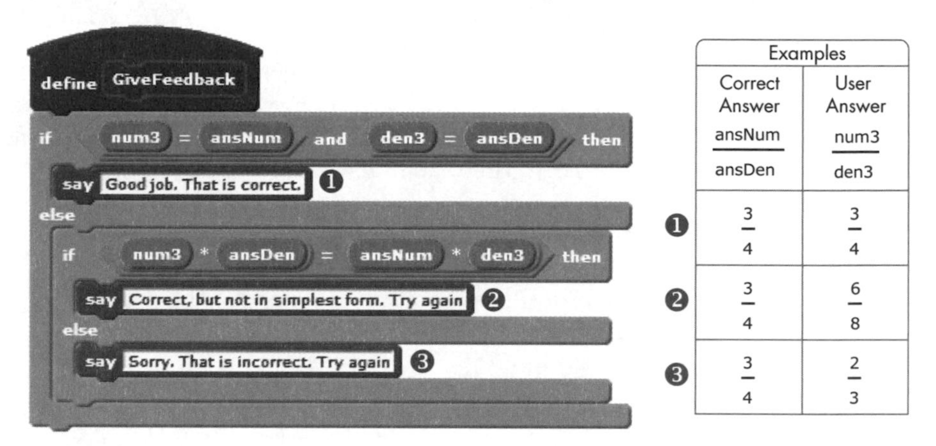

Figure 8-37: The **GiveFeedback** *procedure of the* Teacher *sprite*

TRY IT OUT 8-8

Modify the fraction tutor program to keep track of the number of correct and incorrect answers. Devise a scheme for calculating a score and showing it to the user.

Summary

String processing is an important programming skill. In this chapter, you learned how to access individual characters of a string to combine them, compare them, remove them, and shuffle them around.

We started with a detailed look at the string data type and how strings are stored as sequences of characters. We then wrote several procedures that demonstrated basic string manipulation techniques. After that, we used these techniques to write several interesting and practical applications. The concepts developed in these projects can be applied in many other areas, and I certainly hope they'll help you think of your own projects.

In the next chapter, you'll learn about lists and how to use them to store and manipulate a bunch of values. Equipped with this new data structure, you'll have all the tools you need to write professional programs in Scratch.

Problems

1. Write a program that asks the user to enter a word and then says that word *N* times, where *N* is the number of letters in the input word.
2. Write a program that asks the user to enter a word. The program then determines the number of occurrences of the letter *a* in the input word.
3. Write a program that reads a singular English noun from the user. The program then produces the plural form of that noun. (Hint: Check the last letter and the second from the last letter of the input word.) To keep the program simple, consider only the following rule: If the word ends in *ch*, *x*, or *s*, add *es* for the plural, otherwise just add an *s*.
4. Write a program that reads a single character (between *a* and *z*) from the user and outputs the position of that character in the alphabet ($a = 1$, $b = 2$, $c = 3$, and so on). Uppercase letters and lowercase letters should be treated the same. (Hint: Define a variable named `alpha` that holds the letters of the alphabet, as we did in Figure 8-9, and then use a loop to find the position of the input character within the variable *alpha*.)
5. Write a program that asks the user to enter a letter of the alphabet and then displays the letter that precedes the input letter. (Hint: Use the same technique used in the previous problem.)
6. Write a program that reads a positive integer from the user then finds and displays the sum of its digits. For example, if the user enters `3582`, the program should display `18` ($3 + 5 + 8 + 2$).
7. Write a program that reads a word from the user and then displays the letters in reverse using the **say** block.
8. Write a program that gets a number from the user and then inserts a space between each pair of digits. For example, if the input number is `1234`, the output string should be `1 2 3 4`. (Hint: Construct the output variable by joining the individual letters from the input number with white spaces.)

CompareFractions.sb2

9. In this problem, you'll create a game that lets players compare fractions. The user interface is shown on the right. When the `New` button is clicked, the game randomly picks two fractions to compare. The user selects less than (<), greater than (>), or equal to (=) by clicking the operator button. When the user clicks the `Check` button, the game checks the answer and provides feedback. Open the file *CompareFractions.sb2* and add the necessary scripts to complete the game.

9

LISTS

The programs we've written so far have used ordinary variables to store single pieces of data. Such variables are not as useful, however, when you want to store a bunch of values, such as your friends' phone numbers, names of books, or a month of temperature readings. For example, if you wanted your program to remember the phone numbers of 20 of your friends, you'd need 20 variables! Certainly, writing and maintaining a program with 20 variables would be tedious. In this chapter, we'll explore another built-in data type, called a *list*, which offers a convenient way to group related values. Here's what we'll cover:

- How to create and manipulate lists
- Initializing and accessing individual elements in a list
- Basic sorting and search techniques
- Using lists to create powerful applications

First, I'll explain how to make lists in Scratch, demonstrate the commands you can use with them, and show you how to populate lists with data entered by a user. We'll then discuss numeric lists and common operations performed on them, such as finding the minimum, the maximum, and the average value of their elements. After that, we'll learn one algorithm for sorting the elements in a list. We'll end with several example programs that demonstrate some real-world applications of lists.

Lists in Scratch

A list is like a container where you can store and access multiple values. You can think of it as a dresser with many drawers, with each drawer storing a single item. When you create a list, you name it just as you would a variable. You can then access the individual elements of the list using their storage position in the list. Figure 9-1, for example, depicts a list named dayList that stores the names of the seven days of the week.

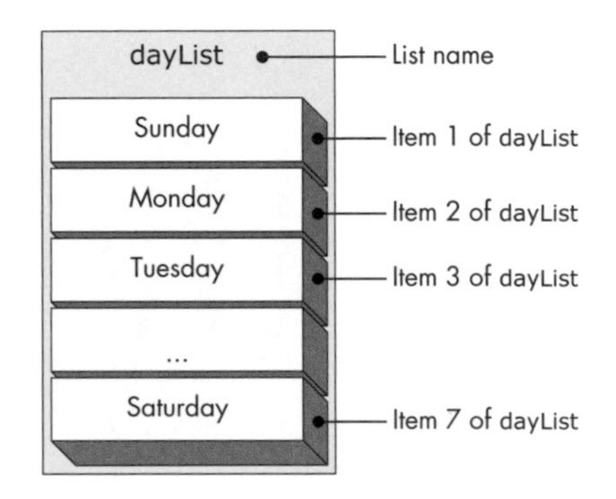

Figure 9-1: A list that contains the days of the week

You can refer to the items contained in a list using their *storage index* (or position). In Scratch, the first item has an index of 1, the second item is 2, and so on. For example, since Tuesday is third in the list, it has an index of 3. Therefore, you can refer to the third element of our dayList using a command of the form "item 3 of dayList."

Let's jump right in and create some lists in Scratch. We'll also look at the commands that allow us to manage and manipulate lists in our programs and learn how Scratch responds to invalid list commands.

Creating Lists

Creating a list is almost identical to creating a variable. Select the *Data* palette and click **Make a List** to bring up the dialog in Figure 9-2 (right). Next, enter the name of the list (we'll use dayList) and specify its scope. Choosing the For all sprites option creates a *global* list that any sprite in your application can access, while the For this sprite only option creates a *local* list that belongs to the currently selected sprite. Local lists can only be read (and written to) by the owner sprite.

When you click **OK** to confirm your input, Scratch creates a new *empty list* and shows the list-related blocks, as illustrated in Figure 9-3. This is similar to what you'd see when you create a new variable. An empty list is a list that does not contain any items.

You can use these new commands to manipulate the contents of your list while your script is running. You can append new items, insert items at specific positions, delete certain items, or replace the values of existing items.

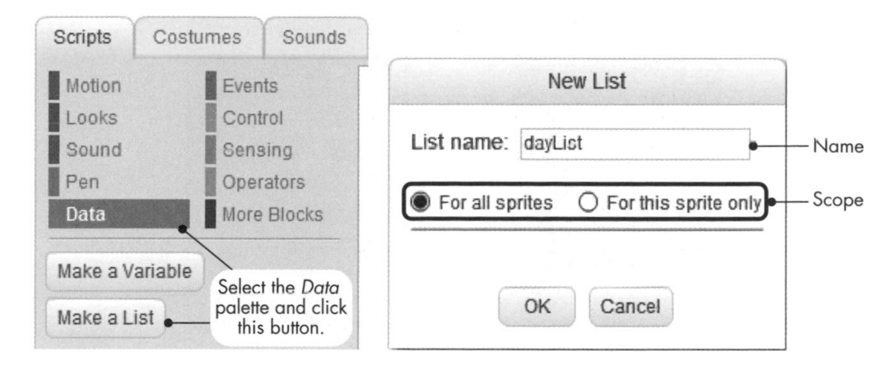

Figure 9-2: Creating a list in Scratch is similar to creating a variable.

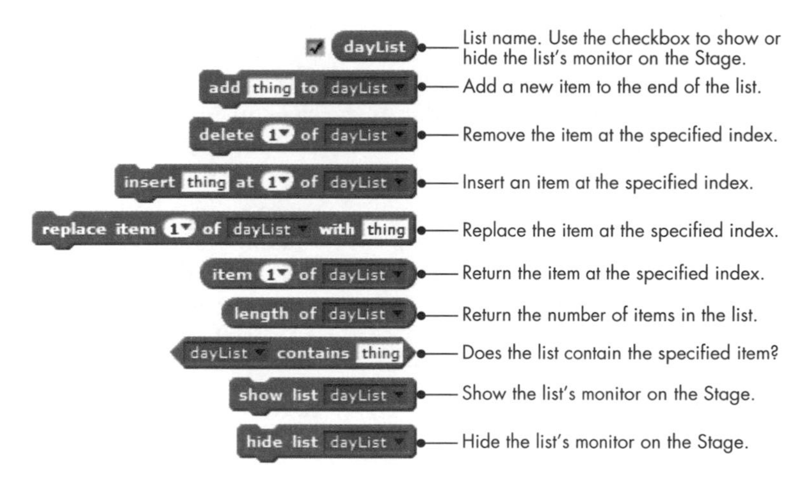

Figure 9-3: Command and function blocks that you can use with lists

When a new list is created, Scratch also shows the list's monitor on the Stage, as illustrated in Figure 9-4. The list will initially be empty, so its length starts at 0. You can use this monitor block to add entries to your list as you design a program.

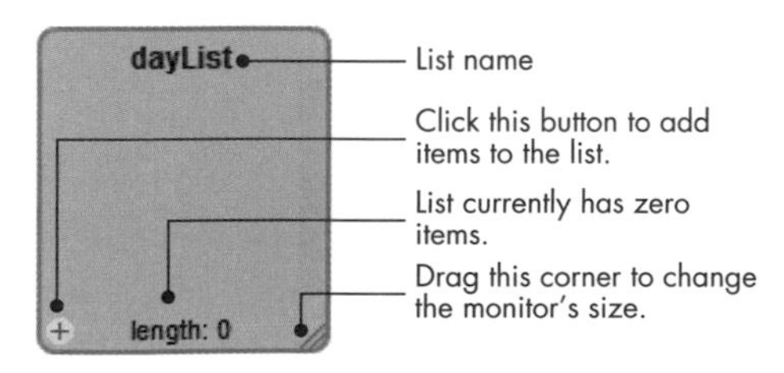

Figure 9-4: The monitor of a newly created list is shown on the Stage.

If you know the data that you want to store in the list (as is the case for our dayList), you can add it to the list at this point. Figure 9-5 shows how you can add days to the dayList using its monitor.

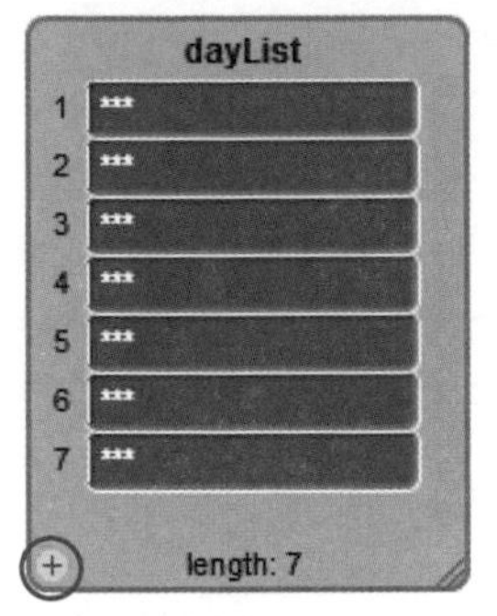

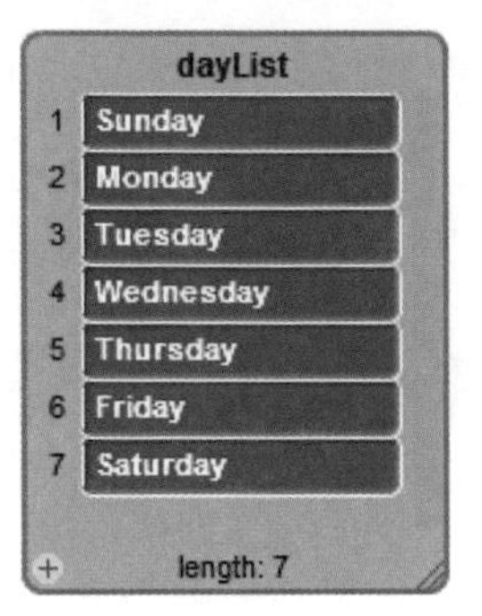

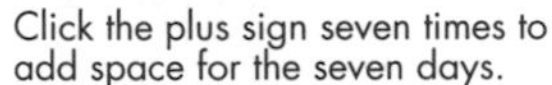

Click the plus sign seven times to
add space for the seven days.

Click inside the edit boxes and type your data.

Figure 9-5: Populating the dayList

Click the plus sign at the lower-left corner seven times to create seven entries and then enter a day of the week inside each edit box. Use the TAB key to navigate through the list items. Pressing TAB once highlights the next list item with a yellow border. Pressing TAB another time highlights the editable text of the selected item and removes the yellow border. If you click the plus sign while the currently selected item is surrounded by a yellow border, the new list item will be added after the current item; otherwise, it will be added before the current item. Try navigating the list!

TRY IT OUT 9-1

Populate dayList with the names of the weekdays, as shown in Figure 9-5.

List Commands

Figure 9-3 described all the blocks that Scratch added when we created our dayList. In this section, we'll look more closely at these blocks to better understand their function.

Add and Delete

The **add** command places a new item at the end of a list, while the **delete** command removes an item from a specific position. Figure 9-6 shows these commands in action.

The script first executes the **delete** command to remove the second item of the list, which is "Orange." The script then puts "Lemon" at the end of the list using the **add** command.

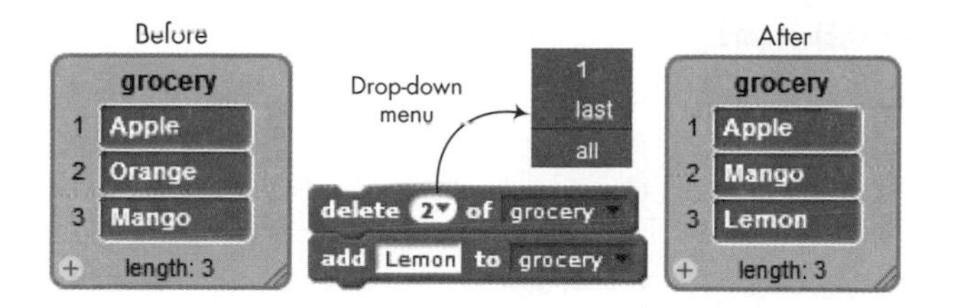

Figure 9-6: A list before and after **add** *and* **delete** *are used to change its contents*

The **add** command is straightforward, but let's examine the **delete** command more closely. You can type the index of the element you want to delete directly into the block's parameter slot, or you can click the drop-down arrow. The drop-down menu (see Figure 9-6) shows three options: 1, last, and all. Select 1 to delete the first item ("Apple") from the list, select last to delete the last item ("Mango"), or select all to delete all the items from the list.

Insert and Replace

Let's say you want to store your friends' names and phone numbers alphabetically in a list, just like the contacts list in your cell phone. As you make your list, you need to insert each friend's contact information at the proper position. Later, if one friend gets a new phone number, you'll need to edit the list to enter it. The **insert** and **replace** commands can help you with these tasks. Figure 9-7 shows an example of using the **insert** and **replace** commands with our phone list.

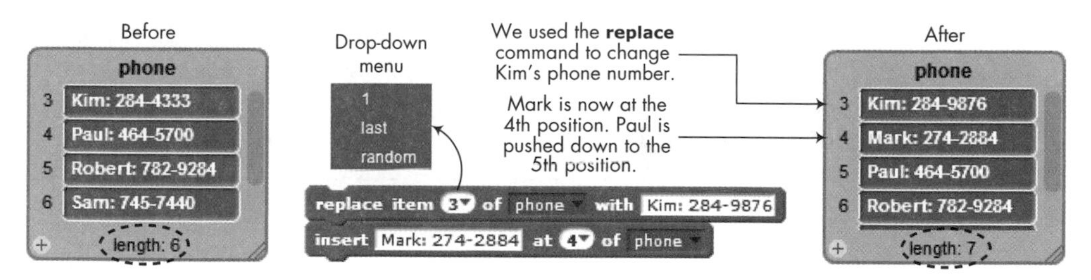

Figure 9-7: Using the **insert** *and the* **replace** *commands to update a list of telephone numbers*

The **replace** command overwrites the current string at slot number 3 with Kim's new phone number. The **insert** command places the phone number of a new friend, Mark, at slot number 4 in the list. Notice that the existing elements moved down one slot to make room for the new entry.

Clicking the item number's down arrow in both the **replace** and the **insert** commands shows a drop-down menu of three options: 1, last, and random (see Figure 9-7). If you select random, the selected command will choose an item number randomly. You'll see some useful applications of this feature later in this chapter.

Accessing List Elements

As we mentioned earlier, you can access any element in a list using that element's index. For example, the script in Figure 9-8 demonstrates using the **item of** block to access the elements of our dayList. The script uses a variable named pos (short for *position*) to iterate through each item of the list, showing the contents via the **say** command.

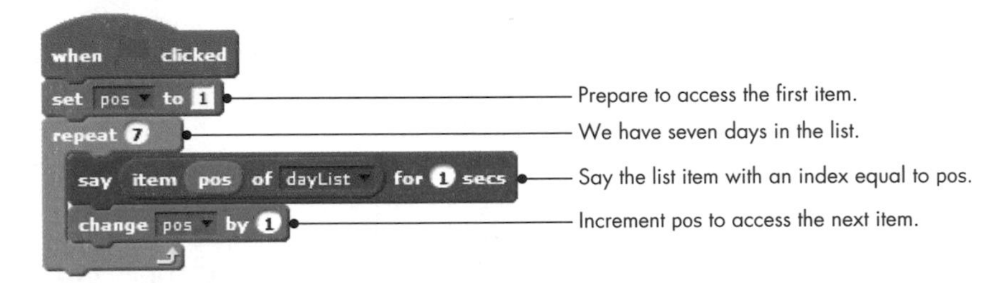

Figure 9-8: This script causes the sprite to display the seven days of our dayList.

The script initializes the value of pos to 1 so it can access the first element in dayList, and then the script enters a loop. The loop's repeat count is set to 7, the number of elements in our list. On each pass, the loop will say the list item with an index equal to pos and increment the value of pos to access the next element. In other words, we're using pos as an index to pinpoint a specific element in the list.

TRY IT OUT 9-2

Replace the literal number 7 in the repeat loop with the **length of dayList** block. This is what you'd normally do to step through a list if you didn't know how many items it contained. Also, select **random** from the first drop-down menu in the **item of** block. This should cause the script to display an item from the list at random.

The Contains Block

You can check whether a certain string is in a list by using **contains**, a Boolean block that returns true or false based on whether or not the list contains your string. The script shown in Figure 9-9 illustrates one use of this block. Since dayList contains the string "Friday", the **say** command inside the **if** block will be executed.

NOTE *The* **contains** *block is case insensitive. The block* **dayList contains friDAY**, *for example, would also evaluate to true.*

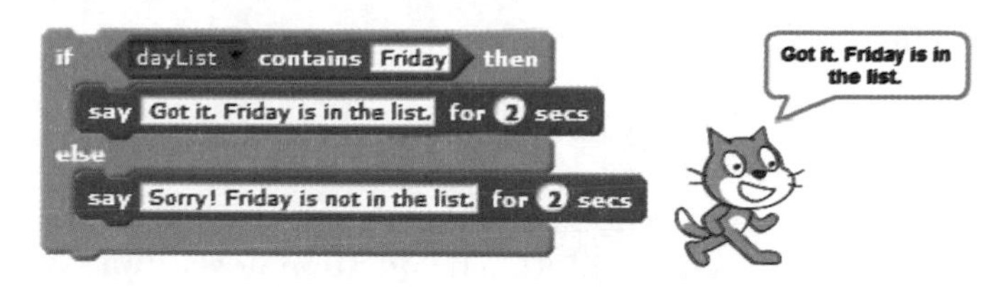

Figure 9-9: Using the **contains** *block to check whether a string is in a list*

Bounds Checking

The four list blocks (**delete**, **insert**, **replace**, and **item of**) require an input parameter that specifies the index of the item you want to access. For example, to delete the seventh element of our dayList, we use **delete 7 of dayList**. But what do you think will happen if you use an invalid index with one of these blocks? For example, how would Scratch respond if you asked it to delete the eighth element of our dayList (which only contains seven elements)?

Trying to access an element past the boundaries of a list is, technically, an error. Rather than display an error message or abruptly terminate your program, however, Scratch silently tries to do something sensible with the offending block. For this reason, the absence of error messages does not necessarily mean the absence of errors. Problems may still exist in your code, and when they do, you still need to fix them. Scratch won't complain about invalid indexes in your blocks, but the outcome usually won't be what you intended. Table 9-1 shows what can happen when you try to access dayList using an out-of-range index.

Table 9-1: Unexpected Results from Bad List Indexes

Command or Function Block	Result
item 8 of dayList	Returns an empty string because dayList has only seven items. The same thing happens if you use an index less than 1.
item 1.9 of dayList	Scratch ignores the .9 and returns the first item of dayList, which is "Sunday". Similarly, if you asked for item 5.3, Scratch would return the fifth item, "Thursday".
insert Newday at 10 of dayList	Scratch ignores this command because it attempts to create a gap in the list. The list remains unchanged.
insert Newday at 8 of dayList	This has the same effect as the **add** command. It adds "Newday" to the end of the list.
delete 8 of dayList	The command is ignored (because dayList has only seven elements), and the list remains unchanged.

The examples in Table 9-1 demonstrate that, although Scratch's blocks try to do something sensible when their inputs are invalid, they won't necessarily do the right thing. You have to provide your program with the right inputs so it works the way you want it to.

Up to this point, our examples have used simple lists that we created manually using their monitors. The question now is this: What if you don't know the contents of a list when you write your program? For example, you may need to make a list of user-entered numbers or fill a list with random values each time the program is run. We'll tackle this problem next.

Dynamic Lists

Lists are powerful because they can grow or shrink dynamically as a program is running. Let's say, for example, that you are writing a grade book application, in which teachers can enter students' test scores for further processing. (The teacher might need to find the maximum score, minimum, average, median, and so on for a class.) However, the number of students may be different for every class. The teacher may need to enter 20 scores for Class 1, 25 scores for Class 2, and so on. How can your program know that the teacher has finished entering the scores? This section will answer that question.

First, we'll introduce two ways to populate lists with data from a user. We'll then explore numeric lists and look at some of the common operations performed on them. Once you understand the fundamental concepts, you'll be ready to adapt these techniques to your own applications.

Filling Lists with User Input

There are two common ways to fill a list with data entered by a user. In the first method, your program begins by asking how many entries there will be and then starts a loop to collect the user's input. A script that demonstrates this technique is shown in Figure 9-10.

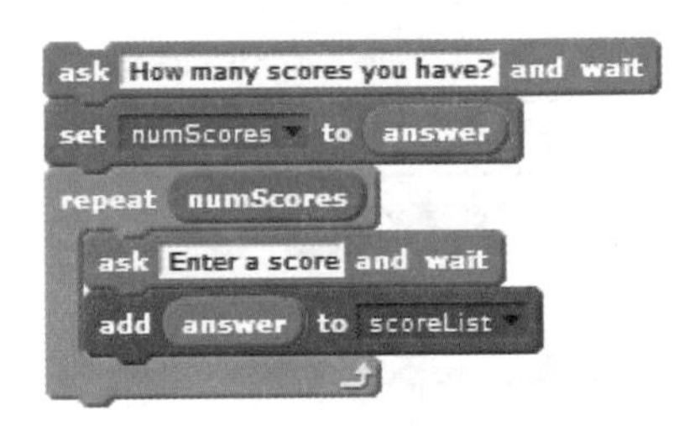

Figure 9-10: Asking the user how many scores will be entered

Once the user tells this script how many scores to expect, the script starts a loop with a repetition count equal to the user's input. Each iteration of the loop then asks the user for a new score and appends that value to the list, called scoreList.

The second way to dynamically populate a list is to have the user enter a special value (known as a *sentinel*) to mark the end of the list. Of course, you should choose a sentinel that won't be mistaken for a member of the list. If you're expecting a list of names or positive numbers, for example, a sentinel of –1 is a good choice. If, on the other hand, the user will enter negative values, then –1 won't be a good sentinel. Using a sentinel of –1 will work for our scoreList, and the script shown in Figure 9-11 uses this sentinel to know when the user is done entering values.

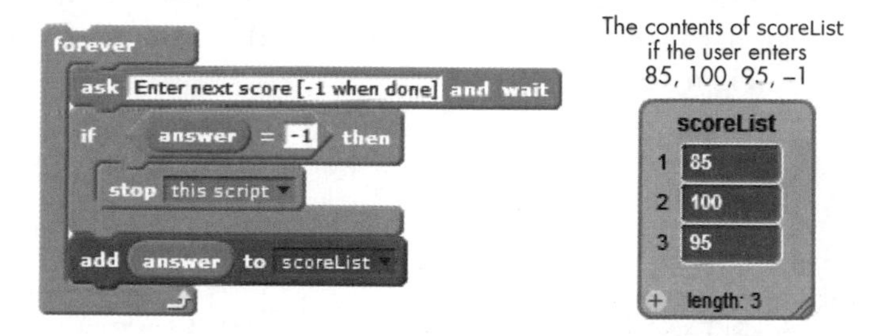

Figure 9-11: Using a sentinel to control list growth

In each iteration of the loop, the script prompts the user to enter a number and compares that value to the sentinel. Note that the script specifies the sentinel (–1 in this case) in its prompt to the user. If the user enters –1, then the script stops because it knows the user is done entering scores. Otherwise, the input value is appended to the list, and the user is prompted for another entry. Figure 9-11 shows how scoreList should look if the user enters three scores followed by the sentinel.

Creating a Bar Chart

BarChart.sb2

As a practical example of collecting user input with lists, let's write an application that draws a bar chart (also called a *histogram*) from the user's numbers. For simplicity, we'll only accept five numbers between 1 and 40. Once the program has received all five numbers, it will draw five bars with heights proportional to the entered values. The user interface for our chart maker is illustrated in Figure 9-12.

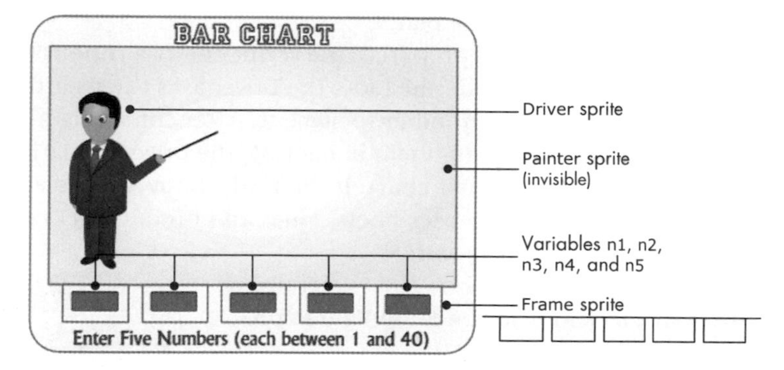

Figure 9-12: The Bar Chart application

This application contains three sprites. The Driver sprite controls the flow of the application; it contains scripts that accept user input, populate the list, and tell the Painter sprite to start drawing. The Painter sprite is an invisible sprite that draws the bar chart. The Frame sprite is purely cosmetic; it hides the bottom of each bar to make it look flat; without it, the bottoms of the vertical bars would have rounded tips. The numerical values for the five bars are shown using five variables, named n1 through n5, whose monitors are located at the right positions on the Stage. When you click the green flag icon to start the application, the Driver sprite runs the script shown in Figure 9-13.

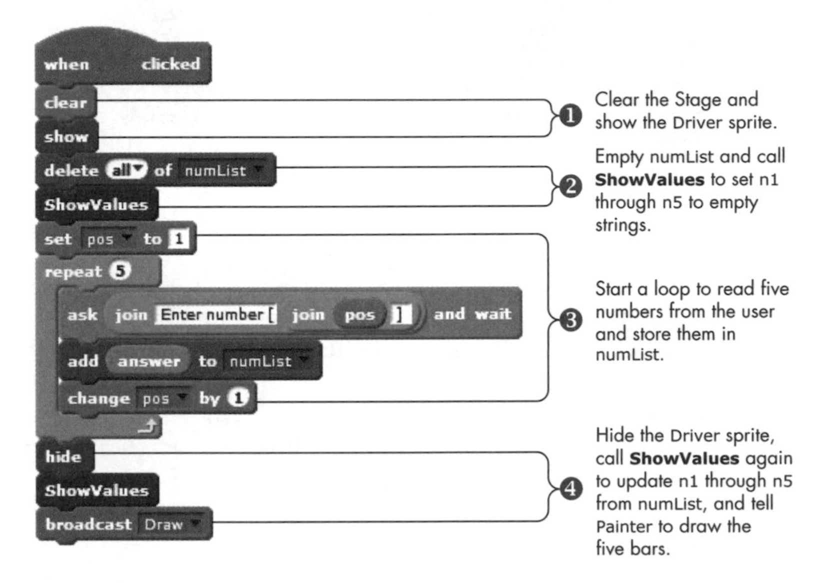
when clicked
clear
show
delete all of numList
ShowValues
set pos to 1
repeat 5
ask join Enter number [join pos] and wait
add answer to numList
change pos by 1
hide
ShowValues
broadcast Draw
❶ Clear the Stage and show the Driver sprite.
❷ Empty numList and call ShowValues to set n1 through n5 to empty strings.
❸ Start a loop to read five numbers from the user and store them in numList.
❹ Hide the Driver sprite, call ShowValues again to update n1 through n5 from numList, and tell Painter to draw the five bars.

Figure 9-13: The main script for the Driver *sprite*

First, the Driver sprite appears on the Stage and clears any previous pen marks ❶. That way, if there is a bar chart already, it will be cleared before the new one is drawn. The script then clears numList so we can use it to collect new entries from the user and calls **ShowValues** ❷ to set n1 through n5 so their monitors will be blank.

When the Stage is prepared, the script enters a **repeat** loop ❸, which iterates five times. Inside the loop, the Driver asks the user to enter a number and appends that number to numList. After collecting all five numbers from the user and saving them in numList, the Driver sprite hides itself ❹ to make room for the bar chart. It then calls **ShowValues** again to update n1 through n5 with the user's new values and broadcasts Draw so the Painter sprite will draw the five bars.

Before examining how the Painter draws the bars, let's look at the **ShowValues** procedure shown in Figure 9-14.

ShowValues simply sets the variables n1 through n5 equal to their corresponding entries in numList. Since the first call to **ShowValues** is made immediately after clearing numList, all five variables will contain empty strings after this call. This results in clearing the five monitors on the Stage,

define ShowValues
set n1 to item 1 of numList
set n2 to item 2 of numList
set n3 to item 3 of numList
set n4 to item 4 of numList
set n5 to item 5 of numList

Figure 9-14: The **ShowValues** *procedure*

which is exactly what we want. When numList contains data from the user, calling **ShowValues** displays the data in those same monitors.

Now let's explore the **Draw** procedure, which is executed when the Painter sprite receives the Draw message. You can see this script in Figure 9-15.

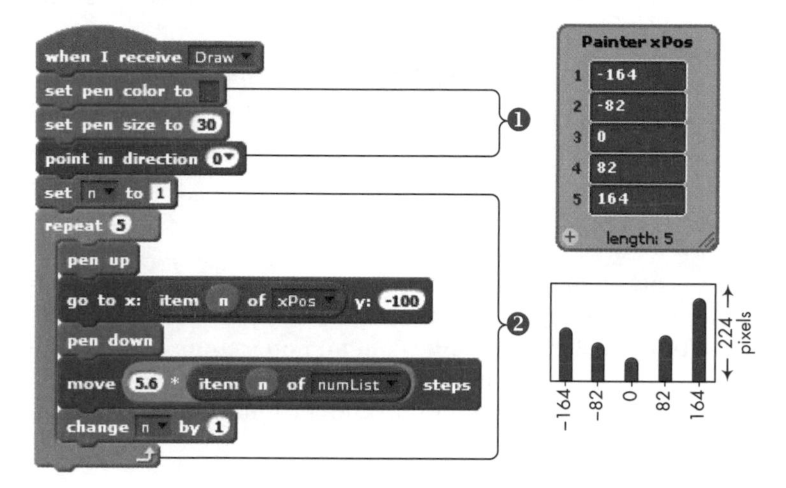

Figure 9-15: The **Draw** *script of the* Painter *sprite*

The sprite first sets the pen color. Then it sets the pen's size to a large value to draw the thick bars. To prepare for drawing the five vertical bars, the sprite points in the up direction ❶.

The script starts a repeat loop to draw the five bars ❷. We knew the *x*-position of each bar in advance, so we created a list named xPos to store those values (also shown in the figure). During each iteration of the loop, the Painter sprite moves to the *x*-position for the current bar, puts its pen down, and then moves up to draw a vertical line.

The height of each line is proportional to the corresponding value in numList. Our chart area on the Stage is 224 pixels tall, and since 40 is the highest value, an input of 40 should have a bar as tall as the chart. To find the height (in pixels) for any number in numList, we need to multiply that number by 5.6 (that is, 224/40). Figure 9-16 shows the output of the application after getting some data from the user. Note that the Frame sprite covers the rounded tip of the wide drawing pen so the bars look flat at the bottom.

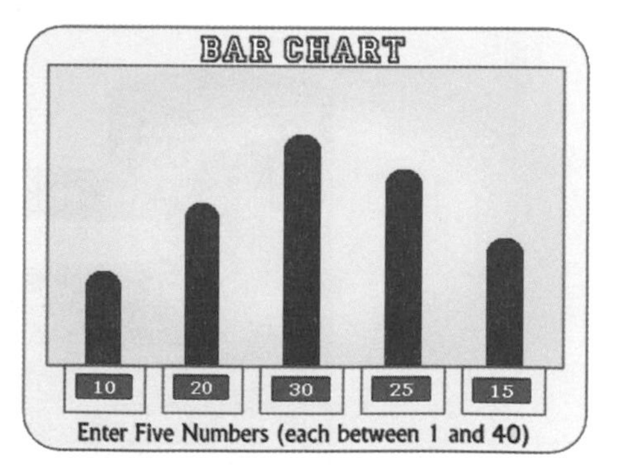

Figure 9-16: A sample output of the Bar Chart application

TRY IT OUT 9-3

Run this application several times to understand how it works. Change the script so that each bar will be drawn in a different color. Hint: Create a new list, named color, for the Painter sprite that stores the color number of the five bars and use the following command before drawing each bar:

Numerical Lists

Lists of numbers appear in many practical applications. We can have lists of test scores, temperature measurements, product prices, and more. In this section, we'll explore some common operations you might want to perform on numerical lists. In particular, we'll write procedures for finding the maximum or minimum value and for finding the average of the numbers stored in a list.

Finding Min and Max

FindMax.sb2

Suppose you're a teacher and you need to know the highest score from the last exam your class took. You could write a program to compare all of those test scores and find the maximum value. Our first example, shown in Figure 9-17, finds the highest number in a list named score.

The **FindMax** procedure starts by setting the value of the maxScore variable equal to the first number in the list. It then starts a loop to compare the remaining numbers in the list with the current value of maxScore. Every time it finds a value greater than maxScore, it sets maxScore equal to that value. When the loop terminates, the value stored in maxScore will be the largest value contained in the list.

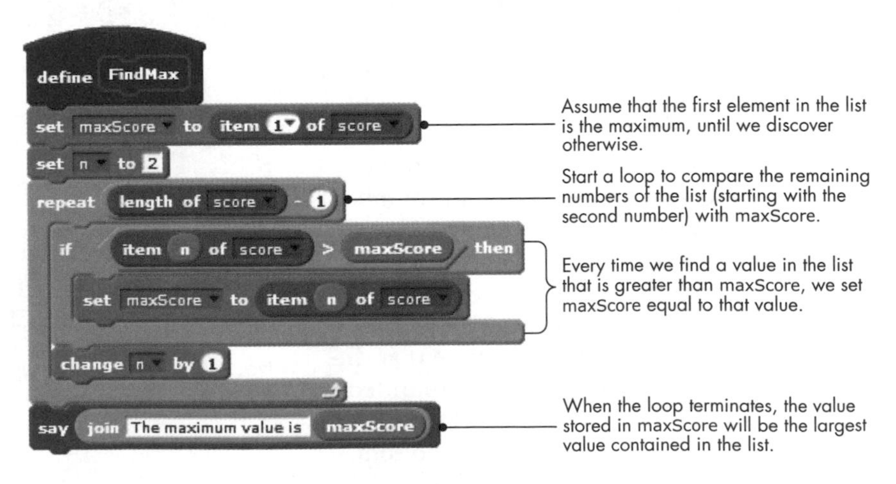

Figure 9-17: Finding the maximum number in a list

Finding the minimum value in a list follows a similar algorithm. We start by assuming that the first element in the list is the smallest element and then use a loop to check the remaining elements. Each time we find a smaller value, we update the variable that holds the minimum value.

> **TRY IT OUT 9-4**
>
> Use what you learned in this section to create a procedure called **FindMin** that finds the minimum value of the score list.

Finding the Average

FindAverage.sb2

In our next example, we'll write a procedure that computes the average score of the numbers stored in our score list. You can find the average of a sequence of *N* numbers by first finding their sum and then dividing the total by *N*. The procedure shown in Figure 9-18 does exactly that.

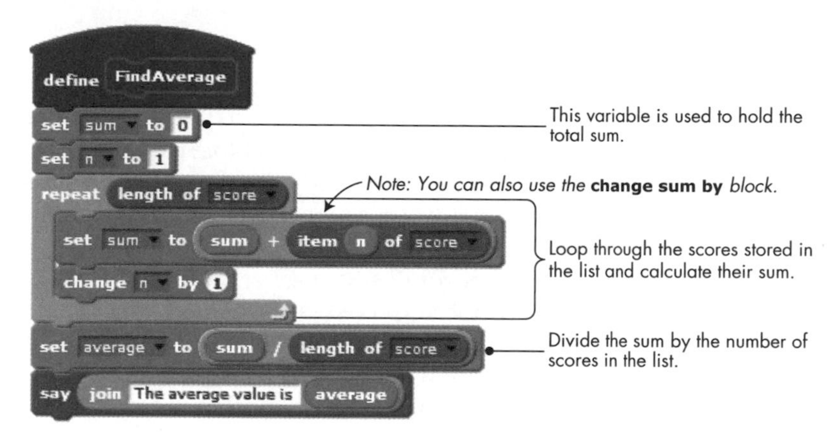

Figure 9-18: Finding the average value of a list of numbers

The **FindAverage** procedure uses a loop to step through the scores stored in the list, add them together, and store the result in a variable named sum. (This variable is initialized to 0 before the start of the loop.) When the loop terminates, the script calculates the average by dividing sum by the number of scores, and it saves the result in a variable named average.

NOTE *Pay special attention to the way we accumulated the* sum *variable inside the loop. This pattern, known as the* accumulator pattern*, comes up very often in programming.*

In the next section, we'll explore how to search and sort lists, two common problems in programming. I'll also walk you through some simple algorithms for performing each operation.

> **TRY IT OUT 9-5**
>
> Combine **FindAverage**, **FindMax**, and **FindMin** into one procedure (called **ProcessList**) that will display the average, maximum, and minimum values for the score list all at the same time.

Searching and Sorting Lists

Suppose you have a list of contacts that isn't in any particular order. If you wanted to organize the contacts, you might *sort* them into alphabetical order based on their names. If you need to know someone's phone number and you have their last name, you'll need to *search* the list to see if it contains that person's contact information. The goal of this section is to introduce basic programming techniques for searching and sorting lists.

Linear Search

SearchList.sb2

Scratch's **contains** block provides an easy way to check whether a list contains a specific item. If, in addition, we'd like to know the position of the item being searched for in a list, then we have to perform the search ourselves.

This section will explain one method for searching lists, called a *linear search* (or *sequential search*). The method is easy to understand and implement, and it works on any list, whether it is sorted or not. However, because a linear search compares the target value with every element in the list, it can take a long time if your list is large.

To illustrate, suppose you're searching for a specific item in a list named fruit. If the list contains the item you are looking for, you also need to know the exact position of that item. The **SearchList** procedure shown in Figure 9-19 performs a linear search on the fruit list to give us the answers we seek.

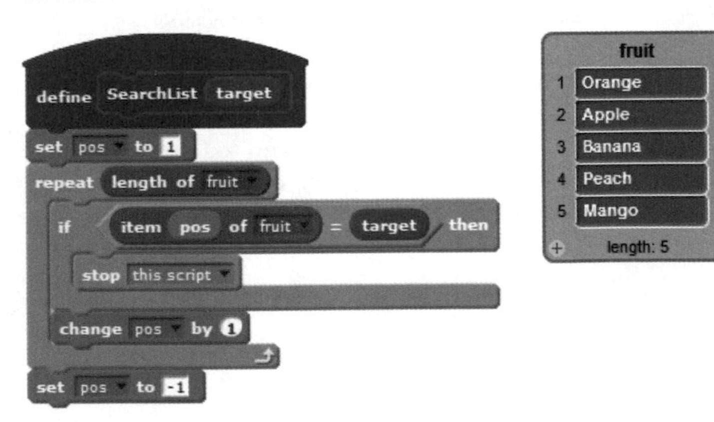

Figure 9-19: The **SearchList** *procedure*

Starting with the first element, **SearchList** compares the fruits in our list, one by one, with the one we're looking for, which is represented by the target parameter. The procedure stops if it either finds the value or reaches the end of the list. If the script finds the value we want, the pos variable will contain the location where the item was found. Otherwise, the procedure sets pos to an invalid value (–1 in this case) to indicate that the target item was not in the list. Figure 9-20 shows an example of calling this procedure and its corresponding output.

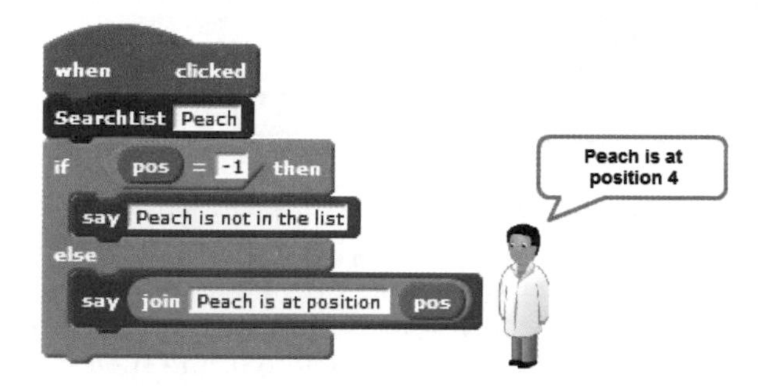

Figure 9-20: Using the ***SearchList*** *procedure*

Examining the value of pos tells the caller two things: (a) whether the item we're looking for is in the list or not and (b) if the item exists, its exact position. Running this script sets pos to 4, indicating that "Peach" was found in the fourth position of the fruit list.

Frequency of Occurrence

ItemCount.sb2

Suppose that your school conducted a survey about the quality of its cafeteria food. Students rated the taste on a 1 to 5 scale (1 = poor, 5 = excellent). All votes have been entered into a list, and you are asked to write a program to process this data. For now, the school only wants to know how many students completely dislike the food (that is, how many gave it a rating of 1). How would you write such a program?

Clearly, your program needs a procedure that counts how many times the number 1 appears in the list. To simulate the students' votes, let's use a list that contains 100 random votes. The procedure that populates the list is shown in Figure 9-21. This procedure adds 100 random numbers between 1 and 5 to a list called survey.

Figure 9-21: The ***FillList*** *procedure*

Now that we have a list of votes, we can count how often a given rating appears in that list. We'll do this with the **GetItemCount** procedure, shown in Figure 9-22.

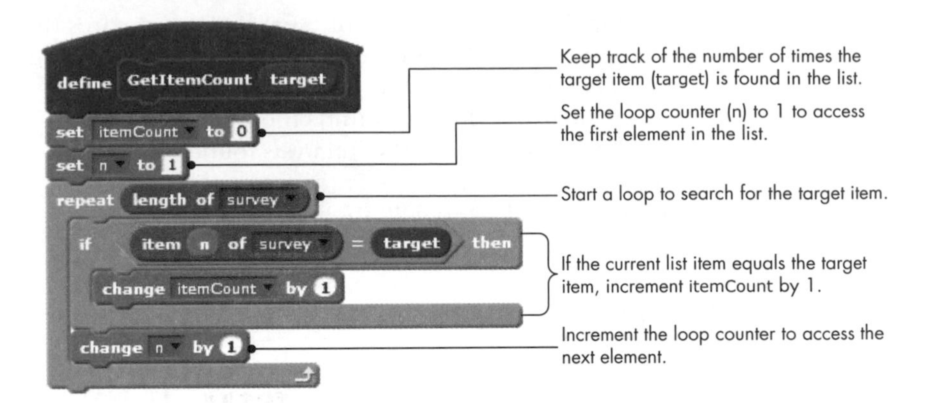
define GetItemCount target
set itemCount to 0
set n to 1
repeat length of survey
if item n of survey = target then
change itemCount by 1
change n by 1
Keep track of the number of times the target item (target) is found in the list.
Set the loop counter (n) to 1 to access the first element in the list.
Start a loop to search for the target item.
If the current list item equals the target item, increment itemCount by 1.
Increment the loop counter to access the next element.

Figure 9-22: Counting how many times an item appears in a list

The target parameter represents the item to search for, while the itemCount variable tracks the number of times the target item is found. The procedure starts by setting itemCount to 0, and then it starts a **repeat** loop to search the list for the value specified in target. During each iteration of the loop, the procedure checks the list item at the location indexed by the loop counter, n. If that item equals the target, the script increases itemCount by 1.

To give the principal information about disgust with the cafeteria's food, we just need to call **GetItemCount** with an argument of 1, as shown in Figure 9-23.

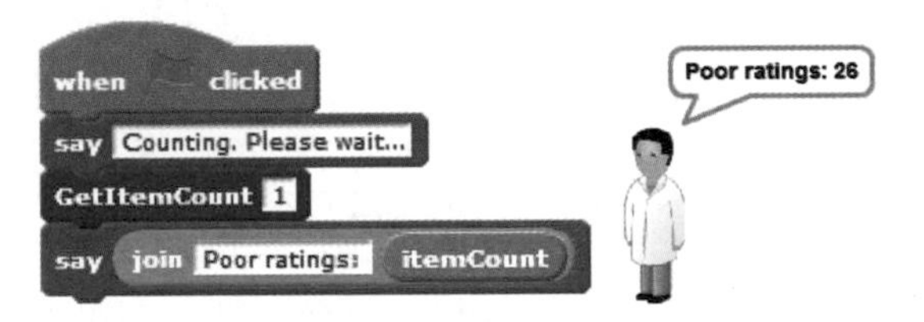
when clicked
say Counting. Please wait...
GetItemCount 1
say join Poor ratings: itemCount
Poor ratings: 26

Figure 9-23: Using the **GetItemCount** *procedure*

TRY IT OUT 9-6

After you provide the answer to this question, the principal suddenly becomes curious about how many students gave the cafeteria an excellent rating. The principal also wants to know how many students participated in the survey. Modify the program and run it again to give the principal the additional information.

Bubble Sort

BubbleSort.sb2

If you have a set of names, game scores, or anything else that you want to show in a particular order—alphabetically, from largest to smallest, and so on—you'll have to sort your list. There are many ways to sort lists, and a *bubble sort* is one of the simplest algorithms. (The name refers to how values "bubble" up through the list to their correct positions.) In this section, we'll learn about bubble sort and write a Scratch program to perform this kind of sort for us.

Let's say that we need to sort the list of numbers [6 9 5 7 4 8] in descending order. The following steps illustrate how the bubble sort algorithm works.

1. We'll start by comparing the first two elements in the list. Since 9 is larger than 6, we can swap their positions, as shown below.

original list

6
9
5
7
4
8

9
6
5
7
4
8

list after swapping the first two elements

2. Now we can compare the second and third elements, which are 6 and 5. Since 6 is larger than 5, the two numbers are already in order, and we can move on to the next pair.
3. We'll repeat this process to compare the third and fourth, fourth and fifth, and finally the fifth and sixth elements. Take a look at the list after these three comparisons, shown below.

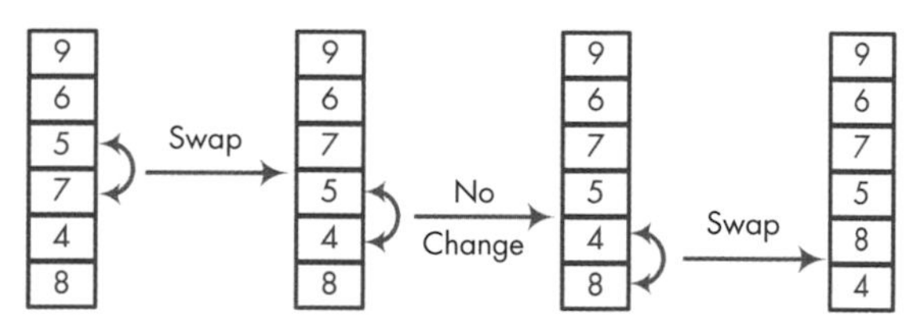

4. This pass of the bubble sort is over, but our list still isn't in the right order. We need to perform a second pass, starting from step one. Once more, we'll compare each pair of elements and swap them if needed. Here's the list after a second pass:

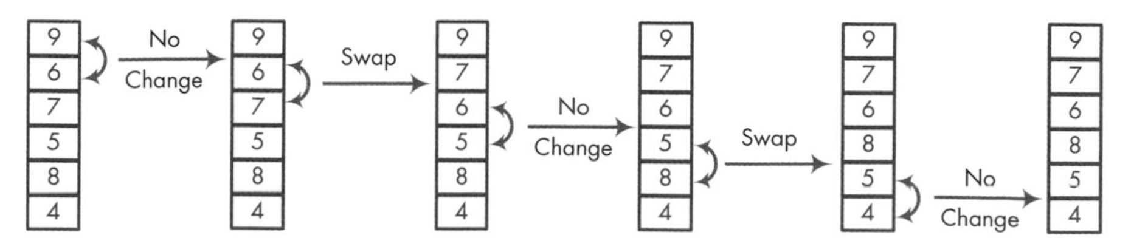

5. We'll repeat the bubble sort process until no numbers are swapped during a pass, meaning that our list is in order. The final three passes of the algorithm are shown below:

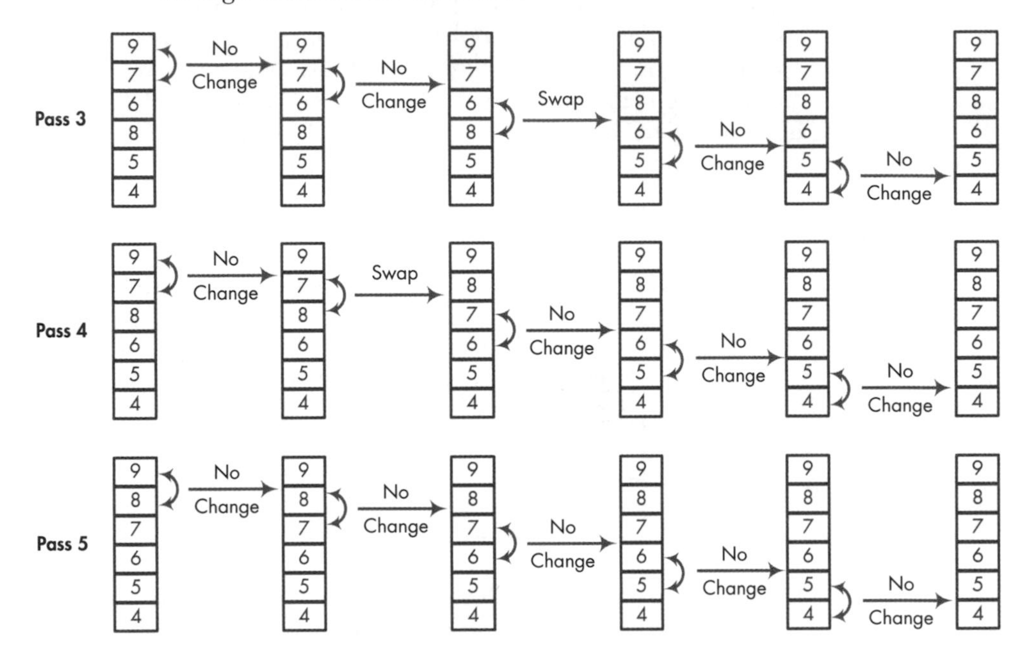

Now that you've seen how bubble sort works, let's implement it in Scratch. The script, shown in Figure 9-24, has two loops. The inner loop cycles through a list, comparing and swapping as needed, and sets a flag (named `done`) to 0 when another pass is needed. The outer loop repeats as long as the `done` flag is 0, because that value means we aren't done sorting. If the inner loop completes one pass without swapping elements, the outer loop will exit, ending the procedure.

Let's explore this procedure in more detail. Since we haven't done any sorting yet, it sets `done` to 0 ❶. The outer loop uses a **repeat until** block to pass through the list until it is sorted (that is, until `done` becomes 1) ❷. At the beginning of every pass, this loop sets `done` to 1 ❸ (that is, it assumes that we won't make any swaps). It also sets `pos` to 1 to start the sort with the first number.

The inner loop then compares each pair of elements in the list. The loop needs to perform $N - 1$ comparisons ❹, where N is the number of items in the list.

If the item at index `pos+1` is greater than the item at `pos` ❺, the two need to be swapped. Otherwise, the procedure adds 1 to `pos` so it can compare the next pair of items. If we do need to swap, this procedure does so with the aid of a temporary variable named `temp` ❻.

Once the current pass through the list ends, the inner loop sets `done` back to 0 if it swapped numbers or leaves `done=1` if it made no changes ❼. The outer loop will continue until the list is sorted.

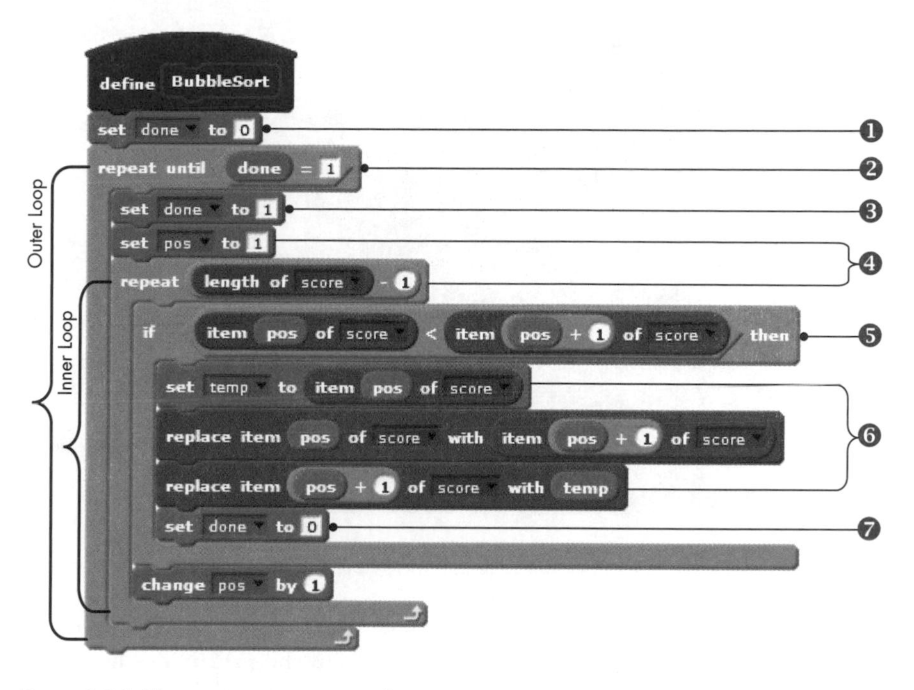

Figure 9-24: The **BubbleSort** *procedure*

TRY IT OUT 9-7

Make a list of names instead of numbers and use the bubble sort script to put the list in order. Does the sort still work as it should? Also, what changes do you need to make to the procedure to make it sort in ascending order?

Finding the Median

Median.sb2

Now that we know how to sort a list, we can easily find the median value of any sequence of numbers. Recall that the median is the middle value in a sorted set of numbers. If we have an odd number of items, we can just take the middle number. If we have an even number, the median is the average of the two middle numbers. We can describe the median for a sorted list of N items as follows:

$$median = \begin{cases} \text{item at index } \dfrac{N+1}{2} & \text{if } N \text{ is odd} \\ \text{average of items at } \dfrac{N}{2} \text{ and } \dfrac{N}{2}+1 & \text{if } N \text{ is even} \end{cases}$$

A procedure that performs this calculation is shown in Figure 9-25. It assumes the list is in order.

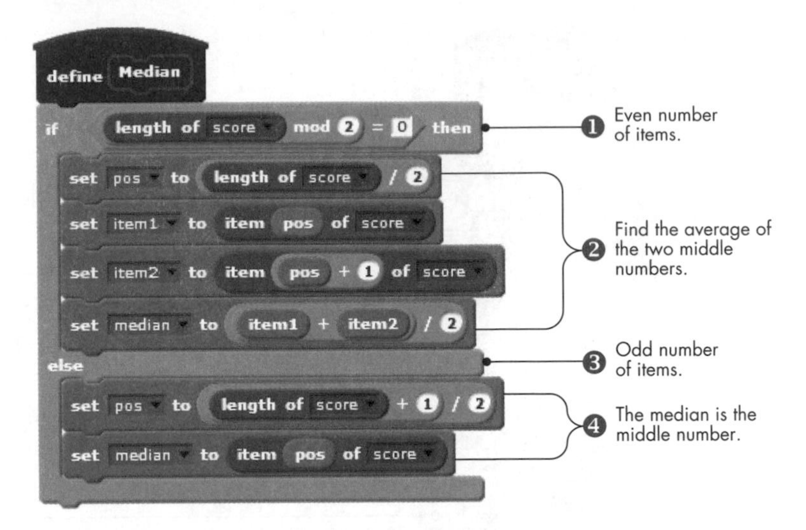

Figure 9-25: Finding the median value of a sorted list of numbers

The procedure uses an **if/else** block to handle the two cases of even and odd lists. If the number of items in the list divides by 2 with no remainder (that is, the list has an even number of items) ❶, the median variable is calculated as the average of the middle two numbers ❷. Otherwise, the list has an odd number of items ❸, and the median variable is set equal to the number in the middle of the list ❹.

We've covered a lot of ground so far, so it's time to apply our newfound knowledge to something more challenging. The rest of this chapter walks through several examples that demonstrate how to use lists in more complex applications.

Scratch Projects

In this section, you'll explore practical Scratch projects that highlight different aspects of lists. I'll also introduce some new ideas and techniques that you can use in your own creations.

The Poet

Poet.sb2

Let's kick off this chapter's projects with a poem generator. Our artificial poet selects words randomly from five lists (article, adjective, noun, verb, and preposition) and combines them according to a fixed pattern. To give our poems a central theme, all the words in these lists are somehow related to love and nature. (Of course, we might still end up with some silly poetry, but that's just as fun!)

NOTE *The idea of this program is adapted from Daniel Watt's* Learning with Logo *(McGraw-Hill, 1983). You'll find the full word lists we're using in the Scratch file for this project,* Poet.sb2.

Each poem is composed of three lines that follow these patterns:

- Line 1: article, adjective, noun
- Line 2: article, noun, verb, preposition, article, adjective, noun
- Line 3: adjective, adjective, noun

With those constructions in mind, let's look at the procedure that builds the first line of the poem, shown in Figure 9-26.

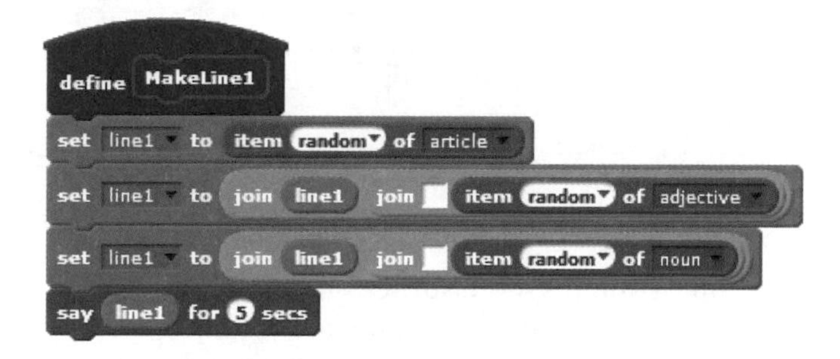

Figure 9-26: "Writing" the first line of a poem

This script selects a random word from the article list and stores it in line1. Then the script appends a white space, a random word from the adjective list, another white space, and a random word from the noun list. Finally, the poet sprite says the complete line. I don't show the procedures for the other two lines of the poem here because they're very similar, but you can open up *Poet.sb2* to view them.

Here are two poems created by our machine poet:

each glamorous road
a fish moves behind each white home
calm blue pond

every icy drop
a heart stares under every scary gate
shy quiet queen

Poet.sb2

TRY IT OUT 9-8

Open *Poet.sb2* and run it several times to see what this machine poet is capable of authoring. Then change the program so that it uses three sprites, with each sprite responsible for one line of the poem, allowing you to read the whole poem on the Stage at once.

Quadrilateral Classification Game

QuadClassify.sb2

Our next project is a simple game that will help you explore different kinds of quadrilaterals. The game shows one of six shapes (parallelogram, rhombus, rectangle, square, trapezoid, or kite) on the Stage and asks the player to classify that shape by clicking the correct button, as illustrated in Figure 9-27.

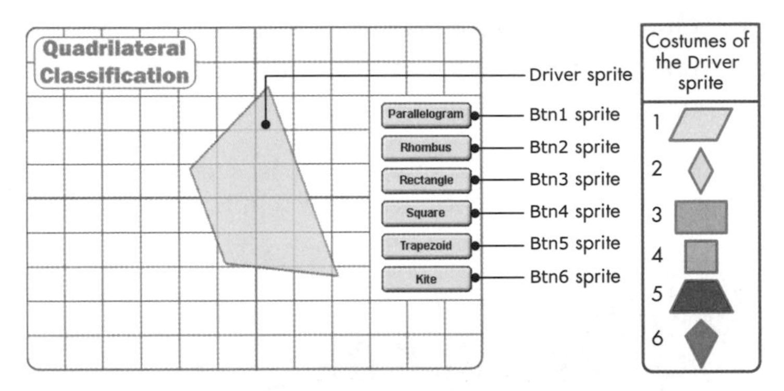

Figure 9-27: The user interface for the quadrilateral classification game

The game contains seven sprites: six for the answer buttons and a seventh (named Driver) that contains the main script. As shown in Figure 9-27, the Driver sprite has six costumes that correspond to the six quadrilaterals in the game. When the green flag icon is clicked, the Driver sprite executes the script shown in Figure 9-28 to start the game.

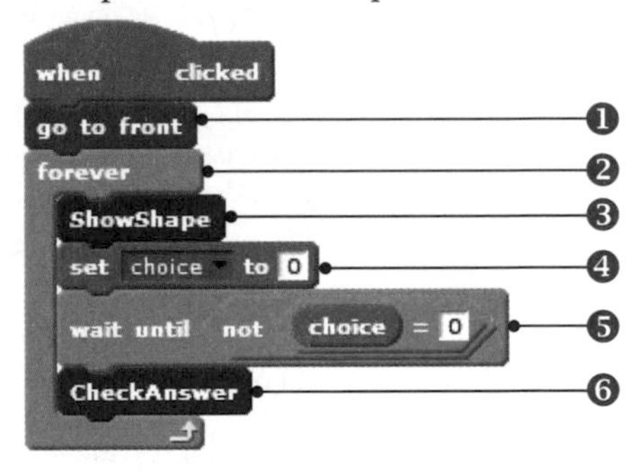

Figure 9-28: The main script of the Driver *sprite*

First, the Driver sprite moves to the top drawing layer ❶ so that no buttons will obscure it. In the main loop of the game ❷, the script shows a random quadrilateral on each pass with **ShowShape** ❸. After showing the quadrilateral, the script sets the global variable choice to 0 to indicate that the user hasn't answered yet ❹.

The script then waits ❺ until choice changes to a nonzero number, which will happen when the player clicks one of the six answer buttons. When the player guesses a shape, the script calls **CheckAnswer** ❻ to tell the player whether or not that answer was correct.

Now that you know how the main script works, let's look at the **ShowShape** procedure, shown in Figure 9-29.

First, **ShowShape** moves the Driver sprite to the center of the stage and points it in a random direction ❶. It assigns the shape variable a random value from 1 through 6 and switches the sprite's costume ❷ to show a quadrilateral for the player to identify.

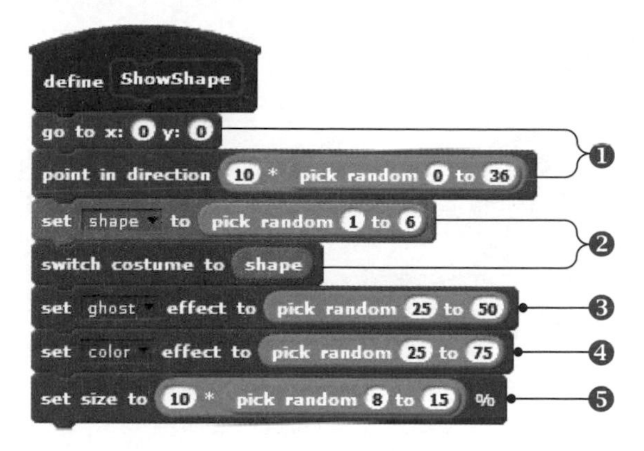

Figure 9-29: The **ShowShape** *procedure of the* Driver *sprite*

To keep the background's grid visible, **ShowShape** sets the transparency level ❸ to a random value between 25 and 50. To give the illusion that it is coming up with a new shape every round, the procedure also sets the color effect to a random value to change the color of the costume ❹ and resizes the sprite to 80%, 90%, ... , or 150% of its original size ❺.

Next, we'll look briefly at the scripts for the six button sprites, shown in Figure 9-30. They're identical except for the value assigned to the choice variable.

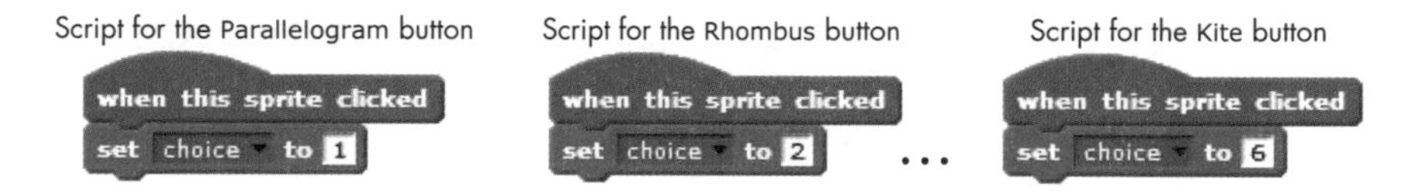

Figure 9-30: Scripts for the button sprites

These one-line scripts each set the value of choice to a different number depending on which button the player presses. Once choice contains the player's answer, the **CheckAnswer** procedure, illustrated in Figure 9-31, can compare it with the value of shape, which specifies the type of the drawn quadrilateral.

If choice and shape are equal, then the player's answer is correct. Otherwise, the answer is wrong, and the sprite will say the right shape. **CheckAnswer** uses the shape variable as an index to a list named quadName, which is also shown in Figure 9-31, to get the correct name of the displayed shape.

QuadClassify.sb2

TRY IT OUT 9-9

Open *QuadClassify.sb2* and run it several times to understand how it works. As written, this game runs forever. Modify the program to add a game-end criterion. Also, keep track of the number of the player's correct and incorrect answers.

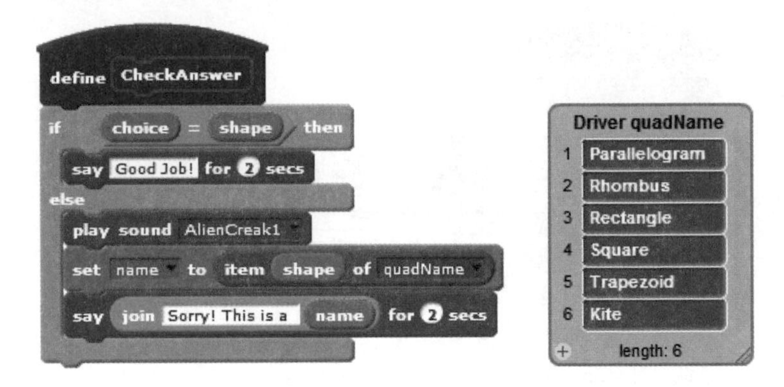

Figure 9-31: The **CheckAnswer** *procedure*

Math Wizard

MathWizard.sb2

This application demonstrates two ways to make lists even more useful. We'll explore how to use lists to store nonuniform records (that is, records with different sizes) as well as how to use one list as an index to another. A *record* is just a collection of related data about a person, place, or thing. In our case, each record consists of a puzzle's answer along with the instructions for that puzzle. Whereas each puzzle has a single answer, the number of instructions varies from one puzzle to another.

Our math wizard asks the user to think of a "secret" number and perform a sequence of mathematical operations on it (double the number, subtract 2, divide the answer by 10, and so on). At the end, after the player performs all these calculations, the wizard uses magical powers to tell the user what number he has, even though the wizard does not know the user's initial number. Table 9-2 illustrates how the game works.

Table 9-2: How the Math Wizard Works

Wizard's Instruction	Your Number
Think of a number.	2
Add 5.	7
Multiply by 3.	21
Subtract 3.	18
Divide by 3.	6
Subtract your original number.	4

After the last instruction, the wizard will tell you that following the instructions has given you the number 4, even though the game doesn't know that you started out with 2. Try this puzzle with different numbers to figure out the wizard's trick!

The interface of the application is shown in Figure 9-32.

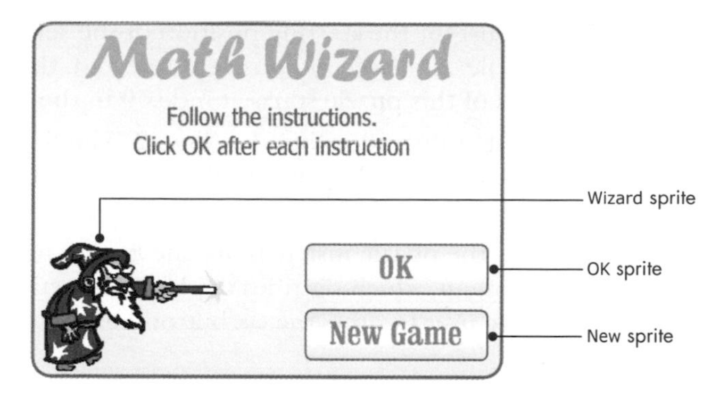

Figure 9-32: The user interface for the Math Wizard application

The application contains three sprites: the Wizard sprite, which gives the instructions to the player, and the OK and New sprites, for the OK and New Game buttons, respectively. It also uses the two lists illustrated in Figure 9-33.

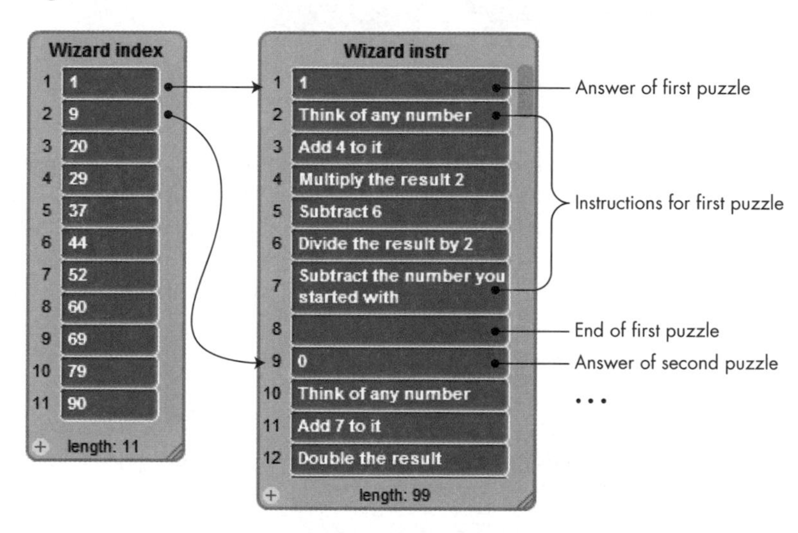

Figure 9-33: The two lists used by the Wizard sprite

The instr list (right) contains 11 puzzle records. Each record includes (a) the answer of the puzzle, (b) the instructions, and (c) an empty element to mark the end of that record. The entries in the list on the left (named index) identify the starting index of each puzzle in the instr list. For example, the second element in the index list is 9, which means the record of the second puzzle starts at the ninth position in the instr list, as illustrated in Figure 9-33. Let's outline a strategy for developing this game:

1. When the user starts a new game, select a random number between 1 and 11 (because our game currently contains 11 puzzles).

2. Consult the index list for the starting position of the selected puzzle's record. For example, if the second puzzle is selected, the index list tells us that the record of this puzzle starts at index 9 in the instr list.
3. Access the instr list at the index found in Step 2. The first element at that index is interpreted as the answer of the puzzle. The following elements represent the instructions that the wizard will say.
4. Let the wizard say the puzzle instructions one by one until encountering the empty element, which signifies the last instruction. The wizard should wait for the user to press the OK button before saying a new instruction.
5. Reveal the answer of the puzzle.

Now that we know how the game should work on a high level, let's look at the scripts for the two buttons, shown in Figure 9-34.

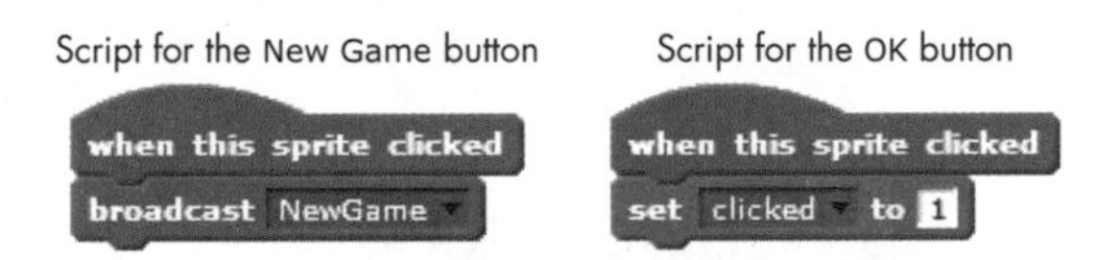

Figure 9-34: The scripts for the two button sprites

The New Game button broadcasts the NewGame message when clicked. When the OK button is clicked in response to an instruction, the sprite sets clicked to 1 to inform the Wizard sprite that the player is done with the instruction she was asked to perform. When the Wizard sprite receives the NewGame message, it executes the script shown in Figure 9-35.

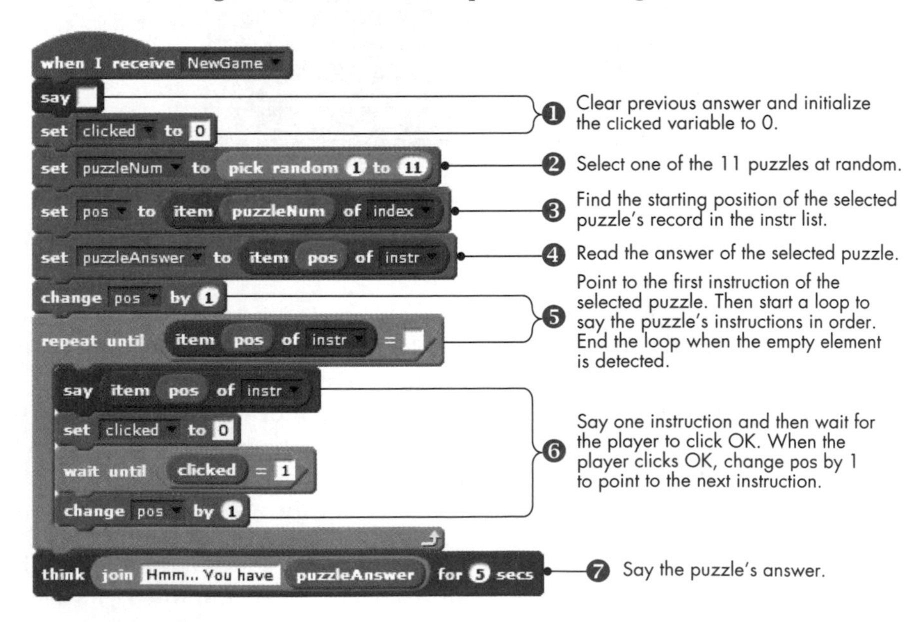

Figure 9-35: The NewGame script of the Wizard sprite

NewGame starts by clearing the speech bubble from the previous puzzle (if any) and initializing the clicked variable to 0 ❶. It then saves the number of the randomly selected puzzle in a variable called puzzleNum ❷. After that, it reads the starting position of the selected puzzle from the index list and saves it in the pos variable ❸. The script then uses pos to read the answer of that puzzle and saves it in puzzleAnswer ❹. Next, the script adds 1 to pos so it points to the first puzzle instruction, and it starts a **repeat until** loop to say the puzzle's instructions in order ❺. After saying each instruction, the script waits for the clicked variable to be set to 1 before moving to the next instruction ❻. When the loop finds an empty element, it exits, and the script says the puzzle's answer ❼.

TRY IT OUT 9-10

If you delete one of the puzzles or change the number of instructions for some puzzles, then you would need to rebuild the index list to match up with the instr list. Write a procedure that automatically populates the index list based on the current contents of the instr list. The key is to search for the empty strings in the instr list, as these indicate the end of one record and the start of the next record.

Flower Anatomy Quiz

FlowerAnatomy.sb2

In this section, I'll use a quiz on the parts of a flower to demonstrate how to build simple quizzes in Scratch. Figure 9-36 shows our example application's interface at the beginning of the quiz and after the program checks the user's answers. Anyone taking the quiz will enter the letters to match the labeled parts of the flower and then click the Check button to check the answers. The program compares the user's answers with the correct ones and provides feedback using the green check mark and the red *X* icons next to each answer.

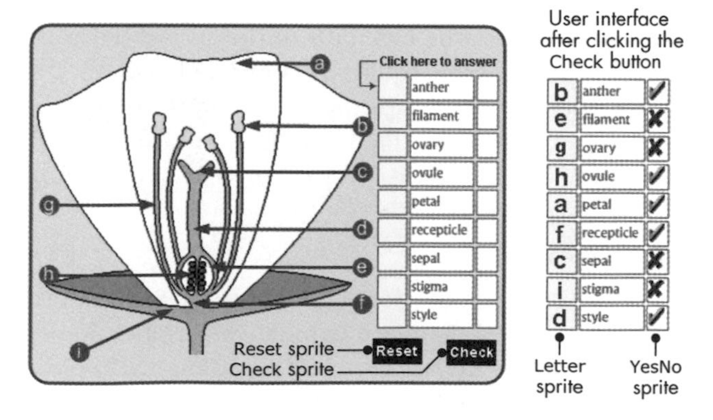

Figure 9-36: The user interface for the flower quiz

This quiz uses three lists. The first (named correctAns) contains the letters that correspond to the right answers for the nine parts of the quiz. The second list (named ans) contains the user's input, and the third list (named cellYCenter) contains the 11 vertical positions used by the Letter and the YesNo sprites (so they know where they should stamp their costumes). When the user clicks the mouse over any of the answer boxes, the Stage sprite detects the mouse click and asks for an answer. The Stage sprite updates the corresponding element of the ans list to match what the user entered and stamps that letter over the answer box. Open *FlowerAnatomy.sb2* to read the scripts that read and display the user's answers.

When the user clicks the Check button, the YesNo sprite, which has the costumes for the check mark and *X* images, executes the script shown in Figure 9-37.

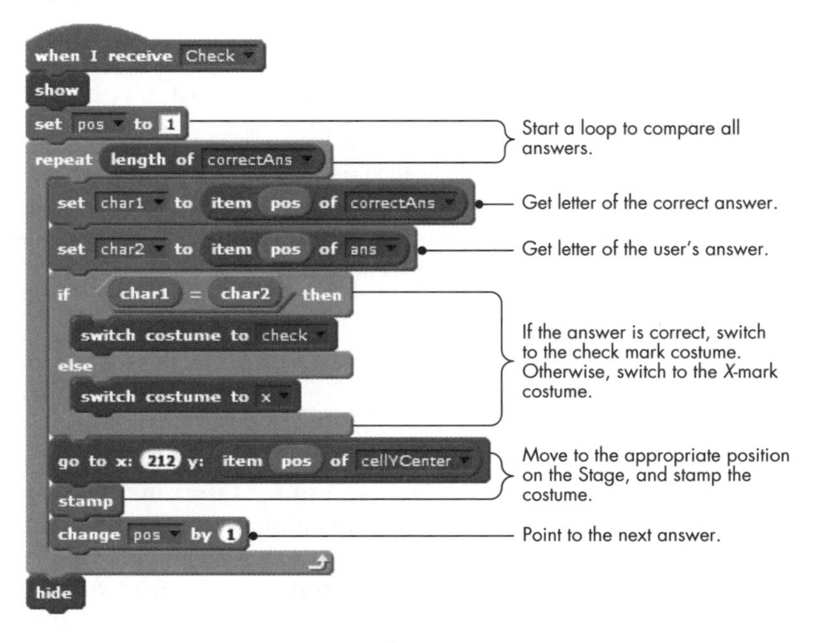

Figure 9-37: The **Check** *procedure of the* YesNo *sprite*

The script compares the elements of the correctAns and the ans lists one by one. If the two values are equal, it stamps a check mark to say the user was correct. Otherwise, it stamps the red *X* where the user's answers were wrong. Either way, Check consults the cellYCenter list to get the correct position for stamping the image. See Try It Out 9-11 on the opposite page.

Other Applications

SayThat Number.sb2

The extra resources you downloaded from the book's website (*http://nostarch.com/learnscratch/*) contain three more applications that you can explore on your own, with full explanations. The first application is a two-player game about sorting fractions and decimals. Each player gets 5 random cards from a deck of 31 cards. Each player is then dealt one card from the remaining set. You can either discard the new card or drag it over one of your current five, replacing the old one. Whoever arranges five cards in ascending order first wins the game.

TRY IT OUT 9-11

USMapQuiz.sb2

Open this application and test it. Then, think of other quizzes in different subject areas that you can create and implement them. One example, shown below, is provided in the file *USMapQuiz.sb2*. Open this file and complete the missing parts to make this quiz work.

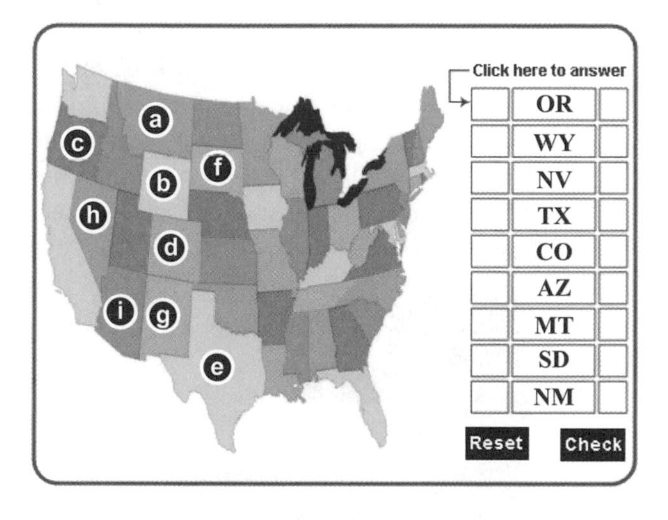

SortEmOut.sb2

The second application is a program that spells whole numbers. It prompts the user to input a number and then says that number in words. If the user inputs 3526, for example, the program will say "three thousand five hundred twenty six." The idea is to break the number, from right to left, into groups of three digits. Each group is then spelled out with a multiplier word (thousand, million, and so on), if needed.

Sieve.sb2

The third program demonstrates the sieve of Eratosthenes, an algorithm for finding all prime numbers less than 100.

Summary

Lists are extremely useful in programming, and they provide a convenient way to store multiple elements. In this chapter, we explored creating lists in Scratch, learned the commands we can use to deal with them, and practiced populating lists dynamically with data entered by the user.

We also examined numerical lists and demonstrated how to find the minimum, the maximum, and the average value of their elements. After that, we learned simple algorithms for searching and sorting lists. We concluded the chapter with several programs that demonstrated the use of lists in practical applications.

Problems

1. Create a list that contains the first 10 prime numbers. Write a script to display these numbers using the **say** block.
2. Create three lists to store personal records. The first list stores names, the second list stores birth dates, and the third list stores phone numbers. Write a program that asks the user the name of the person whose contact information is needed. If the person's name exists in the first list, the program will say the person's birth date and phone number.
3. Create two lists for storing the items sold in a grocery store and their corresponding prices. Write a program that asks the user to enter an item's name and then displays that item's price, if it is found in the list.
4. What is stored in numList after executing the script shown on the next page? Re-create the procedure and run it to check your answer.

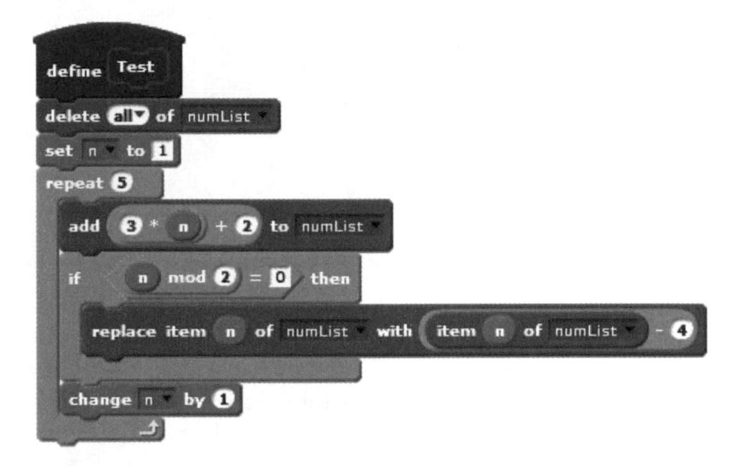

5. Write a program to double each of the elements stored in a numerical list.
6. Write a program that prompts the user to enter students' names and scores and store these inputs in two lists. Stop collecting data when the user enters –1 for a student's name.
7. Write a program that prompts the user to enter the highest and lowest temperatures for the 12 months of a year. Store the input values in two lists.
8. Write a program that prompts the user to enter 10 integers. Store each entered number into a list only if it is not a duplicate of a previously entered number.
9. Write a program that processes a list of 20 scores on a test with 100 items and finds the number of students who scored between 85 and 90.

SHARING AND COLLABORATION

Scratch makes it easy for you to collaborate and share your work with people all over the world, and this appendix highlights features in Scratch 2 that promote connecting with others. In particular, you'll learn how to create an account, how to use your backpack to work with sprites and scripts created by others, how to remix other people's projects, and how to publish your work and share it with the Scratch community.

Creating a Scratch Account

Although you don't need an account to use Scratch, having an account can be beneficial. It gives you the ability to save your work on the Scratch website, communicate with other users, and share your work online. Follow these steps to create a Scratch account:

1. Go to *http://scratch.mit.edu/* and click the **Join Scratch** link at the top right of the screen. In the dialog that appears (see Figure A-1), enter a username and password and then click **Next**.

Figure A-1: First dialog in the account-creation process

2. In the second dialog (see Figure A-2), enter your date of birth, gender, country, and email address. Then click **Next**.

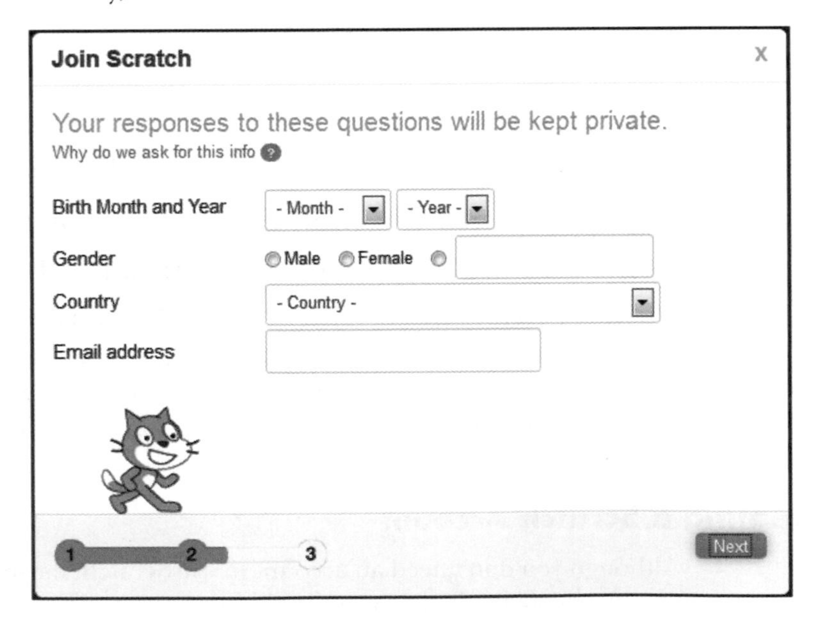

Figure A-2: Second dialog in the account-creation process

3. You'll see a dialog welcoming you to the Scratch user community (see Figure A-3). Click **OK Let's Go!**, and you'll be logged in to your new account.

Figure A-3: Last dialog in the account-creation process

The navigation bar at the top of the screen will show your username, as illustrated in Figure A-4. Use the four links (Create, Explore, Discuss, and Help) in the navigation bar to start Scratch's Project Editor, explore available projects, collaborate with other Scratchers, and find useful guidelines and additional Scratch resources.

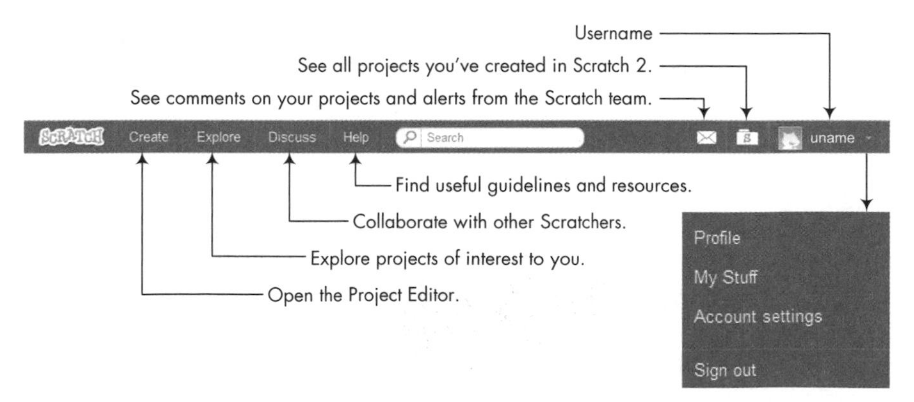

Figure A-4: Navigation bar for a logged-in user

The following sections discuss some of the features that become available when you log in to your Scratch account.

Using the Backpack

The backpack (available only to logged-in users) allows you to copy sprites, scripts, costumes, backdrops, and sounds from any project and use them in your own projects. Click the **Explore** link, shown in Figure A-4, to go to the project exploration page shown in Figure A-5. Here you can try out Scratch projects created by other people.

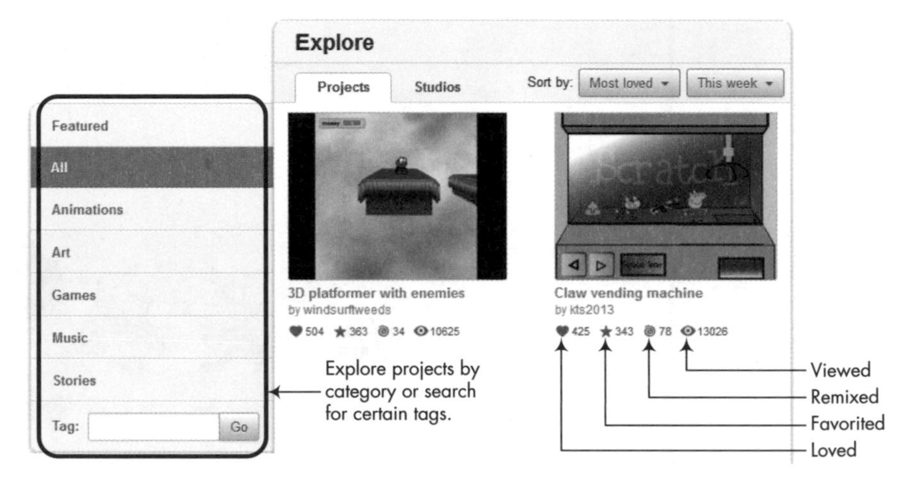

Figure A-5: Project exploration page

You can view projects by category, search for projects that contain certain tags, and sort them according to different criteria (shared, most loved, most viewed, or most mixed). When you find a project that you want to explore, double-click its thumbnail to go to that project's page, as shown in Figure A-6.

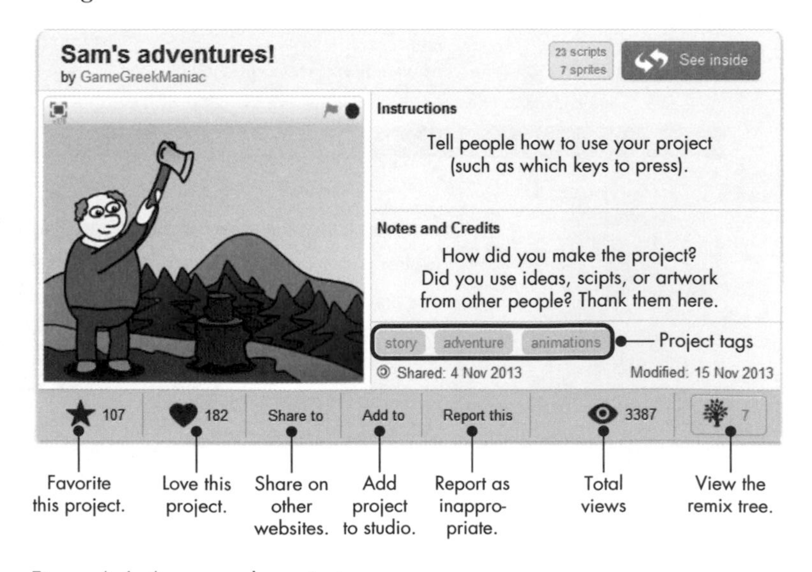

Figure A-6: An example project page

Click the **See inside** button in the upper-right corner of Figure A-6 to see the contents of this project, as shown in Figure A-7.

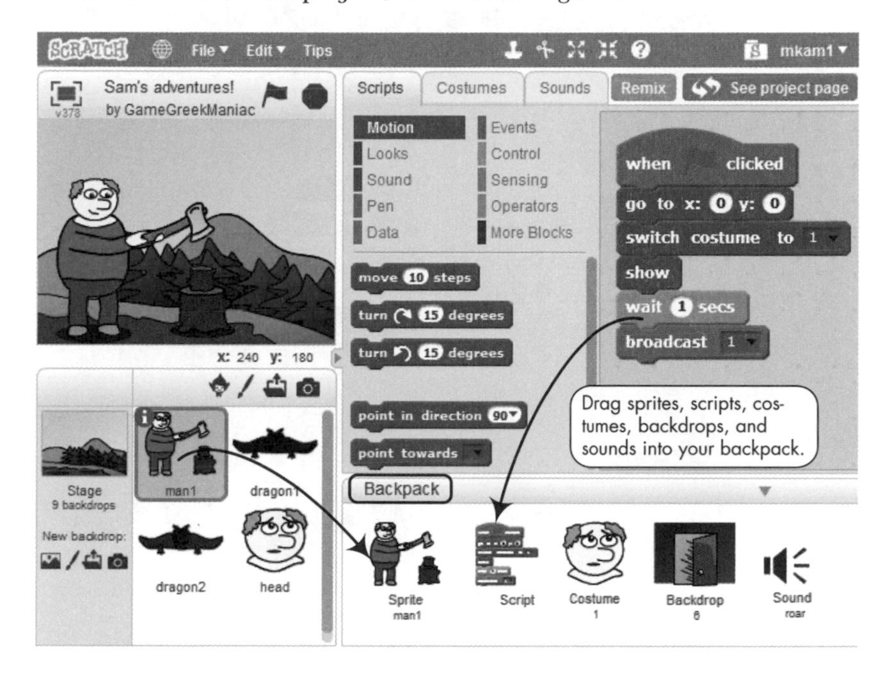

Figure A-7: Viewing the contents of another Scratcher's project

If you want to use parts of this project (sprites, scripts, costumes, backdrops, or sound files) in one of your own applications, just drag those parts onto your backpack. To delete an item from your backpack, right-click it and select Delete from the pop-up menu.

The contents of your backpack are saved on a Scratch server, so you won't lose them when you log off. To use an item from your backpack, just drag it from the backpack onto your project.

Creating Your Own Project

There are many ways to start programming in Scratch. You can create a clean project, remix a project that has been shared on Scratch's website, or open an old project and modify it. We'll look at each of these options.

Starting a New Project

To start a brand-new project, click the **Create** link in the navigation bar to open Scratch's Project Editor, shown in Figure A-8.

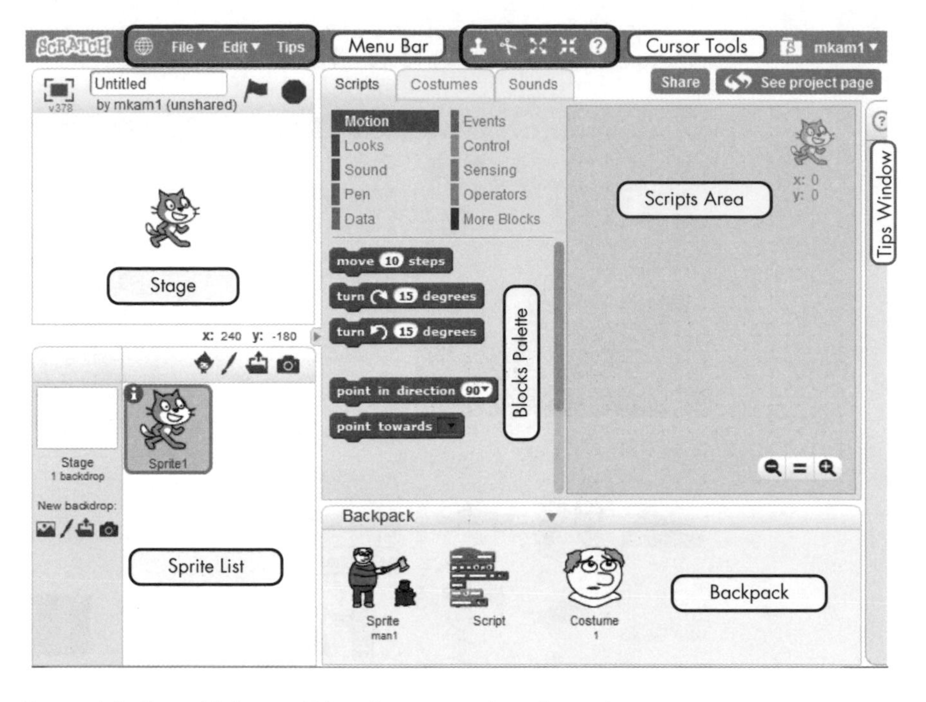

Figure A-8: Scratch's Project Editor for a user who is logged in

This interface is very similar to what you see when you are not logged in, but there are some important differences:

- The backpack pane is visible.
- Two new buttons (**Share** and **See project page**) appear in the upper-right corner.
- The suitcase icon and username show up at the right edge of the toolbar.
- The File menu has new options.

The toolbar and its new options are shown in more detail in Figure A-9.

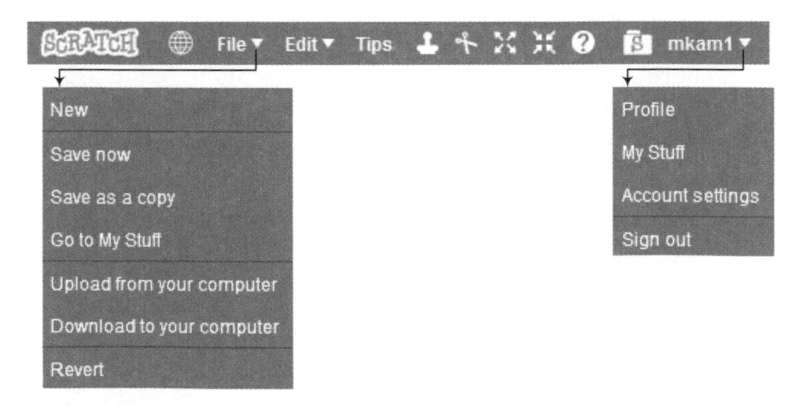

Figure A-9: The toolbar for logged-in users

When you are logged in, Scratch automatically saves your work in the cloud (that is, on the Scratch server), but it's still a good idea to click Save before you exit Scratch. The Save as a copy option saves your current project with a different name. If your current project is named *Test*, for example, the new project will be named *Test copy*. (You can change that name by typing a new one in the project's name edit box.) The Revert option discards any changes you've made since you opened the current project.

If you want to save your projects on your computer rather than in the cloud, use the Download to your computer option. The Upload from your computer option, on the other hand, allows you to load a Scratch project from your computer to the Project Editor. You can use this option to upload projects created with Scratch 1.4 and convert them to the Scratch 2 format.

Remixing a Project

Click the **Remix** button when you have some ideas to add to another Scratcher's project. This will copy the selected project to your account and give you a starting point for your work.

You can also click View the remix tree on the project's page (see Figure A-6) to see how the project has evolved over time and pick the branch that you'd like to copy from.

If you share your remixed project, the project's page will list the original creator(s) and provide links to their projects.

The Project Page

Click the **See project page** button in the upper-right corner of Figure A-8 to edit your project's page, which is shown in Figure A-10. You can enter instructions for people who use your application, give credit to anyone whose ideas or work you used, and specify some tags that will help others find your app.

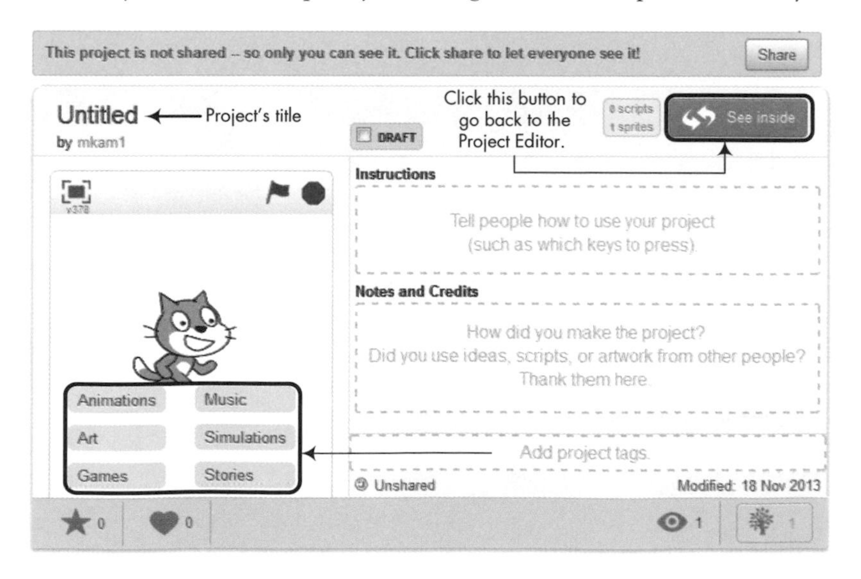

Figure A-10: A project's page

Sharing Your Project

Once you are done with your application, you can share it with the Scratch community by clicking the **Share** button. When you share a project, everyone can find it online and look inside it.

To see a list of all your projects, click the down arrow below your username in the toolbar and select **My Stuff** from the drop-down menu. (You can also click the suitcase icon.) This will take you to the My Stuff page, shown in Figure A-11.

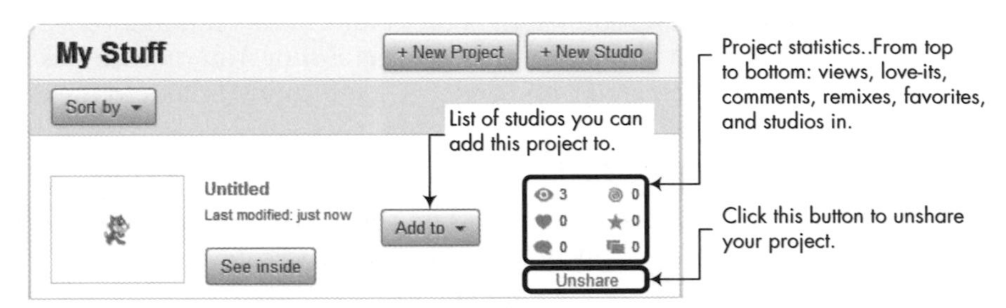

Figure A-11: The My Stuff page

The My Stuff page allows you to control and view various aspects of your projects and studios. You can create, share, edit, unshare, and delete projects from this page. You can also create *studios*—collections of projects—and add projects to them. Studios make it convenient to group related projects together.

NOTE *If you delete one of your unshared projects, the project gets moved to the Trash folder, which acts as a recycle bin for projects. The interface for the Trash folder allows you to restore a deleted project to the My Stuff page.*

INDEX

C

D

N

O

Q

R

S

T

About the Online Resources

You'll find many useful materials in the online resources that accompany this book. Just head over to *http://nostarch.com/learnscratch/* to get started!

As you read, open the Scratch scripts (*.sb2* files) mentioned in each chapter to follow along with the examples. Whenever you solve a practice problem or Try It Out exercise, you can check your answers with the files in the *Solutions* folder. Learn even more about Scratch by reading the information about the Paint Editor, mathematical functions, and drawing geometric shapes in the *Extra Resources* folder. If you want to try out more guided examples, you'll even find extra games and simulations to go along with several chapters in the *Bonus Applications* folder.

Learn to Program with Scratch is set in New Baskerville, Futura, Verdana, and Dogma. The book was printed and bound by Lake Book Manufacturing in Melrose Park, Illinois. The paper is 60# Husky Opaque Offset Smooth, which is certified by the Sustainable Forestry Initiative (SFI).

The book uses a layflat binding, in which the pages are bound together with a cold-set, flexible glue and the first and last pages of the resulting book block are attached to the cover. The cover is not actually glued to the book's spine, and when open, the book lies flat and the spine doesn't crack.

UPDATES

Visit *http://nostarch.com/learnscratch/* for updates, errata, and other information.

More no-nonsense books from  **NO STARCH PRESS**

SUPER SCRATCH PROGRAMMING ADVENTURE!
Learn to Program by Making Cool Games
by THE LEAD PROJECT
OCTOBER 2013, 160 PP., $24.95
ISBN 978-1-59327-531-0
full color

PYTHON FOR KIDS
A Playful Introduction to Programming
by JASON R. BRIGGS
DECEMBER 2012, 344 PP., $34.95
ISBN 978-1-59327-407-8
full color

JAVASCRIPT FOR KIDS
A Playful Introduction to Programming
by NICK MORGAN
NOVEMBER 2014, 252 PP., $34.95
ISBN 978-1-59327-408-5
full color

RUBY WIZARDRY
An Introduction to Programming for Kids
by ERIC WEINSTEIN
DECEMBER 2014, 360 PP., $29.95
ISBN 978-1-59327-566-2
two color

THE LEGO® MINDSTORMS® EV3 DISCOVERY BOOK
A Beginner's Guide to Building and Programming Robots
by LAURENS VALK
JUNE 2014, 352 PP., $34.95
ISBN 978-1-59327-532-7
full color

LAUREN IPSUM
A Story About Computer Science and Other Improbable Things
by CARLOS BUENO
NOVEMBER 2014, 192 PP., $16.95
ISBN 978-1-59327-574-7
full color

PHONE:
800.420.7240 OR
415.863.9900

EMAIL:
SALES@NOSTARCH.COM
WEB:
WWW.NOSTARCH.COM

WITHDRAWN

34.95

2-15

LONGWOOD PUBLIC LIBRARY
800 Middle Country Road
Middle Island, NY 11953
(631) 924-6400
longwoodlibrary.org

LIBRARY HOURS

Monday-Friday 9:30 a.m. - 9:00 p.m.
Saturday 9:30 a.m. - 5:00 p.m.
Sunday (Sept-June) 1:00 p.m. - 5:00 p.m.